THE HISTORICAL SUPPLY CATALOGUE

THE HISTORICAL SUPPLY CATALOGUE

A NINETEENTH-CENTURY SOURCEBOOK

REVISED & EXPANDED EDITION

ALAN WELLIKOFF

CAMDEN HOUSE PUBLISHING

A division of Telemedia Communications (USA) Inc.

Camden House Publishing
Ferry Road
Charlotte, Vermont 05445

Library of Congress Cataloging-in-Publication Data
Wellikoff, Alan.
The historical supply catalogue: a nineteenth-century sourcebook
/Alan Wellikoff. — Rev. & expanded ed.
p.   cm.
Rev. ed of: The American historical supply catalogue, 1984.
Includes index.
ISBN 0-944475-44-2: $17.95
1. United States — Manufacturers — Catalogs. 2. Americana — Catalogs.
I. Wellikoff, Alan. American historical supply catalogue.
II. Title.
TS199.W445   1993
670'.29'473—dc20   93-19057
CIP

Editorial Director: Julie Stillman
Cover and interior design: Eugenie S. Delaney

Trade distribution by
Firefly Books Ltd.
250 Sparks Avenue
Willowdale, Ontario
Canada M2H 2S4

Printed and bound in Canada by
D.W. Friesen & Sons
Altona, Manitoba

First printing May 1993

To Louis Wellikoff, an authentic original

Contents

They shot the railway-train when it first came,
And when the Fords came they shot the Fords.
It could not save them. They are dying now
Or being educated, which is the same.
One need not weep romantic tears for them,
But when the last moonshiner buys his radio,
And the last, lost, wild-rabbit of a girl
Is civilized with a mail-order dress,
Something will pass that was American
And all the movies will not bring it back.

    —Stephen Vincent Benét,
       John Brown's Body, *1928*

The best thing about the future
is that it comes only one day at a time.

    —Abraham Lincoln

Preface

It was natural to be nineteenth century in the nineteenth century, and anyone could do it, but in the twentieth it takes quite a lot of toil.

—Malcolm Bradbury and Michael Orsler, "Department of Amplification," *New Yorker*, July 2, 1960

Much of the material in this book first appeared in the evanescent original edition of *The American Historical Supply Catalogue*. Published to critical acclaim in 1984, that work had just gone into a second printing when a confederacy of forklifts suddenly put the brakes on its success. Forklifts do commerce's heavy lifting—but they would sooner stand idle than teeter up to a loading dock burdened with the offerings of some publisher that didn't pay its warehouse bills. Thus did the first historical catalogue go into suspended animation until another, more estimable publishing house consented to put out a revised edition. With that publisher's imprint on its spine, this is that new book.

Like its predecessor, *The Historical Supply Catalogue* is a compendium of hundreds of replicas, reproductions and century-old products still made. Unlike those items featured in home-restoration catalogs, these cover a broader range of categories to include agricultural equipment, clothing, military goods and much more. The products are selected for their historical and utilitarian interest, as well as for the accuracy with which they conform to past materials, workmanship and design. Nevertheless, it must be emphasized that however true they are to their antique forebears, these objects are only *copies* of historical artifacts. As such, they have no history of their own. None has ever cleaved virgin prairie nor a callow maiden's scalp, or can any claim to actually remember the Alamo.

But this does not mean that replicas and reproductions are just less expensive alternatives to antiques, not notable as cultural phenomena in their own right. On the contrary, it is only replicas and reproductions that are simultaneously illustrative of *two* eras, revealing something of each in concert. Faithfully crafted, they claim a singular status as manifestations of the present's regard for—and society with—the past.

A while ago, a Texas woman of my acquaintance related a story told to her by an aged friend whose father once had dinner with Abraham Lincoln. The father had returned for a visit to his native Illinois, and Lincoln—then a presidential candidate—asked him "How goes Texas?" My friend's friend's father was polite, but distracted by the particles of food that clung unmolested to the railsplitter's new beard.

Apocryphal or not—hell, s*ignificant* or not—this story was in my thoughts again recently.

Looking at a photographic portrait of Lincoln, I was struck by the image. The gently smiling countenance was sharply rendered (and free of crumbs), while the hair and enormous ears were out of focus. As even this humble sourcebook should make apparent, I admire Lincoln; but knowing a story about the prairie Republican that (until now) only a handful of people shared, has made him seem very familiar indeed. Yet Lincoln is a distant icon in history, the achingly remote part of a past that now only exists in unnoticed remnants and prettified restorations. Was the Lincoln of the photograph emerging into clarity, receding into the mists? "The past is a foreign country," says historian David Lowenthal; but in some ways, it is very much like the one we live in now.

Lately, record numbers of Americans have left the cities, grown their own produce, burned wood for heat and otherwise incorporated elements of nineteenth-century life into that of the end of the twentieth. As older technologies, such as those of the windmill and wood stove, are reintroduced to promote business diversity and labor while conserving natural resources, the reason for this is partly economic: the potbelly stove supplants the atomic power plant, the organic farm answers the corporate plantation, and the short-haul railroad wins back some business from the Interstate Highway System.

But economics, while keeping a good accounting of things, cannot explain all this popular atavism. The price of goods will only go so far in helping us understand the surge of interest in such things as horse ownership, Victorian architecture, Shaker design, old house restoration, black-powder hunting, historical reenactments and museum admissions, to name a few. Why has America restored so much of her history to the landscape?

Writing in the 1830s, Alexis de Tocqueville implied that Americans scorned history. Democratic peoples, he said, arrange things so that "the woof of time is every instant broken, and the track of generations effaced." Perhaps it is partly the stress of modern life that has made us want to abandon this trait and gather our history around us for comfort. A prominent architect may have provided some insight here when he noted that a generation of modern architecture caused the most sustained interest in historical restoration that the country has ever seen.

We are a race barely removed from forest and farm, the

descendants of those who lived by agriculture, hunting and the hearth. As our memory of this heritage is indelibly ingrained, we bridle at being carried too far away from it. So as technology advances, we correct it, reserving a place for the farmer, frontiersman and fire builder in us to find expression. Whatever became of those autogyros in which we were all to commute to work? What happened to the little pills that were to make Cuisinarts obsolete by replacing food? They are examples of technologies either too complicated, expensive, unnatural or plain incompatible with the joys of the hearth to be bothered with.

Late twentieth-century society thus merges high tech with low. Today a man can access Telstar 5 from his log cabin without opting for the life of either a frontiersman or cyberpunk. Modern sensibilities have intertwined notions of "past," "present" and "future" into a postmodern cocktail that's gotten the idea of linear progress stinko. "Someone who today makes a buggy whip," said the humorist Jean Shepherd, "performs a modern act." In other ways, the historical past can seem quite recent.

In *The Shootist*, one of John Wayne's last films, an old gunfighter, played by Wayne, seeks out the help of a doctor who tells him he is dying, sick with "the cancer." It is the end of the nineteenth century, and the wildness of the western territories is quickly being consumed by the advance of eastern civilization, for which the shootist's cancer stands as a metaphor. Stunned, yet bearing the dignity of one who has looked down the barrel of many a Remington and Colt, the dying gunfighter shambles back to his Carson City boarding house. There, the landlady sends his clothing—stiff with the dust of cattle towns and frontier camps—out to the dry cleaners.

The formative period of our frontier history is nearer than most of us think. Louis L'Amour, the late writer of western historical fiction, vividly remembered the smell of whiskey on Buffalo Bill Cody's breath when the old scout lifted toddler L'Amour into his saddle and gave him a ride. A couple of old veterans of the Indian Wars got to live long enough to contemplate Woodstock Nation, and a few widows of Civil War veterans still draw government pensions today. In fact, high school kids now sporting neon Mohawks are old enough to have met a man who rode with Jesse James, a man who fought at Vicksburg in 1863, and a man who himself could have met another who fought the Revolution.

So while the idea of a frontier gunfighter having his clothing drycleaned is a surprising one, it is also plausible. It *seems* more anachronistic that it really is. It serves to remind us that history is not made up of static segments of time, but flows and is connected to the present. Bury it in the loam of succeeding events and the past will send up a green shoot to remind us of its proximity.

The Historical Supply Catalogue has been compiled with an eye to those goods that provide this sense of historical dimension. Some aspects of the newly made items I have included—like the Victorian use of aluminum—are surprising for their antiquity; while it's startling to discover objects like the replica Gatling gun available new. Many other replicas, reproductions and items of manufacture for a century or more satisfy the contemporary yearning for substance, scale and historical measure in everyday life. Assembled into a sourcebook intended as useful and informative, they impart the impression of an 1800s trade catalog "come alive" from the past.

The nineteenth-century-style (there's some overlap into the eighteenth and twentieth centuries) products in this book require some clarification of terminology. As used here, a *replica* is an item copied or replicated from one once made in the past. A *reproduction* differs in that to make it, a company (usually the original company) resurrected old molds, dies, formulas, patterns or plans to again produce an item from the same materials. Finally, an item *in continual production* is made as it has always been for almost a century or more, usually by the same company. An example of this is the Hudson's Bay blanket, now more than two centuries old.

Both reproductions and items in continual manufacture are, by definition, authentic. This leaves replicas as the things to be watched. While the shoddy replica invariably gives a bad name to this entire body of goods, for each manufacturer of bad merchandise there are others (e.g., A. Uberti & Company, Prairie Edge Studios, Red River Outfitters) that, due to their standards and devotion to the products and the periods those products represent, make a superior-quality replica of detailed authenticity. While I've tried to limit the replica entries that follow to the latter, I've seen only a small portion of the products described and mostly must rely on the intuition one develops in doing this kind of book. Undoubtedly, some replicas are worse than others, and when this is known, they are liable to criticism. Where I have quoted suppliers it's been because I found their descriptions interesting, colorful or succinctly informative—although sometimes their coyly worded copy is passed along for the reader to use in judgment. Note that neither the author nor publisher makes any claims or guarantees regarding the quality or authenticity of any of the products described in this sourcebook.

Finally, as price and ordering information vary in accordance with the wishes of each supplier, not all prices are listed. As for those that do appear, I strongly recommend that they be used only to infer current prices and that readers correspond directly with the supplier before sending any money. Many of the suppliers included in this book have small businesses sensitive to the vagaries of the marketplace. Thus, prices, addresses, telephone and fax numbers are subject to change without notice, and some suppliers may have gone out of business by the time this sourcebook is in your hands. At which point, of course, their wares will be on their way to becoming collectible antiques.

Acknowledgments

T his sourcebook might have itself become history were it not for Denis Boyles, one of my co-authors on *The Modern Man's Guide to Life*, who brought my idea for a new catalogue to the attention of Camden House Books. I am thankful as well to Camden House's former editorial director, Sandy Taylor, who expressed an immediate interest in the project; and to my agent Meredith Bernstein, who skillfully took matters in hand from there.

My job, of course, was to research and write the updated book, a task made considerably easier by several product leads from Linda Morris of the Baltimore Sun; by my friend Christopher Blair, who told me about the replica Victorian street clock; and by those suppliers I was lucky enough to find who are distinguished by their probity, ability and wit: Ron Barlow of Windmill Publishing, cabinetmaker Keith Diebert, Dick Dabrowski of Shaker Workshops, Billie Gammon at Norlands, Ray Hillenbrand of Prairie Edge Studios, Hank Kluin, Mike Lea, Don Rogers, Maria Laura Uberti, Henri Vaillancourt, Peter Zahn, and especially William S. Courtis and Phil Spangenberger, of the Phoenix Foundry and Red River Outfitters respectively.

I am also thankful for the efforts of Ellen Smith, who typed the manuscript after the dung hit the quaint, brass-filigree ceiling fan authenticated by the Victoria and Albert Museum; to Julie Stillman, who took this book under her wing with the enthusiasm of an acquiring editor; to Wendy Ruopp, who had the graciousness to say nice things about the manuscript even after the laborious task of copyediting its text; and to the Perennial Library's "Everyday Life in America" series of books, edited by Richard Balkin, which aided me greatly in my search for historical lore.

Finally, I owe a debt of gratitude to my brother Michael, to my uncle and fellow Civil War buff, Ephraim Stein, to my friends Stan Charles, George Comtois, Robert Friedman, Sharon Redmon, Alan Rose and Neil Wolfson; and to Elizabeth Grande, who usefully commented on the many draft pages to which she was made to listen, and who had to put up with the mess created by their preparation.

$725.00 AND OUR FREE BUILDING PLANS

WILL BUILD, PAINT AND COMPLETE READY FOR OCCUPANC
THIS $1,100.00 SIX-ROOM COTTAGE

PLANS FOR THIS $725.00 HOUSE, OR ANY ONE OF THE MANY HOUSES W
OFFER, ARE FREE, AS FULLY EXPLAINED ON PAGE 594.

STRUCTURES & PLANS

PARE THIS, OUR $725.00 HOUSE,
house which would cost in your locality from $1,100.00
00. If in doubt send for the plans for this building and
e the exterior, the size, the foundation, the porch work
outer trimmings of this building, then compare the in-
nish, the doors, the windows and trim, hardware, in fact
erials that we specify in these special plans and specifica-
nd you will be immediately convinced beyond doubt that
save you all we claim. This $725.00 house which we show
page represents but one of the many homes
w in our beautiful book of Modern Homes.
you a saving in the same proportion on all t
plans and material for, which will range fro
0. With our plans you can build an $1,800
0, a $2,000.00 house for $1,500.00, a $2,400.
0, etc. This wonderful saving in cost by us
cifications is so great that many persons won
inary values are possible, and to such peop
the enormous saving is only made possible
rk, hardware and other kinds of material
manufacturers' cost plus one small percenta
e you a large chain of profits, profits whi
cturer, the jobber, the retail lumbermen, a
houses with a view of the strictest econom
cut to the very best advantage, which in itse
from 10 to 20 per cent in this commodity a

OU ARE INTERESTED IN B
er how small or how large a house, do not
ful offers. Our building plans and specifi
plainly outlined and described in our spec
Homes, have saved many of our custome
rs. You cannot afford to overlook thi
nity.

PLANS FOR THIS HOUSE
R HOUSE will be sent you the same d
your order. The plans we s
blue prints, plans which are drawn ¼-inch to the foot and
tively accurate in every detail, showing the front and
vation, floor plans, the interior details, etc. All our
re printed by electric blue print process on the finest
paper, showing every line and figure perfect and distinct.

SPECIFICATIONS ARE TYPEWRITTEN
finest grade of linen paper and bound in a very artistic
with an attractive heavy linen cover. These specifica-
onsist of from fifteen to twenty pages of closely typewrit-
tter which gives full instructions for carrying out the
everything is explained in a clear and explicit manner.
ns and specifications are so carefully drawn up that they
made a basis of contract between yourself and the con-
as it fully explains how a contract should be let. The
fine what work must be performed by the contractor.
ork must be performed by the carpenter, specifics what
grade of material must be used; in fact, it would re-
a more definite contract than it would be possible for
me architect to draw up, as it is the result of many years
of some of the best architects in this country.

MATERIALS MAKE GOOD HOUSES.
planning our houses it is a question of how good, not
ap. This statement is easily proven by referring to
the materials we illustrate and describe here below. In
r plans you take no risk of getting poor materials, such
t occur if the work was done by some unscrupulous con
The mill work specified is the best in their respective
You take no risk when building from our plans, as we
ly guarantee every piece of material we specify and, pro-
same is not entirely satisfactory, it may be returned and
oney will be refunded together with all transportation

First Floor Plan.

ILLUSTRATED ABOVE, CONSISTS OF SIX FAIR SIZED ROOMS arranged in such a manner that it can be most economically heated.
First floor, large kitchen, 14 by 11 feet 9 inches; bedroom, 8 feet 6 inches by 11 feet 9 inches; parlor, 12 feet by 10 feet 6 inches. Second floor, front bedroom, 8 feet 3 inches by 10 feet 6 inches; rear bedroom, 8 feet 6 inches by 11 feet 9 inches. One large attic, 14 feet by 11 feet 9 inches. The bedrooms have large roomy closets.

REMEMBER, we can furnish plans for houses ranging in price from $725.00 to $4,000.00 free. Whether it be a modest little home or a mansion, be sure and do not consider building without first sending for our beautiful book of Modern Homes, which will be sent free, post-paid. This special book is illustrated and described on page 594.

Second Floor Plan.

$100.00 FREE BUILDING PLAN OFFER FULLY EXPLAINED ON PAGE 5
BE SURE TO READ EVERY WORD OF THIS GREAT FREE OFFE

THE FRONT DOOR
furnished with our $725.00 house is covered with two coats of paint and handsomely grained to imitate oil finished Red Oak and finished with a heavy coat of varnish, size, 2 feet 8 inches by 6 feet 8 inches, glazed with a sand blast design like illustration. Doors of this quality, as a rule, are only to be found in a much higher priced house. Inside doors, as illustrated to the right, are fine Yellow Pine and will take an elegant oil finish.

SEE THE EXCELLENT HARDWARE
we specify in the construction of our $725.00 house. These locks have genuine cast bronze front, bolts and strike, heavy wrought bronze knobs and 2 ¼ x 7¼-inch outside escutcheons. The raised surface is shown by white lines and the background is in black. Compare these locks with houses in your neighborhood and you will be convinced that the hardware we specify is better than that which is usually furnished in a $1,200.00 house.

All mill work material specified in our houses is made

WONDERFUL VALUES IN HOT AIR FURNACES
QUICK, POWERFUL, FRESH AIR VENTILATING AND HEATING.

FOR $53.94 extra we will ventilate and heat this house to an average of 70 de-
es and in the coldest climate during the coldest weath-
er, with our famous Acme Hummer Soft Coal Furnace.
FOR $56.49 we will heat it with our Acme Tropic Anthracite Coal Furnace, all completely equipped with all hot air pipes and registers.

WRITE FOR OUR BIG FURNACE BOOK

GREAT WOOD MANT
OFFER.

$10.53

Mantel No. 248

$10.53 for this beautiful solid oak Mant
For $10.53 extra we supply this house with splendid cabinet mantel.

$4.00 extra for beauti
colored enamel tile facing
hearth.

$2.93 extra for oxidized
per finish coal grate outfit

**THIS
DSOME
TTAGE
NDOW**
ished in
725.00
The top
size 14x40
is glazed
beautiful
ast design
like illus.
The bot-

13

❧ ORIGINAL LOG CABINS

Because of its intrinsic sturdiness and simplicity, the log cabin has come to be emblematic of the noblest American virtues—honesty, democracy and independence. Perhaps it is for this reason that the structure is widely believed to be an American invention.

It isn't.

The first log cabin to appear on this continent was probably built by Scandinavian settlers at a place near the mouth of the Delaware River they called New Sweden. The year was 1683 and the Scandinavians were erecting structures similar to those they knew in the Old World. But the North American frontier was a place so well suited to the log cabin that soon they were to be found everywhere. "It is not uncommon," Alexis de Tocqueville wrote, "in crossing the new States of the West, to meet with deserted dwellings in the midst of the wilds; the traveller frequently discovers the vestiges of the log-house in the most solitary retreat, which bear witness to the power, and no less to the inconstancy, of man."

To which, from his twentieth-cen-

tury vantage point, Don Rogers adds that "the log cabin remains our most beloved physical embodiment of the early American spirit." Well, if Tocqueville thought that a deserted

1800s log cabin bore witness to man's inconstancy, I wonder what he would have made of seeing Mr. Rogers restore it some 150 years later.

Ever since 1980, Don Rogers has been buying, dismantling and restoring log houses that had been built by settlers who came to the mountains and found the rich bottomlands already taken. "I've been all over South Carolina, Georgia and Tennessee looking for log buildings to work on," relates the man whose company's name is "Old South," "but I've had my best luck way up in the mountains of North Carolina."

It was there where pioneers moved onto the forest coves and steep mountainsides—men who used broadaxes to build a shelter from the surrounding wilderness of poplar, chestnut and oak. Despite its simplicity, writes Rogers, the log house was the best shelter from wind, rain, cold and marauders. "The massive logs with their soft sapwood hewn away protected the family against hostile nature and hostile men. It survived the

seasons and the wear of nearly two centuries because it was in harmony with the land."

And so is Don Rogers. Although he advocates the use of modern techniques to ensure the restored log home's creature comforts, Rogers thinks that most people who rebuild log houses go about true restoration all wrong. Everywhere he looks he sees evidence of designs and materials that seem to be incompatible with the spirit of a log structure.

"I hate to use the word reverence," he says "but at least you need to appreciate the fact that it is an antique. I've seen beautiful logs that were just mutilated—and what you have left is a smorgasbord of jumbled materials and form and design that leaves you with a totally empty feeling. It puts me in mind of one of those country-living magazines I saw with an article titled 'Who Says a Log House has to be Rustic?'

"Well sir, *I* say it does."

Brochure available.

OLD SOUTH COMPANY
3301 Highway 101 North
Woodruff, SC 29388
Tel. 803/877-0538
Fax. 803/848-0025

ADIRONDACK GREAT CAMP GAZEBOS

Late in the nineteenth century, the Adirondack forest was second only to Newport, Rhode Island, as the favored retreat of the northeastern business aristocracy. In the New York woods, rough-hewn palaces known as "great camps" provided a suitable atmosphere for Whitneys, Morgans, Vanderbilts and Astors to rusticate in splendor both natural and man-made.

In those days, that which was man-made was fashioned from the forest itself—using not only its wood, but its bark and stone as well. This wedding of moment and material created buildings that struck a peculiar balance between boreal primitiveness and Victorian splendor. Amid these structures stood the great camp's outbuildings—gazebos and shelters so fanciful that they could serve as grand pavilions in a midsummer's night dream of McKinley-era woodland sprites.

Romancing the Woods got under way as a result of owner Marvin Davis' coveting of a great camp gazebo that stands on a promontory of Overlook Mountain—which overlooks Woodstock, New York. Seeking a similar gazebo to build for himself, the adver-

tising executive could find nothing available but "the junk that one finds in lumberyards all over America." But Mr. Davis' research would soon take him to the nearby Mohonk Mountain House (an historical resort described in the "Tours & Lodging" section of this book) where more than 120 vintage gazebos, shelters and pavilions are located throughout the property. "Everyone who visits wants to take one home," says Davis of Mohonk's gazebos. "Now they can."

They can if they contact Romancing the Woods.

Romancing the Woods builds "shelters, gazebos and summer pavilions in

the authentic nineteenth-century tradition of the great mountain camps." And even if his metaphors might get mixed when saying so, Davis's dedication to his products' authenticity is absolute: "No blue-sky creative shooting from the hip for us," he proclaims. "We're sticklers.... We stick to history." Romancing the Woods' dedication to authenticity requires its woodworkers, cabinetmakers and masons to use nothing but natural materials in their work. Customers select what structures they want from period photographs and drawings, and these buildings are then replicated as faithfully as possible.

Romancing the Woods' pieces start at $750 for a pagoda-covered seating arrangement for two, and can extend to a large octagonal shelter with table and seating for $5,000. Interior and exterior Adirondack furniture is also available.

Free brochure available.

ROMANCING THE WOODS
33 Raycliffe Drive
Woodstock, NY 12498
Tel. 914/246-6976

LOG HOMES

Of the many builders of log homes, the Hearthstone company is the most likely contender for Don Rogers' approval. Hearthstone was founded back in 1971 by James Munsey, who also restored old log cabins, only this time in the mountains of East Tennessee. But unlike Rogers, when Mr. Munsey's stock of restorable cabins grew short, he turned to the business of their replication instead. Today, the company Munsey began cites the 165-year-old John Oliver homestead in Cades Cove, Great Smoky Mountains, as the ideal log structure towards which it strives—something which may account for the distinct Appalachian aspect of its products.

Although capable of referring to these period-style log homes as "building systems," Hearthstone maintains that each one is hand-built, using tools like a foot adze and chain saw to create structures with airtight construction, plumb walls, level ceiling beams and tight notches throughout.

Literature, dealer information available.

HEARTHSTONE HOMES
Route 2
P.O. Box 434
Dandridge, TN 37725
Tel. 615/397-9425

Colonial and ~Victorian~ House Plans

✖ McKIE WING ROTH, JR.

"**The look we are seeking almost exclusively precludes the visible use of materials which were not available prior to the existence of the petrochemical industry,**" claims McKie Wing Roth, Jr. Mr. Roth offers building plans for 35 early New England saltbox, cape, gambrel-roofed

FIRST FLOOR

and colonial homes with contemporary floor plans ranging from 1,000 to 3,200 square feet.

Price for a single set of plans under 2,000 square feet (including a license to build a house from same), $165. A set of plans for a house of 2,000 feet or more, $195.

A 64–page color "Study Folio" is available, $25 postpaid.

McKIE WING ROTH, JR., DESIGNER
Box 31
Castine, Maine 04421
Tel. 800/232-7684

✾ HISTORICAL REPLICATIONS

When native Mississippian Cecilia Reese Bullock despaired at the disappearance of the old-fashioned country homes of the South she loves, she did far more than become wistful: she went into business building them again.

These homes, which combined what are essentially modern floor plans with accurately reproduced traditional and Victorian exteriors, led her into her current business, designing and marketing plans for replicas of authentic late-nineteenth-century residences.

With camera in hand, Mrs. Bullock travels throughout Dixie seeking out houses that have for her a peculiar, not readily definable appeal. The popularity of the designs and plans that result from these journeys prove that Mrs. Bullock's instinct for proportion and grace is right on the mark. Among these are plans for Cedar Lane, a farmhouse built in 1830 in Mount Pleasant, Georgia, by Solomon Graves, a polit-

ical and social leader, and the Webb-Ginn House, an 1835 farmhouse in Gwinnett County, Georgia, with a front of lacy gingerbread "unparalleled for delicacy and grace." Others of Mrs. Bullock's plans have come directly from Victorian house-plan books of the 1880s and 1890s. One of these, she notes, is again a bestseller after more than a hundred years.

Mrs. Bullock's portfolio includes working blueprints for home construction and is available for $16.

HISTORICAL REPLICATIONS
P.O. Box 13529
Jackson, MS 39236

▨ PRIVY PLANS

Although windows in the shape of half-moons were popular on Victorian privies, the outdoor toilet has a long enough history for *gun ports* to have served the dual purpose of its ventilation and defense. Some historians hold that Indian raiders would not attack outhouse occupants, whose methane clouds may have provided them with protection enough. On the other hand, the enclosed privy seems an undesirable place to spark off any black powder.

Plan drawings of American "necessary houses" constructed between 1820 and 1940 are included as part of Ronald S. Barlow's *The Vanishing American Outhouse: Privy Plans, Photographs, Poems and Folklore*. A genuine yet amusing exploration of a long-overlooked aspect of our architectural heritage, this book makes up for lost history.

Price: $15.95, plus $2 shipping for the first, and 50¢ for each additional book ordered. Dealer discounts available.

WINDMILL PUBLISHING COMPANY
2147 Windmill View Road
El Cajon, CA 92020

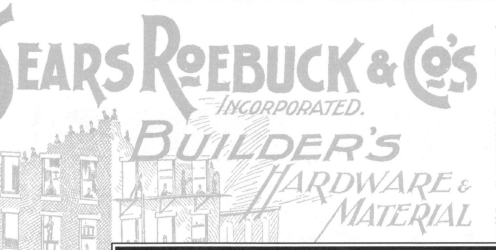

BUILDING SUPPLIES & FIXTURES

Barn D...

No. 13785. ... Hanger, to ... Bolts, screw ... nished free ...

Diameter of wheel, inches,	3	4
Price, per pair,	$0.18	.25
Diameter of wheel, inches,	5	6
Price, per pair,	$0.32	.40

...ck Back Barn Door Hangers.

13788. No screws or bolts furnished ... prices quoted. ...ter of wheel in inches.

	3	4	5	6
...ir,	$0.22	.25	.35	.45

13786. Cast Iron Half Round Rail for above hangers ...nes in pieces 2 feet long. Price, per foot, without ...2c

13789. Double flange Barn Door Rail to be used ...bove hangers, No. 13788; comes in pieces 2 feet long. ...ews furnished at prices quoted. Per foot ...2½c

...nk's Anti-Friction Steel Barn Door Hanger.

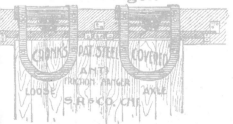

13790. This hanger is made from heavy steel, so it ...arry the door with perfect ease and no trouble. ...ake a round bearing at the ends of the run, so if ...n wider doors than made for, the axle will not ...nto the rider bar, and the round bearings also make ...much easier than it otherwise would, or than any ...hanger that is not made this way. The groove ...hape, so it will not touch or grind on the edges and ...friction, and also having a deep groove, will not ...the track. These hangers are marked with a gauge

No. 13791. This rail, being double braced and double riveted, is the strongest rail in the market. Being braced both ways it will not sag. The joint is made so that it is perfectly solid. It can be used for any grooved wheel hanger, and a heavy door will not make it spring or tremble. Guaranteed to hold a door weighing 2,000 pounds, and used in connection with our Anti-Friction Hangers will work perfectly on large or small doors. If 1¼x10 screws or wire nails are used it will hold any door made.

Comes in pieces 6, 8 and 10 feet long. Price quoted does not include screws. Price, per foot............3c

Barn Door Stay Rollers.

No. 13795. Barn Door Stay Rollers to screw, wrought iron shank. Weight, 14 oz. Price, each, 7c; per doz........65c

No. 13796. Barn Door Stay Rollers, adjustable to any thickness of door. Will always stay in the right position. Price, each, 8c; per doz............85c

No. 13797. Barn Door Pulls, extra heavy japanned. Weight, 10 oz. Price, each, 4c; per doz............40c

Hinges.

Screws are not furnished with hinges at prices quoted. For screws see index.

No. 13806. Light wrought steel T Hinges. Size given is measure from joint to end of hinge.

Size, inches,	3	4	6	8
Size of screw used,	7	8	8	10
Weight, pair,	4 oz.	5 oz.	8 oz.	12 oz.
Price, pair............	$0.03	.04	.05	.07
Doz. pairs............	.33	.40	.54	.75

No. 13808. Extra heavy wrought steel T Hinges.

Size, inches,	6	8	10	12	14
Price, pair............	$0.09	.13	.20	.27	.33
Price, doz. pairs........	.98	1.40	2.20	3.12	3.65

No. 13816. Light wrought steel Strap Hinges. Size given is measurement from joint to end of hinge.

Size, inches,	3	4	5	6
Price, per pair............	$0.03	.04	.05	.06
Price, doz. pairs............	.33	.44	.54	.56

No. 13817. Heavy wrought steel Strap Hinges, without screws.

Size, inches,	6	8	10	12
Price, per pair............	$0.08	.12	.18	.25
Price, per doz. pairs............	.80	1.26	1.92	2.58

No. 13824. Narrow wrought steel Butts.

Width, open,	1	1¼	1½	2
	1¼	1⅜	1½	1¾
Size screw used	5	6	7	8
Weight per pair, oz.	2	3	4	6
Price, per pair............	$0.02	.02	.03	.04
Price, per doz. pairs....	.12	.16	.24	.26

Screws are not furnished with Butts.

No. 13825. Wrought steel Back Flaps.

Width, inches.....	¾	⅞	1	1¼	1½
Length, open......	2¾	2¾	2⅝	3⅜	3⅜
Size screw used..	0	0	6	6	8
Price, per pair...	$0.03	.03	.03	.04	.04
Price, per doz. pairs.	.20	.22	.23	.29	.35

Screws are not furnished with Butts.

No. 13827. Wrought steel Chest Hinges. The ...inch size is 1¼ inches wide and can be used on stuff ...inch thick. The 2 in size is 2 inches wide and can be used on stuff ...inch thick. 1½ inch, pair, 5c; dozen pairs, 50c; 2 inch, per pair, 8c; ...pairs ....7...

Hooks.

No. 13835. Wrought iron Hooks and Staples.

Length, inches...........	3	4	5
Weight, oz...............	3	4	4
Price, each............	$0.02	.02	.03
Price, per doz............	.12	.16	.19

No. 13836. Bright iron Wire Hooks and Screw Eyes.

Size, inches............	2	3
Weight, oz...............	2	2
Price, each............	$0.02	.03
Price, per doz............	.15	.18
Price, per gross............	1.15	1.50

Hasps.

No. 13838. Wrought Iron Hasps and Staples complete with double hook.

Length, in.,	5	6	8
Weight, oz.,	4	5	9
Price, each.,$0.03	.03	.04
Price, doz.,	.24	.28	.36

No. 13839. Wrought Iron Hinge Hasps, like cut.

Length of hasp, in.,	3	4
Whole length, in.,	5⅝	7
Weight, ounces,		
Price, each,	$0.06	
Price, per doz.,	.50	

Rings.

No. 13842. Wrought Iron Rings.

17

Victorian Mill Work

⊞ VINTAGE WOODWORKS

"Heretofore seldom obtainable in this century," boasts Vintage Woodworks of its line of Victorian gingerbread and fretwork. The Fredericksburg, Texas, company offers a wide variety of authentic designs from small fret brackets to running porch rails and fleur-de-lys trim. The "Texas Special" bracket is a stirring Victorian interpretation of eternal Lone Star chauvinism.

Vintage Woodworks' gingerbread is suitable for both indoor and outdoor use as part of the complete restoration of Victorian houses, gazebos, gateways, stables, barns, privies, etc. Special orders are welcomed by the firm.

Catalog available, $2.

VINTAGE WOODWORKS
Highway 34 South, P.O. Drawer R
Quinlan, TX 75474
Tel. 903/356-2158

✄CUMBERLAND WOODCRAFT

Using premium hardwoods the company produces gingerbread, bric-a-brac, carvings, trims, moldings and wainscoting. Also available are bars, back bars, gazebos, paneling, screen and storm doors, medallions and wall-coverings. Included are rails, spandrels, balustrades, brackets, corbels, posts, and wainscoting.

56-page catalog, $4.50.

CUMBERLAND WOODCRAFT COMPANY
Post Office Drawer 609
Carlisle, PA 17013
Tel. 717/243-0064 or 800/367-1884
(outside Pennsylvania only)
Fax. 717/243-6502

✸ NINETEENTH-CENTURY LUMBER

For Europeans like the Massachusetts Bay colonists, being camped on the edge of a vast continental forest brought with it an equal expanse of ambivalence. The Puritans speculated endlessly about their situation: Had they, like Christ, been brought to a demonically wild place as a test of faith? Or was this the site of the New Jerusalem, and they the modern incarnation of the Hebrews, fleeing oppression through a wilderness that led to the establishment of a new covenant?

From the time of Edward Johnson's 1654 *Wonder-Working Providence*, a fascination with the American wilderness and its effect on our character has pervaded our literature and history. Yet 200 years later, during the same century when such men as Jefferson, Emerson, Parkman and Muir were to extol its ennobling influences, the great forest was inexorably depleted. When Frederick Jackson Turner stood before the American Historical Association in 1893 to deliver his famous thesis on "The Significance of the Frontier on American Life," his Chicago audience was unaware that it was participating in what would popularly be remembered as an event that signaled the close of that frontier.

With the western frontier closed, the eastern forest was a worn-out fabric, tattered and rent by agriculture. No longer did stands of huge spruce, hemlock and fir extend solidly from northern New England along the high peaks down to Tennessee. Gone as well was the carpet of oak and chestnut that flourished from New Jersey to northern Virginia, and the pine and oak of the southern forests.

Longleaf pine, a softwood that grew primarily in the southernmost parts of Georgia, Mississippi and Alabama, took 450 years to mature and yielded a heartwood so strong that the keel of the U.S.S. *Constitution* had been made from a single plank. Frequently used during the 1800s in heavy construction, in shipbuilding, and for railroad bridges and coastal pilings, this steely wood was one of our leading exports.

Long since "timbered out," modern civilization has eliminated the conditions required by longleaf pine for regeneration, so today any of it found is likely to be reclaimed nineteenth-century lumber. The Mountain Lumber Company of Ruckersville, Virginia, specializes in this reclamation, salvaging the timber from torn-down structures. The company kiln-dries the wood and resaws it into a variety of sizes for paneling, flooring and other uses.

Free color brochure available.

MOUNTAIN LUMBER COMPANY
P.O. Box 289
Ruckersville, VA 22968
Tel. 804/985-3646
Fax. 804/985-4105

▣ HAND-HEWN BEAMS

The Broad-Axe Beam Company is a family business in Vermont that produces beams of white pine, authentically hand-hewn with a broadaxe. The broadaxe—a chisel-bladed axe—remained the most convenient way to fashion beams even after the introduction of the water-powered sawmill, due to the mill's slowness (it used to be said that you could put a log on the carriage in the morning and then go off to lunch without having to worry about turning it for the next cut).

Broad-Axe Beam's structural timbers are 7-inch-square boxheart beams (meaning that the age rings radiate from the center toward the butt ends), and their decorative beams are simply structural beams sawed in half. All of the company's beams are air-dried for six months. Custom hewing is available.

Structural beams come sawed one side or hewn on all four sides, approximately 7½ inches square, in lengths of 8, 12, 14 and 16 feet. Price: $7 per linear foot.

Decorative beams are approximately 3½ by 7½ inches in diameter, and come in lengths of 8, 12, 14 and 16 feet. Price: $4.50 per linear foot.

Shipping is by commercial trucker to your site.

BROAD-AXE BEAM COMPANY
R.D. 2, Box 417
Brattleboro, VT 05301
Tel. 802/257-0064

▣ MILK PAINT

Homestead Paints & Finishes' milk paint resulted from a search for an authentically early American paint to use on its supplier's replica eighteenth- and nineteenth-century furniture. This product—essentially a re-fabrication of a milk-based one commonly used prior to 1830—has again become popular for its unrefined old look and use of authentic colors. Like a cake mix, the paint arrives as a dry powder to be mixed with water.

Colors available: barn red, bayberry, buttermilk white, oyster white, federal blue, soldier blue, Lexington green, sea green, mustard, pitch black, slate black and pumpkin.

Prices: $2.95 per ounce, $7.95 per pint, $13.45 per quart, $39.95 per gallon (plus shipping costs).

Free brochure and paint card available with SASE.

HOMESTEAD PAINTS & FINISHES
111 Mulpus Road, P.O. Box 1668
Lunenburg, MA 01462
Tel. 508/582-6426

❧ 1886 CEILING FAN

The Hunter Fan Company has been in business for more than a century, and their reproduction limited-edition 1886 ceiling fan elegantly shows just how well they recall their beginnings. Duplicated from original archive drawings and historic research, the original 1886 Hunter was one of the first products of any kind to be powered by electricity. The replica comes with walnut-finished hardwood wing-tip blades that are 52 inches in diameter, and its tear-drop motor housing and matching cast-iron blades are decorated with a floral design in burnished brass. Available in three colors: "burnished brass," "verde" and black. The replica 1886 Hunter can be adapted for lights, and its hanger pole is removable for eight-foot ceilings.

Price: $399.

For distributors, contact:

HUNTER FAN COMPANY
2500 Frisco Avenue
Memphis, TN 38114
Tel. 901/743-1360

GREEK AND ROMAN COLUMNS

As Dixieland is American civilization's repository of classicism, it's fitting that the "authentic replication of Greek and Roman orders" is being undertaken by a Carolina company run by a gentleman named Jeff Davis. Never mind that a promotional press release put out by these inheritors of the southern classical tradition cavalierly reduces the *historic* Jeff Davis to the rank of "a famous Confederate general"; that kind of mistake often occurs when some unlettered factotum bestirs mystic chords of memory in the cause of public relations. There was a Civil War general by the name of Jefferson Davis, but he was a *Union* brigadier—and unlike Confederate President Jefferson Davis, he wasn't all that famous.

But regardless of all that, Chadsworth's "Authentic Replication" line of wooden architectural columns are the most ambitious and far-reaching replications in this book. The columns emerge from designs that are computer-generated from original specifications formulated in 1563 A.D. by "the great Italian Renaissance architect" Giacomo Barozzi da Vignola. (They're right there. We looked it up. Vignola was important enough to have succeeded Michelangelo in charge of work at St. Peter's Cathedral.) Once the design is perfected, the columns are then hand-finished from high-grade lumber.

Free catalog available.

CHADSWORTH, INCORPORATED
Dept. 101, P.O. Box 53268
Atlanta, GA 30355
Tel. 404/876-5410
Fax. 404/876-4492

⊞ TIN CEILINGS

A A Abbingdon Ceilings of Brooklyn, New York, offers a large line of metal ceilings in modern and turn-of-the-century styles.

Brochure available.

A A ABBINGDON
2149-51 Utica Avenue
Brooklyn, NY 11234
Tel. 718/258-8333
Fax. 718/338-2739

⊛ CAST-IRON STAIRCASES

Steptoe & Wife Antiques of Ontario, Canada, carries a line of cast-iron Victorian staircases in kit form. These employ the structural and design features of various nineteenth-century originals, and include treads, risers, side panels and center pole.

The Barclay model is a 5-foot-wide spiral staircase patterned after one purchased by Steptoe & Wife from an old Ottawa paper mill. It bolts together easily and has open fretwork and sides, with a closed step and ornate steel handrail supports. Each rise is 8⅛ inches.

The Kensington is claimed by Steptoe to be the only straight Victorian cast-iron staircase now available. It was adapted by the firm from the designs of several mid-nineteenth-century stairs found in the eastern U.S. and Canada (the staircase at Independence Hall in Wheeling, West Virginia, is cited as a particularly strong influence). The Kensington's riser and side panels are openwork; the tread is closed and employs a diamond-grid design. The stairs are 36 inches wide and have a 7⅝-inch rise. The stairs also have an optional brass railing and have a baked enamel finish.

Prices: Barclay Spiral Stairs, $185 per riser, $225 with brass handrail; Kensington Staircase, $185 per riser (prices include shipping and duty).

Catalog of architectural replicas available, $2.

STEPTOE & WIFE
322 Geary Avenue
Toronto, ON, Canada M6H 2C7
Tel. 416/530-4204 or 800/461-0060
Fax. 416/530-4666

⇒ Bathroom Fixtures ⇒

In December 1855 the big news in New York was not the ascendancy of the Know-Nothings in Congress, but the completion of the Vanderbilt Mansion, which for the first time set aside an entire room for bathing. This "bathroom," which contained both a bathtub and a commode, betokened the growing interest in personal hygiene that soon had Vassar College making each of its girls bathe twice weekly.

✱ PEDESTAL SINK

In the centennial year of 1886, only the best homes had rooms set aside for bathing. This room would have had no commode—which, if indoors, would've been located in a closet or other storage area—and its sink and tub would've been brought in from somewhere else around the house.

Sunrise Specialty's Victorian vitreous-china pedestal sink is an exact replica of one manufactured around 1900.

Price: $400, F.O.B, Emeryville, California.

Price list and color catalog available.

SUNRISE SPECIALTY
5540 Doyle Street
Emeryville, CA 94608
Tel. 510/654-1794
Fax. 510/654-5775

❦ CLAWFOOT BATHTUBS

Sunrise Specialty of Emeryville, California, offers a line of clawfoot bathtubs of the type found in wealthy homes late in the 1800s. These are not replicas but salvaged antiques, restored and refitted with new brass fixtures and oak rims. Sunrise Specialty uses the Chicago Faucet Company's taps exclusively. These have been continuously manufactured by that company since the nineteenth century and are considered the best available. Clawfoot tubs are available in the Emeryville store or by special order.

Prices begin at $1,500.

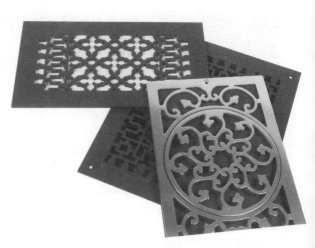

HOT-AIR REGISTERS

The Reggio Register Company manufactures traditional hot-air registers in great variety for ceilings and floors, all made of cast brass, iron or aluminum. They will also accept orders for custom-made grilles and registers.

Catalog available, $1.

THE REGGIO REGISTER COMPANY
P.O. Box 511
Ayer, MA 01432
Tel. 508/772-3493
Fax. 508/772-5513

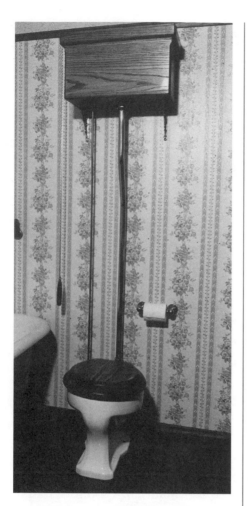

PULL-CHAIN TOILET

The Antique Baths & Kitchens pull-chain toilet is an updated replica of a turn-of-the-century model. Its box is constructed of top-quality solid oak, and is lined with heavy-gauge stainless steel. The valve and flush mechanisms are solid-brass pieces.

The toilet comes with a rosewood flush handle and brass chain. The flush pipe is brass and built in the original offset shape. The bowl is made of first-quality new white china.

Price: $475 (50 percent deposit required; balance billed C.O.D.).

Brochure available, $2.

ANTIQUE BATHS & KITCHENS
2220 Carlton Way
Santa Barbara, CA 93109
Tel. 805/962-8598

COMMODE SEATS

As part of their line of products that "you can bet your assets on," DeWeese Woodworking of Philadelphia, Mississippi, offers solid-oak commode seats with solid-brass hinges. Standard and elongated styles are available.

Brochure available.

DeWEESE WOODWORKING COMPANY
P.O. Box 576
Philadelphia, MS 39350
Tel. 601/656-4951

▣ COPPER WEATHER VANES

A ninth-century papal decree mandated that the image of a rooster be placed atop churches as evidence of good faith and to ward away evil. In time the rooster's talons would grip the roofs of people's homes as well, and throughout the Middle Ages he was a common sight, performing a religious as well as a decorative function there.

Following this tradition, the weathercock became king of the roost on colonial American homes and barns—but by then there were several other beasts in the menagerie. In nineteenth-century agricultural communities the rooster traced the wind's direction along with a barnyard of other critters—cows, horses, sheep, and pigs. In seacoast towns, schools of swordfish, cod and whales swam the wind currents from atop most buildings. During this period two other popular weather vanes were introduced: one was religious, the Angel of Gabriel; the other patriotic, the American eagle.

Good Directions of Stamford, Connecticut, offers more than 50 weather vanes made of pure copper and

brass that "are virtually indistinguishable from original antiques." Available in both polished and patina finishes, these weather vanes depict three sizes of roosters in addition to a deer, the Angel Gabriel, a grasshopper, fish, red Indian and many other figures that turned with the nineteenth century's winds.

Prices range from $75 to $329.

Brochure available, $1.

GOOD DIRECTIONS, INC.
24 Ardmore Road
Stamford, CT 06902
Tel. 203/348-1836
Fax. 203/357-0092

❀ COPPER KITCHEN SINK

Antique Baths & Kitchens' kitchen sink is a replica of a standard nineteenth-century fixture. Formed from heavy-gauge copper, it has a hand-hammered top flange and soldered and riveted seams. Its overall size is approximately 22¼ inches by 32¼ inches by 6 inches; inside measurements are approximately 20 inches by 30 inches. Custom orders are welcome.

Price: $430 (plus packing and shipping charges). A double sink is obtainable for $900.

Literature available, $2.

ANTIQUE BATHS & KITCHENS
2220 Carlton Way
Santa Barbara, CA 93109
Tel. 805/962-8598

BIG REDUCTION IN PRICES

AT $1.39 TO $12.75 We offer you finer iron beds than were ever before shown. Newest designs, first class material, construction and finish. Wonderful values. We challenge the world on quality and price. A lower price than ours means a poorer quality.
THEY ARE INDESTRUCTIBLE AND WILL NEVER WEAR OUT.

THE METAL USED in the construction of our beds is strictly high grade throughout. No rusty scrap iron or corroded refuse metals. The highest and best quality of malleable iron, rolled Bessemer steel and drawn brass tubing.

THE CONSTRUCTION of our metal beds is the best that modern machinery, science and skilled workmanship, can possibly produce. Every part and parcel is carefully modeled, framed and joined. The joints and chills carefully rounded and smoothed. The rails are made of Bessemer steel in angle shape and will not bend or break. Great care is taken in the fitting of the tongue and grooves by which the rail is fastened to the head and foot end. They stand firm and will support any weight of persons.

THE FINISH of our iron beds, we guarantee the best that can be made. The enamel which is used for the several coatings is the highest grade obtainable. Each coat, after being carefully and thoroughly applied, is baked in a large oven heated to a very high degree of temperature, then thoroughly smoothed and polished. This produces a finish that is impervious to water and our iron beds can be cleaned of finger marks or other soiling by washing with soap and water.

THE BRASS TRIMMING which is used in the ornamentation and construction of our metal beds is of the highest quality of drawn brass tubing, highly polished and burnished, coated with the best quality of French lacquer, which absolutely preserves the polish and prevents tarnishing. Lacquer is to brass what varnish is to wood, it preserves the material.

COLOR BEDS. We furnish all our iron beds in ... bed it specifically states w... much more attractive in single solid color only ... ordered in colors, shipment will be made direc... ...ment can be made.

WE CALL YOUR SPECIAL ATTE... ...te, light blue and white, pea green and white ... ...en you wish to order a bed in combination of

WE ESPECIALLY RECOMMEND ... ...shed in the first color mentioned above and th...

VERNIS MARTIN ALL GOLD FINIS... ...rnis Martin. It is a three-coat finish, consistin... ...nze and, lastly, a third coat of the best quality ... ...h grade all brass beds. To produce this hand... ...st be seen, examined and compared with that ... ...e or tarnish.

THE SIDE RAILS on all our iron beds ar... ...to the bed with the re... ...ired. TO SET UP IRON BEDS, place the rai... ...h hammer by striking the wood.

HOW TO ORDER. When ordering a metal bed, be careful to state the width wanted, also the color, otherwise white will be shipped. We illustrate our beds made up with bolster, mattress and covering, but the price quoted is for bed only. Springs, mattresses and pillows are illustrated and described on pages 431 to 435.

FURNITURE

Adjustable Iron Bed Ca...

1K24... illust... shows ...justable for iron... Made of be... high carbo... mer steel. 1⅜ inches ...eter. Soli... hood rods ... thick. Bra... 2 inches in ... Can be se... tached to ... by four ... clamps. When attached to the bed ... canopy measures 86 inches from ... Finished in baked white enamel... solid color. In ordering canopy ... give size of post, width of bed, ... wanted. Shipping weight, about 3...

Price, all sizes ....

$4.98 FOR THIS HANDSOME DESIGN HIGH GRADE, MASSIVE IRON BED complete with best quality steel springs. The bed is one of our special three-piece combina... ...n beds which has no side rails. The long bar ... the spring forms the side rail of the bed. ...e of the finest methods of construction ... ...own and offered exclusively by us. This ... ...thod makes it possible to pack and ship ... ...e bed at less expense. We offer this ... ...mbination outfit to show what it is pos... ...le for us to produce in a strictly high ... ...de bed, spring and mattress at an extremely low ... ...ce, which is offered only as a sample of the won... ...ful values we are giving in our entire bed line. ...ght of the head end of the bed, 56 inches, foot ... ...t, 44 inches. The corner posts are 1 5-16 inches ... ...diameter and are mounted with massive smooth ... ...t ornamental chills. The top rod and filling rods ... ...t ¾ inch thick. These dimensions make an un... ...ally substantial and massive bed. Finished ... ...oughout in best quality white enamel, thorough... ...aked and hardened. The spring frame is made ... ...high carbon steel angle bars, 1¼ inches wide. ...e fabric is made of best quality heavy tinned ... ...e interwoven and interlaced in what is called ... ...rpin style, making it absolutely non-sagging ... ...d noiseless. The fabric is fastened to the steel ... ...me at each end by fifteen high carbon steel spiral ... ...ings. This spring combines the greatest com... ...t and lasting qualities it is possible to obtain. ...e mattress is the finest of its kind that ... ...l and our knowledge of mattress construction ... ...ld enable us to produce. A combination mat... ...ss never before offered, suitable for use in any ... ...mate. The filling is made of white basswood ... ...celsior, thoroughly screened and freed from all ... ...purities. This forms the inner filling only. One ... ...e is covered with a thick layer of the best qual... ...sanitary sea moss, which is not excelled for its ... ...ienic and comfort giving qualities. The other side of the mattress is ...vered with thick layers of elastic felt of good quality. This makes the ...ttress suitable for cold or warm weather and furnishes a firm or soft bed ...may be desired. The ticking is extra quality heavy twill, closely stitched ...d full bound. The mattress is made in the very latest and most up to date ...nner. Diamond tufted with leather tufts, and we place it in competition ...h mattresses sold throughout the country at $6.00 to $7.00.

No. 1K2395 Full size only. Price, Iron Bed and Spring.....$4.98
Shipping weight, about 110 pounds.

No. 1K2395 Full size only. Price, Mattress only...........$3.98
Shipping weight, about 50 pounds.

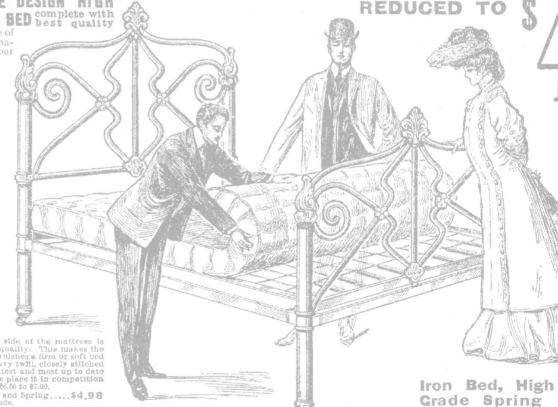

No. 1K2395

REDUCED TO $4...

Iron Bed, High Grade Spring and Mattress.

$1.39

$1.89

$2.69

WINDSOR CHAIRS

The Windsor chair can be traced to the cottage of a peasant that stood near the castle of a king. We have no record of the peasant, but the king was George II—and one dark and stormy night he sought refuge from the torrent in the nameless serf's home. Now, despite allowing England to be drawn into the War of Austrian Succession, George II was a peace lov ing king and—as George Frederick Handel could have told you—a generous patron of the arts. He admired the humble throne that his peasant offered—for its simple design was beautiful while providing much in the way of lightness, strength and comfort. In fact, after the weather cleared, the king put his cabinetmaker to work on a royal replica.

As word of this episode spread, so did interest in these chairs, which were marketed right out of Windsor. By 1725, the Windsor chair had reached Philadelphia, from whence its popularity spread and lasted nearly 150 years.

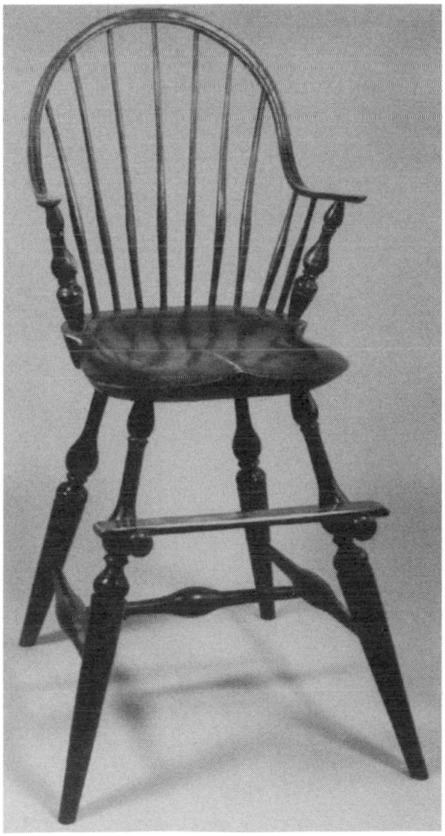

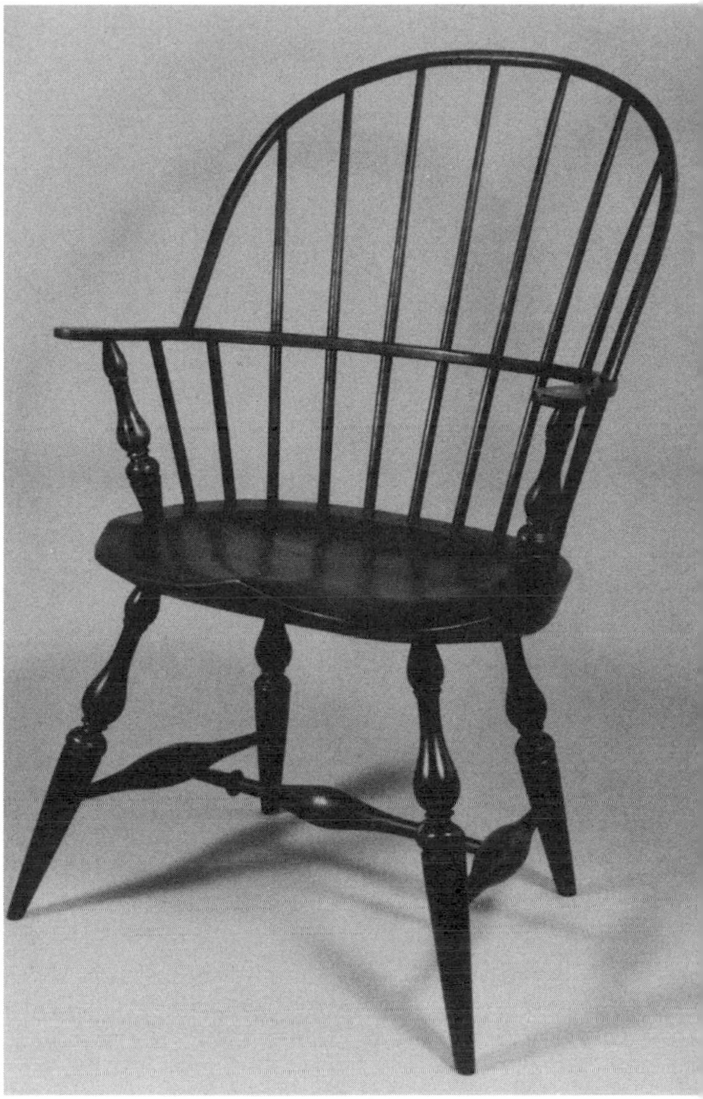

Although, as Wallace Nutting observed, the American Windsor "means a pine seat if it means anything good," the republican chair is a democratic employer of woods. Traditionally, its spindles (there are more of these in the American version than the English one) and arms are made from hickory and ash; its legs from oak or maple; and the bow of its back from hickory again. There are six basic types of backs: low, comb, hoop, loop, fan and New England arm. All employ the slender, round, upright array of spokes or spindles that describe a Windsor chair's characteristically graceful profile.

Windsors were used by the First Continental Congress. Fitted with a small writing desk on the right arm, a comb-back Windsor supported Thomas Jefferson as he drafted the Declaration. But despite that document's intent, we are yet dependent on King George—or at least on one of his peasants—for the chair itself. For ever since the time it was admired by a prince, the Windsor chair's charm has flowed from a ruggedness built of delicacy. It is where, as Nutting went on to put it, "lightness, strength, grace, durability and quaintness are all found in an irresistible blend."

Leonard's Reproductions and Antiques offers replica Windsor chairs in a wide variety of styles. These range in price from $275 for a 1760 bow-back to $1,200 for a camel-back settee finished in crackled milk paint. The unusual high chair pictured costs $410 either stained or painted, and $490 in milk paint. Through six furnished showrooms, Leonard's also does custom restoration of antique furniture, and offers a range of replica eighteenth- and nineteenth-century beds.

Literature and price list available.

LEONARD'S REPRODUCTIONS AND ANTIQUES
600 Taunton Avenue
Seekonk, MA 02771
Tel. 508/336-8585
Fax. 508/336-4884

❧ HITCHCOCK CHAIRS

"L. Hitchcock—Hitchcocks-ville, conn. Warranted," was the legend that Lambert Hitchcock inscribed on each of his chair's seatbacks, with each "N" curiously (if not also quaintly) reversed. According to local legend, "warranted" meant that the chair had survived a fall from the third story of the factory building erected by Hitchcock in Riverton (Hitchcocks-ville), Connecticut, in 1826.

The chairs that Lambert Hitchcock manufactured at his factory had seats made of cat-o'-nine-tails rush, cane or wood. The rush was harvested for him in late summer by local farmers, while the cane had to be imported. For ornamentation, Hitchcock would employ the stencil and striping techniques traditionally used by stagecoach decorators. Rockers, side chairs and armchairs were all made in this way.

In a way, Lambert Hitchcock was

the Ethan Allen of his time (I refer to the miracle-mile furniture showrooms, not the Vermont patriot for whom they are named), for by the time the Hitchcocks-ville factory was complete, its maker was marketing his "fancy chairs" by the thousands and under-selling local cabinetmakers who had previously made chairs for ordinary folk. The low-cost factory-mades that Hitchcock (and other, less well-remembered entrepreneurs) provided, enabled people of modest means to fill their parlors with matched sets for the first time—as well as with more guests to occupy them. But despite this success, Hitchcock became overextended and his factory ended the manufacture of chairs shortly after his death in 1852.

Nearly a century later, John T. Kenney was drifting lazily down the Farmington River on a fishing trip. There he came upon Hitchcock's forlorn chair factory, padlocked and boarded up for decades. Virtually any New Englander would have been well familiar with the story of the Hitchcock chair, but Kenney had even received one as a wedding present. As he continued down the Farmington an idea came to Kenney: "Could it be," he wondered, "that others would be as interested in a revived Hitchcock as I?" Market research soon affirmed Kenney's notion, and on October 17, 1946, the authentic reproduction of the Hitchcock chair was begun.

Hitchcock chairs can be found at company stores located throughout New England, and at selected stores across the U.S.

For more information contact:

THE HITCHCOCK CHAIR COMPANY
Riverton, CT 06065
Tel. 203/379-8531

CHARLESTON BATTERY BENCH

Although it would win the siege that began the Civil War, the Confederacy lost the waltz that preceded it.

Prior to the rebel capture of Fort Sumter on April 14, 1861, there was much confidence that President Lincoln would order its small garrison evacuated. This was based on the notion that a federal withdrawal would keep Dixie's hound dogs of war from hunting for a while, and in recognition of the fact that the fort's location in Charleston's sea channel made its capture by the South inevitable anyway.

Lincoln's advisors overwhelmingly favored abandoning Sumter, and seeing the new President as little more than a mid-chart Darwinian specimen, figured he'd obediently cede the fort to the rebels. But Lincoln had different plans: with his April 6 dispatch of an armed naval expedition to reinforce Sumter, the President confounded advisors and adversaries alike by putting the latter in the position of either backing down from their threats against the fort, or launching an attack upon it. Such an attack would not only mark the fledgling Confederacy as aggressor in a war it didn't want, but would, as Jeff Davis was warned by his Secretary of State, Robert Toombs, "wantonly strike a hornet's nest which extends from mountains to ocean," resulting in "a civil war greater than any the world has yet seen."

Few men were as steadfast as was Davis when he thought a principle was involved—and believing that Lincoln's advancing naval force would cause the world to view the U.S. as aggressor whoever shot first, the Confederate President would not back down. So in spite of Toombs' dread prophesy, Davis issued an order on the 10th for Gen. P.G.T. Beauregard to demand that the federal troops quit Sumter, and, if refused, "to proceed in such a manner as you may determine to reduce it."

Beauregard sent out two soldiers in a rowboat to pow-wow with Maj. Robert Anderson, Sumter's commander. Anderson, who had been Beauregard's artillery instructor at West Point, sorrowfully declined the terms demanded by his former student's emissaries; and saying, "If we do not meet again in this world, I hope we meet again in the better one," saw them away from the wharf. Within hours, the "honor" of firing the first shot of the war would fall to one of these soldiers—a Virginian named Roger Pryor. Only days before, Pryor had stood on a Charleston balcony exhorting Carolinians to "strike a blow" for the Confederacy; but when the lanyard to that blow was offered, he declined with emotion, saying that he could not fire the first gun.

Less squeamish and more sesech (secessionist) was Edmund Ruffin. A crusty old-line rebel and the editor of an agricultural newspaper, the 67-year-old Virginian was so cantankerous he might have gone on to be played by Lionel Barrymore in some knockoff of *Gone With the Wind*. It was no doubt with a curmudgeonly display of brio that Ruffin touched off the Civil War's first mortar at 4:30 on the morning of the 12th. As seen from the Battery, the ten-inch shell traced a crimson ellipse through Charleston's sea and sky before bursting above Sumter and into a fusillade of four year's duration.

The Charleston Battery Bench is made from the original mold pattern of those benches lining the Battery in the mid-1800s. "It is a very authentic piece of Charleston history," says Andrew Slotin, director of Charleston Battery Bench, Inc., "given that its manufacture has been continuous since the middle part of the nineteenth-century and is still being made *exactly* as was done some hundred-plus years ago." The bench uses Carolina cypress dip-painted in the traditionally-dark Charleston green, and depicts in its heavy-weight castings the flora and fauna indigenous to the state during its nineteenth-century period of secessionist fervor. The maker asks you to note that, as it is with New Orleans, ironwork is closely attached to Charleston's history. Hence the bench's "inverted parrot, fox and hound, and extensive use of a foliate motif overall."

Dimensions: 48 inches long, 28 inches high, 21 inches deep. Weight: 75 lbs.

Price: $119.50.

Free brochure available.

CHARLESTON BATTERY BENCH, INC.
191 King Street
Charleston, SC 29401
Tel. 803/722-3842

▣ VICTORIAN GLIDERS

The porch had its beginning in the eighteenth-century South, where weather and hospitality conspired to elaborate on the stoops and entryways of colder climes. But beginning in 1850, these places would also adopt the porch, effectively making it the architectural prerequisite of the American Victorian home.

By the turn of the century, the porch had to some degree replaced the log cabin as a symbol of political virtue.

Both structures were folksy, but physically and metaphorically the porch was located much farther from the forest. "A rambling front porch was worth 300,000 votes," observed one party boss, who, like those advising William McKinley and Theodore Roosevelt, recognized that their candidates' images of rugged frontier individualism had to be tempered with some respectable Victorian domesticity.

But mostly, the porch became ubiquitous for the pleasures it offered as a kind of Victorian HBO. More than just a setting in which the passing midsummer evening and its community of players was framed, the porch became a place for children to play, and—in the sway of porch swings and gliders—for courtship to progress.

Natural oak or white-painted replicas of Victorian porch swings and gliders are available from Green Enterprises of Hamilton, Virginia. Prices for swings begin at $324.50, and for gliders at $574.50.

Color brochure available, $1.

GREEN ENTERPRISES
43 South Rogers Street
Hamilton, VA 22068
Tel. 703/338-3606

❀ ENGLISH HAT STAND WITH UMBRELLA RACK

Here's the hat rack for the Grand Vizier of Victoriana's curlicued miters— a spacecraft ripped from the pages of Jules Verne's *Rocket Ship to Roccoco*, complete with an umbrella-festooned launch gantry. Anything more ornate might have made even Victoria and Albert a bit dizzy.

Actually, while Victoriana may never die (historian Asa Briggs has said that as we head towards our own *fin de siècle*, interest in the style will escalate) the time may soon come when certain segments of society will be running around in Cassini-edition AMC Matadors to gush over abandoned strip malls of the 1970s. Someday soon, Ms and Mr. Sunday Style Section, you may find yourselves sipping your Constant Comment from the shadow of a restored Photomat kiosk. Styles change, and you do with them. So what if all Victoriana is not beautiful? That's the beauty of it.

For good or ill, the Moultrie Manufacturing Company's "Old South Collection" are one-of-a-kind items, manufactured by a family firm. Faithfully recreated in aluminum are—in addition to the hat-and-umbrella stand featured—such formerly cast-iron Victorian pieces as garden furniture (some of it replicated from originals patented in 1846), garden fountains, a bar stool, a gazebo, a music rack, and more. The hat rack's overall height is 71 inches, its width 25 inches and its depth 10½ inches

Catalog available.

MOULTRIE MANUFACTURING COMPANY
P.O. Box 1179
Moultrie, GA 31776-1179
Tel. 800/841-8674

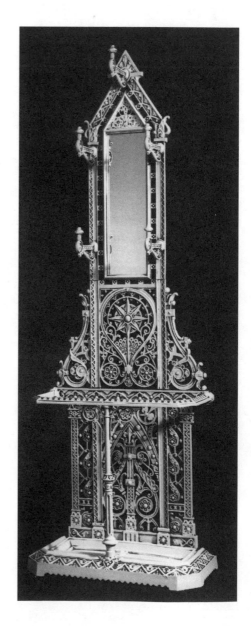

❦ VICTORIAN MAILBOXES

Delivery of residential mail began during the 1860s, introducing to the everyday American landscape both the mailbox and the postman making his rounds. But the assorted shapes, sizes and colors of the former would be, until 1902, a matter determined by recipients—with rural lard pails, coal cans and apple and cigar boxes sometimes pulling postal duty.

The Antique Hardware Store's elegant Victorian mailbox more closely resembles something that might have housed the correspondence between Lloyd George and George Sand, had there been any. It is freestanding, made of cast iron, and has a brass flap fore and lockable door aft for the respective deposit and removal of mail.

Dimensions: 47 inches high by 16½ inches wide.

Price: $279, plus postage, handling and insured delivery charges.

Free color catalog available.

ANTIQUE HARDWARE STORE
9718 Easton Road
Route 611
Kintnersville, PA 18930
Tel. 215/847-2447 or toll-free order line
*   800/422-9982*
Fax. 215/847-5628

⊷ Iron and Brass Beds ⊷

Brass beds, which reached the height of their popularity at around the turn of the century, have enjoyed a sustained revival of interest during the past 20 years. To the current standard of flimsy, brass-clad replicas, here are a couple of exceptions:

❖ THE BED FACTORY

Purveyors of "heirloom quality" iron and brass beds in period styles.

Catalog available, $5 (refundable with purchase).

THE BED FACTORY
112 Harding Way West
Galion, OH 44833
Tel. 419/468-3861

❧ THE BEDPOST

The Bedpost disdains the use of such "modern" materials as aluminum (invented in the 1880s, aluminum was used during the turn of the century, although not for bedframes) and keeps instead to cast iron, steel rods and pipe. The firm also employs an antique-style bedframe design for its superior structural strength.

The company's iron and brass beds feature several types of ornamentation, the designs of which have been faithfully copied from originals. They estimate that their gauge of brass is about 25 percent heavier than that of the competition. Both king- and queen-size models are available.

Packet of literature, $3.

THE BEDPOST
32 South High Street
East Bangor, PA 18013
Tel. 215/588-3824

❈ CHARLES P. ROGERS BRASS BEDS

Established in 1855, the Charles P. Rogers Brass Bed Company is the country's oldest manufacturer. Their solid-brass beds are available in a good range of antique styles and reflect in their structure and design the manufacturer's allegiance to traditional construction techniques.

Color catalog available, $3.

CHARLES P. ROGERS BRASS BEDS
899 First Avenue
New York, NY 10022
Tel. 212/935-6900 or 800/272-7726
(outside New York State)

Bedding House of CHAS. P. ROGERS & CO.,

248 Sixth Avenue, N. Y.

Corner 16th Street.

January 1st, 1890.

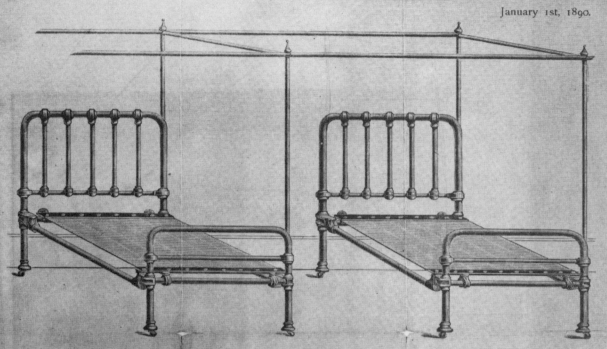

We would respectfully call your attention to

Our Improved Institution Iron Bedstead.

We refer by permission to the following Institutions where they are in use, and are found to meet all the requirements of a first-class **Hospital** or **Institution** Iron Bedstead.

References:—

Convent of the Sacred Heart, N. Y. City.
Isabella Home, N. Y. City.
Sisters of Charity, New Providence.

Franciscan Sisters of St. Mary's Brooklyn, N.Y.
Berachah Home, N. Y. City.
and many others.

This Bedstead is made of the best material throughout. The frames are made of inch tubing, with $1\frac{1}{2}$ inch Tubular Sides and ends, are fitted with best quality woven wire, spring mattress with adjustable screws that prevent sagging, made with rubber feet, or castors and japanned, any plain color.

Sizes, - - - - 2 ft.-6. 2 ft.-9 3 ft. 3 ft.-6 wide.
Price, - - - -

We are prepared to furnish estimates for all kinds of Mattresses, Pillows, etc., suitable for **Institution** or Hospital use.

Mattresses and Pillows remade and renovated at Short notice. (Special Prices.)

✹ BALL-AND-BALL BED

The ball-and-ball bed is named for its distinctive turnings at the top of each post. Popular in the antebellum era, the bed's use of heavier timber than that of earlier styles gave it an imposing presence. The ball-and-ball posts vary in height from just over 3½ feet to about 6 feet. Many of these higher posts support "cannonball" beds, named for the larger size of their turnings. Southern beds of this style will often have holes at the top of each post in which dowels are placed to accommodate mosquito netting.

Alan W. Pease's replica ball-and-ball beds are handmade in the same fashion as the originals, but in standard sizes. They are available in a variety of woods and types, per your order.

Price for standard ball-and-ball bed, $1,370.

Catalog of beds and other period-style furniture, $4.

THE COUNTRY BED SHOP
Alan W. Pease, cabinetmaker
Rural Route 1, P.O. Box 65
Ashby, MA 01431
Tel. 508/386-7550

Shaker Furniture

The following seven items are all from Shaker Workshops. See page 38 for ordering information.

▨ TAPE-BACK DINING CHAIRS

These replicas of the dining chairs used by Mount Lebanon Shakers employ bent backposts and curved backrails to comfortably accommodate people of any height. Rock maple is used throughout, and dimensions are said to have been thoughtfully worked out by the Shakers.

Height of back, 40¾ inches; height of seat, 17½ inches; width, 20¾ inches; depth, 17⅛ inches.

For the armchair (not shown) kit, $150 (plus 5.95 for shipping and handling); assembled and finished, $300 (plus $10.55 for shipping and handling). For the side chair kit, $128.75 (plus $5.65 for shipping and handling); assembled and finished, $257.50 (plus $10.55 for shipping and handling).

❋ HANGING SHELVES

A replica of a set of nineteenth-century shelves now in the collection of Hancock Shaker Village.

Made of clear pine with a height of 25 inches and a width of 27 inches, the three shelves are approximately 5, 6 and 7 inches deep, respectively.

Price: Kit, $62.50, plus $4.55 for shipping; assembled and finished, $125, plus $8.80 for shipping and handling.

⊞ MOUNT LEBANON SETTEE

"This piece would never have left the community," writes Mr. Richard Dabrowski of Shaker Workshops, regarding the Shaker Mount Lebanon settee. Further described as "the rarest of all Shaker furniture," the double armchair that this se ttee replicates follows one originally built at Mount Lebanon, New York, toward the end of the nineteenth century.

With a frame of rock maple, the settee has a height of 37½ inches, a width of 43½ inches, and a depth of 19 inches.

Price: Kit, $263.75, plus $9.10 for shipping and handling; assembled and finished $527.50, plus freight collect by truck.

⊞ TOWEL RACK

Freestanding floor racks such as this were commonplace in Shaker retiring rooms, kitchens and wash houses. This one, still in use by Shakers at Maine's Sabbathday community, is well suited for airing quilts and blankets, hanging towels or drying wet socks and mittens.

Made of hard maple, the rack is 33 inches high, 34 inches wide and 6½ inches deep.

Price: Kit, $55, plus $4.20 for shipping; finished piece, $110, postpaid.

❈ WEAVER'S CHAIR

Huge Shaker handlooms demanded chairs with high seats to allow the weavers to sit close to their work. The same chairs were also used at shop desks and at laundry and ironing tables.

This weaver's chair is made of rock maple, and when finished stands 39 inches high (with a seat height of 26 inches) and 18¾ inches wide.

Price: Kit, $82.50 (plus $5.40 for shipping and handling); assembled and finished $165 (plus $10.55 by UPS).

❀ REVOLVING CHAIR

This ingenious hard-maple chair was first produced at the Shakers' Mount Lebanon chair factory around 1860. A threaded steel rod allows the height of the chair to descend from 21½ inches to 17½ inches with a quick spin. The chair's bent back adds an additional 10¼ inches to its height, and the seat is 15½ inches in diameter.

Price: Kit, $75 (plus $4.55 for shipping and handling); assembled and finished, $150 (plus $8.80 for shipping and handling).

▣ HANCOCK STEPSTOOL

The tall chests of drawers and built-in cupboards commonplace at Shaker villages required some means of access. Shaker Workshops' Hancock stepstool duplicates one in use at the Hancock, Massachusetts, Shaker community during the nineteenth century. Although that stepstool was green, this kit comes without any stain; but the original and other paint colors are available through the Shaker Workshops catalog.

Made of Eastern white pine, the Hancock stepstool measures 24 inches in height, 17¼ inches in width, and 14¼ inches in depth. Its steps are each 4½ inches deep.

Price: Kit, $77.50 (plus $4.55 for shipping and handling); assembled and finished, $155 (plus $8.80 for shipping and handling).

Seasonal catalog available, $1.

SHAKER WORKSHOPS
P.O. Box 1028
Concord, MA 01742
Tel. 508/646-8985
Fax. 508/648-8217

❋ 1802 TRUNK

During the seventeenth and eighteenth centuries, the dower chest was part of every maiden's world. She began filling it with linens and laces from the time she began to sew, laying away her first samplers and linens against that day when she would marry. Made of pine, poplar and walnut, these chests were generally three- to four-feet long and placed in the parlor or bedroom. The chests were built by farmers and carpenters and generally decorated by itinerant artists. These men covered them with a background color of soft blue, against which were often painted the year, the tulips that recalled the distant gardens of the Rhine for Pennsylvanians, and the unicorn that had been the guardian of maidenhood since medieval times.

The Country Store of Concord, North Carolina's 1802-dated "trunk" has been designed to resemble these dower chests. Against a pale back-

ground, it bears flowers, trees and a black-and-Williamsburg-blue vase.

The trunk measures 23 inches high by 38 inches wide by 13 inches deep.

THE COUNTRY STORE
130 Cabarrus Avenue East
P.O. Box 625
Concord, NC 28026
Tel. 704/784-1526

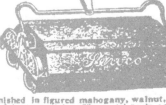
39

ANTIQUE HARDWARE STORE

The Antique Hardware Store, a classic example of the harder-trying "Avis" in its field, has been in business since 1982. In addition to a varied line of period-style brass hardware, the company's mail-order catalog features bathroom fixtures and plumbing, lighting fixtures, weather vanes and more.

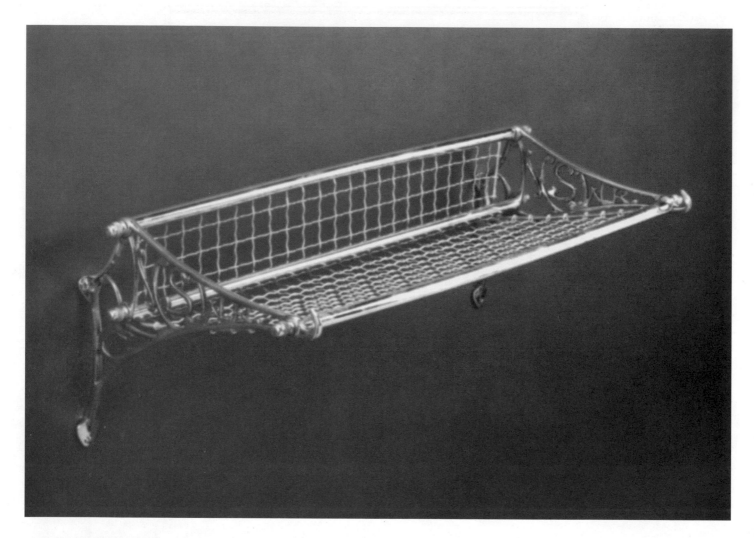

VICTORIAN TRAIN RACK

Victorian racks were settings for the display of the cultural biases and accomplishments of their owners through a jumbled medium of exotic animal or botanical prints, family photographs and foreign views. On the other hand, Victorian *train* racks generally just conveyed hats, bags and the like—but here their replicas have been adapted to ride the display route at home.

The Antique Hardware Store's train rack is made of solid brass, has a gently sloping shelf, and measures 29½ inches in length.

Price: $129, plus postage, handling and insured delivery charges.

Free color catalog available.

ANTIQUE HARDWARE STORE
9718 Easton Road, Route 611
Kintnersville, PA 18930
Tel. 215/847-2447 or
*   800/422-9982 to order*
Fax. 215/847-5628

✻ FIREBACKS

Although still used in parts of continental Europe, the cast-iron fireback has been virtually unknown in America since the middle of the nineteenth century. But now, an addendum to the history of the American fireback may be written.

A fireback is a cast-iron plate that, when placed behind the fire of a hearth, absorbs the heat of the fire and further protects the rear wall of the fireplace. Lately the decorative qualities of firebacks have renewed an appreciation of their utility.

The earliest English fireback yet found was made back in 1548 and reflects the influence of the firebacks that had been popular both in Holland and Germany for the previous hundred years. In the English-speaking American colonies, the use of firebacks followed the example of the mother country, and employed embossed decorative patterns based on the designs of coats-of-arms, illustrated allegories and "loose stamps." Although the use of firebacks waned in England early in the nineteenth century, they persisted in the U.S. until around 1840, when the sealing-off of fireplaces was hastened by the invention of the airtight stove.

Pennsylvania Firebacks offers a large selection of firebacks, including such replicas as "Hereford Stove Plate" and "Floral Panels."

PENNSYLVANIA FIREBACKS, INC.
2237 Bethel Road
Lansdale, PA 19446
Tel. 215/699-0805

▦ ROXBURY FLYTRAP

He could take a reference & fall into the Right Course (he carrying a flie-trap slung on his Back to assist him on such Occasions).
— *Uria Brown,* Journal, *1816.*

Because they represent such a small, idealized part of it, even the best replicas and reproductions invariably misrepresent the past. Theirs is a selective memory, as dreamily lit as a Victoria magazine layout of a bunch of 1880s aristocrats playing lawn tennis. "You think about your Hitchcock chairs, or Coca-Cola bottles, or old-fashioned Sears-Roebuck catalogues," says historian Jack Larkin, "and basically you don't have to deal with what's uncomfortable about history." Buy a reproduction kerosene lamp, in other words, and relegate to the shadows all the slavery, broken treaties and murderous epidemics that were so charmingly lit by the glow of the original.

To this rule, the Roxbury Flytrap is a heroic exception. Handmade of finished pine and harness leather, it enables flies to die in the same way as did their Victorian insect ancestors about 300 million generations back. Moreover, the "authentic necessity for all Victorian homesteads" is about as pretty as the job it does.

Price: $40 plus $3.50 for handling (Kansas residents add 4 percent sales tax).

Brochure available, $1.

ROXBURY FLYTRAP COMPANY
P.O. Box 33
Roxbury, Kansas 67476

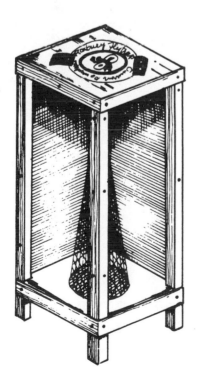

OLD STURBRIDGE VILLAGE CANDLESTICKS

❀ HEART-HANDLED CHAMBERSTICK

A traditional heart design has been pierced into the handle of this solid-brass chamberstick, a precise replica of a Sturbridge Village original.

Dimensions: 2¼ inches by 8½ inches by 4½ inches.

Price: $62 apiece (plus $5.50 for shipping and handling).

▦ PORTER CANDLESTICK

OSV's pewter candlestick follows an 1835 original bearing the mark of pewterer F. Porter of Westbrook, Maine. It stands 6¼ inches high on a ¾-inch base.

Price: $50 apiece (plus $5.50 for shipping and handling).

Catalog available.

OLD STURBRIDGE VILLAGE
One Old Sturbridge Village Road
Sturbridge, MA 01566
Tel. 508/347-3362

NAILHEAD-STUDDED LEATHER TRUNKS

Sometimes termed "hair trunks" because their leather covering often had patches of animal fur left on the hide, nailhead-decorated trunks like those replicated by Steve Lalioff were frequently used in the eighteenth and early nineteenth centuries. In addition to Mr. Lalioff's uniform hair trunk of 1750-1800 depicted here (in ascending order) is his circa-1805 bark-tanned travel trunk, his circa-1855 Jenny Lind jewelry box, and a letter box duplicating one that dates from around 1800.

Mr. Lalioff, who received his training at Williamsburg, Virginia, also reproduces key baskets, Toby mugs, tavern kegs, saddlebags and painted fire buckets—all made of leather in historical fashion.

For further information contact:

TRADITIONAL LEATHERWORK COMPANY
4030 East 225th Street
Cicero, IN 46034
Tel. 317/877-0314

TAVERN WALL BOX

Found during colonial days in the large homes, country inns and taverns of the eastern seaboard, three-tier wall boxes like these were used to store eating utensils or candles, or to keep cooking herbs and spices out of the grasp of rodents. The village carpenter would craft wall boxes from wide pine and poplar woods, assembling it with square-cut nails made by the local blacksmith.

"Today antique boxes command a very high price and are rarely sold on the open market," relates Peter E. Pasquariello of The Heritage Shop.

"With my boxes and shelves, I hope to have captured the beauty and simplicity found throughout America during an earlier day." Mr. Pasquariello uses the same materials to fashion his wall boxes as did the eighteenth-century village carpenter.

Dimensions: 25½ inches tall, 11 inches wide and 5 inches deep.

Price: $160, postage paid.

Catalog available, $2 (refundable with purchase).

THE HERITAGE SHOP
Dept. SC, P.O. Box 172
Boiling Springs, PA 17007

❦ BANDBOXES

Early in the nineteenth century, when travelers boarded coaches on overland journeys, they carried along an item of luggage that really has no counterpart today—the bandbox. These relatively fragile containers made of pasteboard and wallpaper were used by women as storage for such necessaries as jewelry, scarves, combs, ribbons and sundry bagatelles. By the second quarter of the century even women of modest means generally owned several bandboxes in varying shapes and sizes.

But use of bandboxes was necessarily wedded to the stagecoach era. After 1850, when passage by steamboat and rail required stouter luggage, the bandbox was often treated with cedar oil and put to use as a mothproof container in which finery was stored. Original bandboxes are now said to be beyond the means of all but the wealthiest collectors, but replicas like those made by Box Lore of Omaha, Nebraska, are available. Owner Beth Ramsey's bandboxes are covered with early twentieth-century wallpaper and lined with the same kind of veneer used to make cedar chests. We count 30 varieties, from a $42 trinket box to a $239 limited edition baby's box.

Portfolio available, $5.

BOX LORE
P.O. Box 4381
Omaha, NE 68104
Tel. 402/571-8426

NANTUCKET LIGHTSHIP BASKETS

They were called "Nantucket mink" once: "Nantucket" because they'd be about as genuine as Siberian bourbon if made anywhere else, and "mink" because women—young and old, on-island and off—coveted them so greatly.

Legend has it that the baskets were adapted from those made by local Indians who used clay and willow twigs to fashion them. Of course they weren't yet known as "lightship" baskets then—that came later, during the nineteenth century when seamen aboard the Nantucket lightships took to making them to help while away the hours spent bobbing in the North Atlantic.

"Nantucket lightship baskets endure as a link to the independent spirit that birthed the island and this historic form," says John E. McGuire, a teacher and author of books about New England basketry. From his home in upstate New York, Mr. McGuire employs methods "correct to the nineteenth century" to replicate more than a dozen types of Nantucket lightship baskets—including the evening purse depicted.

Catalog available with SASE.

JOHN C. McGUIRE
398 South Main Street
Geneva, NY 14456
Tel. 315/781-1251

HAND-STITCHED BROOMS

All early American brooms were made from broomcorn, a plant first grown in America by Benjamin Franklin. Some say that Franklin was also first to import the sorghum (for *Sorghum vulgare* is what broomcorn is) from England. The brooms—or "besoms" as they were then known—were made by simply tying a handful of twigs to a wooden handle. Shakers improved upon this arrangement by stitching "shoulders" of broomcorn into the sweeper for greater rigidity. The Shakers sold their first "new style" brooms in 1798.

Rocky Mountain Broomworks does not reflect much of this history, but its equipment does date from before 1900, a time when Colorado was known for its broom industry. Each of its brooms is hand wound and stitched using colored broomcorn, traditional sewing cuffs and double-ended needles. They are available in the company's shop only, in varieties ranging from small whisk to large workshop brooms.

Price: $6 to $18 (colored broomcorn additional).

ROCKY MOUNTAIN BROOMWORKS
The Victor Trading Company and Manufacturing Works
114 South Third Street, P.O. Box 53-M
Victor, CO 80860
Tel. 719/689-2346

✳ SHAKER OVAL BOXES AND CARRIERS

Shaker Workshops credits the work of Brother Delmar C. Wilson (1873—1961) of the Sabbathday Lake community with the inspiration for these oval boxes and carriers. They are entirely handmade by a process that steams and bends select cherry wood and secures it with copper nails to tops and bottoms made of clear pine. The Shakers used oval boxes for the storage of sewing notions and for kitchen items. I've used them as wedding gifts and know them to be of remarkably fine quality.

The oval carrier (W521) is 13¼ inches long, 9⅜ inches wide, and 2¾ inches deep, and costs $37.

There are six oval boxes made, ranging in size from 4⅜ by 1½ inches and costing $34.50 (W510), to 13¼ by 9⅜ by 5¾ inches and costing $62 (W515).

A nested set of all six boxes (W510–W515) costs $250; a nested set of the three smallest boxes (W510–W512) costs $90.

Seasonal catalog available, $1.

SHAKER WORKSHOPS
P.O. Box 1028
Concord, MA 01742
Tel. 508/646-8985
Fax. 508/648-8217

⌘ FIREPLACE BELLOWS

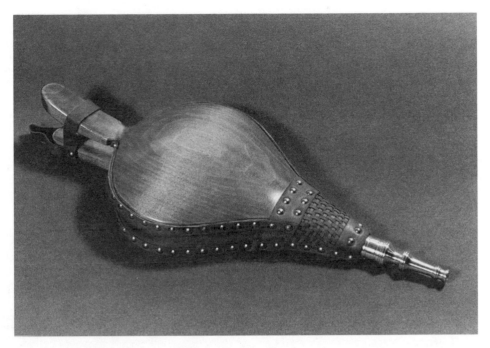

Bellows have been around since the sixteenth century, but the earliest recorded American pair was made by Paul Revere. Although this was a simple affair of turned wood, leather and brass—it wasn't long before patriot utility would replace it with the nineteenth century's taste for ornament. In the early 1800s, a woodcarver from Salem, Massachusetts, named Samuel McIntire fashioned a bellows festooned with a basket of flowers with swags and wreaths of roses. And in 1820, the company of Eckstein & Richard patented their "Elegant Convex Japanned Parlour Bellows," decorated with a painting of a woman and a basket of flowers on one side, and a landscape on the reverse.

In their Revere-like simplicity, George Soucy's turtle-back bellows nearly resemble fine violins. Pear-shaped, and individually crafted from basswood and selected soft leather, the bellows' nozzles are produced from one-inch solid brass bar stock.

Prices: For a small bellows with an overall length of 15 inches, $55; for a regular bellows of 16½ inches, $65; for a large bellows of 20 inches, $85.

Authentic restoration and repair of old and antique bellows also available. Free brochure.

BELLOWS BY SOUCY
1532 West Shore Road
Warwick, RI 02889

⌘ COFFEE GRINDER

If this is coffee bring me tea, but if this is tea, please bring me a cup of coffee.
—attributed to Abraham Lincoln

Before the revolution, Americans drank tea as avidly as any of King George's subjects. It was in fact the revenue potential created by all this colonial tea drinking that resulted in the imposition of one of George III's most despised taxes—the Townshend Acts of 1767. With these duties commenced the notion of coffee drinking as a patriotic display, leaving tea to the Tories.

With lordly indifference to this, the British Parliament passed the Tea Act in 1773, which gave a monopoly in tea to the British East India Company, resulting in even higher prices for the drink. By December, the Boston Tea Party had sealed tea's fate and would help make coffee our national cup.

The Mr. Dudley Company of Oceanside, California, carries 16 models of replica Early American coffee grinders. These are not exact duplicates as they vary in size and detail from the originals.

For dealer information write:

DUDLEY KEBOW, INC.
2603 Industry Street
Oceanside, CA 92054
Tel. 619/439-3000 or 800/447-2600
Fax. 619/967-8032

PYRAMID TOASTER

Toast.

Cut stale bread into slices one-fourth inch thick; dry in the oven. Then put on a toaster or fork, move it gently over heat until dry, then allow it to become a light brown by placing it nearer the heat and turning constantly; or, light gas oven and heat five to eight minutes. Place bread in toaster or pan, one inch from gas, in lower or broiling oven. When brown on one side turn and brown on the other. Bread cut into triangles and toasted are called toast points, and are used for garnishing.

— From the 1903 "Settlement" Cookbook, compiled by Mrs. Simon Kander and Mrs. Henry Schoenfeld.

Whew! Lehman Hardware's turn-of-the-century pyramid toaster can put you right into this picture, diffusing its heat for even browning and "all-the-way-through" crispness. The pyramid toaster works equally well on an open fire, a wood stove, or over a gas burner, toasting two slices at a time.

Price: $6.95.

"Non-Electric" Catalog, $2.

LEHMAN HARDWARE & APPLIANCES
4779 Kidron Road
Kidron, OH 44636
Tel. 216/857-5441
Fax. 216/857-5785

IRONWARE

The Lodge Manufacturing Company is a fourth-generation family business incorporated in 1896. The extensive selection of ironware includes skillets, old-style griddles, camp ovens, country and straight kettles, and cornstick and muffin pans.

Price list and order form available.

LODGE MANUFACTURING COMPANY
P.O. Box 380, Railroad Avenue
South Pittsburgh, TN 37380
Tel. 615/837-7181

GRANITEWARE

First produced in 1870 by the St. Louis Stamping Company, enameled graniteware's special glaze made cooking and cleaning a lot easier. By the turn of the century there were many varieties available—some mottled, some marbled, some spattered, some speckled—and a 24-piece set was advertised in the Sears catalog for $4.37.

Although the American Graniteware Association maintains that none of the currently manufactured graniteware can come even close to the original in quality, they allow that the ware manufactured by the General Housewares Corporation is about the best available. Their "Frontier Campware" offers a nice variety of spattered enamel graniteware, including a huge 20-serving coffee boiler.

Brochure and order form available.

GENERAL HOUSEWARES CORPORATION
Consumer Services
P.O. Box 466
Terre Haute, IN 47804
Tel. 812/232-1000

✤ TIN TEA- AND COFFEEPOTS

"This is a distinctive style reappearing throughout the 1700s," writes tinsmith Bruce Panek of his side-spout coffeepot. A European adaptation of an Arabian design, this coffeepot carries the same type of handle as were found on several vessels in General Washington's mess kit.

Also available as a result of Panek's handiwork is an oval teapot of the type associated with Paul Revere (first executed in silver, these were later copied in tin for the middle classes), and a gooseneck coffeepot that is a replica of one in the Ohio Historical Society's collection. A compatible, nineteenth-century-style cream and sugar set is also obtainable.

For further information, contact:

BRUCE PANEK, TINSMITH
Ohio Historical Society
1985 Velma Avenue
Columbus, OH 43211
Tel. 614/297-2680

▨ TINNED WARE

Although copper has many properties that make it a superior cooking vessel, its chemical composition causes certain foods to react adversely to it. "One-hundred and fifty years ago," relates Indiana coppersmith Michael Bonne, "unscrupulous vendors soaked pickles in vinegar in copper kettles. It made the pickles a prettier green—but poisonous."

So for centuries, copper has been made safe by coating it with tin. In his smithy, Mr. Bonne employs the ancient method of ladling molten tin over a well-heated copper surface, wiping and spreading it as he goes. This procedure leaves behind the small bumps and swirls that are recognized as the hallmark of a hand-tinned copper vessel.

The design of the fish server

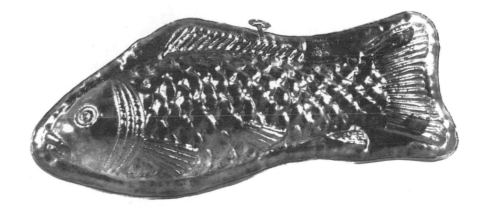

depicted was taken by Mr. Bonne from an 1870s cast-iron fish cake pan in his collection. It is but a single item in a wide offering that includes tinned boilers, cutters, scoops, measures, toys, baking pans and more.

Literature available with SASE.

MICHAEL BONNE, COPPERSMITH
RR #1, P.O. Box 177
Carthage, IN 46115
Tel. 317/565-6521

✖ SUGAR KETTLE

Early in the nineteenth century, American sugar consumption grew to the point where a lump of the sweetener was regularly enjoyed by the *lumpen,* either in the form of a refined "loaf" or as less expensive molasses. Like coffee, sugar was more likely to grace the tables of the gentry during the 1700s, but by 1830 it had become so "entrenched in the public appetite" according to one New England chronicler, that the poor considered it to be a necessity.

Cumberland General Store's sugar kettles may be used for rendering lard or cooking food as well as for boiling syrup. They come in 6-, 10½-, 23- and 33-gallon sizes, measuring from 16½ inches to 27 inches in diameter.

Six-gallon kettle, $195.39; 10½-gallon kettle, $240.48; 23-gallon kettle, $353.37; 33-gallon kettle, $494.32.

General Merchandise Catalog, $3.

CUMBERLAND GENERAL STORE
Route 3, Box 81
Crossville, TN 38555
Tel. 800/333-4640 for orders
or 615/484 8481

▦ DOUGH BOXES

I jist grabbed the Dough-box and split it plumb over his head!
— *William T. Porter,* A Quarter Race in Kentucky, and Other Sketches, *1846*

If Porter's protagonist was out to make the 1800s fastest dough-nut, he was probably successful. But even in the Kentucky, this was not the dough box's intended use.

One of the most useful and ubiquitous of all eighteenth- and nineteenth-century kitchen appurtenances, dough boxes were used to provide an environment in which bread could rise prior to baking. The top, taken off and turned upside down, was used as a surface for kneading the dough.

Keith Dibert, a native of Bedford County, Pennsylvania, is a master cabinetmaker who produces both tabletop and standard self-supporting dough boxes like those that were originally crafted to meet the needs of Allegheny Mountain settlers and farmers. The hand-turned legs and dovetailed, hardwood chest of these dough boxes are characteristic of early nineteenth-century central and southern Pennsylvania-style pieces. Mr. Dibert's range of early nineteenth-century local pieces also includes bench seats with drawers, two-piece corner cupboards and Allegheny water benches. All are made from cherry, walnut, maple and other stock, hand-picked and milled under Dibert's supervision. Many are from trees grown on the cabinetmaker's own lot.

Prices for a Dibert dough box start at $350 for a tabletop model fashioned from local cherry.

KEITH DIBERT, CABINETMAKER
Route 3, Box 470
Everett, PA 15537
Tel. 814/652-6678

✸ TWO-PIECE "SAD" IRON

Based on the turn-of-the-century Potts sad (meaning heavy) irons that first featured detachable handles, an innovation that allowed the ironer to keep one base warming while the other was in use. The Lehman sad iron has a hand-ground bottom to ensure snag-free operation, a hollow cast-iron base, and a wooden handle.

Prices: sad iron bases, $19.95 apiece; handle, $16.95 (Lehman Hardware recommends that you purchase two bases with a single handle).

"Non-Electric" Catalog available, $2.

LEHMAN HARDWARE & APPLIANCES
4779 Kidron Road
Kidron, OH 44636
Tel. 216/857-5441
Fax. 216/857-5785

✸ PLANS FOR AN OAKEN ICEBOX

Beginning in the 1880s, any well-equipped Victorian kitchen would include an icebox, often located along an outside wall to enable the ice man to make deliveries from a back porch without entering the home.

The Hammermark company's plans lack the tin insulation and other features of a functional icebox, but otherwise faithfully replicate one advertised in the Sears catalog of 1904.

Catalog available, $1 (refundable with order).

HAMMERMARK ASSOCIATES
P.O. Box 201
Floral Park, NY 11002
Tel. 516/352-5198 or 516/354-2787

HOUSEWARES FROM AMAZON VINEGAR & PICKLING WORKS

In Buffalo, New York, there once was a fern bar named Mother's Bakery. Directly across the street stood another called The Butcher Shop. The only baked goods in the former were those little gold-fish crackers, and the only meat in the latter was best left to the reader's imagination. While it's true that Anglo-Americans have traditionally given silly names to gin mills, today all sorts of "olde timey" businesses have things in their monikers as rare to them as buffalos are to Buffalo. Amazon Vinegar & Pickling sells neither.

I dunno, perhaps the mail-order outfit is housed in a former pickling plant. Maybe the pickles produced there were known as "Amazons." Let's hope so. But while we're at it, let's point out that Amazon Vinegar also puts out a wonderfully varied catalog of nineteenth-century replicas. Below are a couple of their housewares.

❧ BRASS INKWELL AND TWO FEATHER QUILLS

Amazon's inkwell is a small brass cylinder set on a broad base. The accompanying quills have no nibs cut into them and will require the use of a penknife.

Price: $9.95 (plus $3 for shipping).

❧ BRASS PADLOCKS

Each brass padlock comes with two keys and a lock guard and drain hole. You have a choice of two sizes: the smaller to lock your camp chest, Saratoga trunk or carpetbag; the larger for use on shipboard or boxcar doors.

Prices: Small padlock $9.50, large padlock $18.95 (plus $2 each for shipping and handling).

Catalog of "Items for the Nineteenth-Century Impression," $2.

AMAZON VINEGAR & PICKLING WORKS DRYGOODS, LTD.
Dept. AH, 2218 East 11th Street
Davenport, IA 52803
Tel. 319/322-6800 or 800/798-7979 for orders
Fax. 319/312-4003

▨ DESK BOX

Frye's Measure Mill, the only original water-powered measure mill in the U.S. still remaining, makes and sell reproductions of Shaker and colonial wood products. Their square-lapped eighteenth-century desk box measures 7 inches in length by 5 inches in depth. It is fastened with copper tacks and is available in either fruitwood or maple.

"Frye's Measure Mill," a newsletter "for the collector, historian and enthusiast of early American woodenware" available, $5 per year (2 issues). In Canada, $7.50 per year.

FRYE'S MEASURE MILL
Wilton, NH 03086
Tel. 603/654-6581

CUMBERLAND GENERAL STORE HOUSEWARES

From supermarkets to shopping malls, the descendants of the traditional American general store exist today in their several overly air-conditioned forms. If you still want to see the real thing though, one place you can go is Crossville, Tennessee.

Crossville lies at the heart of Eleanor Roosevelt's mid-1930s Homesteads Project, an experiment to provide rural Volunteer Staters with jobs and low-cost homes during the Depression. The Cumberland General Store was something of an outgrowth of Homesteads.

More than a potbelly stove surrounded by an array of basic goods for the home and farm, Cumberland annually publishes a kind of commercial, mail-order version of this book. Below are just a sample of the housewares that Cumberland sells from among its "all new goods in an endless variety for man and beast."

❋ HIP BATH

It was during the 1830s when, in preparation for the Sabbath, the Saturday-night bath became an American institution. Sitting in a big tin tub before the fireplace or kitchen stove, the bather awaited kettles full of hot water for scrubbing. Soon, wash-tubs were replaced with more formal bathtubs, such as this one sold by the Cumberland General Store. The galvanized tub, which measures 30 inches high and 31 inches wide, provides complete back support and features both soaprests and armrests.

Price: $198.

❋ BASKET-STYLE POPCORN POPPER

There was a basket of popcorn and several 'poppers' and the crowd of young folk were soon shelling corn and popping it.
— Alice Emerson, *R. Fielding at Snow Camp,* 1899

Cumberland General Store's "shakin'" type popcorn maker employs a full sliding wire cloth lid and an enameled grip. The pan size is 7 by 9 by 2½ inches. The overall length is 26¾ inches. Shipping weight is 3 lbs.

Cumberland catalog #4296, $10.95.

❖ LOVELL CLOTHES WRINGER

"The life of a wringer," proclaimed the Sears catalog of 1908, "largely depends upon its rolls." Quite right too. Cumberland's wringer employs semi-soft "balloon" rollers for just this reason. These, in addition to the wringer's all-steel frame, gray baked-enamel finish, rustproofing and hard maple bearings, make for a durable appliance.

It can be attached to stationary or portable tubs (round or square), its clamps open to 1¾ inches, and it is equipped with 12-by-1⅞-inch rollers.

Price: $151.60.

❋ BRASS WASHBOARD

This washboard is fashioned from specially rolled heavy spring brass supported by a five-truss rod. It has an open back and sanitary front soap drain, according to the store's catalog, and its cross rails are flush with the rubbing surface.

Washing surface is 10⅞ inches by 11 inches.

Price: $13.27.

COPPER WASH BOILER

This copper wash boiler was built for the Cumberland General Store by the same company that developed the original boilers a century ago. Excellent for water-bath canning, it will fit over two burners, holds 13¾ gallons, and comes complete with lid.

Dimensions: length 22 inches, width 12 inches, height 13 inches.

Price: $49.50.

BEATEN BISCUIT MACHINE

The castings for Cumberland's beaten biscuit maker have been made from an 1880 original. The replica's rollers are made of stainless steel to original dimensions, and are set upon cast-iron end frames. The machine includes a table with cast-marble top and iron legs. Black finish, 92 lbs.

Price: $885.

General Merchandise Catalog, $3.

CUMBERLAND GENERAL STORE
Route 3
Crossville, TN 38555
Tel. 615/484-8481
or 800/333-4640

SOAPSAVER

Save soapsuds if you have a garden, for they form a very useful manure for flowers, as well as shrubs and vegetables. It is well to have a sunk tub in every garden where the soapy water can stand until required for gardening.
—*"Useful Hints" from the 1900 Farmer's Almanac*

Cumberland's soapsaver, a once-common device for making use of soap slivers, can help here. "Swish it in your water for lots of suds," says Cumberland.

Price: $10.50.

APPLE PARER

Made of cast-iron and brass according to a design patented in 1878 by a small family foundry, this apple parer peels any firm apple you can spike on its nickel-plate holding fork. Ten inches high, clamps to any surface one inch thick.

"Non-Electric 'Good Neighbor' Heritage Catalog, $2.

LEHMAN HARDWARE & APPLIANCES
4779 Kidron Road, P.O. Box 41
Kidron, OH 44636
Tel. 216/857-5757 or 216/857-5441
Fax. 216/857-5785

HAND-CRANKED ICE CREAM FREEZER

In 1778, during the "Winter of our Discontent," Gen. George Washington knelt in the snow and prayed, it's not cynical to suggest, that the Continental Congress would grant his army enough money to keep it from starving.

In 1790, during the course of a sweltering New York summer, President Washington reputedly blew several hundred dollars on ice cream.

Somehow it's comforting to know that the light that shines on the memory of the Father of our Country isn't so blinding that it hides his weaknesses. This is particularly true of those weaknesses we all share, for ice cream is a favorite food of Americans.

Of course our beloved frozen con-coction was very expensive in Washington's time, and might still be today were it not for the invention of the ice cream freezer by Nancy Johnson, a New Jersey woman, in 1846.

The design of what *Money* magazine called "the best traditional hand-operated ice cream machine" now on the market was turned out about a century ago. Made of maple-stained white pine, braced with copper wire, and emblazoned with White Mountain's forest-green Old Man of the Mountain logotype, the best available is also the handsomest imaginable.

Available in 2-, 4-, 6-, 8- and 10-quart sizes.

For prices and ordering information write:

WHITE MOUNTAIN FREEZER COMPANY
Winchendon, MA 01475
Tel. 508/297-0015

HOUSEWARES FROM CHOP-RITE TWO

Chop-Rite of Harleysville, Pennsylvania, manufactures several traditional kitchen utensils.

❀ CHERRY STONER

"Pits every cherry—will not miss." The Chop-Rite cherry stoner will pit the fruit without otherwise disfiguring it. The stoner cleans easily, and will not rust.

✳ MEAT CHOPPER

The Chop-Rite meat chopper is available with a one-piece cast-iron stand, cylinder and hopper. It will not be affected by rust or acids. All parts are easily removed and cleaned.

᪥ SAUSAGE STUFFER, LARD OR FRUIT PRESS

This is actually three implements in one: it stuffs sausage casings, presses lard or cheese, and squeezes fruit and vegetables. It features cast-iron cylinders bored perfectly true. The Teflon-coated cylinder lies within the cast cylinder to enable the operator to remove hot cracklings without inconvenience. Nontoxic black finish. Capacity: 8 quarts. Height: 22 inches.

CHOP-RITE TWO, INC.
531 Old Skipjack Road
Harleysville, PA 19438
Tel. 215/256-4620
Fax. 215/256-4363

CROCKERY
❧❧

...elle Pattern.

Manufactured by John-son Bros., Hanley, Eng.

h semi-porcelain ware; thin and pure white. The glaze is burnt on and ...ick or chip with ordinary use. The shape is of the very latest design ...ised scroll work is handsomely ornamented with neat gold decorations. ...e dinner ware of this quality with gold decoration is unusually attrac-...ure to please. We shall be pleased t...

Order No. 540...

	Per doz.		Per...
...ps and Sau-		10 Bone Dishes......	$
...cups and		11 Bowls, 1 pt......	
...rs...........	$1.87	12 Oyster Bowls, 1	
...Cups and		pint......	
...2 cups and		13 Oatmeal Bowls, 1	
...rs...........	2.18	pint......	
...scalloped			
...inches...	1.06	14 Bakers, 8-inch...	
...scalloped		15 Nappies, 8-inch...	
...nches...	1.28	16 Platters, 8-inch...	
...scalloped		17 Platters, 10-inch...	
...nches...	1.52	18 Platters, 12-inch...	
...scalloped		19 Platters, 14-inch...	
...nches...	1.75	20 Platters, 16-inch...	
...lates, 7		21 Covered Dish, 8-	
	1.52	inch............	
...ishes, 4-in.	.71	....	.94
...ual Butter			
	.47		

31 Tea Pot and Cover.	.63	
32 Sugar Bowl and		
cover	.54	
33 Cream Pitcher....	.26	
34 Cake Plate........	.31	

Manufactured by Henry All-cock & Co., Hanley, England.

...n Pattern.

...r grade of English Royal semi-porcelian, decoration of small forget-me-..., handsomely put on under the glaze; all the pieces are shapley and have ... trimmed edges and handles, plates are scalloped on the edge. This is a ...some table set and can be furnished in two colors, fawn and pencil, both ...ractive. When ordering be sure to state which color you prefer.

Order No. 54005.

	Per doz.		Per doz.		Each.
...ps and Sau-		13 Bowls, 1pint......	$2.00	30 Pitchers, 1-quart..	$ .30
...dled......	$2.00	14 Oyster Bowls, 1		31 Pitchers 2-quart..	.51
...Cups and		pint......	2.00	32 Pitchers 3-quart..	.75
...handled..	2.35	15 Oatmeal Bowls, 1		33 Covered Dishers,9	
...inner Cof-		pint......	2.00	inch......	1.00
...and Sauc-				Each. 34 Casserole (square	
...dled......	1.67	16 Platters, 8-inch..	$0.22	covered dish)9-inch	1.12
...inches..	1.12	17 Platters, 10-inch..	.38	35 Soup Tureen and	
...inches...	1.38	18 Platters, 12 inch..	.63	ladle (no stand)...	3.75
...inches...	1.63	19 Platters, 14-inch..	.87	36 Sauce Tureen with	
...inches...	1.88	20 Platters, 16-inch..	1.38	ladle and stand....	1.26
...Plates, 7		21 Bakers, 7-inch....	.26	39 Sauce Boat.......	.34
	1.63	22 Bakers, 8-inch	.38	40 Pickle Dish.......	.26
...ates.....	.75	24 Scalloped Nappies		41 Cake Plate.......	.34
...ual Butters		7-inch.........	.26	42 Covered Butter	
	51	25 Scalloped Nappies		Dish............	.75
..., 3-inch		8-inch..........	.38	43 Teapots..........	.67
...side dishes)	1.75	29 Pitchers, 1-pint..	.28	44 Sugar Bowls.......	.56
...ishes......	1.75			45 Cream Pitchers.	.26

Manufactured by Johnson Bros., England.

...bia Pattern.

Order No. 54007.

	Per doz.		Per doz.		
1 Tea Cups and Sau-		13 Oyster Bowls, 1		27 Sauce Tureen,with	
cers with handles ..	$1.47	pint........ ...	$1.47	ladle and stand ...	$0
2 Coffee Cups and			Each.	28 Sauce Boat........	
Saucers with handles	1.71	14 Bakers, 7 inches...	$0.19	29 Pickle Dish....	
3 Plates, scalloped		15 Bakers, 8 inches...	.28	30 Covered Butter	
edge, 5 inches.....	.83	16 Bakers, 9 inches..	.38	Dish............	
4 Plates, scalloped		17 Platters, 8 inches.	.16	31 Covered Vegetable	
edge, 6 inches.....	1.02	18 Platters, 10 inches.	.28	Dish............	
5 Plates, scalloped		19 Platters, 12 inches.	.47	32 Casserole (square	
edge, 7 inches.....	1.19	20 Platters, 14 inches	.64	covered dish)......	
6 Plates, scalloped		21 Platters,16 inches	1.02	33 Tea Pot.........	
edge, 8 inches.....	1.38	22 Scalloped Nappies,		34 Sugar Bowl	
7 Plates, scalloped		7 inches...........	.19	35 Cream Pitcher....	
edge, 7-in., soup ...	1.19	23 Scalloped Nappies,		36 Cake Plate.......	
8 Fruit Saucers, 5-in.	.55	8 inches...........	.28	37 Pitcher, 3 quarts.	
9 Individual Butters	.38	24 Scalloped Nappies,		38 Pitcher, 2 quarts.	
10 Bone Dishes.......	1.28	9 inches...........	.38	39 Pitcher, 1 quart..	
11 Bakers (used for		26 Soup Tureen,with		40 Pitcher, 1 pint..	
side dishes), 3-inch.	1.28	ladle and stand ...	3.65	41 Pitcher, ½ pint.	
12 Bowls, 1 pint.....	1.47				

Oregon Pattern.

Manufactured by Mellor, Taylor & Co., Burslem, England,

Genuine English Semi-porcelain ware. A delicate anemone flower spr... decoration in a steel gray color put on under the glaze; warranted not to wear ... or to crack. The shapes are new and gracefully moulded For a low priced p... tern it is unexcelled, as to finish, decoration and durability, and is a decid... change from the ordinary brown prints.

Order No. 54010.

	Per doz.		Each.		Ea
1 Tea Cups and Sau-		13 Platters, 8-inch..	$0.14	30 Soup Tureen(with	
cers, handled....	$1.40	14 Platters, 10-inch..	.27	ladle and stand)...	$3.
2 Coffee Cups and		15 Platters, 12-inch..	.43	31 Sauce Tureen	
Saucers, handled..	1.64	16 Platters, 14-inch..	.61	(with ladle and	
3 Pie Plates, 5-inch.	.78	17 Platters, 16-inch..	.96	stand)...........	
4 Plates, 6-inch.....	.96	18 Bakers, 7-inch..	.18	32 Sauce Boat.......	
5 Plates, 7-inch....	1.13	19 Bakers, 8-inch..	.27	33 Pickle Dish......	
6 Plates, 8-inch....	1.31	21 ScallopedNappies,		34 Covered Butter	
7 Soup Plates, 7-inch.	1.13	7-inch...........	.18	Dish	
8 Fruit Saucers	.53	22 ScallopedNappies,		35 Covered Vegetable	
9 Individual Butters.	.05	8-inch	.27	Dish	
10 Bakers, 3-inch (for		25 Pitchers, ½ pt....	.14	36 Casserole (square	
side dishes)..........	1.23	26 Pitchers, 1 pt....	.18	covered dish)......	
10½ Bone dishes.....	1.23	27 Pitchers, 1 qt....	.21	37 Teapot	
11 1 pt. Bowls.......	1.40	28 Pitchers, 2 qt....	.35	38 Sugar Bowl	
12 1 pt. Oyster Bowls..	1.40	29 Pitchers, 3 qt.....	.54	39 Cream Pitcher ...	
Oat Meal Bowls,5-inch	1.40			40 Cake Plate.......	

Lexington Pattern.

Manufactured by Johnson Brothers, Hanley, England.

English semi-porcelain, a very pretty shape, decorated with a light brown ... gonia leaf, enameled with blue forget-me-nots and warranted not to wash or we... off; scalloped edge plates, gold traced handles. We shall be pleased to have ... order for any quantity, no matter how small.

Order No. 54011.

	Per doz.		Per doz.		Ea
1 Tea Cups and Sau-		12 Bakers (used for		24 Pickle Dish	$0.
cers with handles	$1.87	side dishes),3-in..	$1.64	25 Covered Butter	
2 Coffee Cups and Sau-		13 Oyster Bowls, 1		Dish.............	
cers with handles..	2.18	pint...............	1.87	26 Covered Vegetable	
4 Plates, scalloped			Each.	Dish, 9-inch......	
edge, 5-inch.....	1.06	14 Bakers, 7-inch..	$0 26	27 Casserole (square	
5 Plates, scalloped		15 Bakers, 8-in.. ..	.35	covered dish)......	
edge, 6-inch.....	1.28	16 Platters, 8-in.....	.20	28 Tea Pot	
6 Plates, scalloped		17 Platters, 10-in...	.35	29 Sugar Bowl	
edge, 7 inch.....	1.52	18 Platters, 12-...		30 Cream Pitcher...	

SALT GLAZE POTTERY

Westmoore Pottery produces a small selection of salt glaze and red-ware pottery it has replicated from specific seventeenth-, eighteenth- and nineteenth-century pots. Their specialty is pottery that was used in the early days of North Carolina, which includes pottery made in England, Germany, New England, Pennsylvania and the North Carolina piedmont. The salt-glazed stoneware is burned in an old-style "groundhog" kiln in which the pots are stacked atop one another from rim to rim in the traditional way. Doing this leaves small "stacking marks" on most of the pots, providing additional variation to the gray-to-brown patina of early American salt glaze. While some of these salt glaze pots are plain, others are decorated in cobalt blue, a color that actually ranges from brilliant blue to navy, depending on the patterns of wood smoke in the kiln.

Literature available with SASE. Special price lists obtainable for living history groups.

WESTMOORE POTTERY
Route 2, Box 494
Seagrove, NC 27431
Tel. 919/464-3700

REDWARE POTTERY

Redware pottery is made from the red clay common to most of the eastern seaboard. Its workable qualities were immediately apparent to early settlers, and by 1630 American potters were fashioning it into stew and bean pots, pitchers, chamber pots, flower pots, pipes, roofing tiles, and the like. The distinctive charm of redware is produced by the mottled coloration of the glaze and the brushing of green and brown that are allowed to flow down the surface of the piece. Redware was popular into the 1850s.

In his book, *The Reshaping of Everyday Life: 1790-1840,* historian Jack Larkin tells of how in 1803 redware potter Hervey Brooks "dug and carted his clay, ground it in a horse-drawn pugging mill, mixed and kneaded it to a proper consistency, and 'turned ware' or shaped it into vessels on his foot-powered wheel." Brooks' pot shop was located in Goshen, Connecticut, a short drive through the land-of-steady-habits from where Paul D. Lynn and Kathryn Woodcock-Lynn have been producing redware pottery since the early 1970s. The couple base many of their designs for reproduction redware bowls, mugs, pitchers, porringers and jugs on eighteenth- and early-nineteenth-century examples similar to Brooks's.

Free brochure available.

WOODSTOCK POTTERY
Woodstock Valley, CT 06282
Tel. 203/974-1673

TRADITIONAL MAINE BEANPOT

Although Henry David Thoreau never laid eyes on Rowantree's hand-made beanpot, a well-known admirer of his who had never been any-where near Maine once did. Rowantree's founder, Adelaide Pearson, considered pottery making only "recreational activity" at the time she showed her work to a friend, Mahatma Gandhi, in 1936. Gandhi, who felt that the "oldest craft known to mankind" deserved greater devotion, admonished Pearson to take her work more seriously. Thus charged, Ms. Pearson began the production of earthen-ware the quality of which has warranted its being grouped among the Madison Chinese Export and Eisenhower Gettysburg Service shown at the Smithsonian Institution's American Presidential China Exhibit.

Rowantree's two-quart beanpot is made of a secret combination of Maine ores. It is ovenproof and has ridges for nonslip handling. The company will pack and ship earthenware to any part of the United States.

Free literature available.

ROWANTREE'S POTTERY
Blue Hill, ME 04614
Tel. 207/374-5535

DEDHAM POTTERY

Toward the end of the nineteenth century Hugh Robertson, a fifth-generation master potter from Dedham, Massachusetts, uncovered the ancient Chinese secret of crackle glazing. Combining this process with a variety of distinctive hand-painted patterns that became his trademark, Robertson incorporated the Dedham Pottery Factory.

Public acceptance of Robertson's Dedhamware was great, and before very long his pieces, often carrying the cobalt-blue rabbit motif, were well known. In the five decades that Robertson's business continued to manufacture Dedhamware, supply never caught up with demand.

Dedhamware was revived in 1975, when Chotsie Starr began redirecting her basement-based pottery hobby into fashioning reproduction Dedham pottery. She quickly found that interest in this pottery had only been lying dormant since Robertson's day, and with her two sons she founded the Potting Shed in 1977.

Like the originals, the Potting Shed's Dedham pottery is fully hand-

crafted, relying on a painstaking sequence of molding, painting, firing and finishing that takes a week to complete. To distinguish reproductions from originals, the bottom of each piece is marked with the Potting Shed trademark, a star.

Catalog available, $3.

THE POTTING SHED
P.O. Box 1287
Concord, MA 01742
Tel. 508/369-1382
Fax. 508/369-1416

Genuine Rich Cut Glass.

The demand for cut glass has induced us to offer a few items of the best value to be found. The Strawberry Diamond and Fan "Cutting" is one of the most beautiful patterns, every piece splendidly cut and highly polished in the most brilliant manner. It is as useful as silverware and is more beautiful to offer for presents, wedding gifts, etc. The illustrations are not expected to do it justice, as it is beyond comparison with the ordinary pressed glassware.

54900 Cut Glass Salad Bowl, 8 inches in diameter, genuine Strawberry diamond and fan cutting. Each.... $6.65

54901 Cut Glass Salad Bowl, 7 inches in diameter. Each.......... $5.35

54903 Cut Glass Berry or Fruit Bowl, 8 inches in diameter, genuine strawberry and fan. Each....

54904 Cut Glass Handled Jelly or Olive, genuine strawberry and fan cutting. Each..........

54905 Cut Glass Bottle, genuine strawberry diamond and fan cutting. Each.....

54906 Cut Glass Table Tumbler, genuine strawberry diamond and fan cutting. Each.......... $0.42

54907 Cut Glass, Sugar and Cream Tete-a-tete or afternoon tea size; genuine strawberry diamond and fan cutting. Per set..... $5.35

54917 Genuine cut glass strawberry diamond and fan cutting. Globe shape, silver plated top, salt and pepper shakers. Each, 25 cents, per dozen............. $2.70

Czarina Crystal Pattern.

An exact imitation of the celebrated strawberry diamond and fan genuine cut glass pattern, which came to prominence during the World's Fair. The shapes are very pleasing and novel. Color of glass pure crystal. We guarantee finish to be the very best obtainable. This is undoubtedly the handsomest pattern out this season and one we feel sure will please you in every respect.

55018 Table set, containing four pieces as illustrated. Per set............ $0.55

55021

55019 Czarina Half Gallon Pitcher. Each.... $0.40

55022 Czarina Oil or Vinegar Bottles. Each........ $0.20

55023 Czarina Syrup Pitcher, nickel plated top. Each.......... $0.23

55022   55023

55024 Czarina Salt and Pepper Shakers, silver plated tops. Specify salt or pepper when ordering. Each............ $0.10
Per dozen.................... 1.08

55026 Czarina Berry Dishes.

Inches in diameter.	Price, each.

55032 Czarina Footed Jelly Dish
Each.......... $0.12
Per dozen.................. 1.35

55034 Czarina Flower Vases.

	Each.	Per doz.
7 inches high	$0.15	$1.62
8 inches high	.18	1.95
10 inches high	.30	3.24

Czarina Ruby and Crystal Pattern.

The shapes in this pattern are the same as our crystal czarina. We recommend this pattern above all others to lovers of colored ware. The ruby is put on in a very pleasing manner, aside from this the prices are lower than any other pattern ever produced in ruby and crystal colors.

55035 Ruby and Crystal Czarina Table Set, same number of pieces and same shape as No. 55018.
Per set.......................... $1.05

55036 Ruby and Crystal Czarina Half Gallon Pitcher, for illustration see No. 55019.
Each.......................... 1.00

55038 Ruby and Crystal Czarina Half Pint Tumblers, see No. 55021 for illustration.
Per dozen.......................... 1.35

55039 Ruby and Crystal Czarina Oil or Vinegar Bottles, see No. 55022 for illustration.
Each.......................... .35

55040 Ruby and Crystal Czarina Salt and Pepper Shakers plated top, specify salt or pepper, when ordering see No. 55024 for illustration.
Each.... .18
Per dozen.......................... 1.95

55042 Ruby and Crystal Czarina 8-inch Berry Dishes, see No. 55026 for illustration. Each. .40

55043 Ruby and Crystal Czarina 4½-inch Berry Nappie. See No. 55027 for illustration.

St. Bernard Pattern.
Crystal Engraved.

We aim at all times to offer the latest and pleasing patterns. As a novelty the St. Bernard pattern cannot be equaled. All the covered pieces have handles. The figure, as illustrated, is the image of a St. Bernard dog. The plain surface is decorated by a very attractive engraving, which with part of the face in figured relief, makes the effect a very pleasing one. All the pieces are extra large, and finished by the latest and best process known to manufacturers.

St. Bernard Engraved Table Set Contains four pieces as illustrated. Per set......
St. Bernard engraved berry bowls.

	Price.
9 inch, each	$0.20
	.30
10 inch, each	.35
	.95

55052 St. Bernard engraved Covered Berry Bowls.

Diameter	
7 inches	
8 inches	

55054 St. Bernard Engraved Half Gallon Water Pitcher.
Each.......... $0.50

55056 St. Bernard Engraved Half Gallon Tankard. Each......

55059 St. Bernard Engraved Pint Tankard. Per doz.

55060 St. Bernard Engraved Celery Holder. Each.......... $0.24

55063 St. Bernard Engraved 4½-inch Berry Dishes.
Per dozen.... $0.90

55067 St. Bernard Engraved

▨ STERLING SILVER MINT JULEP CUPS

The inhabitants of Maryland...were notoriously prone to get fuddled and make merry with mint julep and apple toddy.
—*Washington Irving,*
A History of New York, *1809*

Copying an original made in Shelbyville in 1795, the Wakefield-Scearce Galleries produces the only authentic Kentucky mint julep cup available. The following information came from the firm's president, Mark J. Scearce:

Mint Julep cups got their name in Kentucky in the latter part of the eighteenth century.... The Julep cups have long been associated with horse racing and shows, and often were awarded as racing trophies in lieu of a purse.

Our cup is unusual in that it is hand-beaded both on top and at bottom and is marked "Shelbyville, Ky." It also bears a little American eagle mark, underneath which the current president's initials are engraved. We change these with each new administration and the old ones are never made again, so the cups become collector's items.

Free catalog of fine imported antiques available.

WAKEFIELD-SCEARCE GALLERIES
Historic Science Hill
Shelbyville, KY 40065
Tel. 502/633-4382

⚜ OLD SOUTH JERSEY GLASS

"Don't come expecting Anchor-Hocking," Jim Travis told the fellow calling from the Philadelphia Museum of Art, "we've got nothing here but a chicken coop and a garage." Travis was talking about Clevenger Brothers Glass Works (of which company he is president), but what probably was bringing the museum guy up from Philly was its product—replicas of old South Jersey glass.

Here are the Cliffs Notes on the subject:

Early in the eighteenth century, a peculiar method was developed for producing glass vases, pitchers, jugs and flasks from the molten silica mass that is the primordial swamp of all such products. Known as "green-glass blowing," the process involved gathering up the molten glass from the furnace with the aid of a long blower's stem that itself had a glass tip. This goo was then "free-blown" into whatever shape was

desired. Colonial-era glass was usually lime-green in hue, and New Jersey was famous for its green-glass blowing centuries before Springsteen ever played Asbury Park.

The Clevenger Brothers Glass Works got its start after Tom, Reno and Allie Clevenger—all of whom had been employed by a series of Jersey glass factories since the 1880s—decided to ride out the Depression by bootlegging replicas of South Jersey glass as the real antique McCoy. However fraudulent their ends, their means to them were authentic, and they free-blew the glass until the 1940s, when an original nineteenth-century mold was found in a nearby barn. This "Booz Bottle" became the Clevengers' first mold-blown piece.

James Travis acquired the defunct Clevenger Brothers from Allie's widow in 1966 and resumed the replication of eighteenth-century South Jersey glassware using nineteenth-century formulas and mold-blowing techniques. More than 60 bottles, jugs, flasks and other glassware are now available from Clevenger Brothers in amethyst, azure

and cobalt blue (the last is limited), original Jersey green and forest green. Each one is made from molds taken from original early South Jersey pieces, and is marked "CB" to identify it as a replica.

Average retail prices range from $22 to $25.

A free color brochure is available from Clevenger Brothers' distributor:

CHARLES ZAHN, IMPORT MERCHANT, LTD.
P.O. Box 75
Milford, NH 03055
Tel. 603/673-1908

✿ PEWTER

From the days of the Pilgrims until about 1850, pewter was an indispensable metal in American homes. The material of all kinds of tablewares, the "poor man's silver" was also used for such household objects as candlesticks, lamps, inkstands, picture frames, door latches, clock dials, nursing bottles, and buckles and buttons.

Pewter is an alloy composed principally of tin, with copper, antimony and bismuth as additional ingredients. In the early days, lead was also sometimes used, and pewtermaking consisted essentially of pouring molten metal into a brass mold that gave a piece its form. The casting thus made was turned on a lathe, or "skimmed," to smooth the surface. Some hollowware pieces, though not all, were then hammered to increase their strength.

About 1800, an English alloy called Britania was introduced in this country. Britania was a superior grade of pewter, developed to meet the competition of new and relatively inexpensive kinds of china. Forty years after the Revolution, the name had apparently regained some of its panache, as clever pewterers took to referring to their product generically as brittania. By 1825, the lead-free metal had virtually replaced older pewter.

At this same time, a new method of shaping pewterware was adopted. Termed "spinning," the process gave shape to a flat sheet of metal by pressing it, on a lathe, against a wooden form called a chuck. Spinning eliminated the casting and hammering processes, and made it possible to fashion lighter vessels in a greater variety of shapes. Due in part to these innovations, among today's collectors "old" American pewter refers to that made prior to 1825.

Thomas Jefferson was once so taken by the design of a set of sake cups he'd ordered from the Orient that he commissioned a pewterer to replicate them in three sizes. Replicas of *these* cups are available from Three Feathers, a small Ohio pewtery owned by Sharon and David Jones. Along with a full line of pewterware that includes plates and trays, server sets, saltcellars, candlesticks, snuffers, sconces, jewelry, buttons and frontier "trade silver," the Joneses offer a large mug, and a bowl replicating one that aided in the establishment of Paul Revere's reputation as a pewterer. All the hollowware produced by Three Feathers is in the simple-lined style of the late eighteenth and early nineteenth centuries. Using a lead-free formula, it is hand-spun over rock maple forms just as was done 200 years ago. The Joneses also accept special orders by commission.

Catalog and price list available, $3.

THREE FEATHERS PEWTER
P.O. Box 232
221 Jones Street
Shreve, OH 44676
Tel. 216/567-2047

✹ SHEAF O' WHEAT PLATE

Glass pressing, a technique developed by Deming Jarvis in 1830, eliminated the need to blow glass. When Jarvis's Sandwich, Massachusetts, factory began production of pressed-glass drinking vessels, his employees nearly went on strike at the prospect of being thrown out of work.

Marked by the "OSV" logotype to distinguish it from an original in its collection, Old Sturbridge Village pressed-glass Sheaf o' Wheat plate is 10 inches in diameter. The plate bears the legend "Give Us This Day Our Daily Bread."

Price: $24 (plus $5.75 for shipping and handling).

OLD STURBRIDGE VILLAGE
One Old Sturbridge Village Road
Sturbridge, MA 01566
Tel. 508/347-3362

Zenith Hall Lamp.

No. 2R816 Zenith Hall Lamp. Just the thing for a small hall. Ruby, opal or pink globe. This is the cheapest and best hall lamp in the market. In ordering state which color globe you prefer. Shipping weight, 25 pounds.
Price............ $1.49

Square Hall Lamp.

No. 2R819 Square Hall Lamp. This is a larger and better lamp than the Zenith and costs very little more. In two colors, crystal etched or ruby etched glass as desired. Be sure to state color desired. This hall lamp is handsome enough for any dwelling. It is an exact reproduction of the high priced gas lamp that has always been so popular. Length, 36 inches. Complete with burner and chimney. Shipping weight, 25 pounds.

No. 2R816 Our price........ $2.49   No. 2R8...

Store Lamps.

No. 2R825 Store Lamp. The best ... cheapest in the market. For large areas where good light is required only the ... lamps should be ... cured. We keep t... and guarantee ev... lamp we sell to give ... fect satisfaction. Juno gives a steady and white light. Just the thing to throw light on a window display. Complete as illustrated, 15-inch tin shade, suitable for store or window lights, 65-candle power. Shipping weight, 40 lbs. Price, brass finish, $2.00. Price, nickel finish, 2.25

No. 2R830 Same lamp as No. 2R825 only trimmed with 10-inch white porcelain dome shade which makes a much neater lamp without much greater cost. Shipping weight, 50 pounds.

...ice, brass finish.............. $2.45
...ice, nickel finish.............. 2.75

The Juno Mammoth Store and Hall Lamps.

...o. 2R834 Juno Mam-...th Store and Hall Lamp, ...-candle power. The ...ngest and best finished ...p on the market. The ...r movement is perfect ...so simple that a child ... rewick the lamp. Patent ... ring to hold fount in ... obviates all danger of ...t jarring out of frame. ...nt taken out from below ... filling. You are taking ...hances with this lamp ...we guarantee every one ...ive perfect satisfaction, ...e will replace them and ... all expenses. The lock ... used to hold the Juno ... great convenience. The ...t can easily be taken ... from below for refilling. ...plete, as illustrated, 14-... plain dome shade, ...able for churches, halls, ...es, etc. Each lamp is ...fully packed in a barrel ...sure safe delivery. Ship-... weight, 40 pounds.

...ice, complete, brass finish.............. $3.69
...ice, complete, nickel finish.............. 4.25

...o. 2R836 Same lamp as above only it is ...med with a 20-inch tin shade, making a cheaper ... more suitable lamp for saw mills, factories, etc. ...ice, complete, brass finish.............. $3.25
...ice, complete, nickel finish.............. 3.50

...o. 2R838 Same lamp as above, trimmed with 14-... white dome shade and fitted with an automatic ...ng extension so it can be lowered for cleaning ...hting without the use of step ladder or chair.

Our $7.15 Chandelier

Chandelier, with patent automatic extension for raising and lowering. A handsome chandelier at a price that puts it within the reach of all. This beautiful parlor fixture, useful as well as ornamental, is finished in rich gold bronze, and completed with etched globes of a very popular shape. The burner is of a new design that can be lighted and trimmed without removing the globe or chimney, thus avoiding the possibility of ...

The burners can be lighted and trimmed without removing globes or chimney. We can furnish this chandelier in either three or four-light.

No. 2R872 Price, complete, three lights... $11.95
Shipping weight, 60 pounds.
No. 2R874 Price, complete, four lights..... 13.60
Shipping weight, 90 pounds.

Patent Extension Chandelier.

Patent Extension Chandelier. Length, closed, 36 inches; extended, 57 inches. This chandelier is elegantly finished in rich gold, has colored metal center; trimmed with unique burners, which can be trimmed and lighted without removing chimney or globes. Trimmed with fine etched crystal globes. Shipping weight of three-light chandeliers, about 75 pounds; the four light, 90 pounds.

No. 2R878 Price, complete, three lights... $13.65
No. 2R879 Price, complete, four lights.... 16.25
Church or Hall Chandelier. Same chandelier as above, except burners. This fixture is trimmed with the celebrated B. & H. No. 1 center draft burners, each light 50-candle power.
No. 2R882 Price, complete, three lights... $16.35
No. 2R883 Price, complete, four lights.... 18.85

Our 98c Banquet Lamp.

No. 2R890 We have reduced the price of this beautiful banquet lamp from $1.55 to 98 cents, bringing the price within the reach of all, so that there is no reason why any family should not have a banquet lamp to help decorate their home. The lamp is 21 inches high, and has a tinted globe and bowl, shading from white to green, with beautiful floral decorations, as illustrated. It is furnished with a No. 2 brass burner and rests upon a cast brass base. When securely...

Our Very Finest Lamp for $6.9...

No. 2R8...
$6.95 ... you one ... largest ... somest, ... banquet ... made, a ... equal to ... that ret... double the ... It stands ... high, has ... globe and ... bowl, res... gold plate... Both gl... bowl a... cately ti... the de... consists ... ural color ... put on b... before the ... ing by fr... work so ... will not ... rub off. T... is remove... made of ... pressed ... The la... equipped ... best larg... Royal 10... power ... draft b... This la... large an...

...at no illustration can do it justic...
...packed in a barrel and weighs 40 po...
special price........

Our $5.90 Cerise Banquet La...

...902 This ... elebrated ... Cerise ... which is ... nly manufac-... tured by one fac-... tory in the ... United States. ... Both globe and ... bowl are of the ... one dark red ... shade with the ... velvet finish, ... making a very ... soft light at night. ... This cerise color ... is not on the out-... side of the globe ... or bowl, but is in ... the glass itself, ... giving a much ... better light than ... those which are ... tinted on the out-... side of glass and ... hand decorated. ... It is an ornament ... to any parlor ... either day or ... night. It is 25 ... inches high with ... a 12-inch globe ... and 14-inch bowl. ... It has a No. 2 ... Royal center ... draft burner and ... removable brass ... oil fount. Packed ... securely in a barrel, weighing 40 pounds.
Our special price........

Our Big $5.65 Vase Banquet L...

No. 2R9... handsome... nearly th... pattern ... 2R900, bu... ly smaller ... and differ... oration. ... popular ... globe a... with the ... free hand ... tion, mak... ornament ... home. It ... cast bra... plated bas... brass oil fo... No. 2 cen... burner. ... 24 inches ... a 10½-inch ... and 12½-in... The burne... our cent... lamps ar... taken ... cleaned an...

✿ LAMPPOSTS

Brandon Industries hand-casts Victorian lampposts from aluminum, using methods claimed by the company to be generations old. Shown here are two of Brandon's more popular models, representing their single- and multiple-globe offerings. The lampposts are available in heights ranging from 7 feet 8 inches to over 10 feet tall. Matching interior wall sconces are also obtainable.

Color brochure of interior and exterior lighting, Victorian planters and mailboxes available.

BRANDON INDUSTRIES
4419 Westgrove Drive
Dallas, TX 75248
Tel. 214/250-0456

CUMBERLAND GENERAL STORE KEROSENE OIL LAMPS

❈ SEWING LAMP

An original-pattern sewing lamp of the type once found in every home. It holds 26 ounces of fuel, stands 14 inches tall, and has a shipping weight of 6 lbs.
Price: $12.95.

✹ WALL BRACKET LAMP

Complete with a No. 2 burner, wick, chimney, cast-iron wall bracket and Mercury Mirror reflector. Shipping weight: 15 lbs.
Price: $71.28.

▦ DAISY HEART PATTERN LAMP

The Victorian daisy heart pattern is shown in intricate detail from its petal-footed base to its six-hearted font. Comes complete with crimp-top chimney, wick and glass burner. The overall height is 18 inches. Shipping weight: 6 lbs.
Price: $35.64.

General Merchandise Catalog available, $3.

CUMBERLAND GENERAL STORE
Route 3, Box 81
Crossville, TN 38555
Tel. 615/484-8481 or
800/333-4640

MARLE REPLICA LIGHTING FIXTURES

After the Second World War, the Marle Company's use of New England craftsmen to produce period lanterns in copper and brass was restarted with a Yankee foreman who began working with the firm in his seventieth year and retired in his eightieth. This legacy of devotion to small-scale craftsmanship and attention to detail has resulted in the Marle Company's "hundreds and hundreds" of lanterns to be seen in historic buildings, fine residences, office buildings and shops.

Among the nineteenth-century replicas produced by Marle's craftsmen is a whale-oil lantern of copper and brass, a hall lantern and a turn-of-the-century gas light with leaded glass.

Catalog and price list available; showroom visits encouraged.

MARLE COMPANY
35 Larkin Street, Box 4499
Stamford, CT 06907
Tel. 203/348-2625

DOCTOR'S LANTERNS

For portability, the doctor's lantern was designed as a collapsible eighteenth-century lantern that could be readily set up with a candle. A.J.P. Coppersmith's replicas are electrical adaptations using mirrored reflector panels.

Available in two sizes: Twelve inches high by 4 inches wide, by 4½ inches deep. Fourteen inches high by 5 inches wide by 5½ inches deep.

Catalog $3.

A.J.P. COPPERSMITH & COMPANY
20 Industrial Parkway
Woburn, MA 01801
Tel. 617/932-3700 or 800/545-1776 (outside Massachusetts)

R.E. DIETZ LANTERNS

The citation for "Dietz Celebrated Tubular Lanterns" in the Sears catalog of 1908 attests to the company's boast of manufacturing the lanterns that "lit America's history."

The Dietz company was founded in 1840 by Robert E. Dietz, who gave up his job in a hardware store at the age of 22 to buy a small lamp-and-oil business in Brooklyn, New York. Until the mid–1850s, when kerosene was first produced as a distillate of petroleum, Dietz manufactured whale-oil lamps and wall-lamp fixtures.

Around 1867, R.E. Dietz acquired the patents and rights to manufacture a tubular lantern, which the Original #76 described below reproduces. Used by Yankee seamen and Confederate guerrillas, on Mississippi riverboats and beside California prospectors, these lanterns are surviving standard-issue nineteenth-century Americana.

THE ORIGINAL #76 HURRICANE LANTERN

A reproduction of the nineteenth-century tubular model, the Original #76 is flat black with brass trim and stands 10 inches high. Recommended fuel: common lamp oil.
Price: $15.95.

PIONEER ESTATE POST LANTERN

A "true replica" of the Dietz street-and-railway-platform lamp of the late 1800s, this post lantern has been converted from kerosene to electricity. Constructed of steel, with a black enamel finish, it stands 22 inches high and 15 inches wide.
Prices: Black, $129.11; Solid Brass, $193.83.

BRASS HURRICANE LAMP

A reproduction from Dietz's 1840 dies in a solid-brass special edition; each lamp is serially numbered.
Price: $44.95.

Literature and order forms available.

R.E. DIETZ COMPANY
225 Wilkinson Street
Syracuse, NY 13204
Tel. 315/424-7400

The Original #76
Hurricane Lantern

❊ PROGRESS VICTORIAN LIGHTING

The Victorian era, which takes its name from the long reign of Queen Victoria (1837–1901), encompasses a period of remarkable social advance and technological change.

During this time in America, the Civil War was fought and slavery abolished, 28 states came into the Union; mass production introduced inexpensive machine-made items to a burgeoning middle class; and magnificent steamships and railroads expanded the possibilities for travel.

This rapid transformation of society brought about a concomitant nostalgia for the past, and interest in such designs as Greek and Roman classicism, American colonial revival, rococo, and Oriental and Italianate was reflected in much of what was produced. Although the Victorian era is remembered as one with excessively ornate design, its truly "eclectic" nature included many spare, linear forms.

This wide range of Victorian design is fully represented in Progress Lighting's collection of gas and electric fixtures. Emphasizing the company's commitment to absolute authenticity (which relies on the use of old dies and molds), its products are accompanied by a testimonial by Dr. Roger Moss, executive director of Philadelphia's Athenaeum, an independent research library established in 1814 to collect materials "connected with the history and antiquities of America."

The Classical Revival chandelier illustrated here is based on an original manufactured by the Victorian era's leading producer of lighting fixtures, Cornelius & Company of Philadelphia. This was the same firm that supplied fixtures to the U.S. Capitol when it was refurbished during the Civil War.

Dimensions: body height, 32 inches; diameter, 29 inches.

Catalog of lighting fixtures available, $2.50.

PROGRESS LIGHTING
Erie Avenue and G Street
Philadelphia, PA 19134
Tel. 215/289-1200
Fax. 215/537-0887

NOWELL'S LIGHTING FIXTURES

Nowell's manufacture of reproduction Victorian lighting fixtures started out in the parts bin. In 1954, Nowell's began restoring old lamps and fixtures ("In San Francisco, we mean Victorian when we say 'old,' because everything here was built after the Gold Rush"—not to mention the earthquake), undertaking projects for the M.H. de Young Museum and the Haas–Lilienthal Mansion, among others. As these contracts required the use of old techniques to refabricate parts from original materials, before long Nowell's was making Victorian fixtures from scratch. "A few dozen projects like this," as one staff member put it, "and we had enough jigs and patterns and molds and sources for obscure parts to make the San Francisco Line."

The San Francisco Line numbers 70 fixtures in all, and Nowell's has graciously sent us 10 representatives.

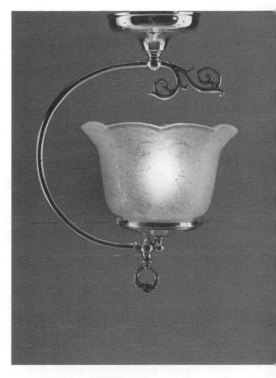

❧ THE POLK GULCH

This is described as a small gas-type hall light designed for low ceilings. Finished in polished or antique brass.

Dimensions: width, 10 inches; standard height, 16 inches.

▦ THE EMBARCADERO

The Embarcadero is a 12-light gas fixture with etched floral ball shades. It is suitable for the grand entry or the ballroom.

Dimensions: width (with glass), 70 inches; standard height, 60 inches.

❋ THE EMPEROR NORTON

This 12-light gas or electric fixture comes in polished or antique brass.

Dimensions: width (with glass), 50 inches; standard height, 72 inches.

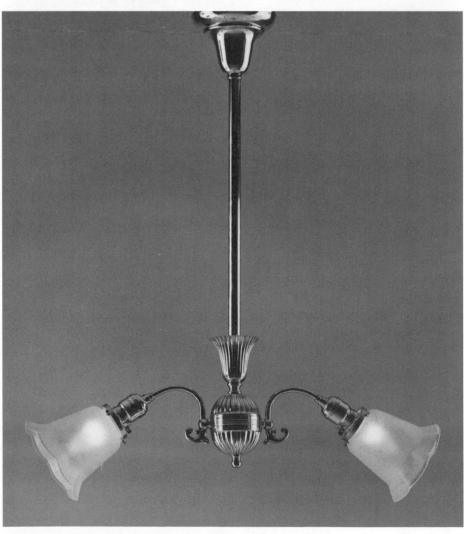

❋ THE NATIONAL HOTEL

Recommended as a hall, bath, kitchen or pantry fixture, the National Hotel is finished in polished or antique brass.

Dimensions: width (with glass), 22 inches; standard height, 39 inches.

▣ THE MEIGGS WHARF

A good gift for anyone who considers Victorian design a lot of overly ornate folderol; 680 of these fixtures were purchased by the U.S. government for installation in the Treasury and Old Executive Office buildings.

Dimensions: width (with glass), 40 inches; standard height, 40 inches.

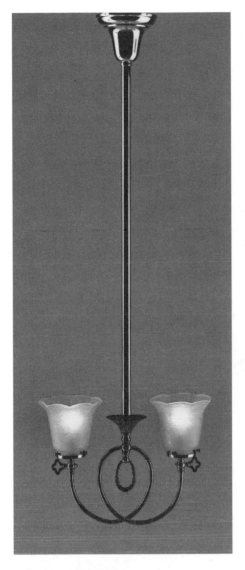

❀ RINCON HILL

This was recreated from a hall light, casting the gas cocks from the original and using the same hand-assembly techniques.

Dimensions: width (with glass), 14 inches; standard height, 42 inches.

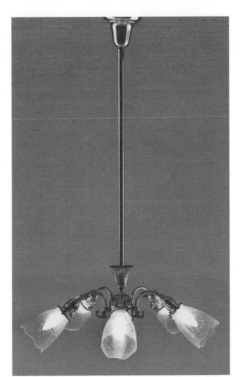

❧ THE OLD WALDORF

A five-light electric parlor fixture with optional full-ribbed or half-ribbed body, the Old Waldorf is finished in polished or antique brass.

Dimensions: width (with glass), 22 inches; standard height, 39 inches.

✾ THE NATOMA

A single-light Victorian hall fixture, the Natoma's small smoke bell originally shielded the ceiling from the flame of the gas jet.

Dimensions: width, 9 inches; standard height, 42 inches.

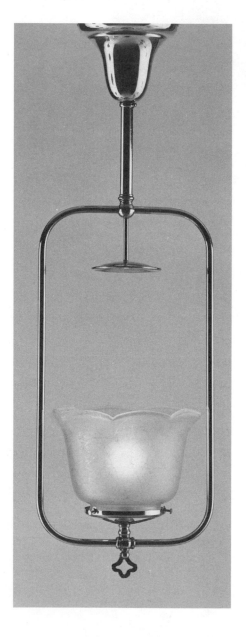

❧ THE PACIFIC CLUB

An adaptation of a period ballroom gas-and-electric fixture, the Pacific Club is assembled by hand and comes in polished or antique brass.

Dimensions: width (with glass), 36 inches; standard height, 42 inches.

THE TIVOLI

A five-light fixture with heavy crystal prisms, the Tivoli is "about as Victorian as you can get," says Nowell's. It comes in polished or antique brass.

Dimensions: width (with glass), 40 inches; standard height, 42 inches.

Catalog of Victorian chandeliers, sconces, post lights and glass shades available, $5.

NOWELL'S, INC.
P.O. Box 295
Sausalito, CA 94966
Tel. 415/332-4933
Fax. 415/332-4936

PHOENIX CARBON-LOOP LIGHT BULBS

In 1880 Thomas Alva Edison's first commercially practical light bulbs had filaments made from *bamboo*. In time, however, the man who said, "Show me a thoroughly satisfied man and I'll show you a failure," replaced these with a carbon-loop filament that emitted a soft, yellow light.

In its series of Phoenix Historic Light Bulbs, Bradford Consultants of Alameda, California, replicates two carbon-loop bulbs. The Century, a copy of an 1890s clear-tipped bulb complete with original style "hairpin" carbon filament, stands six inches high and produces 12-30 watts consumption. The Imperial, an early twentieth-century twin-loop carbon filament, produces 60 watts.

Prices: Century, $8.95 each; Imperial $6.25 each; packing and UPS shipping additional.

Descriptive literature available.

BRADFORD CONSULTANTS
P.O. Box 4020
Alameda, CA 94501
Tel. 415/523-1968

ANTIQUE HARDWARE STORE'S VICTORIAN LIGHTING

✳ SINGLE-ARM VICTORIAN GAS-STYLE FIXTURE

Gaslight offered a welcome alternative to the use of kerosene for those gaslight-era swells who could both afford to install such fixtures and had homes near enough to the gasworks. The Antique Hardware Store's "single-arm Victorian gas-style fixture" comes with the etched French shade shown.

Price: $179, plus postage, handling and insured delivery charges.

▨ COUNTRY STORE FIXTURE

In 1859, the Sutter's Mill of kerosene occurred in Titusville, Pennsylvania. Following its discovery, "kero" become so important a fuel in Victorian homes that (until the acceptance of the internal-combustion engine) gasoline was seen as its relatively inconsequential by-product. In rural areas especially, kerosene lamps enabled folks to discard such older means of illumination as tallow candles, oil lamps that burned lard, whale, cottonseed and castor oils, turpentine or camphor.

Made of heavy cast iron, the Antique Hardware Store's country store lamp is an electrical fixture that can be converted to gas or oil. It has an opal glass font, shade and smokebell; the chimney is included. Hanging height is adjustable with gas as fuel.

Price: $279, plus postage, handling and insured delivery charges.

❀ PARTNERS DESK LAMP

By the 1880s gas had begun to lose in its battle for residential illumination to electricity, although many feared the latter for its "magical" nature. Not only were fires, explosions, and electrocution attributed to electricity, but so were several ailments, including—in one instance—freckles. This was the time when portable lamps capable of being plugged into outlets became available, although they were still too costly for widespread use.

The Antique Hardware Store's brass partners lamps come complete with two green shades.

Dimensions: 17 inches high by 15½ inches wide by 10½ inches deep.

Price: $119, plus postage, handling and insured delivery charges.

Free color catalog available.

ANTIQUE HARDWARE STORE
9718 Easton Road
Route 611
Kintnersville, PA 18930
Tel. 215/847-2447, or order line
    800/422-9982
Fax. 215/847-5628

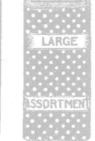

36K3711 Shirting ... Prints. All full ... goods in weight, ... and finish. You may ... tly be able to buy ... calicos at as low a ... as our full standard ... t this special price of ... ts. Don't do it. Save ... oney by purchasing ... ade goods originally. ... alicos will last so much ... and always look so ... etter—in short you'll ... much more real satis... out of the use of our ... hat the economy of ... vestment will be at ... parent. We are con... adding new styles so ... interest our calicos have created ... they go may not be lessened. New, ... styles, embracing everything that is ... dots, figures, checks and stripes, ... rounds with red, blue or black figures, ... ight blues, Garibaldi red and blacks, ... d reds, red and whites, wines, cadets, ... black and whites, indigo blues, browns, ... d checks in black and white, pink, ... een and brown, chambrays, chocolates, ... beige effects, tans and a full line of ... etc. Be sure to state color wanted. ... 25 inches.
per yard 6½c
piece of about 50 yards, per yard . 6¾c

BEST DRESS PATTERNS.

No. 36K3783 Wide and Heavy Pure German Indigo Dress Print. The real old fashioned heavy calico that has been the stand-by for so many years. Very few manufacturers beside our own have maintained the original quality, and although print cloths have advanced sharply we are still away below all competition on prints as well as all other lines of merchandise. Neat styles, figures, dots and stripes. Mention style wanted. Width, 31 inches.

Price, per yard 11c
Full piece of about 45 yards, per yard .. 10½c

7c OIL BOILED CALICO, RED, BLUE OR BLACK

No. 36K3813 Guaranteed oil boiled and fast col... ...

RIVER VIEW ROBES

6½c FANCY COMFORTER PRINTS, HIGH GRADE GOODS, NEW DESIGNS.

No. 36K3835. No better Fancy Comforter Print made than this number. Handsome scroll patchwork, floral and oriental patterns in a full line of colors. As a rule, one does not expect much of anything in the way of style in a low priced print, but we have selected the very best patterns for our line this fall, and really never saw better work in these goods. Width, 24 inches.

Price, per yard 6½c
Full piece of about 50 yards, per yard 6¾c

11c NEW COMFORTER SILKOLINES, BEAUTIFUL PATTERNS.

No. 36K3847 Handsome Figured Silkoline in a choice selection of new and up to date patterns.

THE leading paper pattern distributors are now bringing out garment patterns especially designed for 24-inch goods. Printed calicos will, therefore, have an increased demand. See our Standard Calico No. 36K3711 on this page.

6½c FANCY COMFORTER PRINTS GUARANTEED OIL RED.

No. 36K3843 Gem Oil Boiled Comforter Print, Red grounds with black s... and other tasty designs. T... who have once used these ... and blacks may be cou... on for repeated orders. T... make friends everywhere. ... are showing a variety of ... designs this fall, inclu... patchwork patterns. F... standard goods in every ... spect. Color warran... Width, 24 inches.

Price, per yard 6½
Full piece of about yards, per yard 6½

TURKEY RED

16c Fancy Comforter ...eens, Handsome P... terns.

No. 36K3849 For those who feel that they must have something heavier and better than the SILKOLINES for COMFORTER USE we have added this fine and beautiful figured SATEEN. We always invite comparison and before buying comforter sateens which may seem as low as ours, do yourself justice by sending for our samples. We have gone over the comforter sateen market thoroughly and after examining the lines of every first class manufacturer, have placed our contracts on these goods on a basis that shows you a saving of 25 to 30 cents on a comforter bought elsewhere. The patterns are all new and especially designed for comforter work. They will appeal you the moment you see them. Illustration in black and white cannot do the justice. The colors are dark green, green, rose pink, light blue, cream, red white ground with appropriately tinted flo... patterns like illustration. Be sure to st... color wanted. Samples free on request ... necessary. Width, 36 inches.

Price, per yard 16
By the piece of about 40 yards, per yd. 15

DRY GOODS

FLANNELS AND FLANNELETTES

Shirting Flannels.   California Shirting Flannels.   Canton Flannels.   Domet or Shaker Flannels.   Elderdowns.   Embroidered Flannels.   Fleeced Back Flannele...
Guinea Hen Mottled Flannels.   Mackinaw Flannels.   Outing Flannels, Plain and Fancy.   Shirt Patterns, Flannel and Flannelette.   White Wool Flannels.

7½c FANCY OUTING FLANNELS, CHECKS, PLAIDS, STRIPES. GOOD NAP.

No. 36K3862 Fancy Outing Flannels. Good weight and nicely napped. We could not buy this cloth from the mill today in one hundred case lots at the price we quote you. This only serves to show how you benefit by our anticipation of the market advances. A new assortment of pretty checks, plaids and stripes, both light and dark, as well as plain pink, light blue and cream. Be sure to state color wanted. Width, 27 inches.

Price, per yard 7½c
By the piece of about 50 yards, per yard 7¼c

PLYMOUTH

10½c FANCY OUTING FLANNELS, OUR HEAVIEST AND BEST QUALITY.

No. 36K3872 Our Heaviest and Best Fancy Outing Flannel. This is a cloth that retails ordinarily for 15 cents per yard, and considered good value at that price. The very newest styles in both staple and fancy checks, plaids and stripes are to be found in the assortment, which covers a handsome variety of colorings, light and dark. Many of the styles shown are copied from dress goods patterns. A very warm and durable outing flannel. No better made. Be sure to mention whether light or dark color is wanted. Width, 27 inches.

Price, per yard 10½c
By the piece of about 40 yards, per yard 10c

CHELSEA OUTINGS

9½c DAISY CLOTH OR BABY FLANNEL, PINK, BLUE, CREAM OR WHITE.

No. 36K3890 Baby Flannel, medium heavy weight, of beautiful soft texture. Has a well defined flannel twill, with pretty soft nap on both sides. Comes in solid colors only. Cardinal, pink, light blue, pure white or cream color. It is much used for babies' wear, as well as for ladies' dressing sacques, kimonos, tea gowns, night dresses, etc. At 10 cents per yard this is really an exceptional value. Be sure to give color wanted. Width, 28 inches.

Price, per yard 9½c
By the piece of about 50 yards, per yard 9c

TULIP FLANNEL

7c GUINEA HEN FLANNEL, NICE MO... TLED EFFECTS. GOOD WEIGHT

No. 36K3900 Cho... Guinea Hen Flannel. The stock cloth. Well napp... soft and warm. Wears sp... didly. Our Guinea H... Mottled Flannels are ... ished on both sides, m... ing a much more desira... cloth than the general ... of these goods. Colors ... mottled pink, blue, gray ... brown. Be sure to st... color wanted. Width, ... inches.

Price, per yard, ... 7c
By the piece of about yards, per yard 6¾c

BEAVER

10c GUINEA HEN FLAN... NEL, EXTRA WARM CLOTH. FOUR COLOR

No. 36K3925 Our Best and Heaviest Mott... Flannel, or Guinea Hen, as it is commonly called. This is a stout cotton flannel, ha... ing a delightfully soft fleece and is wonderful warm. Gives the greatest service imaginable Comes in mottled pink, blue, gray or brow Be sure to state color wanted. Width, ... inches.

MOTTLED

Price, per yard 10c
By the piece of about 55 yards, per yd. 9½c

13c FANCY DRESS FLANNELETT EXTRA FINE AND WIDE.

No. 36K3960 Our Best and Widest Fine Dress Flannelette. We have pink, light blue, tan, cardinal, navy, brown or black in figures like illustration, also new and handsome plaids in red, green, blue and brown combinations, black and white shepherd checks, as well as staple dots and a few choice fancy stripes. Be sure to state color wanted. Width, 34½ inches.

9½c FANCY OUTING FLANNELS, PRETTY CHECKS, PLAIDS AND STRIPES.

36K3868 Extra Fancy Outing Flannel, well napped. Will give ... service. The cloth ... and nicely finished. ... es are very pleasing, ... both light and dark ... d variety of checks, ... d stripes. There are ... eral fancy bourette ... hich are worthy of ... on in much higher ... alities. We recom... e purchase of a full ... these goods which ... u an additional sav... cents on your pur... Width, 28 inches.
... per yard, ... 9c
... piece of about 40 ... yard 8¾c

QUINCY OUTINGS

9½c PLAIN OUTING FLANNELS, DARK, SOLID COLORS. SERVICEABLE.

No. 36K3887 Firm Fast Colored Outing Flannels in plain dark colors only. Well napped and a cloth that will give excellent service. This is a flannel that will thoroughly please you, not only in appearance, which is fully equal to outing flannels quoted by any other dealer at 12½ cents per yard, in depth of color and natural warmth, which pronounce it a household favorite everywhere. Looks and feels like a piece of the French flannels that have been so much in demand. Colors are wine, medium gray mixed, dark gray mixed, navy, dark brown or black. Be sure to state color wanted. Width, 27 inches. Price, per yard 9½c
By the piece of about 50 ...

HARMONY OUTINGS

Fancy Figured Flannelettes.

Samples free on request if necessary.

10c HANDSOME DRESS FLANNELETTES, ALL THE POPULAR NEW STYLES.

No. 36K3930 An elegant assortment of stylish Dress Flannelettes at a very low price. The cloth is firm, well woven and will give extra wear. Has a nice dressy appearance. Back of fabric is lightly napped. Among the many new styles shown will be found several appropriate kimono ideas as well as others adapted for wrappers, waists and children's wear. Colors are navy, wine, cardinal, reseda green, tan, pink, light blue, brown, gray or black. Figures, stripes or dots, as desired. We also have tasty plaids in red, blue, green or brown. Be sure to state color wanted. Width, 28 inches.
Price, per yard 10c

HUDSON'S BAY POINT BLANKETS

By the third week in December [1865] everything was in readiness, and about two thousand warriors began moving south… The weather was very cold, and they wore Buffalo robes with the hair turned in, leggings of dark woolen cloth, high-topped Buffalo fur moccasins, and carried red Hudson's Bay blankets strapped to their saddles.

—*Dee Brown,* Bury My Heart at Wounded Knee, *1971*

By the time these Sioux embarked on what became known as Red Cloud's War, the Indians of North America were long familiar with the Hudson's Bay point blanket. Introduced into trade in 1779, it was used to barter with natives all across the American and Canadian wilderness, the "points" (indicated by parallel black bars woven into the fabric) denoting the number of pelts required to equal the blanket's value. Continuously manufactured in England for two centuries, the Hudson's Bay point blanket has never slackened in either its usefulness or appeal.

Made of 100 percent pure virgin wool, it is available in three sizes, four point (regular), six point (queen) and eight point (king). Colors and patterns are: scarlet, gold, green, white with blue stripe, white with gold stripe, and candy-stripe. Eight-point available in candy-stripe only.

Contact:

L.L. BEAN, INC.
Freeport, ME 04033

or the Hudson's Bay exclusive agents in the United States:

PEARCE WOOLEN MILLS
Woolrich, PA 17779

JACQUARD COVERLETS

"Bundling," as defined by Noah Webster's 1828 *American Dictionary of the English Language*, was a practice that permitted courting couples "to sleep on the same bed without undressing"—with, as was later added, "the shared understanding that innocent endearments should not be exceeded." Well, maybe that's what Webster's teenage daughter told *him,* but like the "bundling maid" in one 1820s broadside song who "sometimes say when she lies down / She can't be cumbered with a gown," historical evidence shows that ardor progressed with courtship, and bundling was no more chaste a ritual then than spring break in a beer tent is now.

The wool pulled over Noah Webster's eyes might resemble Robert Black's handwoven jacquard coverlets as the latter "are in the style and construction that was woven in this country from the 1820s to the 1880s." In fact, Mr. Black claims to be the only weaver in America today handweaving coverlets on a jacquard—a French loom capable of intricate designs that was introduced into the U.S. in 1824. The jacquards are made with a natural cotton warp and crossed with cotton and wool in the nineteenth-century fashion. They are double woven and reversible, and can be "signed" by having Mr. Black weave his name (or the customer's) into the fabric. Other custom designs, or a reproduction of an antique jacquard, can also be effected.

Prices: throws (48 inches by 72 inches) $500; double (76 inches by 110 inches) $1,300; queen (84 to 86 inches by 110 inches) $1,400; king (94 to 96 inches by 110 inches) $1,600. A 25 percent deposit is required with orders. Once a design has been settled on, six to eight weeks are required for its completion.

Brochure available.

Noah Webster: Did bundlers pull the wool over his eyes?
(Library of Congress)

THE BLACK'S HANDWEAVING SHOP
Box 1, 597 Route 6A
West Barnstable, MA 02668
Tel. 508/362-3955

⊛ RAG RUGS

Because of their folksy charm, most people wrongly associate rag rugs with the eighteenth century. In point of fact this colorful floor covering is a postindustrial furnishing that followed the availability of machine-made yarns in the 1830s. These lowered the cost of materials while providing a good source of scraps for homemakers to weave into small hearth- and bedside rugs.

Heritage Rugs of Bucks County, Pennsylvania, weaves its rag rugs on an antique loom that permits widths of up to 15 feet and lengths of up to 35 feet. As each rug is custom-made, it is assigned a number and is registered as a Heritage original.

Company proprietors Sherry and Martin Shulewitz suggest that with your order you send along samples of the colors you'd like woven into your rug.

Prices: 4 by 6 feet ($215), 5 by 7 feet ($315), 6 by 9 feet ($485), 8 by 10 feet ($720), 9 by 12 feet ($975), 10 by 15 feet ($1,350), 12 by 15 feet ($1,620), 15 by 15 feet ($2,025).

Brochure available, $1.

HERITAGE RUGS
Sherry and Martin Shulewitz
Lahaska, PA 18931
Tel. 215/794-7229

⊰ Carpetbags ⊱

Long before the business and political opportunists known as "carpetbaggers" headed south to exploit the situation created there by the Reconstruction Act of 1867, carpetbags were a common sight.

They began to appear in 1840, six years following the U.S. patent for an in-grain-carpet power loom was issued. But by the 1870s, Reconstruction had so tarnished the carpetbag's reputation that its popularity waned. In time the word "carpetbag" became so kindred to "scoundrel" that in 1884 the Kingston, New Mexico, *Clipper* would remark: "An effort is being made to remove more of the job-bers, bloodsucks, and renegade carpet-bag scrubs from our territory."

If after that characterization you still want one, Bob Porter of Lynchburg, Virginia, produces a line of carpetbags the authenticity of which have been refined by years of work with Civil War reenactors.

❧ METAL-FRAME CARPETBAG

Had Confederate Gen. Robert E. Lee won at Gettysburg in July of 1863, history might now record that his army went on to occupy Philadelphia, and—if that didn't result in peace negotiations—even New York. But Lee lost Gettysburg, and according to historian D.S. Freeman in his book *Lee's Lieutenants,* it was because Gen. Thomas Jonathan Jackson "is not here."

Stonewall Jackson was an ingenious tactician, and his Shenandoah Valley campaign ranks with the most brilliant in history. As Lee's strong right arm, Jackson executed the bold plan that resulted in a rebel victory at Chancellorsville. During this battle, he was mortally wounded by one of his own men.

Another of Jackson's sobriquets, "Old Blue Light," was not a description of a secessionist Sinatra, but a reference to the incandescent quality that the general's eyes took on in battle. As Freeman describes him, Jackson is a man of "contrasts so complete that he appears one day a Presbyterian deacon...and the next a reincarnated Joshua. He lives by the New Testament and fights by the Old."

Patterned after an artifact at the Stonewall Jackson House in Lexington where the general lived while a professor at the Virginia Military Institute, this steel-framed carpetbag was the most popular style in use both during and after the war. It has a wooden bottom with brass studs, leather rope handles attached with copper rivets and burrs, and either leather closure straps with roller buckles or an antique brass clasp with a lock. The bag also has an inside pocket, and a lining of either cotton muslin, black chintz or any coordinating chintz. Outside, the fabric can be heavy upholstery velvet (like old carpeting) or exotic tapestry fabric per your choice.

Dimensions: 20 inches long by 14 inches high by 6½ inches thick.

Price, $95; with detachable shoulder strap, $110. Either bag requires an additional $6 for delivery and insurance.

❋ LARGE TRAVELING BAG

This carpetbag has solid walnut handles that are hand carved and rubbed. It is fully lined with either chintz, moiré or cotton and has a removable wooden bottom.

Dimensions: 18 inches high by 22 inches wide by 8 inches deep.

Price: $80, plus $6 for delivery and insurance.

Catalog of carpetbags, purses, chests and trucks available, $1.

THE CARPETBAGGER
P.O. Box 15055
Lynchburg, VA 24502
Tel. 804/525-5473

▨ AMISH AND MENNONITE QUILTS

Like the husking bees, spinning bees, and road- and church-building bees that came before, the quilting bees that began in the early 1800s were happy social gatherings for the purpose of getting a particular kind of work done.

Following the Civil War, the Amish surpassed most quilters in the graphic quality of their coverlets. Geometric images were created by piecing together cottons and wools in arresting and vivid combinations against a background of the dark blue, brown, purple, green and black favored in Amish dress.

The Old Country Store of Intercourse, Pennsylvania, purveys traditional Amish and Mennonite quilts still handmade by Lancaster County craftswomen. These quilts are made from new fabric (not pieced together from worn-out clothing as quilts once were), but the technique and designs—including the dramatic Lone Star, the Oriental-influenced Fan, and the Colonial Star depicted—are ancient.

"Quiltalog" available, $2.

THE QUILT ROOM
Old Country Store
Main Street, P.O. Box 419
Intercourse, PA 17534

A quilting bee as depicted in *Gleason's Pictorial Drawing Room Companion* of 1854.
(Library of Congress)

DECORATION

pair. doz. pair.
...amped Muslin Pillow Sham, ...nmed. Assorted patterns, 28x $0.20 $2.00

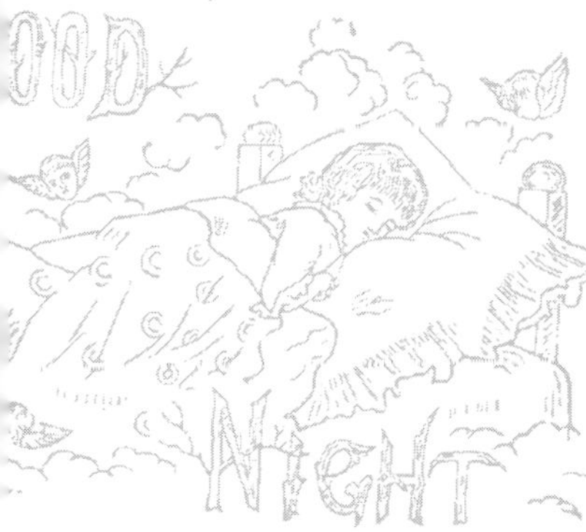

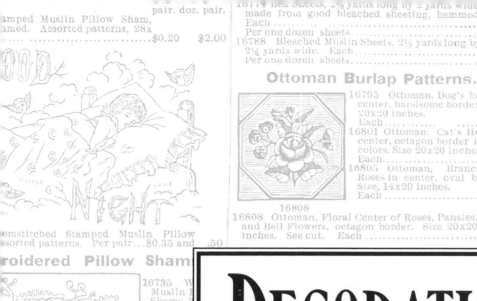

...emstitched Stamped Muslin Pillow ...ssorted patterns. Per pair...$0.35 and .50

...roidered Pillow Sham...

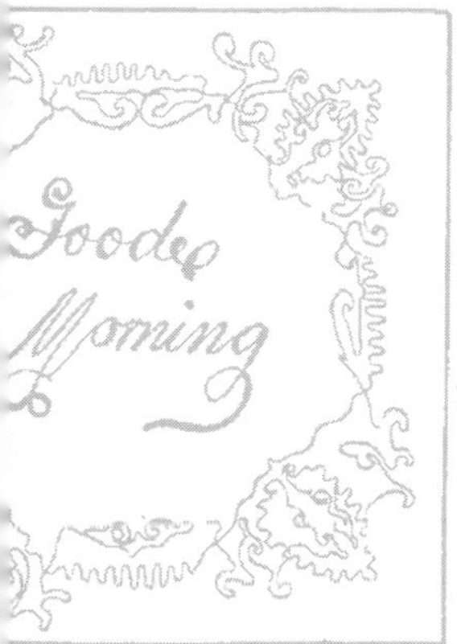

16735 W... Muslin ... Shams, 3... Embroid... in fast d... with ... Night o... and ... Morning... the other... Per pair, ...

16743 W... Muslin ... Shams, 30x30. Embroidered in white, with Good Night on one and Good Morning on the other. Per pair, $0.35

16735—43

16748 White Muslin Pillow Shams, 30x30. Embroidered in fast dye red. Per pair, $0.43

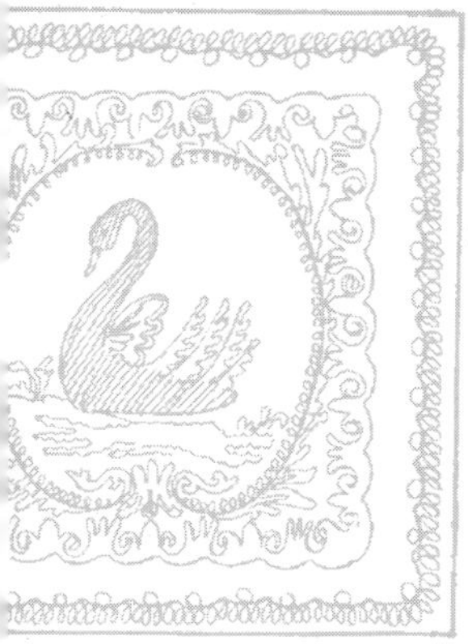

16752 White Muslin Pillow Shams, 30x30. Embroidered in fast dye red. Per pair, $0.60

...Muslin Pillow Cases.

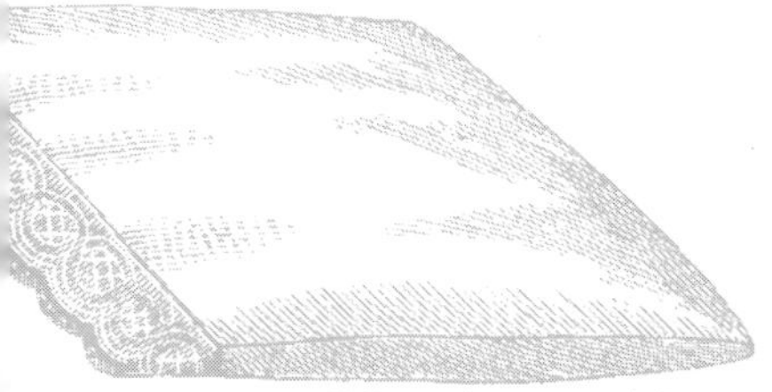

...ached. Hemmed Pillow Cases, with ... lace. Size, 22x35. Per pair..........$0.40 ...pairs.............. 4.35

16774 Bed Sheets, 2½ yards long by 2 yards wide, made from good bleached sheeting, hemmed. Each............ $0.50
Per one dozen sheets............ 5.75
16788 Bleached Muslin Sheets, 2½ yards long by 2¼ yards wide. Each............ .60
Per one dozen sheets............ 6.75

Ottoman Burlap Patterns.

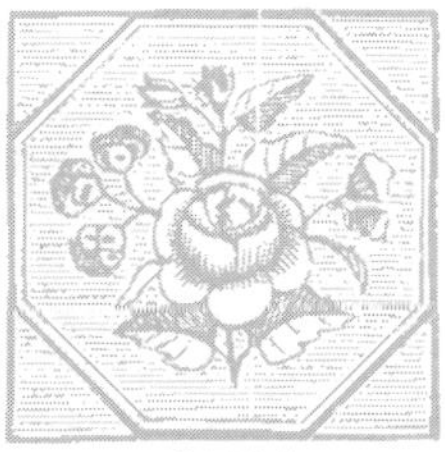

16808

16795 Ottoman, Dog's head in center, handsome border, size, 20x20 inches. Each............$0.12
16801 Ottoman, Cat's Head in center, octagon border in two colors. Size 20x20 inches. Each............$0.12
16805 Ottoman, Branch of Roses in center, oval border. Size, 14x20 inches. Each............$0.10
16808 Ottoman, Floral Center of Roses, Pansies, and Bell Flowers, octagon border. Size 20x20 inches. See cut. Each............$0._2

...frame as shown in the cut, stretching tightly and square. Then proceed to work the pattern by following the lines with the various colors designated.

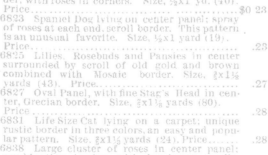

16815 Turkish Design. Size 16 in. by 1 yard; price, 23 cents. Similar to cut (136).

16820 Bouquet of Roses in center, surrounded by scroll in old gold and brown; geometric border, with roses in corners. Size, ½x1 yd. (40). Price............$0 23
16823 Spaniel Dog lying on center panel; spray of roses at each end, scroll border. This pattern is an unusual favorite. Size, ½x1 yard (19). Price............ .23
16825 Lilies, Rosebuds and Pansies in center surrounded by scroll of old gold and brown combined with Mosaic border. Size, ⅝x1⅛ yards (43). Price............ .27
16827 Oval Panel, with fine Stag's Head in center, Grecian border. Size, ⅝x1⅛ yards (80). Price............ .28
16831 Life Size Cat lying on a carpet; unique rustic border in three colors, an easy and popular pattern. Size, ⅝x1⅛ yards (24). Price............ .28
16838 Large cluster of roses in center panel; combination border, with handsome scrolls. Size, ¾x1¼ yards (96). Price............ .35
16840 Spaniel Dog lying on Mosaic carpet, surrounded with a unique oval, with twined ash leaves, scroll in corners of plain border. Size, ¾x1¼ yards (36). Price............ .35
16841 Turkish Design, similar to 16815. Size, ¾x1¼ yards (150). Price............ .37
16843 Stag by the Lake; heavy rich border of scroll work; beautiful landscape in center. Size, ¾x1½ yards (22). Price............ .42

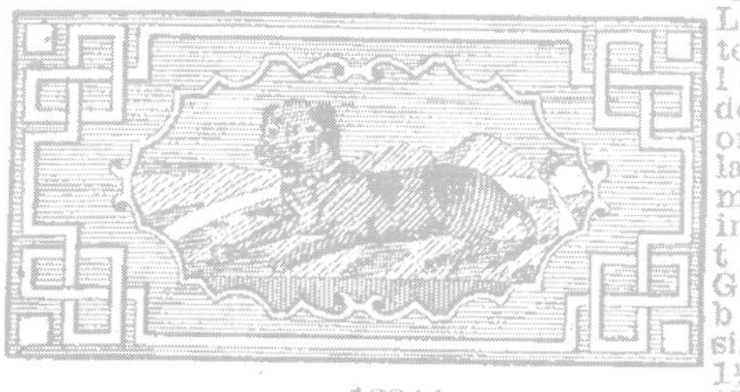

16844

16844—Large, intelligent-looking dog lying on a lawn, lake and mountain in the distance. Grecian border. size ¾ x 1½ yards (91.) Price............$0.42
16849 Cat and Three Playful Kittens, with handsome scroll border. Size ¾x1⅛ yards (39). Price............ .42
16855 Bouquet of Morning Glories, Lilies, etc., in center; Grecian border. Size ¾x1½ yards (90). Price............ .42

Patterns.

Every household has its supply of odds and en... rags and ravelings, which can be woven into article... beauty and utility. Rags worked into the proper p... terns with the improved rag machine produce v... rich and handsome rugs and ottomans, having a tap... try effect which gives no suggestion of the cheapn... of the material.

Some prefer to work colored yarn with their ra... others use fancy yarns altogether. In the latter case ... may be estimated that it will require from one-quar... to one-half pound of yarn to every square foot of ca... vas worked, according as you want the article, light... heavier. One-half pound of good yarn to the squa... foot will make a rug nearly three-quarters of an in... thick.

Colored Rug Yarn.

Order No. 16881.

Yarn especially manufactured for this purpose a... kept in stock by us can be supplied in any quantity. The average amount of yarn required to fill our p... terns is shown in the following list; but for the weig... of each separate color we refer you to our yarn li... which we will send when asked for.

Pounds
...1⅝ "
...2 "
..., 80...2¾ "
..., 150...3½ "
..., 91...4½ "
...4¾ "
...5½ "
...3, 7, 8...⅞ "
...2...¾ "
...ngrain carpet yarn, assorted colors, 4 ...pound. Per skein............$0.

...em Tufting and Embroider... Machine.

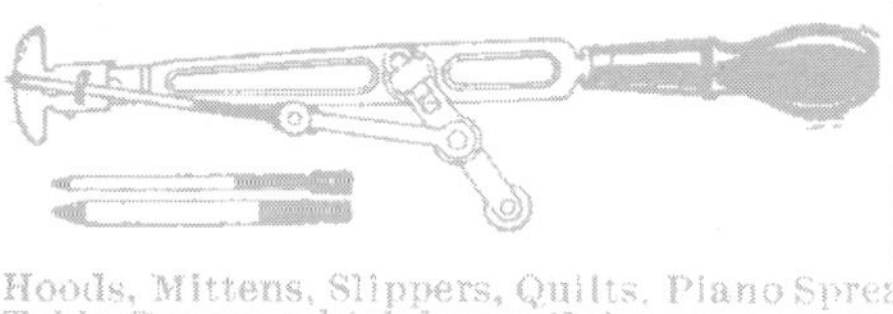

16888 Has four needles. Will work rags, yarn, zeph... and silk. ... machi... for $1. ... that mak... Turki... Rugs, Ott... mans, Cu... tains, Sta... Carpe... Hoods, Mittens, Slippers, Quilts, Piano Spreads or Table Covers, which have all the gorgeous appearance of the genuine Turkish or Persian design. So simple that a ten year old child can operate it. With this machine you can beautify your homes and teach your children to be industrious. Special instructions with each machine. Postage 7 cents. Each............$1.

Canvas.

16890 Java Canvas, white, 18 in. Per yard... $0
16892 Penelope Canvas, 27 in. Per yard...

Ladies' Gingham Aprons.

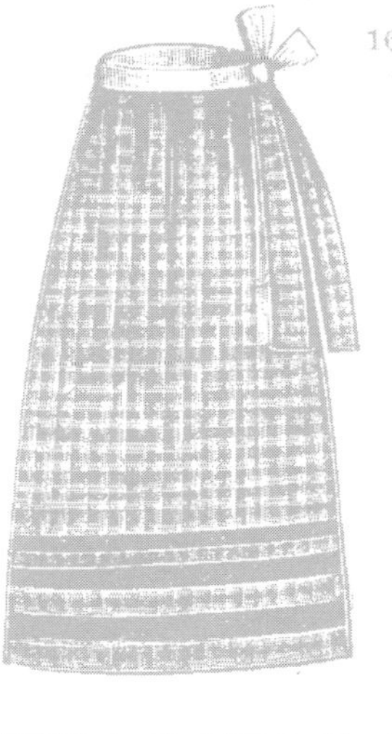

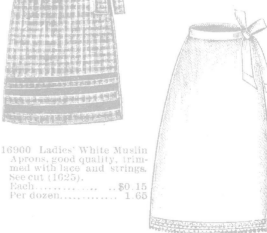

16895 Ladies' Good Gingha... Aprons, assorted checks, ... brown, green and blue, ... inches long, 45 inches wid... See cut. Each ......$0.... Per dozen............ 2....

Ladies' White Aprons.

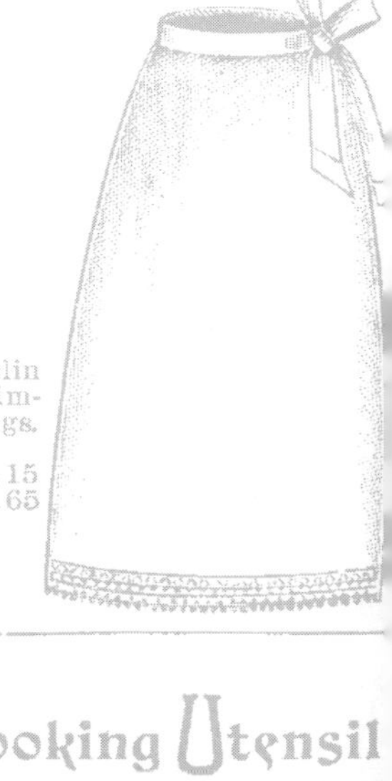

16900 Ladies' White Muslin Aprons, good quality, trimmed with lace and strings. See cut (1625). Each............$0.15
Per dozen............ 1.65

Aluminum Cooking Utensil...

LITHOGRAPHS ON CANVAS

By means of a process in which the ink from oil-painting lithographs is impregnated onto canvas under pressure, Old Grange Graphics has reproduced a survey-course full of Early American artwork. The paintings are stretched over wooden stretchers, framed (if desired by the customer), and completed with picture wire, title and bumpers. The entire process is done by hand on the premises of the Old Grange Hall in Hopewell, New Jersey, where the company is located.

Under such categories as "American Folk Art," "The Federal Period" and "The Hudson River School," etc., are 105 landscapes and portraits, including several by Edward Hicks (1780–1849), best known for "The Peaceable Kingdom"; John Singleton Copley's "Paul Revere"; paintings of sailing ships by William A. Coulter; the "Merced River, the Yosemite Valley," by Albert Bierstadt (1830–1902); and Charles Osgood's 1840 portrait of the young Nathaniel Hawthorne shown here. During this period of his life, Hawthorne worked at a customs house and stayed at Brook Farm, in West Roxbury, Massachusetts—a cooperative of transcendental intellectuals that the writer portrayed in his 1852 book, *The Blithedale Romance.* As shown, the Hawthorne portrait sells for $166; other completed lithographs range from $84 to $260.

Old Grange will transfer your prints to canvas as well as conduct a search for any specific or genre painting that you want reproduced.

Catalog available, $4 (refundable with first purchase).

OLD GRANGE GRAPHICS
P.O. Box 297, 12-14 Mercer Street
Hopewell, NJ 08525
Tel. 800/282-7776

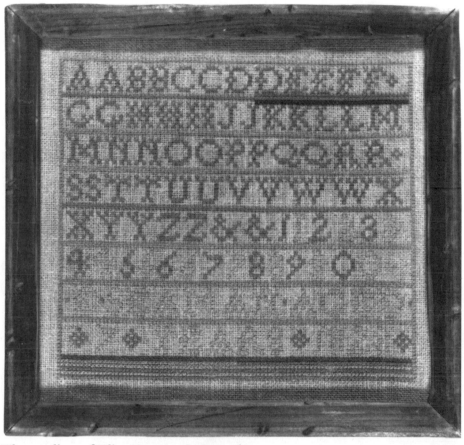

The replica of Eliza Seaman's Sampler.

❊SAMPLER KITS

The Early American "examplar," or sampler—an article of linen embroidered to show the alphabet or a verse—has been replicated into kits for needleworkers by the Examplarery of Dearborn, Michigan.

Using antique samplers, many with historic significance, the Examplarery reproduces them with an exactitude that extends to the use of naturally dyed linens with imported floss.

The sampler depicted is a replica of one made in 1823 by eight-year-old Eliza Seaman. Miss Seaman, whose original sampler is part of the Detroit Historical Museum's textile collection, was to achieve wide renown as an abolitionist and suffragette. Married in 1836 to Augustus Leggett, the couple numbered Walt Whitman, Ralph Waldo Emerson and Louisa May Alcott among their friends.

Kit catalog available, $3.

THE EXAMPLARERY
P.O. Box 2554
Dearborn, MI 48123
Tel. 313/278-3282

Eliza Seaman Leggett

✳ VICTORIAN WALLPAPERS

"A white wall is appropriate for lavatories and pigsties," said the avant-garde wallpaper designer **Christopher Dresser.** A proponent of the Victorian notion that art serves to edify, Dresser appeared to advance the belief that blank walls be used only in those places where an inflammatory thought might create hazards. But elsewhere in Dresser's late nineteenth-century world there were walls, wainscoting and cornices suitable for his elaborate designs—designs that the Bradbury & Bradbury company has been replicating (along with those of several other Victorian schools) since 1976.

This "art wallpapers" collection is the result of the meticulous researching of designs created in England and America during the last quarter of the nineteenth century. Some wallpapers and ceiling designs—such as those done in the Neo-Greco style—are replicas; others employ adaptations of stenciled and hand-painted decorations; while yet other wallpapers use new styles created by designers "working in the tradition established over a century ago."

To eliminate the need for middlemen, Bradbury & Bradbury uses mail-order exclusively. Hand-printed samples of designs selected through their catalog's informative "Roomset" chapters are shipped the same day they are requested. In keeping with the company's evident efforts to anticipate customers' needs, a professionally staffed design service is also available.

Catalog available, $3.

BRADBURY & BRADBURY ART WALLPAPERS
P.O. Box 155
Benicia, CA 94510
Tel. 707/746-1900
Fax. 707/745-9417

▣ FAIRY-TALE TILES

Replicas of tiles originally manufactured in 1870 by the English tile-works Minton–Hall are sold by the Hudson River Museum of Westchester County, New York. Chosen from a series of eight original fairy-tale tiles mounted in the Great Hall mantelpiece of the Museum's Trevor Mansion are tiles depicting "Bluebeard," "The Frog Prince," "The Little Tailor" and "The Six Swans." All were illustrated by the English artist J. Moyr Smith. The 6x6-inch tiles are rendered in brown on white, as are the originals.

Price: $2 each, plus tax if sold within New York State, and shipping.

Literature, dealer information available.

THE HUDSON RIVER MUSEUM OF WESTCHESTER
511 Warburton Avenue
Yonkers, NY 10701
Tel. 914/963-4550

⊞ TURN-OF-THE-CENTURY PRINTS

As early as the 1840s, root beer was a drink highly favored by children and temperate adults alike. Young men grew up, stayed sober and got old sipping the carbonated concoction before the Hire's Root Beer ad that Nostalgia Decorating so faithfully duplicates appeared on the scene. Accompanying Hire's are more than 100 other full-color advertising prints including ones extolling Burpee's Seeds and Grape-Nuts, which cereal was a part of C.W. Post's 1890s launch of the breakfast-food industry. Nostalgia Decorating also carries a large selection of Victorian and nineteenth-century prints including the popular 'Suspense' by artist Charles Burton Barber.

Prices: $4.75 per print (plus $2.25 for shipping and handling).

Full-color brochure, $2.

NOSTALGIA DECORATING COMPANY
P.O. Box 1312
Kingston, PA 18704
Tel. 717/472-3764
Fax. 717/472-3331

❦ SHAKER "HEAVENLY TREE" PRINT

A Shaker "gift drawing," replete with multicolored fruits, flowers and leaves reproducing one painted by Sister Polly Collins at Hancock Shaker Village in December of 1855. Individually silk-screened on parchment, the unframed print measures 23 by 18 inches.

Prices: $30 postpaid.

Color catalog of Shaker crafts available, $1.

SHAKER WORKSHOPS
P.O. Box 1028
Concord, MA 01742
Tel. 508/646-8985
Fax. 508/648-8217

❀ CURTAIN POLE FINIALS

The Ground Floor of Charleston, South Carolina, offers period curtain-pole finials in motifs like bursting seedpods, thistles, and the pineapple depicted.

　　Prices: $100 each pair; poles, rings, brackets and curtain cord pulls are available.

Brochure and price lists available.

THE GROUND FLOOR
95½ Broad Street
Charleston, SC 29401
Tel. 803/722-3576

❧ VICTORIAN STENCILS

With such styles as rococo, Persian and griffins, Victorian stencils were generally more ornate than earlier American versions. The job of stenciling would fall to the housewife, who would compound the complexity of these designs by combining the stencils and painting them on colored backgrounds. At times, different colors would be used above and below the chair and picture rails. Stencils were readily available from major paint manufacturers like Sherwin-Williams or from stencil companies like Excelsior.

　　After unsuccessfully searching for Victorian stencils to use to decorate period homes, Kim Black turned to the original stencil catalogs. Using these, Ms. Black cofounded Epoch Designs to sell the replicated stencils to the vast modern-day Victorian design market.

Catalog available, $3.

EPOCH DESIGNS
P.O. Box 4033, Dept. 050
Elwyn, PA 19063

4R70

CERTIFICATE OF GUARANTEE
No
TRADE MARK
CHEAPEST SUPPLY HOUSE ON EARTH THE WORLD
THIS CASE IS MADE OF TWO PLATES OF SOLID GOLD OVER A COMPOSITION OF FINE METAL

TIMEPIECES

❋❋

4R72

4R76

4R74

THIS ILLUSTRATION of our Edgemere movement is engraved expressly for us by our artist direct from the movement itself. The Edgemere is manufactured expressly for us. This movement is solid nickel through and through; the top plate is beautifully damaskeened in gold and nickel. It has 12 fine ruby jewels, each jewel finely set in polished settings, polished patent regulator, double cut expansion balance wheel, genuine Breguet hair spring, goldine timing screws. The dial is fine French enamel with marginal figures, the entire movement is perfectly finished in every detail, timed and regulated. We guarantee it for a term of five years and know it will give entire satisfaction.

GUARANTEED 20 YEARS

.25 AND UPWARDS
FOR THE HIGHEST GRADE
SCREW BACK AND SCREW BEZEL
T PROOF, GOLD FILLED WATCHES MADE

OUR SPECIAL GRADE 20-YEAR GUARANTEED GOLD FILLED CASES, THE FINEST MADE.

E GOLD FILLED CASES are made under contract for us by the best gold filled case makers in America, and we believe are t exception **THE BEST GOLD FILLED CASES MADE.**

FACE, 18-Size, Screw Back and Screw Bezel and guaranteed absolutely dust proof, stem wind and t; made from two plates of solid gold over an inner lined plate of hard ition, and is guaranteed by special certificate, which accompanies every case, and retain its color for 20 years. All cases are beautifully engraved, deco- polished and finished. The best gold filled watch possible to turn out.

and up, according to movement, is a great reduction and far lower than the same grade of watch has ever been sold.

PECIAL PRICE OF $6.25

AKE NO RISK. BEAR IN MIND. If after you receive one of these watches, you don't find it exactly as described, return we will refund your money.

CHOICE OF CASES ILLUSTRATED, with any of the following movements, at prices named:

Jeweled Seth Thomas..	$ 6.25
Jeweled No. 208 grade Elgin or No. 18 grade Waltham....	7.50
JEWELED EDGEMERE, SEARS, ROEBUCK & CO.'S SPECIAL MAKE..	7.45
JEWELED No. 218 GRADE ELGIN OR No. 820 GRADE WALTHAM....	9.25
JEWELED SEARS, ROEBUCK & CO.'S SPECIAL...............	9.10
JEWELED ELGIN OR WALTHAM, Adjusted.................	11.00
JEWELED DUEBER, GRAND HAMPDEN, Adjusted.........	12.50
JEWELED G. M. WHEELER, ELGIN OR P. S. BARTLETT, WALTHAM, Adjusted.	13.60
JEWELED APPLETON, TRACY, WALTHAM, Adjusted.......	21.00
JEWELED NEW RAILWAY HAMPDEN, Adjusted..........	23.15
JEWELED B.W. RAYMOND ELGIN, Adjusted.............	24.85
JEWELED CRESCENT ST., WALTHAM OR FATHER TIME, ELGIN, Adjusted..	24.20
JEWELED JOHN HANCOCK, HAMPDEN, Adjusted........	30.50
JEW'D VANGUARD WALTHAM, No.150 GRADE ELGIN OR VERITAS, ELGIN, Adjus'd	36.10
JEWELED VERITAS, ELGIN, Adjusted....................	35.00

89

✶ VICTORIAN STREET CLOCKS

The period following the Civil War marked the moment in history when methods for marking moments in history changed. Time, which in antebellum days had been measured in the rotation of harvests and stars, began conforming to the factory whistles and railroad clocks of the industrial age. Yet despite the march of progress, time's trackless frontier was not subdivided into little boxes of ticky-tack continuance all at once. In rural areas particularly, time was measured by the seasons and in the pages of almanacs long into the 1870s. And in cities and towns, public clocks continued to be set to noonday by the overhead position of the sun.

The Electric Time Company's Two-Dial Howard Post Clock is cast from the original 1890 patterns of the E. Howard Clock Company of Waltham, Massachusetts. The aluminum street clock is approximately 15 feet 4 inches high and has backlit dials. A control that automatically resets the clock after power failures and for daylight-saving-time changes is located in the base. The clock's standard finish is a forest-green polyurethane—although additional colors are available. Other designs for tower and street clocks are obtainable from the manufacturer, including one for a four-faced Victorian model.

Price: Two Dial Howard Post Clock, $13,500 plus freight cost.

ELECTRIC TIME COMPANY, INC.
45 West Street
Medfield, MA 02052
Tel. 508/359-4396
Fax. 508/359-4482

CLOCKS BY FOSTER S. CAMPOS

Foster S. Campos is a master craftsman who has been building fine clocks for more than 30 years. His replicas of 12 nineteenth-century clocks have all been handcrafted using selected woods and American-made, solid-brass pendulum movements. The maker claims that they are "faithful to the originals in every detail."

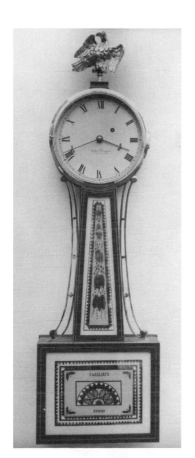

❧ WILLARD BANJO CLOCK

The banjo clock, designed to hang on the wall with a small gilt bracket to support it, was devised and patented in 1802 by Simon Willard. Typically, the frame of the clock was in the shape of a banjo and had a finial in the form of an eagle or other motif above the round dial. Brass brackets beside the long center panel, and decoration there and on the rectangular glass panel of the bottom section completed its presentation.

The Campos replica of a Willard banjo clock made around 1802 has a solid mahogany case with a cross-banded inlay, a cast-brass bezel, sidearms and eagle finial. The glass panels are hand-painted.

Dimensions: height, 40 inches; dial diameter, 7¼ inches.

Price: $1,200.

❧ GRANDMOTHER CLOCK

Small clocks in the form of tall clocks, but only four feet high, more or less, were made in the late 1700s and early 1800s. Predictably, these reduced grandfather clocks were called *grandmothers.*

The Campos grandmother clock is a scaled-down version of a Willard grandfather model. It has a solid-mahogany Roxbury-style case with three, solid-brass capitals, a rich inlay and hand-rubbed finish. Available with a weight-driven pendulum; with a

drop-off hourly strike; or with an hour, or hour-and-half-hour striking German weight-driven movement. Rocking ship or hand-painted floral dials are optional.

Dimensions: height, 61 inches; width, 12 inches; depth, 6 inches.

Price: Willard Grandmother Clock, $2,600. All shipments require a $40 fee for packing and UPS clock crating.

Catalog available, $2.

CLOCKS BY FOSTER S. CAMPOS
213 Schoosett Street, Route 139
Pembroke, MA 02359
Tel. 617/826-8577

▦ AARON WILLARD CLOCK KIT

Aaron Willard and his brother Simon of Roxbury, Massachusetts, were among the most renowned and prolific clock makers of the turn of the nineteenth century. Their "coffin clock" (circa 1800) reflects the beautifully clean lines of its grim namesake.

Like death itself, the coffin clock is severe; but unlike the Grim Reaper, it's available from the manufacturer only based on demand. The Willard coffin clock has a quartz movement and sounds a gong on the hour. The pine case, with glass-covered dial and pendulum window, is 36 inches high, 10 inches wide and 5 inches deep. Four hours are required out of your life for assembly.

Price: $264.

Catalog of reproduction furniture kits available, $3.

COHASSET COLONIALS
834 X Ship Street
Cohasset, MA 02025
Tel. 800/288-2389

▣ SCHOOLHOUSE CLOCK

Victorian sensibilities greatly expanded primary schooling in both scope and length, as the average number of days required for attendance doubled between the years 1870 and 1918. In many elementary schools, Benjamin Franklin's admonition that "Time Is Money" was well understood—and so school clocks were watched with a desperation equal to that found in the most Dickensian of workhouses.

Portsmouth Clock Company's schoolhouse clock replicates one originally produced in upstate New York during that region's service as domestic mecca for Arts & Crafts design. Today, the clock is produced from quarter-sawn red oak by craftsmen in New Hampshire and Maine. It features a silk-screened face plate and retaining ring that are made of 24-gauge steel, solid-brass hardware, and a lifetime warranty on electrical components.

Price: $199, plus shipping and handling.

PORTSMOUTH CLOCK COMPANY
P.O. Box 4247
Portsmouth, NH 03802-4247
Tel. 603/433-6120

MASON & SULLIVAN'S NINETEENTH-CENTURY CLOCKS

The firm of Mason & Sullivan of Cape Cod has been manufacturing replica clocks (both in kit form and with fully finished cases) for 45 years. They have an excellent reputation for quality that has resulted from their high standards in wood, joinery, movements and detailing. The following is a sample of their replica nineteenth-century clocks:

❦ SHAKER WALL CLOCK

"The clock is an emblem of a Shaker community because everything goes on time," wrote a visitor from the outside world in 1887. This replica Shaker clock was designed after one in the collection of the Groton (Mass.) Historical Society. Suitable for use on a wall or shelf, the clock has a cherry case with pine backing. The kit comes complete with a painted wooden dial, quartz-regulated pendulum (guaranteed for three years), hands and round glass.

Dimensions: case measures 20½ inches high by 13½ inches wide by 4 inches deep.

❋ SHAKER CLOCK

Designed by master clockmaker Isaac N. Youngs (1793-1865), the original from which this clock has been replicated can be found at the Hancock Shaker Village.

Dimensions: height, 41¾ inches; width, 14¾ inches; depth, 5¾ inches.

☸ POCKET WATCH

The timekeeping triumph of nineteenth-century America was the "dollar watch," the wonder of European visitors. These timepieces were not made for ease of repair and seemed not worth repairing. Although priced at $22.39, the Cumberland General Store's "Conductor" pocket watch appears to preserve this tradition. With a locomotive depicted on its "gold-color" case, the Conductor comes with a matching chain. Shipped weight, 1 lb.

General Merchandise Catalog available, $3.

CUMBERLAND GENERAL STORE
Route 3, P.O. Box 81
Crossville, TN 38555
Tel. 800/334-4640 for orders
or 615/484-8481

✸ BRISTOL SHELF CLOCK

The company of Smith and Goodrich of Bristol, Connecticut, produced attractive miniature shelf clocks that were popularly priced for the mid-nineteenth-century. Mason & Sullivan's kit replica is made from select oak, with a hand-screened glass and dial, brass hardware and a precision, pendulum quartz movement.

Dimensions: height, 11⅜ inches; width, 7⁹⁄₁₆ inches; depth, 3⅞ inches.

✸ VIENNA REGULATOR CLOCK

The clocks known popularly in America as "Vienna Regulators" were derived from nineteenth-century German and Austrian clocks highly valued for their craftsmanship. Mason & Sullivan's version replicates a Vienna Regulator at midcentury—its movement not yet overpowered by scrollwork.

Dimensions: height, 42 inches; width, 12¾ inches; depth, 8 inches.

Seasonal catalog of replica clocks available.

MASON & SULLIVAN COMPANY
586 Higgins Crowell Road
West Yarmouth, MA 02673
Tel. 800/933-3010
Fax. 508/775-5581

BURNS ANY KIND OF FUEL, HARD OR SOFT COAL, WOOD, COKE OR CORN COBS.

A REDUCED PRICE.

We offer this wonderful new 1908 pattern Acme Progress Steel Cook Stove as the very latest and very highest grade steel cook stove offered on the market, the equal of any steel cook stove you can buy at double our price. It will burn hard or soft coal, coke, wood, or any other fuel; it will be found to be the most adaptable steel cook stove you can buy, and

IT IS SOLD TO YOU UNDER OUR POSITIVE BINDING GUARANTEE OF SATISFACTION OR YOUR MONEY BACK.

THE BODY of the Acme Progress Steel Cook Stove is made of heavier steel than is used by other makers. The heavy steel ...es are accurately cut and punched for riveting and they are very care-...y milled and fitted together; they are securely hand riveted, thoroughly ...ed, and so thoroughly are they designed and so carefully are they ...e that an Acme Progress Steel Cook Stove will be in better condition ...r five years of constant use than the ordinary light weight or cast iron ... stove would be after but one year's use.

...E MAIN TOP. The main top, cover and centers are made of the very finest cast stove plate from the purest pig iron, should not be confused with malleable top ranges which other manufac-...rs sometimes call "steel" with the deliberate purpose to deceive you. No ...eable iron top ever made can compare in lasting quality with the cast ... plate tops used in the manufacture of our stove.

...E FIRE BOX is well constructed of proper ... vide enough heat for the oven ... the two end pieces removed and the cast iron ...ched, the fire box is easily prepared for burning w... ...length of fire box for wood 23½ inches. We equip ...ress with duplex grate, which can be used for ... wood, or any other fuel, as shown on page 637.

...E PERFECT OVEN of the Acme Progress ... Stove is made from ex... ... plate, hand riveted with wrought rivets, careful... ...ughout, and with our arrangement of flues and ... a very quick, fine and satisfactory baker. It is ... ...ions, being 17½x20x12 inches in size, and it h... ...terbalanced drop oven door on the right side, wi... ...handsomely nickeled medallion center plate and ... ...om of our Progress Steel Cook Stove is made of ... ...cted stock sheet steel, so constructed, bolted, bra... ...ys remain level, and there is absolutely no possi... ...agging. The oven top is protected with a hes... ...serves to distribute the heat to all parts of the o... ...t side (the left side left blank). The door opens ... ... ranges, forming a large, commodious shelf. ...g and ornamented with a beautifully nickel pla...

...IS STOVE is furnished in numbers 8-20 or 9 ... has four holes and the size of the ... is 42½x26 inches. The height from floor to mai... ...box for wood, 23½ inches; size pipe to fit collar. ...plete with lifter, shaker and scraper for removin...

THE LA... RESERVOIR ... is made of the best ... of cast iron, white ... lain lined to ... rusting. Easily kep... and removable. I ... capacity of 17 ...
DAMPERS ar... venient to rea... so placed tha... are easily reg... POUCH FEED... Progress Steel ... Stove has a ... pouchfeed for ... coal or coke a... also permit ... insertion of a ... over the fire...

...to the left and is ...ted to prevent ...lling to the floor ... DOOR is extra ... standard grade ... under the ash door, which prevents the ashe... The bottom edge is reinforced with heavy ... ...he stove and strongly riveted to the steel pl... ...will be seen by referring to the illustration ...e Progress Four-Hole Steel Cook Stove, the ...ry newest rococo pattern.

Prices, strongly crated and delivered on cars at our foundry at Newark, Ohio:

No. 22K205 Price, No. 8-20, with reservoir and 8-inch lids ....$15...
On this stove the fire box is 8½ inches wide and 5½ inches deep, its length for coal is 18 inches and for wood 23½ inches. Capacity of reservoir, 17 quarts. Shipping weight, 340 p...
No. 22K206 Price, No. 9-20, with reservoir and 9-inch lids ....$15...
Prices do not include pipe or cooking utensils. For cooking utensils, see pages 461 to 466.

IF DESIRED WITHOUT RESERVOIR BUT WITH END SHELF, DEDUCT $2.00 FROM EITHER SIZE.

...CME ROVER GENUINE STEEL FOUR-HOLE COAL AND WOOD STOVE $6 7...

A REDUCED PRICE.
WITH RESERVOIR
MODEL OF 1908
Three sizes, direct from our foundry, offered at $6.75, $7.75 and $8.75, according to size, as listed below.
ONLY

COMPARE THE PRICES with any prices you have ever seen or he... in either a steel or cast iron reservoir cook stove, and you will find th... we are offering on this reservoir steel cook stove less than one hal... others charge, and it is positively THE GREATEST STOVE VALUE... WORLD HAS EVER SEEN.

COMPARED WITH THE LOWEST PRICES we could possibly mak... on any of our cast iron reservoir cook stoves we save you easily from ... to $7.00, and compared with any other steel cook stove we could se... we show you a saving of from $6.00 to $8.00; and compared with an... any other maker or dealer could offer you we show you a saving in cost on this, OUR... ROVER STEEL COOK STOVE WITH RESERVOIR, of easily $7.00 to $15.00.

THE BODY is made of the highest grade sheet steel, thoroughly bolted, braced, reinforced throughout, the very best oven construction; our new special flue, draft damper and circulating system, made to burn hard coal, soft coal, or wood. With each stove we furnish a special grate for wood. Has a cast top—the exact same grade of top that we use in our highest grade stoves and ranges; four lids, cut centers, supported by our own special system of construction. At the special price named, the stove is furnished with a detachable or removable reservoir, as shown in illustration. In shipping the stove we pack the reservoir inside of the oven, and the stove is crated in a way that there is no chance of its reaching you in bad condition—in fact the stove is unbreakable.

WE HAVE A LARGE STOCK OF these stoves on hand, ready for immediate shipment. It will just take a few days for you order to reach us and the stove to reach you. The stove being made of sheet steel is comparatively light and the freight charges will amount to next to nothing. This stove can be shipped from 100 to 500 miles at from 35 cents to 75 cents; from 500 to 1,000 miles at from 50 cents to $1.00; greater or lesser distances in proportion.

REPAI... PART... We will always ... a complete stoc... repairs and ... parts in years ... come; even ten y... hence we will be ... to deliver you ... piece or part to ... place or repair ... defective part ... *his at actual ... a mere fraction ... what other st... dealers charge.

THIS ILLUSTRATION, engraved by our artist from a photograph, showing our new 1908 model Acme Rover, four-hole, reservoir, all steel cook stove, which we offer at $6.75, $7.75 and $8.75, will give you a good general idea of the appearance of this stove.

NOTE OUR REDUC... IN PRICE

DETAILED DESCRIPTION

THE BODY is built of heavy smooth steel plate, is substantially put together, riveted with wrought iron rivets, strongly reinforced and bra... every part. The heavy plates are well riveted and jointed.

THE MAIN TOP. In manufacturing this, our Acme Rover, we have constructed the main top and covers of good stove plate. It has four cooking... and with ordinary care and usage the main top and covers will last years. All parts of the main top are carefully fitted, with sufficient allowance for heat expa...

THE LARGE FIRE BOX. It has an extra large fire box, provided with practical cast iron ...gs, with shaking and dumping grate. With every stove we include, free of cost, an ... grate for wood, so you can burn hard coal, soft coal or wood.
THE FIRE DOOR is beautifully designed and swings to the left.
THE DRAFT SLIDE is in front, of more than usual capacity.
THE ASH PIT is large and roomy and is provided with a large ash pan.
THE OVEN is of very generous proportions, perfectly square, is a very satisfactory, quick ... even baker, and is furnished with a heavy wire oven rack.
THE OVEN DOOR is on the right side (the left side left blank). It is our latest swing ...rn, attractive rococo design, steel lined, perfectly square, and fits snug to the body of ... stove, thus retaining all the heat in the oven.

THE FLUES are ample and provided with cleanout in rear of ash pit, which is re... from the front of the stove.
THE RESERVOIR is made of galvanized iron, heats by direct contact with the ... the stove, is removable and can be used on either end or rear side at pleasure, or can b... on top of stove as occasion requires.
GOOD SERVICE. The long looked for steel cook stove for practical people, neat ...act, serviceable and cheap. No such value in a cook stove ever offered before. ...cme Rover Steel Cook Stove, is shipped ready to set up, the four legs and all other ... parts packed inside. When received you have only to put on the legs, pipe and othe... parts, when it is ready for fire, the same as if you were moving an old stove from on... to another.

94

...CES FOR OUR ACME ROVER STEEL COOK STOVE, FOR COAL AND WOOD, WITH RESERVOIR, FOUR COOKING HOLES, DUMPING GRATE, LARGE ASH PAN, OVEN RACK, GALVANIZED RESERVOIR ADJUSTABLE TO EITHER END, SIDE OR BACK.

⊞ RESTORED ANTIQUE RANGES AND STOVES

Good Time Stove, Richard "Stove Black" Richardson's 22-year-old operation, is just off the main road leading into Goshen, Massachusetts—not far from where the first parlor cookstove was built in 1845. The stoves that emerge from Good Time's barn-red shop there—restored nineteenth-century parlor

stoves, kitchen ranges, potbellies, and others—are daunting in their intricate beauty. The evidently old-fashioned workmanship and gauge, the magnificent rise and monumental heft of such as the Glenwood Oak (1898), Railway King (1885) and Base Burner Six Door (1896) make Richardson's showroom something of a Smithsonian of wood and coal burners. It is the rarity of antiques such as these that usually gives them their value, but Good Time's restored stoves and ranges are here to do a job. Thus quaint patina is unceremoniously discarded and resurrection comes in a glitter of renickeled newness that can transport you right back to the loading dock of some late-nineteenth-century foundry.

Richardson claims that his restored antiques go their modern counterparts better in more than workmanship and looks: "After all," he says, "these stoves were produced in an era when wood was split by hand and hauled by horse. There were no gas-powered chain saws, hydraulic lifters, or even backup heating systems. The stoves had to use precious fuel as efficiently as possible."

Catalog and video available. Visitors welcome.

GOOD TIME STOVE COMPANY
Route 112
Goshen, MA 01032
Tel. 413/268-3677

⊛ ROME COOKSTOVE

This cast-iron stove is the reproduction of a design from the 1820s—a time when several improvements in American stove design coincided with a rise in firewood prices wrought by a century-and-a-half of deforestation. The newfangled stoves, perceived by Benjamin Rush to burn "but a fourth or a fifth part of what is commonly burnt in ordinary open fireplaces" (the actual amount was about

a third) constituted the first significant change in domestic heating since the fireplace itself came along in the Middle Ages.

Cumberland's 1820s cookstove is available in a gas-burning as well as a wood-and-coal-burning model. It is obtainable in three separate sections: a stove base (28⅜ inches high by 31 inches wide by 26 inches deep), oven (9½ inches high by 15 inches wide by 14½ inches deep) and splashback with warming box. The cooking area is 22 inches deep by 31 inches wide.

Price: $1,167.50 for the gas model, $817.50 for the wood-burning model. Both shipped freight collect.

General Merchandise Catalog available, $3.

CUMBERLAND GENERAL STORE
Route 3, Box 81
Crossville, TN 38555
Tel. 800/334-4640 for orders
*   or 615/484-8481*

✻ STANLEY IRON WORKS' STOVES AND RANGES

The Stanley Ranges are replicas of turn-of-the century woodburners. Unlike the Waterford Stanleys on page 100, they are domestically produced. With nickel-trimmed black-iron exteriors, these ranges have each been outfitted with four modern electrical or gas components. The electric burners are seated in stainless steel and surmounted by an oven with both bake and broil elements. The gas stove has a bake element only. Both ranges carry a one-year warranty.

The Stanley A is 36 inches wide, and the B is 42 inches wide and offers six burners, or four with a grill. Both stoves are 29 inches deep, 34 inches to the cook top and 65 inches tall with their roll-top ovens (if this is forsaken in favor of a simple upper shield, the height is 55 inches). The oven in each stove is 20 inches wide, 18 inches deep and 13 inches high.

Prices for Stanley A are $1,550, plus $200 with the upper oven; Stanley B is $2,000, plus $200 for the upper oven. Normal delivery is four to six weeks following the receipt of an order.

Brochure and catalog of restored antique stoves available.

STANLEY IRON WORKS
64 Taylor Street
Nashua, NH 03060
Tel. 603/881-8335

Stanley A

Stanley B

❦SOAPSTONE STOVE

In addition to its subtle beauty, soapstone has the remarkable ability to store (and slowly release) twice as much heat as either cast iron or steel. But building stoves made of soapstone requires a degree of patience and attention to detail that precludes mass production. For this reason, soapstone stoves were manufactured in small quantities even during their mid-nineteenth-century heyday, receiving heirloom status the moment they left the gate.

In its revitalization of soapstone manufacture, the Woodstock Soapstone Stove Company maintains a reverential approach to this tradition. Patterned after a stove made in northern New England in the 1860s, these stoves are authentically detailed and built one at a time by a single craftsman.

The Woodstock Soapstone Stove is a 28-by-26-by-22-inch woodburner providing a maximum heat output of 55,000 Btus per hour over a 10-to-12-hour period. An internal catalytic combustor increases heat output and virtually eliminates pollution. The stove has airtight construction and can heat up to 1,500 square feet. UL listed. EPA certified.

Price: Approximately $1,500.

WOODSTOCK SOAPSTONE STOVE COMPANY, INC.
Airpark Road, Box 37H
West Lebanon, NH 03784
Tel. 800/866-4344
Fax. 603/298-5958

PORTLAND STOVE'S RANGES AND STOVES

THE QUEEN AND PRINCESS ATLANTIC KITCHEN RANGES

When they first appeared, cookstoves would bring into the nineteenth-century home the same admixture of excitement and bewilderment for which personal computers have since come to be known. When a cookstove was installed into the basement kitchen of Millard Fillmore's White House, it reportedly so perplexed his cook that the future Know-Nothing candidate was forced to abandon the affairs of state in order to run over to the Patent Office for operating instructions.

By the turn of the century, however, a wood- or coal-burning kitchen range would grace virtually every home. The stove was used not only for cooking and baking, but also to provide the household with hot water and to heat adjoining rooms. By the early part of the twentieth century full-size kitchen ranges were being built by the hundreds of thousands all across the country.

Portland Stove's Queen Atlantic has been in continuous production since its introduction in 1906. From among such royalty of the time as the Star Kineo, the Home Comfort, the Crown Acorn and the Glenwood, only she still reigns. Like her slightly smaller (but more ornate) sibling, the Princess Atlantic, the Queen is 100 percent cast iron, available as either a wood- or coal-burner, and has long and deep fireboxes to accommodate long-burning loads. Both ranges also have six-lid tops, keep-ash pits, optional hot-water reservoirs, and warming ovens. The Queen Atlantic is the largest cast-iron kitchen range now made.

The Queen Atlantic

The Princess Atlantic

Dimensions: Queen Atlantic 32¼ inches high (to range top), 30 inches deep and 57 inches wide (including end shelf).

Prices: Queen Atlantic, $2,450; Princess Atlantic, $2,350. Optional items: hot-water reservoir (Queen only), $475; warming oven, $375.

THE ATLANTIC BOX STOVE

During the mid-nineteenth century, the utilitarian boxstove brought, in Portland Stove's phrasing: "welcome warmth … to one-room schools and logging camps. To shanties and stone-built sanctuaries. To countless homes on Main Street or R.F.D." Portland's Atlantic Box Stoves are made from a superior grade of 100 percent cast iron. The side panels—raised Gothic on the outside—are inwardly recessed to eliminate the need for liners or fire brick. Whole logs may be loaded from the front or top, where a cooking surface is provided.

Dimensions: Height, 26¾ inches; width, at hearth, 22¾ inches; length, 41¼ inches; firebox length, 28½ inches; stove pipe size, 6 inches. Average burn time: 9 hours.

Price: $675.

✖ B&M STATION AGENT STOVE

Portland Stove is one of the last remaining manufacturers of potbelly stoves. Their Station Agent measures from 42 inches in height to 22½ inches in outside diameter. The firepot diameter is 15 inches and the lid size is 10 inches. Coal burning time is 16 to 24 hours and the stove requires a 6-inch stovepipe.

Price: $1,050. Crating fee for all Portland stoves, $75.

Literature, $2.

PORTLAND STOVE COMPANY
P.O. Box 37, Fickett Road
N. Pownal, ME 04069
Tel. 207/688-2254

▦ WATERFORD STANLEY COOKSTOVES

An Irish import, the Waterford Stanley is an up-to-date version of an 1870 bog-burner that used peat for fuel. It has both a primary and secondary combustion system, an airtight firebox and a long smoke path for greater heat retention. Standard on each are a built-in thermometer, griddle, hot plate, two simmering plates and a damper control. Options are a top-exit flue exhaust, a plate rack, a warming oven, a side shelf, a coal-conversion kit and a stainless-steel hot-water jacket. The stove is available in matte black, or beige and brown enamel finishes.

Specifications: Height to top of warming compartment, 58½ inches; height to cook top, 34½ inches; width 35½ inches; depth, 24¼ inches; flue diameter, 6 inches; oven size, 15 inches deep by 13 inches high by 15½ inches wide (large enough for a 25-pound turkey); weight, 520 lbs.; Btu Rating, 32,000/hour; hours of burn, 8.

Free literature available.

WATERFORD IRISH STOVES
16 Airpark Road, Suite 3
West Lebanon, NH 03784

THE HEARTLAND OVAL COOKSTOVE

The Heartland Oval is an airtight replication of the Findlay Oval stove, first introduced in 1908 by the Findlay Brothers Foundry near Ottawa, Ontario. Until its demise in 1956, the Findlay Oval was sold as the "Queen of the Cookstoves" to three generations of Canadian Mennonites. It was, in fact, their devotion to the Oval cookstove that brought about its remanufacture.

In the early 1970s, Tom Hendrick, a hardware dealer from Elmira, Ontario, was doing all he could to scrounge old Findlay Oval replacement parts for stoves owned by area Mennonites. Hardly a day would pass when an Amish customer didn't pull his horse and buggy up to Hendrick's place to inquire after these parts and then extoll the old Oval's virtues.

So with the idea of having parts remanufactured, Hendrick went over to the Findlay foundry one day in 1976 to find the stove's original castings rusting behind the plant. The wood-stove revival of the late 1970s was only an ember then undetected by the Findlay people, who were uninterested in Hendrick's suggestion that they bring their stoves back. So after mulling the idea over for a while, he decided that he'd go it alone. Hendrick slapped down the money for parts for about 50 stoves, and embarked upon the production of new models that would last 14 years.

Today Oval stove manufacture is in the hands of Heartland Appliances of Kitchener, Ontario, which acquired Elmira in 1990. Like its smaller sibling the Sweetheart, the Heartland Oval is airtight, has a thickened stove top for heat retention, and makes extensive use of porcelain enamel and nickel trim. An optional reservoir replaces a portion of the firebox to produce from eight to ten gallons of hot water an hour. Heartland also produces electric, natural gas and propane ranges that strongly resemble its wood-burning counterparts, and all are sold through an extensive North American dealer network.

The body of the Heartland Oval is black, with door-fronts and decorative panels available in either white or almond porcelain enamel. For a $200 surcharge, an all-black model can be obtained. There is also an optional "Williamsburg" backsplash (the panel behind the cooking surface) of either white or almond enamel with stenciling done in blue porcelain enamel.

Prices range from $2,400 to $4,000.

Literature, current price list and dealer information available.

HEARTLAND APPLIANCES, INC.
5 Hoffman Street
Kitchener, Ontario
Canada N2M 3M5
Tel. 519/743-8111
Fax. 519/743-1665

OUR WONDER VALUE DISC HARROWS.

$14 55

STEEL FRAME

LIGHT XES.

We offer these high grade up to date ble Lever Disc Harrows at prices lower I have ever been attempted upon discs of most inferior quality. There are no more able or perfect working disc harrows on the ket and at our prices they are value which ther house can duplicate.

o. 32K435 8-16-Inch Disc Harrow. 460 lbs. Price..................$14.55
o. 32K436 10-16-Inch Disc Harrow. 480 lbs. Price..................$15.95
o. 32K437 12-16-Inch Disc Harrow. 500 lbs. Price..................$17.35
o. 32K438 14-16-Inch Disc Harrow. 515 lbs. Price..................$18.95
o. 32K439 16-16-Inch Disc Harrow. 530 lbs. Price..................$20.65

WONDER VALUE PONY GANG PLOWS

$12 87

ese Walking Gang Plows are old time rites. Perfectly adapted for all kinds of low plowing and especially desirable for ard cultivation. Each plow bottom is 9 es wide and the entire width of cut of the s 27 inches. Price is for the plow com-, as shown in the illustration. Plows chilled or combination bottoms furnished three extra chilled shares, but no extra ts are furnished with No. 32K432.

o. 32K430 Chilled Pony Gang Plow. 295 lbs. Price..................$12.87
o. 32K431 Combination Pony Gang 295 lbs. Price..................$14.55
32K432 Steel Pony Gang Plow. 295 lbs. Price..................$17.85

WONDER VALUE BRUSH AND GENERAL PURPOSE PLOWS.

7 35

is is one of the most popular styles of s on the market. It serves the purpose brush plow and its shape also makes it ble to use it for tame sod or stubble ing. Moldboard, landside and share are lid steel. This is a strong, serviceable and one for which every farmer has . Price is for the plow complete, as n in the illustration.

o. 32K415 12-Inch Brush Plow. Wt., Price..................$7.35
o. 32K416 14-Inch Brush Plow. Wt., s. Price..................$7.70

OUR WONDER VALUE ROD BREAKING PLOWS.

5 75

ese are the highest grade and best built s of their type. Have solid steel beam are well braced throughout. Adjustable rods take the place of a moldboard. e and fin cutter are of solid steel. Price plow complete, as shown in the illustra-and one extra share.

32K420 12-Inch Rod Breaking Wt., 35 lbs. Price..................$5.75
32K421 14-Inch Rod Breaking Wt., 04 lbs. Price..................$5.95
32K422 16-Inch Rod Breaking Wt., 67 lbs. Price..................$6.15

OUR WONDER VALUE PRAIRIE BREAKING PLOWS.

$7 37

This is the most popular style of Prairie Breaking Plow on the market and is too well known to need further de-scription. Price is for the plow complete, as shown in the illustration and with one extra share. We will furnish plow with gauge wheel and rolling coulter for $1.85 extra.

No. 32K425 12-Inch Prairie Break-ing Plow. Wt., 135 lbs. Price..$7.37

NOW IS THE TIME FOR YOU TO BUY.

We can save you big money on farm implements and machinery of all kinds. The articles shown on this page are selected from our regular stock and are but examples of the astonishing value represented by every farm implement and machine shown in this catalogue.

WHILE OUR PRICES ARE ABOUT ONE-HALF WHAT OTHERS ASK,

no one can furnish you with a superior quality of goods. If extra fine quality, absolutely perfect and up to date goods at a saving of nearly one-half to you will bring your order, we are entitled to all of your business on farm machinery. Our guarantee to please you in every way or return your money (an offer which is made by no other house in the world) is so very liberal that our farm machinery for our own protection must be right.

WE GUARANTEE TO SATISFY YOU

or you get every cent of your money back and freight charges both ways, and we repeat, if you are not satisfied in every way with any piece of farm machinery purchased from us, return it at our expense and we will refund your money along with any freight charges you may have paid out.

You will always find our quality the highest and our prices the lowest.

OUR WONDER VALUE STEEL WALKING PLOWS

OTHERS ASK $12.00 TO

7 73

HIGH LIFT

SOFT CENTER STEEL MOLD-BOARD, LANDSIDE AND SHARE.

BEAM HITCH

Here is positively the great-est Sulky Plow offer ever made. No one else has ever been able to offer such high grade, first class sulky plows for prices so low as we here quote. We furnish these plows in either stubble or turf and stubble bottom. Price is for the plow complete with pole, neckyoke, three-horse evener, weed hook and rolling coulter. When ordering state which you want.

No. 32K405 14-Inch Sulky Plow. Wt., 455 lbs. Price..................$24.75
No. 32K406 16-Inch Sulky Plow. Wt., 460 lbs. Price..................25.65

OUR WONDER VALUE STEEL GANG PLOWS

$39 95

EQUAL IN EVERY WAY TO GANG PLOWS WHICH OTHERS SELL FOR FROM $50.00 TO $60.00

HIGH LIFT

SOFT CENTER STEEL MOLDBOARD, LANDSIDE AND SHARE

BEAM HITCH

PRICE INCLUDES TWO ROLLING COULTERS

These are strictly up to date High Lift Gang Plows and superior in many ways to almost any gang plow which any other concern can offer you. Our price represents positively the greatest value ever offered in a gang plow. We furnish these plows in either stubble or turf and stubble shape. When ordering specify which you want. Furnished complete with pole, neckyoke, weed hooks, two rolling coulters and four-horse evener.

No. 32K410 12-Inch Gang Plow. Wt., 675 lbs. Price..................$39.95
No. 32K411 14-Inch Gang Plow. Wt., 680 lbs. Price..................40.85

OUR WONDER VALUE SWEEP HORSE POWERS.

These powers are of standard design, strongly constructed, and will give splendid service and con-tinued satisfaction. Shafts are steel and boxes babbitted; have high and low speed shafts. Illustra-tion shows a two and four-horse power. Six-horse powers have four sweeps. Price includes about 20 feet of tumbling rod, three couplings, rod block, platform, and spring hitch for each sweep. Lead poles are furnished with two and four-horse powers.

No. 32K465 Two-Horse Power. Wt., 725 lbs.

OUR WONDER VALUE CULTIVATOR

$17

This is one of the most desirable co Riding and Walking Cultivators on th ket. All steel, excepting the pole and Wheels have wide tires and dustpro tight long distance bearings, and adjusted from 4 to 5 feet wide.

No. 32K450 4-Shovel Break Pin vator. Wt., 410 lbs. Price......$17
No. 32K451 6-Shovel Break Pin vator. Wt., 425 lbs. Price......$18
No. 32K452 8-Shovel Break Pin vator. Wt., 435 lbs. Price......$18
No. 32K453 4-Shovel Spring Tr tivator. Wt., 435 lbs. Price......$
No. 32K454 6-Shovel Spring Tr tivator. Wt., 465 lbs. Price......$20

OUR WONDER VALUE ANGLE BAR HARR

$3 43

This is one of the most satisfactor frame harrows made. Will harrow wise of sod and not track. Frame of se oak, strongly riveted at each tooth and braced. Teeth are ½ inch square. includes draw bar.

No. 32K440 48-Tooth Angle Ba row. Wt., 125 lbs. Price..........$3
No. 32K441 60-Tooth Angle Ba row. Wt., 150 lbs. Price..........$4
No. 32K442 72-Tooth Angle Ba row. Wt., 190 lbs. Price..........$5
No. 32K443 90-Tooth Angle Ba row. Wt., 210 lbs. Price..........$5

OUR WONDER VALUE SPRING TOOTH HARR

$5

These bar-rows are too well known to need de-scription. Frames are of seasoned o fitted with stump guards around the sid front. Teeth are standard size, made o quality tempered spring steel and are secured. Price includes draw bar.

No. 32K445 16-Tooth Harrow. Wt lbs. Price..........$5
No. 32K446 18-Tooth Harrow. Wt lbs. Price..........$6
No. 32K447 20-Tooth Harrow. Wt lbs. Price..........$7

OUR WONDER VALUE COMBINED F CUTTER AND SHRE DER.

$18 95

You cannot buy the equal of this machine elsewhere for less than $30.00. It cuts the fodder into short lengths and at the time shreds each piece into small parts. be run by either hand or power. Can from one to two-horse power to run it. 11-inch cylinder head, with thirty knives. Price includes crank and pulle

No. 32K460 Feed Cutter and der. Wt., 325 lbs. Price........$18

$2075

⊞ NINETEENTH-CENTURY FOOD CROPS

The Seed Savers Exchange is a nonprofit organization dedicated to the preservation of endangered vegetables, fruits and grains. Gathering its seeds from those passed down from the Massachusetts Bay colony to today's "gardeners and farmers in isolated rural areas and ethnic enclaves," the exchange's members maintain thousands of these heirloom varieties, including traditional Indian crops, Amish and Mennonite garden seeds, and varieties no longer appearing in any seed catalog. SSE members receive three publications—a *Seed Savers Yearbook,* a *Summer Edition* and *Harvest Edition* —each containing 500 pages of horticultural information and access to thousands of heirloom varieties not available anywhere else.

Prices: U.S. membership fee, $25 (Reduced, Canadian, Mexican, Other Foreign, Supporting and Lifetime memberships also available).

Brochure available, $1.

SEED SAVERS EXCHANGE
Route 3, Box 239
Decorah, IA 52101

✹ HISTORIC TREES

Famous & Historic Trees is a project of The American Forestry Association, the country's oldest conservation organization. Their historical reproductions are biological ones as well.

Famous & Historic Trees researches and identifies the lineage of trees significant in American history. The program then collects and grows the seeds of these trees, carefully tending them until they are of suitable size to plant. Money from the sale of individual plantings goes to historic preservation groups, and has already benefited such sites as Walden, Gettysburg and Andersonville.

Among the scores of historic tree seedlings available are the descendants of "Goliad," a Live Oak used as a hanging tree in the days of the Texas frontier; the Diamond Willow that shaded a North Dakota site where the Lewis and Clark expedition camped; the Black Locust from Robert E. Lee's birthplace; and the Tulip Poplar that George Washington sowed at Mount Vernon.

Laudably combining historical preservation with environmentalism, Famous & Historic Trees also sponsors America's Historic Forest near Des Moines, Iowa, and the community-based Historic Groves program.

Price: $35.25 per tree.

Free information available.

FAMOUS & HISTORIC TREES
P.O. Box 7040
Jacksonville, FL 32238
Tel. 800/677-0727 (credit card orders only)

THE BAKER RUN-IN-OIL WINDMILLS AND TOWERS

The following have been reproduced from the Heller-Aller catalog:

Price list and literature available, $1.50.

THE HELLER-ALLER COMPANY, INC.

Corner Perry & Oakwood
P.O. Box 29
Napoleon, OH 43545
Tel. 419/592-1856

BAKER RUN-IN-OIL WINDMILLS

"Old Reliable"

Thousands of users have nicknamed the Baker Windmills Why? Because they have proven themselves capable of giving a life time of economical and dependable water pumping service. All working parts are running in a bath of oil. Requires oiling but once a year. More sails to the wheel. Simple and sturdy throughout. Will fit any make tower.

For Sale By

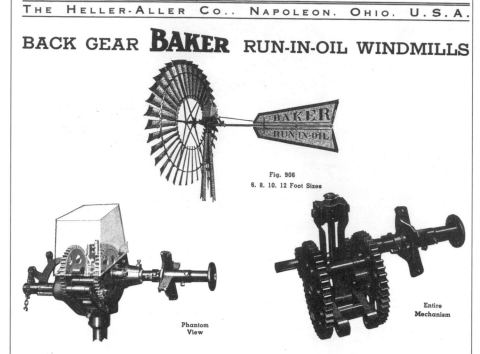

THE HELLER-ALLER CO., NAPOLEON, OHIO, U.S.A.

BACK GEAR **BAKER** RUN-IN-OIL WINDMILLS

Fig. 906
6, 8, 10, 12 Foot Sizes

Phantom View

Entire Mechanism

The "Baker" Windmill is a powerful and sturdy mill with smooth and easy running qualities.

The wheel is designed with a multiplicity of blades correctly curved and pitched to convert the maximum amount of energy from the prevailing winds to pumping power. Through the back gear arrangement, the wheel makes three revolutions to produce one complete pumping stroke.

The back gear design provides two pinion gears pinned to the main shaft against the interior sides of the oil bowl. The pinion gears drive the two large gears mounted on the stud shafts which project into the bowl from the hubs on either side of the bowl. The use of two sets of gears, one on either side of the bowl, distributes the load evenly assuring less wear and longer life of the mechanism. The pitman is connected from the offset hub of the large gears to the center of the rocker arm. The rocker arm, which is connected to boss provided at the back end and is an intergral part of the bowl, carries the side straps which run upward and are secured to the pump rod casting. As the wheel turns the main shaft, the train of the mechanism produces the up and down stroke of the pump rod.

The vane made of high grade galvanized steel, is of larger area and long so as to serve postively as a rudder to keep the wheel into the wind.

DISTINCTIVE FEATURES OF THE BACK GEARED BAKER WINDMILL

1. A Perfect Product - Over 80 years experience in windmill production results in the finest. Simple in design and use of the best materials available.

2. Gray iron castings and cold rolled shafting team up to provide the most rigid construction, and the best wearing surfaces in this windmill.

3. The complete operating mechanism runs in the pool of oil contained in the bottom of the one piece cast iron bowl, lubricating all moving parts and bearing surfaces. There are no parts above the bowl to become dry. This is POSITIVE OILING.

4. Leverage Advantage - The underslung rocker arm gives the Baker Windmill direct upward lifting motion providing the greatest power transferal and resulting in an easy operating windmill.

5. Two pinions and 2 large gears on either side of the pump rod distributes the load, giving smoother action and longer life.

6. Compact and Simple Design - A minimum of working parts, all brought together within the bowl, produce the most compact train of power transmission.

7. Bearings - All bearings are made of the best grade of cast iron and because of the graphitic content of gray iron, an excellent bearing surface is created in this useage. The main removeable bearing is provided with an oil grove the full length of the bearing surface permitting the oil which is picked up by the pinion gear, to move through the bearing to the oil seal at the far end where the oil is trapped and dropped into an oil return channel taking the oil back to the bowl.

8. The Baker Wheel - After many years of experience and thorough testing, this wheel was developed to capture the maximum amount of energy from the wind and transform it into pumping power. The result is a windmill easily able to activate a pump in a slight wind.

9. The Baker Vane - Extra long and with Maximum area of galvanized steel to serve as a rudder to keep the wheel into the wind under variable conditions. The vane is "Automatically Self Governing" so that when the wind reaches a high velocity, it will take the windmill out of gear to avoid damage.

10. Ball Bearing Turntable - Two iron castings with chilled ball bearing races are provided to accept a complete ring of ½" ball bearings. The main casting is secured to the top of the tower and the second casting rides on the ring of ball bearings. The mast pipe of the windmill goes through the center of the two castings and is thereby free to revolve easily on the tower so that the wheel may always face the wind.

11. Will Fit Any Make of Existing Tower - Different styles of turntables and truing centers are available to fit many towers. If the Baker turntable cannot be adapted to the existing tower we can furnish, at small additional cost, stub towers which can be added to any tower and which will accommodate our equipment.

12. Easily Erected - Baker windmills are simple to assemble and erect.

THE HELLER-ALLER CO. — BAKER WINDMILLS

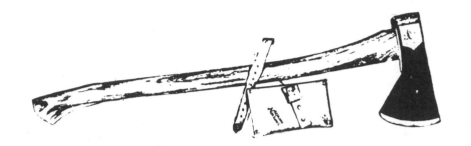

Axes

🏵 PENNSYLVANIA BROAD AXE

In the United States, local blacksmiths were the primary source for axes until one Mr. Samuel Collins of Hartford, Connecticut, built the first true axe factory in 1826. Like the Kent axe below, the Pennsylvania broad axe was used by settlers to hew rough timber into posts and beams; unlike it, this tool is hand-forged from high-carbon steel by a blacksmith. Shipped weight, 12 lbs.

Prices: Broad Axe head, $54; Broad Axe Handle, $7.95. F.O.B., Crossville, TN.

General Merchandise Catalog, $3.

CUMBERLAND GENERAL STORE
Route 3, Box 81
Crossville, TN 38555
Tel. 800/334-4640
for orders or
615/484-8481

🏵 HUDSON BAY AXE

There are two theories about the origin of the Hudson Bay Axe. The most popular is that it was developed from the tomahawk for use in the fur trade with the native population in northern Canada. It was unquestionably a trade axe, but some scholars believe that the trade axe itself evolved from earlier European axes, particularly the medieval Iberian axe. Whatever its origin, the fact remains that the Hudson Bay Axe's design gives it the greatest amount of blade area for the lowest weight, making it a good axe for softwoods.

Cumberland General Store's reproduction of the Hudson Bay Axe claims to follow the original pattern of those carried by eighteenth-century voyageurs and fur traders. Curved handle, 26 inches. shipped weight 6 lbs.

Price: $28.20. F.O.B., Crossville, TN.

🏵 KENT BROAD AXE

Although often mistaken for a big and clumsy felling axe, the Kent broad axe (also described in the entry for the Broad-Axe Beam Co., page TK) was actually used as a striking chisel for hewing square beams from round logs. Woodcraft Supply's Kent broadaxe has an offset eye, permitting the hewer to cut flat strikes on surfaces with ample clearance. The head has a 6-inch cutting edge and weighs 5 lbs.

Price: $34.95; 34-inch axe handle, $10.95.

Color tool catalog, $3.

WOODCRAFT SUPPLY CORPORATION
P.O. Box 4000
Woburn, MA 01888
Tel. 800/225-1153
Fax. 304/428-8271 (for orders only)

🏵 FROE

Colonists used a knifelike wedge called a froe (or frow) to split shingles, staves and clapboards. The froe is used by striking it with a short maul known as a "froe club." Lehman's froe has a 16-inch hardwood handle and a 15-inch steel blade. Weight: 4 lbs.

Price: $34.75. Hardwood mallet froe club, $21.50.

"Non-Electric" catalog, $2.

LEHMAN HARDWARE & APPLIANCES
4779 Kidron Road
Kidron, OH 44636
Tel. 216/857-5441
Fax. 216/857-5785

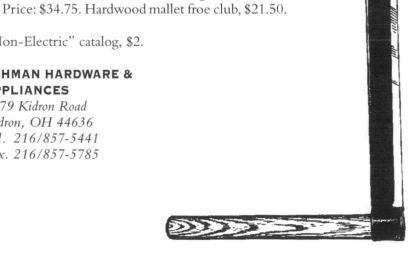

CUMBERLAND GENERAL STORE
FARM IMPLEMENTS

❈ FARM BELL

This No. 2-size farm bell is black-finished cast-metal. It can be heard from up to a mile away in clear weather. Shipping weight, 58 lbs.
    Price: $196.30.

❈ GEM WATER ELEVATOR CHAIN PUMP

The Gem chain pump is made of galvanized steel, painted gray, varnished, lettered and trimmed in black. It has malleable iron castings, a round iron sprocket, and a wooden handle, black. The Gem measures 8 by 16 inches at its outside base and is 36½ inches high. Shipping weight: 40 lbs.
    Price: $146.25.

❈ FOUR-TINE WHITE OAK PITCHFORK

The style of these pitchforks antedates the mass-produced iron pitchforks of the late nineteenth century. Crafted according to a centuries-old method that begins with selecting the right tree, felling it and skidding it home, Cumberland claims that their oak pitchforks are highly valued by collectors. Shipping weight: 8 lbs.
    Price: $60.50.

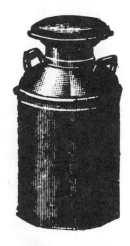

❈ HEAVY-DUTY MILK CANS

These 10-gallon milk cans have been used and have worn finishes, so Cumberland sells them "as is." The store requests that you state your preference for either the recessed- or umbrella-lidded can, but must ship what is available nonetheless. Shipping weight: 28 lbs.
    Price: $35.25 each.

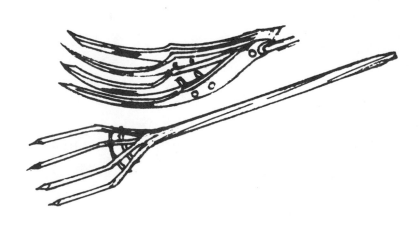

GEORGIA PLOW STOCKS

"Lamon," Abe Lincoln said to his friend Ward Lamon as the President resumed his seat, "that speech won't scour." This phrase, whispered against a background of desultory applause, was used during the President's boyhood to describe a plow that wouldn't shed earth as it sheared through prairie. Lamon was to further learn from the nonscouring speech's (and the Union's) deliverer that he considered the address "a flat failure" and a disappointment to those who had gathered to hear it.

While making no claim to the status of the Gettysburg Address of plow stocks, Cumberland's Georgia stock will use any type of blade that takes a heel bolt—and will likely scour. The stock also comes with varnished beam and replaceable handles and a wrought-iron, pivot-mounted standard.
Price: $96.25.

WOODEN BUCKSAW

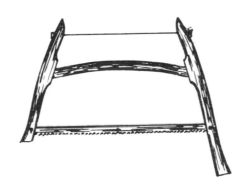

Selected Cumberland County hardwood makes an old-fashioned bucksaw with perfect balance and feel. Its 1-inch-by-30-inch blade is made of Swedish steel, hardened, tempered and precision-filed to a razor sharpness. Mortise-and-tenon joints throughout the frame. Shipping weight: 4 lbs.
Price: $29.95.

FERGUSON PLANTER

"An exceedingly substantial and desirable planter," the Ferguson is an old-style hill-type planter. This means that it drops corn every 24 inches and beans every 21 inches for a "hill" or grouping of the corn and beans planted together. One-row team or horse model. Shipping weight: 120 lbs.
Price: $475, not including transportation or postage costs.

General Merchandise Catalog available, $3.

CUMBERLAND GENERAL STORE
Route 3, Box 81
Crossville, TN 38555
Tel. 800/334-4640 or
615/484-8481

PITCHER PUMP

At one time a pitcher pump was standard in every country kitchen. Located by the sink, it supplied water for cooking and washing. Today, not only have less vigorous means of water delivery rendered the pitcher pump obsolete, but the drop in both water tables and quality have eroded its use. Nevertheless, Lehman Hardware's turn-of-the-century pitcher pump is one of several it offers its Amish customers. Made with appropriately ornate Victorian castings, it can be used only with a cistern or shallow well with less than a 20-foot drop to the reservoir. The pump features a one-piece cast-iron body with a smoothly grounded and tough enamel finish. Its extra-long downspout is fully enclosed.

Also available from Lehman are deep-well pump head, cylinders, drop pipe and rods.

"Non-Electric 'Good Neighbor' Heritage Catalog," $2.

LEHMAN HARDWARE & APPLIANCES
4779 Kidron Road, P.O. Box 41
Kidron, OH 44636
Tel. 216/857-5757 or 216/857-5441
Fax. 216/857-5785

❖ CUT NAILS

In Wareham, Massachusetts, on the site of a mill burned by a British raiding party during the War of 1812, the world's oldest nail factory is still turning them out.

Founded in 1819, the Wareham Nail Company is a survivor of the iron industry that once flourished in and around Wareham. All during the nineteenth century local bog iron (still to be seen in the reddish soil around the town's cranberry bogs and the great heap of slag that forms an embankment beside the Wareham River) provided the basic resource for small, water-powered industries. In addition to nails, Wareham likewise produced pots, pans, wagon treads and ship's fittings back then.

Although not intentionally archaic, the Wareham factory's old wooden buildings—with their huge foundation stones, hand-hewn beams, and array of overhead belts and drives—evoke a feeling for the kind of American industriousness that itself has grown musty. It's the modern value of its old cut nails

that sustains Wareham.

Cut nails are sliced from a flat piece of steel by a machine-driven knife blade; the result is a four-sided nail that tapers toward the head. Such nails were common during colonial times, but because of their superior fastening ability they are still indispensable to use with masonry and (when galvanized) to shipbuilding.

Inevitably, Wareham's cut nails have not been overlooked by folks who restore antiques and old buildings. The company's fasteners have been driven into projects at Old Sturbridge Village, Colonial Williamsburg, the Harper's Ferry National Monument, Old Bethpage Village Restoration, and other historic sites. Several types of cut nails are available for every type of restoration.

Catalog available.

WAREHAM NAIL COMPANY
8 Elm Street, P.O. Box 111
Wareham, MA 02571
Tel. 508/295-0038

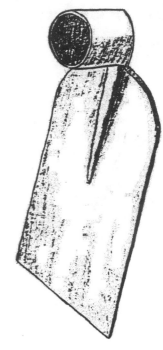

❖ HOES

According to the Forge & Anvil catalog, hoes like the one depicted were being made in Virginia by the 1750s and continued to be factory-manufactured late into the nineteenth century. Other, specific varieties of the tool—designed for weeding, hilling, and turnip, carrot, fluke and onion raising—are also available from the company.

Price: $41.40, including shipping and handling.

Catalog of period tools and hardware available, $1.

FORGE & ANVIL
P.O. Box 51
Newman, IL 61942
Tel. 217/352-0803

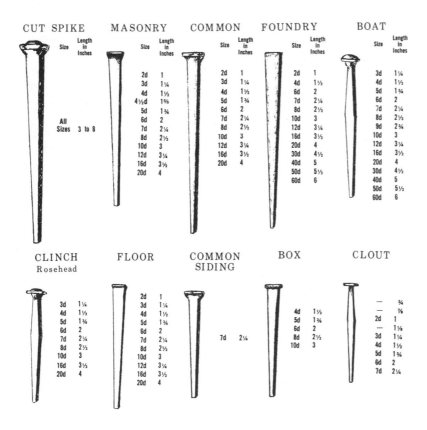

CUT SPIKE		MASONRY		COMMON		FOUNDRY		BOAT	
Size	Length in Inches	Size	Length in Inches	Size	Length in Inches	Size	Length in Inches	Size	Length in Inches
		2d	1	2d	1	2d	1	3d	1¼
		3d	1¼	3d	1¼	4d	1½	4d	1½
		4d	1½	4d	1½	6d	2	5d	1¾
		4½d	1⅝	5d	1¾	7d	2¼	6d	2
		5d	1¾	6d	2	8d	2½	7d	2¼
All Sizes	3 to 8	6d	2	7d	2¼	10d	3	8d	2½
		7d	2¼	8d	2½	12d	3¼	9d	2¾
		8d	2½	10d	3	16d	3½	10d	3
		10d	3	12d	3¼	20d	4	12d	3¼
		12d	3¼	16d	3½	30d	4½	16d	3½
		16d	3½	20d	4	40d	5	20d	4
		20d	4			50d	5½	30d	4½
						60d	6	40d	5
								50d	5½
								60d	6

CLINCH Rosehead		FLOOR		COMMON SIDING		BOX		CLOUT	
		2d	1					—	¾
3d	1¼	3d	1¼					—	⅞
4d	1½	4d	1½			4d	1½	2d	1
5d	1¾	5d	1¾			5d	1¾	—	1⅛
6d	2	6d	2			6d	2	3d	1¼
7d	2¼	7d	2¼	7d	2¼	8d	2½	4d	1½
8d	2½	8d	2½			10d	3	5d	1¾
10d	3	10d	3					6d	2
16d	3½	12d	3¼					7d	2¼
20d	4	16d	3½						
		20d	4						

⊛ BUTTER CHURNS

Butter nowadays is often sent to distant markets, and it becomes a matter of the first importance to pack it properly. The readiness of a sale will depend very much upon it. The utmost care should be taken in the first place to free the butter entire from milk by washing and working it after churning, at a temperature so low as to prevent it from losing its granular texture and becoming greasy. Of course, every good butter maker knows that the quality of the product will depend, in a great measure, on the temperature at which the milk or cream is churned…which should be from 60 to 65 degrees Fahrenheit.
— Farmer's Almanac, *1889*

The Ross Farm Museum represents a Nova Scotian family farm of the period from 1816 to 1917. As the museum includes a farm workshop, cooperage, stave and shingle mill and blacksmith shop, it is able to replicate several period items. Among the woodenware it offers for sale are hand-made butter churns. Draft animal accouterments, barrels, butter prints, spoons, hay rakes and snowshoes are also available.

For information, write or call:

ROSS FARM MUSEUM
New Ross Route 12
Lunenburg County
Nova Scotia, Canada B0J 2M0
Tel. 902/689-2210

❀ McCONNON'S UNIVERSAL HEALING BLACK OINTMENT

This old-time salve has been of benefit in the treatment of livestock-galls, harness sores, sore teats, contracted hoofs, and as an anti-pick treatment for poultry. "Safe for Man, Beast & Poultry Use," reads the cautionary copy. "Do not use on cats!"

Price: $4.64, plus shipping and handling.

General Merchandise Catalog available, $3.

CUMBERLAND GENERAL STORE
Route 3, Box 81
Crossville, TN 38555
Tel. 800/334-4640 or
*   615/484-8481*

❁ SHAKER SEED BOX

"Your gardening seeds is fine, and if I should sow 'em on the Rock of Gibraltar probably I should raise a good mess of gardening sass." Thus Artemus Ward, during an 1866 visit to the New Lebanon, New York, Shaker community, placed his benediction on nearly four-score years of Shaker seed production and marketing.

It was in the communities of New Lebanon and Watervliet, New York, that the Shakers began the first commercial seed nursery in the United States during 1789. By 1795, the New Lebanon community was actively growing seeds for sale to the "world's people," a business that increased steadily into the next century. By innovatively marketing the seeds in small paper packets and distributing them by wagon to general stores throughout the country, in time the Shakers would have this "lucrative and agreeable employment" accounting for a large portion of their revenues.

Shaker seed boxes were made to serve several functions—as a container for seed packets, as an accounting system for sales, and as a counter display. At first somberly colored, by the late 1800s the seed boxes bowed to the demands of the worldly marketplace and sported bright plumage.

Shaker seed boxes, appropriately decorated with color labels, are available from Marty Travis of Fairbury, Illinois.

Brochure available, $2.

MARTY TRAVIS
Rural Route 1, P.O. Box 96
Fairbury, IL 61739
Tel. 309/377-2271

MILLS FROM
THE PHOENIX FOUNDRY

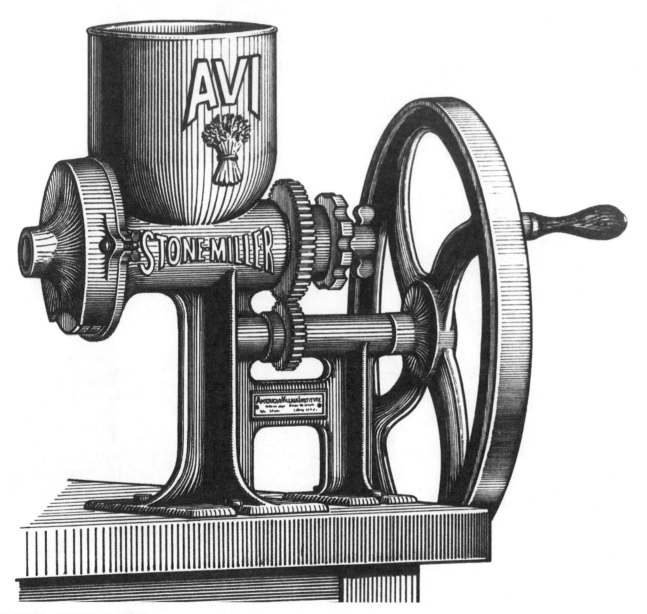

❧ STONE-MILLER FLOUR MILL

The Stone-Miller is a ruggedly built flour mill designed to reduce the effort needed to grind wheat into fine flour. Although primarily designed for hand operation, this mill is also very efficient when driven by a mechanical power source, such as an electric motor.

The mill is of heavy cast-iron con-struction. Machine-cut steel gears for smooth, noise-free operation provide a 2 to 1 reduction for easy grinding. Stones are 5 inches in diameter, fed by a cast auger. The auger shaft is sup-ported by a ¾-inch tapered roller bear-ing for a long, trouble-free life. Adjustment from course to fine is made with a positive lock control. Each "click-stop" changes the distance between stones by 0.005 inch.

The hopper holds eight cups of grain. The output of fine flour from whole grain in a single pass is about 12 cups (four pounds) per hour, and about 36 cups (12 pounds) using an electric motor with a one-inch pulley.

Height above the table is 15 inches. Total weight is about 55 lbs.

Prices: $231 for the no-frills model, $348 with a stone cover and V-belt grooved flywheel.

✽ AMERICAN HARVESTER CIDER MILL

The American Harvester double-tub cider mill combines the best features found in many different presses manufactured around the turn of the century. The Harvester is a hand-operated mill, capable of producing the most cider from the fewest apples with a minimum of effort. The double-tub feature makes it possible to grind and press at the same time. This is a practical advantage when processing large quantities of apples.

The quantity of apples that this mill will process depends on the type used, as well as the speed and endurance of the operators. On average, two people working at a steady pace can produce as much as 80 gallons a day.

The frame is of laminated construction for overall strength and to prevent twisting with age. All joints are dadoed and cross-bolted for strength and structural rigidity. The 12-inch-high by 13½-inch-diameter tubs have beveled hardwood staves for easy cleaning.

The 1½-inch-diameter press screw is Acme thread and passes through the cast-iron cross arm. A cast-iron foot distributes the pressure on a wooden press plate that fits inside the tub. The grinder housing is all cast iron, with a laminated-wood grinding cylinder provided with stainless-steel teeth. The 1 to 3 gear ratio is complemented by a heavy cast-iron flywheel, which can store a significant amount of energy, making grinding smooth and fast.

Dimensions: (overall size) about 22 inches wide, 35 inches long and 45 inches high. Shipping weight: about 200 lbs.

Prices: $395 to $664 depending on hardware, wood options and design (three-leg as illustrated, or four-leg). For hardware kits (no wooden parts), $230 to $309, depending on options chosen. Single-tub presses also available, $310 to $418. Hardware kits, $198 to $216.

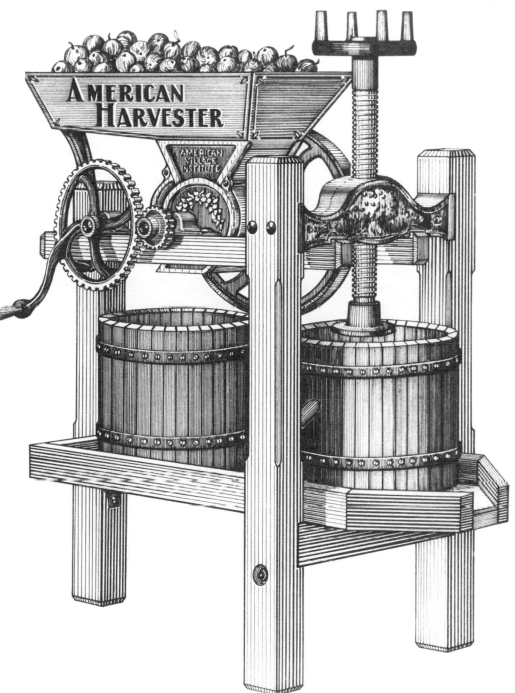

Price list available.

THE PHOENIX FOUNDRY
P.O. Box 68 H
Marcus, WA 99151
Tel. 509/684-5434

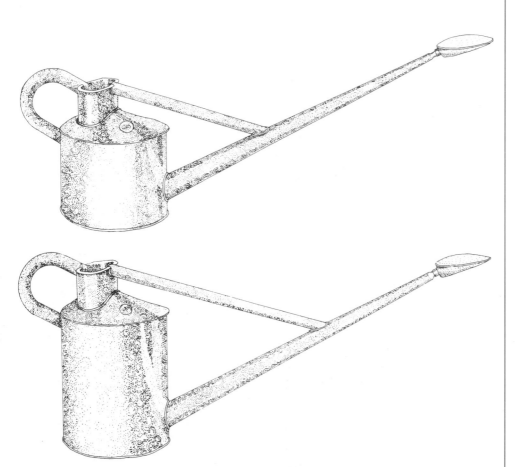

❋ HAWS WATERING CANS

"The New Invention," as described by John Haws's 1885 patent, "forms a Watering Pot that is much easier to carry and tip, and at the same time being much cleaner and more adapted for use than any other put before the Public."

Haws' patent coincided with the tremendous rise in English professional gardening; in fact, throughout the reign of Queen Victoria, large glass-house nurseries were being established in and around London in record numbers. This, combined with the perfect balance and improved watering rose offered by the Haws can, ensured its success.

SMITH & HAWKEN TOOL COMPANY
25 Corte Madera
Mill Valley, CA 94941
Tel. 415/383-2000

❦ GARDENING SPADE

The Forge & Anvil zealously consults library and museum sources as well as its own extensive collection of period tools, drawings and books to produce its replica axes, garden, woodworking and agricultural tools. This, their tilling spade, follows the design of one that was introduced during the eighteenth century and remained in use (albeit with declining popularity) into the twentieth. Made by welding together two sheets of iron while leaving a pocket open between them to receive a handle, it is approximately 22 inches in length from the tip of its straps to the end of its blade. The spade is not available with a handle, although these are periodically obtainable from the company.

Prices: $98.90, complete with shipping and handling.

Catalog available, $1.

FORGE & ANVIL
P.O. Box 51
Newman, IL 61942
Tel. 217/352-0803

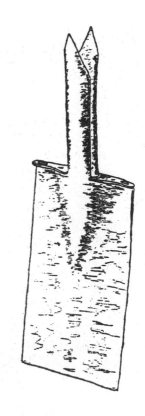

$4.95

GUARANTEED TWO YEARS.

THE QUEEN OF OUR AMERICAN BEAUTIES, THE GREATEST SELLING BUGGY OF OUR AMERICAN BEAUTY LINE, IS CARRIED IN WAREHOUSES AT DIFFERENT POINTS FOR IMMEDIATE SHIPMENT, AS FULLY EXPLAINED ON PAGE 98 AND 99. DON'T FAIL TO READ ABOUT OUR WONDERFUL AMERICAN QUEEN, ILLUSTRATED AND DESCRIBED ON PAGE 99, THE MOST POPULAR BUGGY OF OUR AMERICAN BEAUTY LINE, THE GREATEST SELLER OF THEM ALL.

This line of American Beauties represents great value, and the leader of them all, the largest seller, the greatest buggy ever built outside of our highest grade Solid Comfort Buggies, is fully illustrated and described on page

$46.75

VEHICLES
❦ ❦
& HARNESS

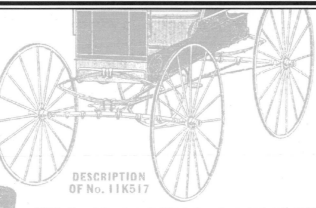

DESCRIPTION OF No. 11K610

—29½ inches; panel spring back and box cushion; seat ends padded and lined; up- in heavy dark green body cloth or extra moroccoline leather. BODY—Piano box style; wide by 55 inches long; hardwood frame; rear of body; carpet; toe carpet on front leather dash, fitted with nickel dash rail. Three-bow genuine leather quarter top; padded back stays; rubber roof and lined back curtain; wool faced head lining; patent fasteners; heavy side curtains; roll-up straps; propnuts; storm apron. GEAR—15-16- axles; long distance dust and mudproof hickory axle caps; double reach, ironed and bearing fifth wheel, three and four-plate tempered springs; new style center bearloops. WHEELS—Sarven's patent style; screwed rims, full ¼-inch oval edge steel inches front and 42 inches rear. SHAFTS y shafts, trimmed with leather 22 inches tip, flat straps; double braced; quick naft couplers. PAINTING—Body, rosewood, ancy design on seat risers; gear, wheels and h blood carmine, striped. TRACK—4 feet r 5 feet 2 inches. State width desired. 11K610 Price, complete with double afts and steel tires.........$44.05 Shipped from Evansville, Indiana.

DESCRIPTION OF No. 11K612

—Deep side panel phaeton seat; 29½ inche ing overstuffed panel back and spring cushio s padded and lined; handsome seat handle red with dark green body cloth or extra gra line leather. BODY—23 inches wide by 55 inch long, piano box style; 8-inch panels; hardwood fram drill fiber boot on rear of body; carpet; leather das TOP—Three-bow leather quarters and leather back stay wool faced head lining; back stays padded and line lined back curtain; heavy side curtains; stitched valanc two roll-up straps; patent curtain fasteners; storm apro GEAR—Arched axles, 15-16-inch; hickory axle caps; lo distance dust and mudproof bell collar spindles; doub reach, ironed; oil tempered, easy riding, three and fou plate springs; new style center bearing body loop WHEELS—¾-inch screwed rims, fitted with ¼-inch ov edge steel tires; full bolted; Sarven's patent style; 38 inch front and 42 inches rear. SHAFTS—Double braced hic ory shafts; trimmed with leather 22 inches back from t point, flat straps; quick shifting shaft couplers. PAIN ING—Body, plain black; gear, wheels and shafts, da Brewster green, striped. TRACK—4 feet 8 inches or feet 2 inches. State width desired. No. 11K612 Price, complete with double brac shafts and steel tires.........$46.75 Shipped from Evansville, Indiana.

DESCRIPTION OF No. 11K517

SEAT New style auto seat; 29½ inches; fancy back and cushion, fitted with plenty of springs; upholstered with heavy dark green body cloth or extra grade moroccoline leather. BODY—Piano box style; 23x55 inches; hardwood frame; boot on rear of body; carpet; toe carpet on front panel; leather dash, fitted with nickel dash rail. TOP—Genuine leather quarters and back stays; rubber roof and back curtain; back stays padded and lined; wool faced head lining; lined back curtain; two roll-up straps; heavy side curtains; patent curtain fasteners; storm apron; nickel top propnuts; three bows. GEAR—15-16-inch steel axles; long distance, dust and mudproof bell collar; hickory axle caps; special fifth wheel; elliptic end springs; center bearing body loops; double reaches, ironed full length. WHEELS—Sarven's patent; ¾-inch screwed rim; full ¼-inch oval edge steel tires; 38 inches front and 42 inches rear. SHAFTS—Hickory shafts; double braced; trimmed with leather 22 inches back from the tip, flat straps; quick shifting shaft couplers. PAINTING—Body, black, striped and decorated; fancy seat risers; gear, wheels and shafts, blood carmine, striped with black. TRACK —4 feet 8 inches narrow or 5 feet 2 inches wide. State width desired. No. 11K517 Price, complete with double braced shafts and steel tires,.........$47.85 Shipped from Evansville, Indiana.

$5.75

$43.95

DESCRIPTION OF No. 11K514

29½ inches; solid panel l spring back and box frame hion; padded and lined seat ends; upholstered in heavy dark y cloth or extra grade moroccoline leather. BODY—23x55 ano box style; hardwood frame; 8-inch panels; boot on rear of et; leather dash. TOP—Leather quarter top and back stays; padded and lined, fancy stitched; heavy waterproof side cur- lined back curtain, wool faced head lining; raised, stitched wo roll-up straps; patent curtain fasteners; three bows; water- m apron. GEAR—15-16-inch arched axles; dust and mudproof s; long distance spindles; hickory axle caps; double reach, ree and four-plate oil tempered elliptic springs; new style center dy loops. WHEELS—Sarven's patent; ¾-inch screwed rims, ¼-inch oval edge steel tires; 38 inches front and 42 inches rear. FTS—Double braced hickory shafts; trimmed with leather 22 the tip, flat straps; quick shifting shaft couplers. PAINTING

113

DESCRIPTION OF No. 11K619

SEAT—Georgia drop back; spring cushion, 25½ inches; padded and lined seat ends; double bar nickel arm ralls; upholstered in heavy dar green body cloth or extra grade moroccoline leather. BODY—20 inche wide by 55 inches long; hardwood frame; piano box style; boot on rear body; carpet; toe carpet on front panel; patent leather dash. TOP—Tw and one-half-bow; leather quarters and back stays; back curtain lined; heav side curtains; wool faced head lining; patent curtain fasteners; two roll-u straps; storm apron. GEARS—15-16-inch axles; long distance dust an mudproof bell collar; hickory axle caps; long easy riding side springs; doub reaches. WHEELS—38 inches front and 42 inches rear; Sarven's paten style; ¾-inch screwed rims; ¼-inch oval edge steel tires, full bolte SHAFTS—Hickory shafts, trimmed with leather 22 inches back fro

▓ STAGECOACHES

Although, as abolitionist William Lloyd Garrison observed, they required a "prodigious sacrifice of bodily ease," stagecoaches were the most popular form of long-distance transport in nineteenth-century America. Starting out as large freight wagons with boxes built atop to accommodate passengers, stage coaches branched out after 1790 into a dense network of routes extending through Massachusetts, Connecticut, Rhode Island, eastern Pennsylvania and southern New York. By the mid-1820s, you could board one of these Greyhounds of the Grange and travel, with connections, anywhere from Boston southward to New Orleans, or west to St. Louis.

It was in St. Louis where frontier travel by stagecoach got under way when the Overland Mail Company was established by John Butterfield in 1859. Mr. Butterfield's coaches hauled passengers and mail to San Francisco, calling at 160 stations along the 2,800-mile route (it sagged south to El Paso at the behest of southern politicians, but was straightened out again by the Civil War), and making the trip in about 24 days.

Butterfield used Concord coaches—leaf-sprung, enclosed, nine-passenger wagons (a tenth paid full fare to ride shotgun with the driver) weighing 2,500 pounds and costing around $1,250. In 1866, Butterfield sold his company to Harry Wells who had formed Wells, Fargo & Company in 1852.

Today, Concord coaches, (the name is taken from the New Hampshire city where the coaches were first built in 1827), are still produced by a handful of buggy-makers, most of whom, according to wagon-builder Joseph Edwards, are a "whole lot of people who don't know any more than the man in the moon" what the job takes. Edwards, whose line also includes "1884" doctor's surreys and box surreys, spring wagons, road wagons, hunting wagons and an elegant turn-of-the-century Victoria carriage, is devoted to making his conveyances as faithful to the originals as possible. Recognizing that the wood on most of the old carriages now in museums is as solid today as it was when they were built, Edwards realized that his materials would have to be of equal quality if his vehicles were to be honest replicas. In pursuit of this ideal, the wheels and shafts of his vehicles are made of hickory, while cottonwood and marine plywood form the bodies. Axles are made of sturdy red oak, and fenders of white oak for that wood's flexibility. In addition, special jigs and tools are used to carve many of the intricate wooden pieces and metal parts that Edwards' vehicles require. "I don't build anything in comparison with anyone else," says the Georgia wagon-maker. "Pricewise I don't compare, and my quality is way above."

Pricewise: Concord Coach, $50,000.

Brochure of "Handcrafted Horse Vehicles with Authentic Fabrication and Style of the Nineteenth Century" available.

EDWARDS HORSE-DRAWN BUGGY WORKS AND HARNESSES
U.S. Highway 19 South
Putney, GA 31782
Tel. 912/787-5307

VEHICLES FROM THE CUMBERLAND CARRIAGE WORKS

The Cumberland General Store's Carriage Works will custom-build these horse-drawn vehicles to your order. The carriages they sell are newly manufactured from original plans and specifications, using the original machinery, and in a few cases, second- and third-generation buggy and wagon craftsmen. "They are absolutely the finest conveyances built," claims Cumberland's catalog, "being continuously manufactured since 1884." The following appears as it does in the Cumberland catalog:

General Merchandise Catalog available, $3.

CUMBERLAND GENERAL STORE
Route 3, Box 81
Crossville, TN 38555
Tel. 800/334-4640 or
615/484-8481

Shown
With Drop Axle

CUMBERLAND'S GENERAL PURPOSE BUGGY

MODEL H-1 & H-5

This buggy speaks for itself and in points of finish, style, quality, etc., has no equal. Built to meet your approval, Cumberland's General Purpose Buggy is most reliable. This is a splendid carriage in every respect and is very desirable. Custom built to to your order, this is one of the best horse-drawn vehicles every made available. You may choose from two styles; Model H-5 without top or Model H-1 with top. No matter what your selection, you will not be dissapointed!

GEAR: 1" arch standard track axles; 12" double reach fifth wheel; elliptical springs front and rear; wrought Bailey loops or hickory spring bars.
WHEELS: Sarven patent best hickory with screwed rims; ¼" flat steel tires, 1" tread, height 36-40"
BODY: 24x56" poplar panels and floor; hardwood sills.
SEAT: Solid panel seat upholstered in red artifical leather.
SHAFTS: Hickory high bend substantially braced at cross bar and heel
PAINTING: Gear, wheels and shafts red with neat striping; body and seat black.
EQUIPMENT: Leather dash securely braced; whip socket; full length carpet.
CRATED WEIGHT: 535 pounds.

MODEL H-1 WITH TOP
With steel tires
7040 . . . . $4912.50
With rubber tires
7041 . . . . $5000.00

SIDE CURTAINS: Optional. They unsnap and roll-up for removal in nice weather.
3780 . . . . $160.00

MODEL H-5 WITHOUT TOP
7042 Complete with steel tires $4287.50
7043 Complete with rubber tires $4375.00

Price Picked Up At Our Dock.

Spring Wagon →

Model H–15

Two Models To Choose From:

Model H–15
A stylish, easy running, comfortable wagon. It's made of the best grade materials and is very carefully finished. Makes a wagon we are as proud to sell as you are to own.
Shipping Weight: 615 pounds crated.
#7068 Complete with steel tires
#7069 Complete with rubber tires

Model H–16
This wagon is exactly the as Model H–15 except it comes without the rear seat.
Shipping Weight: 615 pounds crated.
#7070 W/ Steel tires $3600.00
#7071 W/ Rubber tires . . . $3687.50

Specifications

Gear: 1-1/8" steel axles, 12" fifth wheel with double reaches, front spring 1-1/2" leaves, rear springs half-platform style.
Wheels: Sarven patent best grade hickory with screwed rims; 1-1/4" steel tires, height 36–40".
Body: 34"x 90" with drop end gate.

Seats: Solid panel style; well ironed throughout, trimmed in red artificial leather. Rear seat is removeable.
Shafts: Heavy easy bend surrey shafts well ironed with cross and heel braces.
Painting: Gear is painted red with neat striping. Body and seats are black with fine line striping on the body and risers.

Cumberland's Buckboard

A Handsome Rig!

Now available in natural finished body and painted gear

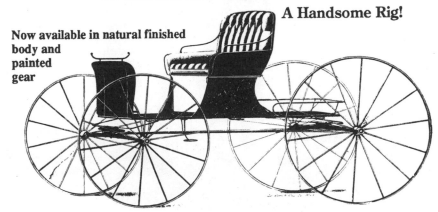

Specifications

Gear: 1" steel axles; 56" track.
Wheels: Sarven patent or bolted hub roller bearing best hickory; 1"tread with 1/4" flat steel tires; height 36–40".
Body: 25 x 66" slatted floor with neat rail back of seat to prevent packages from dropping out. Especially nice for carrying picnic baskets.
Seat: 32" cushion, lazy back type.
Shafts: Bent hickory with singletree.
Painting: Gear, wheels and shafts black with neat pin striping; body & seat black
Equipment: Bent wood dash and whip socket
Shipped Weight: appx 450 lbs crated
#8244 Complete with steel tires
#8245 Complete with rubber tires
#8246 Natural finish body & painted gear

Utility Wagon does not have scroll design as shown.

Surrey With The Fringe On Top for horses & ponies

There are several models of this romantic carriage to choose from. Let us know what your needs are and we'll help you pick the one best suited.

Model
H–10 &
P–10

Two Seater

Horse Model:

Gear: 1" arch long distance axles; 12" double reach fifth wheel; elliptical springs front and rear; hickory spring bars.

Wheels: Sarven patent best hickory with screwed rims; 1/4" flat steel tires 1" tread; height 36–40"

Body: 28 x 70" body of high grade poplar; well reinforced.

Seats: Two solid panel spring backs and cushions trimmed with red artificial leather. Lined seat ends.

Top: Canopy top lined, thrimmed with red fringe.

Shafts: Circle bar shafts of select hickory, triple braced and well ironed.

Painting: Gear, wheels and shafts red with neat striping; body and seats black.

Equipment: Leather dash securely braced; whip socket.

Model H–10

Shipped Weight: 715 pounds crated.
#7052 Complete with steel tires
#7053 Complete with rubber tires

Pony Model:

Same as horse model, but made on a smaller scale. For use with ponies.

Body: Measures 22 x 60"

Wheels: 1" tread; diameter to suit size of pony.

Shipped Weight: 550 pounds crated.

Model P–10
#7056 Complete with steel tires
#7057 Complete with rubber tires

Please Note:
The specifications for these buggies are basically the same.

Two Seater Without The Top

Same Models without the top.

Horse Model: Model H–11

Shipped Weight: 615 pounds crated.
#7054 Complete with steel tires
#7055 Complete with rubber tires

Pony Model: Model P–11

Shipped Weight: 450 pounds crated.
#7058 Complete with steel tires
#7059 Complete with rubber tires

Three Seater

Horse Model Only:

Similar design to one above with three seats and longer body. (34 x 102" and steps to accommodate all seats from both sides.) Axles and wheel tread 1-1/4"

Model H–12

Shipped Weight: 950 pounds crated
#7060 Complete with steel tires
#7061 Complete with rubber tires

Model H–12

Three Seater Without The Top

Same as above model without the top.
Shipped Weight: 840 pounds crated

#7062 Complete with steel tires
#7063 Complete with rubber tires

Price Information is available upon request: because each buggy or wagon is made one at a time, when ordered, we are unable to quote prices until we know exactly what you want—please call or write.

CUMBERLAND'S
UTILITY WAGON

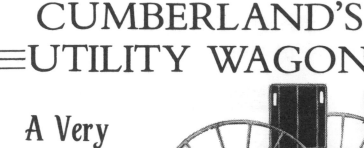

A Very Attractive & Fine Appearing Wagon

A fine general purpose wagon. Cumberland's Utility Wagon very convenient for carrying parcels and gear. Hinged lids close to protect enclosed items.

GEAR: 1'' arch long distance axles; 60'' wide track. Double elliptical rear spring. Hickory spring bar.
WHEELS: Sarven Patent best hickory with screwed rims; ¾'' flat steel tires, 1'' tread, height 38'' and 42''.
BODY: 28''x60''. Poplar panels and floor; hardwood sills.
SEAT: Lazy back type upholstered in red artificial leather.
SHAFTS: Bent hickory shafts with singletree.

PAINTING: Gear, shafts and wheels painted red, neatly striped. Body and seat are black. Utility wagon does not have scroll design as shown.
EQUIPMENT: Leather dash securely braced; whip socket. Full length carpet.
CRATED WEIGHT: About 600 lbs.
3744 Complete with steel tires
3776 Complete with rubber tires

A GOOD CHOICE FOR THE BEGINNING HORSE AND DRIVER!

CUMBERLAND'S
High Grade
ROAD CART

This cart is as well known among users of road carts as any staple article in a merchandise store.
SEAT: It has wide seat for two passengers; slat bottom with full seat rail; hung on hickory supports; oil tempered steel spring hung in adjustable loops on heel of shafts.
WHEELS: Sarven patent, 44 inches high, 1 inch best steel tire.
GEAR: Axle is 1 inch, the best refined steel. Width of track, 4 feet, 8 inches.

BODY: Seat, posts, foot rack, shafts, cross bar and single tree are made of the best carefully selected material.
PAINTED: Red.
CRATED WEIGHT: About 150 lbs.
3778 Complete with steel tires
3779 Complete with rubber tires

Specifications

Gear: 1" long distance axles; 12" fifth wheel; double reaches; wood spring bar; elliptical springs.
Wheels: 1" sarven patent best hickory with screwed rims; 1/4" flat steel tires with 1" tread.
Please specify height: 36&40" or 38&42".
Body: 28 x 70" with roomy high panel seat.
Seat: Regular panel upholstered in deep red or black leatherette. (**Please specify color**).
Shafts: Heavy easy bend surrey shafts, well ironed with cross and heel braces.
Top: Heavy rubber roof; black curtains and head lining.
Painting: Gear, wheels and shafts red with neat striping; body and seat black.
Equipment: Patent leather dash and rear fenders securely braced; whip socket.
Shipped Weight: Appx 600 lbs crated
#3742 Complete with steel tires
#3743 Complete with rubber tires

Extension Top Carriage
A truly splendid carriage in every respect!

Rear seat & top are removable!

The Town & Counrty Delivery Wagon is of the highest quality—built by experts, and will bring you many, many years of pleasure and dependable use! One of the most versatile wagons that we offer!

Town & Country Delivery Wagon
Handsome & Serviceable, too!

Specifications

Gear: 1-1/8" long distance axles, heavy fifth wheel with double reaches, ironed full length and well braced. Heavy leaf front spring and two springs in rear.
Wheels: Sarven patent best grade hickory with screwed rims; 1-1/4" tread; 1/4" steel tires. Height: 36 & 40".
Seat: Wagon style as illustrated with cushion trimmed in red artificial leather.

Bed: 84" long by 34" wide with extension toe board, fitted winged flare boards as shown and drop end gate.
Shafts: Heavy easy bend surrey shafts well ironed with cross and heel braces.
Painting: Gear painted red with neat striping. Body and seat are black with fine striping on body and risers.
#7050 Complete with steel tires
#7051 Complete with hard rubber tires

CARRIAGE WORKS' HORSE-DRAWN VEHICLES

▨ AUTO CUT UNDER SURREY

This surrey is a replica of one introduced after the turn of the century just as the automobile was becoming popular. Built to negotiate tight corners, the surrey represents the type of fancy carriage then used for travel to church or town.

The Carriage Works' Auto Cut Under Surrey has hydraulic brakes and roller-bearing-equipped wheels.

Prices: $9,000. Harness $1,200.

▨ ALBANY CUTTER

Guide my wild Parnassian pony, Till our aerial cutter runs athwart 'a Wilderness of suns!'
—*Thomas G. Fessenden,* Terrible Tractoration!, *1804*

Unlike Fessenden's Dedalus flyer, this cutter origi-inated in Albany, New York's earthly precincts where sleighing has been a favored pastime ever since the time of Dutch rule. Of a gay, 1752 Albany sleighing party, one Anne Grant wrote:

In the winter, the river, frozen to a great depth, formed the principal road through the country, and was the scene of all those amusements of the skating and sledge races, common to the north of Europe. They used in great parties to visit their friends at a distance and having an excellent and hardy breed of horses, flew from place to place over the snow or ice in these sledges with incredible rapidity.... The night never impeded these travellers, for the atmosphere was so pure and serene, and the snow so reflected the moon and star-light, that the nights exceeded the days in beauty.

The Carriage Works' Albany Cutter is a replication of a distinct type of Albany sleigh developed in 1813.

Prices: $3,600. Harness, $1,200.

THE CARRIAGE WORKS
707 South 5th
Klamath Falls, OR 97601
Tel. 503/882-0700
Fax. 503/882-9661

⚙ WAGON WHEELS

Established in 1868, the George E. Daniels Wagon Factory has been manu-facturing wagon wheels using the same equipment at the same location ever since.

Price list available on request.

GEORGE E. DANIELS WAGON FACTORY
Daniels Road
Rowley, MA 01969
Tel. 508/948-3815

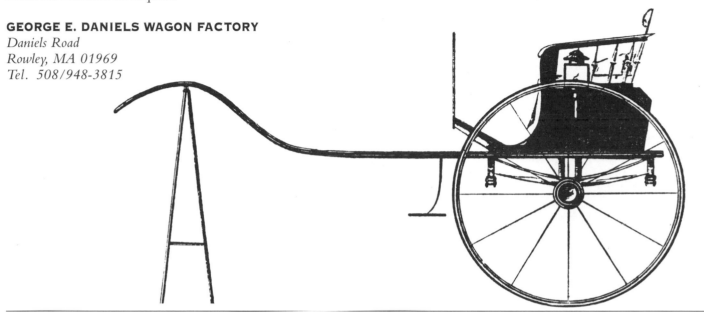

❧ HARNESS

The increasing use of draft animals may again make the harness a common article of farm and riding equip-ment. Big Sky Leatherworks' team harness, horse collars and hames are made in the old way.

Catalog available, $3.

BIG SKY LEATHERWORKS
5243 Highway 312 East
Billings, MT 59105
Tel. 406/373-5937

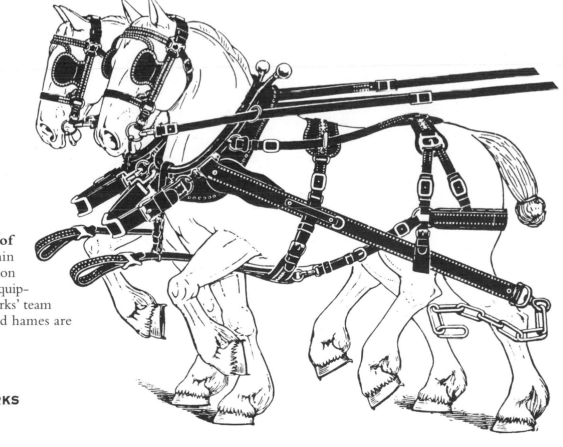

✤ENGRAVED BRASS SLEIGH BELLS

Crazy Crow derived the designs for their engraved brass sleigh bells from those found on antique-store bells. Available in three sizes, with tang backs for easy installation.

Catalog available, $3.

CRAZY CROW TRADING POST
P.O. Box 314-AMS
Denison, TX 75020
Tel. 903/463-1366

✲BUGGY UMBRELLAS

Gohn Brothers is a retail supplier to Amish and Mennonite communities throughout the U.S. and Canada. Their large (50-inch diameter) black buggy umbrellas come with either a wooden or metal shaft.

Prices: No. 8 (metal shaft) costs $15.98, and No. 16 (wood shaft) costs $14.49 (plus $2.90 each for postage and handling).

Catalog of Amish and plain clothing available.

GOHN BROTHERS
Box 111
Middlebury, IN 46540
Tel. 219/825-2400

▣HIGH-WHEELER BICYCLES

Around the turn of the century, the most fashionable sports were mobile ones. In the 1870s, high-wheeler bicycles (or "penny-farthings," as they were often called) rode along en route to besting roller skates in popularity. In the 1880s, bicycles would become *haute volée* as sports equipment until the 1910s, when Americans could ditch them for automobiles.

Ungainly unless under way, the high-wheeler bicycle would take a good deal of skill to maneuver, and its lofty configuration made it especially problematic for modest women in skirts. John Kemp Stanley's 1884 "safety" bicycle, which joined two equal-sized wheels with a steel frame, would begin to put this right; and by 1887, the Victor, a safety bicycle with a dropped frame and no crossbar, completed the bicycle's evolution towards feminine suitability. Three years later, 150,000 men and women would be cycling gaily throughout America; and by 1895, the city of Chicago alone could boast of 500 cycling clubs—each with its own colors and uniform.

Rideable Bicycle Replicas has been building new, old-fashioned, full-sized replicas of nineteenth-century bicycles in Oakland and Alameda, California, for nearly 20 years. Several models are offered, including a 38- and 48-inch Penny Farthing; a copy of the 1878 Columbia; an 1882 Rudge Sociable; and an 1891 New Mail.

"To keep the old-fashioned look," Rideable Replicas' bicycles are handmade, and designed to provide maximum strength and reliability. Each bicycle has been fully tested and is guaranteed. Company owner Mel Baron welcomes custom orders, such as those he recently completed for Euro Disneyland.

Brochure and price list available.

RIDEABLE ANTIQUE BICYCLE REPLICAS
2329 Eagle Avenue
Alameda, CA 94501
Tel. 510/769-0980
Fax. 510/521-7145

your freight charges, and the saving you make, therefore, on these items will be absolutely clear; besides you will get a test of the values we
omething that you owe to yourself to make if you have not as yet tried our grocery department. We want to save you one-third on your gr
e can, and remember, we guarantee to furnish the best grades on the market. If you are disappointed in the least, all you have to do is to re
s at our expense and we will refund your money. REMEMBER, WE ARE QUOTING LOWEST CHICAGO WHOLESALE PRIC
ES. THAT IS WHY OUR PRICES ARE SO LOW.

100 pounds it will not add a single

SEE OUR GREAT FREE GROCERY PRICE LIST OFFER ON PAGE 534

79c

2 pkgs. 20c   No. 7K43112

3 1-lb. pkgs. 24c   No. 7K66623

Per box of 25 99c

5 gal. can $1.89

6 No. 1 cans 59c   No. 7K52616

6 cans

2456 59c

3 lb. pkgs. 24c   No 7K66633

6 tins 2

3 cans 63c

1½-l can

K53656 7c

3 cans 63c   No. 7K532

3 ¼-lb. pkgs.

ISLAND Pineapple   No. 7K49293

No. 7K7258

No. 7K5390

No. 7K51036

Princess GRATED PINEAPPLE   No. 7K49313

No. 7K66653

½-lb. tin 25c

Per box of 50 $1.98

4¾-lb. box 50c   No. 7K6985

1-lb. tablet 12c   No. 7K5432

6c 1-lb. tin 25c   No. 7K4054

1-lb. box 36c   No. 7K3800

No. 7K4049

No. 7K8085

6 No. 2 cans $1.11

100 bars 60

5983

No. 7K52296

SPANI PEANUT ST   No. 7K7344

Per box of 50 $1.20

Pail, 30 Fish 7

No. 7K54007

123

❧ GRANULAR- CURD AMERICAN CHEESE

Although he never seemed to say it when posing for a photograph, the word "cheese" was an important one in Calvin Coolidge's vocabulary. In 1890, the Plymouth Cheese Company of Plymouth, Vermont, was founded by the future president's father, and for decades now it's been run by Calvin's son John, whose enthusiasm for the business seems unaffected by semi-retirement.

Yankee flintiness is a misunderstood thing. The dour facade is used as an effective foil against charlatans, the mask of people whose natural friendliness may need restraint. It's a bluff, a dog barking while his tail wags with abandon. John Coolidge is as arid as any old Vermonter, but the revelation that I was calling from Springfield, Massachusetts (his boyhood was partly spent in nearby Northampton), released so ready a *bonhomie* as to make me wonder if his father's fabled frostiness might not be relegated to that part of the Smithsonian reserved for such bogus presidential lore as Washington's wooden teeth.

In his youth John apparently loved the sights and smells of his grandfather's little industry, but six years after he was graduated from Amherst it began to fail. "I couldn't stand to see it go to wrack and ruin," he confided; "it was a boyhood thing with me."

The Kraft slices that the term "American cheese" brings to mind have little to do with Plymouth Cheese's product. The term originally arose after the Revolutionary War when Americans, missing the English Cheddar they were accustomed to, developed a domestic version with a good republican name. Plymouth's American follows an authentic early Vermont process of agitating Cheddar and plat curd in the vat, and has won the praise of even the most xenophilic devotees of imported varieties. "We make old-fashioned rat-trap store cheese," says Mr. Coolidge in response to praise, "and we're the only purists in the business, I think."

Visitors welcome.

PLYMOUTH CHEESE COMPANY
P.O. Box 1
Plymouth, VT 05056
Tel. 802/672-3650

JOSIAH BENT'S CELEBRATED WATER CRACKERS

In the rural town of Milton, Massachusetts, by the Blue Hills and the Neponset River, along which ran the trails of the few remaining Indians of the Ponkapog tribe, lived a man whose name has become a household word, not only in the United States, but the entire world. This man was Josiah Bent. He made the first Water Cracker bearing that name. At first they were made in small quantities, and he traveled from town to town selling the crackers from saddlebags across the horse's back, employing his own children to make them; he made good and provided for his family.

This was the infancy of the world-famous Water Cracker of the present day ...

Sounding for a moment like Longfellow when he was in school, the above "History of the Bent's Water Cracker" is the work of George H. Bent, one of Josiah's

Bent's
BAKERY SPECIALTIES
SINCE 1801

descendants. Written in 1914, it evokes the wish that the "powder keg that was Europe" might not have erupted so that the world could lavish its attention on the Bent's Water Cracker a while longer. But the Great War proved uncommonly cruel, and would spare the Water Cracker's fame no more than it would an Alsatian farmhouse.

Some people might therefore be surprised to learn that the Josiah Bent Water Cracker never left us.

Hearty enough to have found its way onto tea traders and whaling ships, and genteel enough to have been an integral part of the nineteenth-century Boston Brahmin's dinner (served with cheese), the honest good flavor of the Bent's Water Cracker comes from its 191 years of using only pure spring water and stone-ground wheat flour. No salt ever goes into one.

So if the celebration of Triscuits is as unfathomable to you as it is to me, and if you think you'd like a cracker you can sink your teeth into ("provided you have good teeth," says the company), then try Josiah Bent's Water Crackers.

Here's a recipe for cracker pudding provided by the Bent company:

G.H. Bent's 100-Year-Old Recipe for Common Cracker Pudding

1 pint (2 cups)cracker crumbs
3 pints milk
1 cup sugar
1 tsp. salt
¼ tsp. cinnamon
1 Tbsp. butter
1 cup raisins

Soak cracker crumbs in milk, and mix in sugar, salt and cinnamon. Butter a deep-dish earthenware container, pour in crumbs and other already-mixed ingredients, and bake. While mixture is baking, puff up the raisins over steam, and after half an hour of baking, stir the raisins into the mixture, adding additional milk around the edges (not in the middle). Bake for another 2½ hours (maybe less).

Prices (postage included): 6 packages, $17.75; 8 packages, $22.75; 10 packages, $27.25; 12 packages, $32.00.

G.H. BENT COMPANY
7 Pleasant Street
Milton, MA 02186
Tel. 617/698 5945

NEW ENGLAND COB-SMOKED TURKEY AND HAM

Harrington's of Vermont is a century-old business famous for their hams and turkeys that are slowly smoked over maple wood and corncobs ("we don't use hickory, never have") in the nineteenth-century Vermont fashion.

Seasonal catalog of mail-order foods available.

HARRINGTON'S
618 Main Street
Richmond, VT 05477
Tel. 802/434-3411

▣ ARBUCKLE'S ARIOSA COFFEE

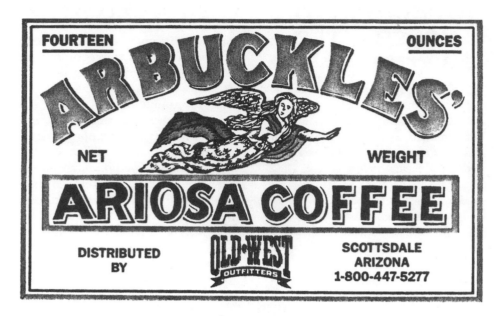

Although coffee had been drunk in Ethiopia 500 years before the discovery of America, the post-Columbian brew compounded its equatorial essences into a New World resource. American coffee was the culinary equivalent of coal—a rich, black, energy-producing commodity that could drive the building of nations; and if looked at perversely enough, U.S. history itself can be seen as a saga of Coffee Achievers on a transcontinental jag. Was it not patriot C.A.s who dumped tea into Boston harbor, fought the Revolution and, by the 1830s, established the cuppa joe as an American staple? And who but coffee-achieving pioneers would individually require *15 pounds* of the stuff to steam on the dashboards of their Conestogas while braving hostiles, cholera and the Rockies along the continental commute from the Missouri to California?

Like those faux Algonquins at the Boston Tea Party, real Navajos liked coffee and drank it in prodigious amounts. In keeping with the chuck wagoneer's dictum that there was no strong coffee, only weak men, the Navajos took theirs black and hearty enough to float a horseshoe, but boiled with sugar in the pot. When obtaining coffee from trading posts, the Indians always asked for *Hosteen Cohay*—or "Mr. Coffee" in the Navajo tongue. What they invariably got was Arbuckle's Ariosa.

Arbuckle's was universally found around the campfires and in the ranch kitchens of the Old West, and Ariosa—a combination of Rios and Santos coffees—was its most popular blend. But whatever its other virtues, the brand's monopoly in cowboy coffee was less a matter of Manifest Destiny than an exercise in marketing genius.

Until John Arbuckle came along, coffee beans were generally sold green, as roasting caused them to quickly lose the volatile oils that gives the brew its flavor and aroma. But once you got green beans home you first had to pick them clean, then place a single layer of them in a roasting pan, and then stir them over a fire while on guard against the first sign of burning—as one burnt bean would spoil a whole batch. Mr. Arbuckle eliminated the need for this bother by finding an economical way to roast the beans at his store, and then coating the roasted beans with egg whites and sugar to preserve their freshness. In 1865, Arbuckle put these up for sale in one-pound packages—an innovation considered hilarious at the time, but one that enabled him to ship his coffee around the country. By 1881, Arbuckle's angel-emblazoned brand had won the West about as well as the cavalry, sod busters, flathead Fords, the Bureau of Reclamation, Sangre de Christo Estates, Hollywood trash and cowmen themselves have done then and since. These last, says one historian, "never knew there was any other kind" of coffee.

Today, Arbuckle's Ariosa is as incompletely remembered as it is distributed. But what's that you say, Joe DiMaggio? Folks can still brew Arbuckle's at home in their own Hosteen Cohays? Packaged with a copy of the original 1870s label, a pound of the cattleman's favorite coffee will be sent to you by Old West Outfitters if you first pony up $7.99, plus shipping and handling.

Catalog of western outdoor wear and gear available, $3.

OLD WEST OUTFITTERS
7213 East First Avenue
Scottsdale, AZ 85251
Tel. 800/447-5277
Fax. 602/951-8633

❧ "1852 BRAND" HONEY

Honey was a common sweetener in both England and the American colonies, where honeybees were introduced (to Massachusetts Bay) in 1639. C.F. Diehnelt, a beekeeper in Germany before he came to Wisconsin, began the production of honey there is 1852. Today his descendants, who still own Honey Acres, preserve the memory of this event with their 1852 Brand honey, a "gourmet-quality" line packaged in replica nineteenth-century glass jars.

Prices: two 4-oz. "mini" jars are available for $4.90; two 1-lb. jars cost $12.90.

HONEY ACRES
Ashippun, WI 53003
Tel. 414/474-4411

⊛ BOTTLED BEER

Portland's Blitz-Weinhard Brewery makes a regional beer—an important enough distinction when the alternative brews are usually undifferentiated amber wash—and although it's the oldest brewery in continuous operation west of the Mississippi, it's not famous.

Blitz-Weinhard was founded in 1856 by Henry Weinhard, an immigrant from Germany, where he was a master brewer. The company was originally located in the Oregon Territory near Fort Vancouver, where the beer was quaffed with the kind of hearty appreciation one might expect from cavalrymen. But lest the Weinhard Brewery's early reputation rely solely on the palates of soldiers, it should also be noted that a contemporary newspaper described it as being "unsurpassed by any other native product of its kind."

As good as this standard brew seems to have been, it wasn't as good as Henry Weinhard's premium, which he prepared in small batches to serve to his friends. Using superior Cascade hops, substantial amounts of the Klamath Basin's rare two-row barley, and their founder's nineteenth-century brewing techniques, Blitz-Weinhard has lately succeeded in reproducing Henry's premium. The beer has been christened "Henry Weinhard's Private Reserve," and bears a label design taken from the one on the founder's old beer glass. Because of its "handmade" character (they just about double the time

required to brew standard beer) and the fact that it still can be made only in small quantities, Henry Weinhard's is still somewhat private. Patience may be required when ordering it from beyond the pale of the brewery's market area, but the rewards are worth it.

THE BLITZ-WEINHARD BREWERY
1133 West Burnside
Portland, OR 79209
Tel. 503/222-4351

✱ PURE SORGHUM

Cumberland General Store's sorghum is grown, processed into syrup, and packed by their Amish neighbors. The new crop "comes ready" in the early fall, and the store may run out of it during the following year. The sorghum is put up in quart jars weighing 40 ounces (shipping weight: 6 lbs.).
Price: $5.95 per jar.

General Merchandise Catalog available, $3.

CUMBERLAND GENERAL STORE
Route 3, Box 81
Cumberland, TN 38555
Tel. 615/484-8481 or 800/333-4640

HAROLD'S CABIN CHARLESTON SPECIALTIES

Despite the rustic sound of its name, Harold's Cabin doesn't operate in a copse of plantation pine, but out of a Charleston supermarket. Of course, Charleston being the place that it is, this supermarket isn't just any downtown foodliner. What it is, according to Harold's brochure, is "the fabled Meeting Street Piggly Wiggly."

There is perhaps no city on the continent that can offer a history buff more than does Charleston. But a *fabled* Piggly Wiggly? I hope the National Trust has looked into this.

▣ "SLAVE BENNE"

Regarding the history of the benne they sell, Harold's Cabin offers the following:

When slaves first came to the coastal areas of Georgia and South Carolina, they brought with them—as their most valued possession—a little handful of benne seed (Sesamum indicum) which they believed hold for them the secret of health and good luck.

Planted near the slave quarters of the early plantations, benne became a traditional part of "the Old South." Cooks in the "Big House" kitchens knew just how to use this rich, spicy honey-colored seed to make delicious and exotic concoctions that have since been famous recipes of "dabuckra" [as whites are referred to in the Gullah dialect that was spoken by slaves and can still be heard in the Carolina low country].

Price: Dark or light, $3.75 per 7-oz. tin.

▩ PEPPER-COATED COUNTRY HAMS

"Cured from a famous old plantation recipe." Average weight is 12 lbs.

Price: about $49 for an approximately 12-lb. ham.

❋ "SLAVE RECEIPTS"

Harold's Cabin also sells a variety of candies once prepared by the plantation slaves of the Carolina low country.

Peach Leather costs $3.50 a quarter pound, $7 for a half pound.

Brochure of Charleston and Carolina low-country specialties available.

HAROLD'S CABIN
In the Fabled Meeting Street Piggly Wiggly
445 Meeting Street
Charleston, SC 29403
Tel. 803/722-2766

❧ BELL'S SEASONING

The military-green herb seasoning for stuffing that for generations has been the very aroma of Thanksgiving was created by William G. Bell, a trained engineer who was a pioneer in the development of refrigeration. Bell founded his company in 1867 and owned it until 1917, when it was purchased by the D.L. Slade Company of Boston, a regional spice concern. Today both companies are owned by Brady Enterprises, Inc.

Throughout its history Bell's Seasoning has never changed its formula—including rosemary, thyme, marjoram, oregano, ginger, pepper and Dalmatian sage, which contributes the most to its distinctive flavor.

THE WILLIAM G. BELL COMPANY
P.O. Box 99
East Weymouth, MA 02189
Tel. 617/337-5000

TABASCO PEPPER SAUCE

As if geographically destined for historic importance, Avery Island rises dramatically out of the Louisiana coastal swamp, some 162 feet of solid salt covered by tidewater forest. After the beginning of the War Between the States, John Marsh Avery, scion of the family who owned Avery Island, worked its brine springs for salt to supply the rebel army. This made the island a military target, and in April 1863 Federal troops under the command of Union Gen. Nathaniel P. Banks advanced from New Orleans to destroy the island's salt mines. Judge D.D. Avery and his family fled into Texas for safety.

In the summer of '65, the war over, the Averys returned to ruination. Although everything on the island appeared destroyed, in the midst of the old judge's kitchen garden one plant flourished: the fiery capsicum (chili) pepper—an ancient Central American plant that had taken root there only a decade before. Taken with the piquant flavor of the peppers, the jurist's son-in-law Edmund McIlhenny began to experiment with them—first crushing and straining them into a mash, then adding salt and vinegar, and aging the mixture in wooden barrels. The hot sauce he developed lent some needed zip to the plain fare of Reconstruction, and by 1868, Mr. McIlhenny was selling hundreds of single-ounce bottles of what he called "Tabasco Pepper Sauce." Within two years the sauce received its patent, and by 1872 McIlhenny had opened a London office to handle the European demand. Today the pepper sauce from the plant unbowed by Federal occupation is an American classic.

Reconstruction Hopping John

Owing to the scarcity imposed by Reconstruction, pea- and bean-based meals were household staples. Hopping John, which was a popular Civil War-era dish traditionally eaten on New

Year's Day, benefits greatly from the addition of pepper sauce. The McIlhenny Company supplied the following 1868 recipe:

- 1 lb. dried blackeye peas
- 2 tsp. bacon fat
- 3 pints cold water
- 2 medium onions, chopped
- ½ lb. sliced salt port or bacon
- 1 cup uncooked long-grain rice
- 1 tsp. Tabasco sauce
- 1½ cups boiling water
- 1 tsp. salt

Cover the peas with cold water in a large kettle. Soak overnight [the modern method for cooking dried peas involves bringing them to a boil, simmering them for two minutes, and let-ting them stand for an hour]. Add salt pork, Tabasco and salt. Cover and cook over low heat for about 30 minutes. Meanwhile cook onions in bacon fat until yellow and add to peas with rice and boiling water. Cook until rice is tender and water is absorbed, about 20 to 25 minutes, stirring occasionally. Yield: About eight servings.

Free recipe booklet available.

McILHENNY TABASCO COMPANY
Avery Island, LA 70513

✳ WILBUR'S BUDS

A pound and a half of Wilbur's Breakfast Buds, made according to the original 1894 formula, is available through the company in this replica of that era's breakfast cocoa can. Indicate preference for milk chocolate or "dark sweet chocolate buds."
    Price: $15, delivered.

Chocolate products catalog available.

WILBUR CHOCOLATE COMPANY, INC.
48 North Broad Street
Lititz, PA 17543
Tel. 717/626-1131

❋ HEINZ TOMATO KETCHUP

For one who in 1888 built an immense industrial complex in Pittsburgh that included a palatial stable with a Turkish bath for his horses, H.J. Heinz was an uncommonly modest man. For why else—in the age of Buffalo Bill, J. Walter Thompson, the snake-oil circuit and the ballyhooing broadside— would the purveyor of more than 200 varieties of packaged food lay claim to only 57? Why was this man, who didn't hesitate to euchre (or, for that matter, to chow-chow) his beloved pickles, at the same time so respectful of the credulity of a buying public long inured to overstatement? Why, it's as if McDonald's were suddenly to announce: "Many Thousands Sold!"

    Some argue that the modesty of Heinz's two-digit boast has long since been swept away by the frequency with which it's been made. But a modest man or not, H.J. was certainly an uncommon one—particularly for a robber baron (that Pittsburgh plant, incidentally, also included a roof garden, swimming pool, gymnasium and auditorium for its employees).

    The key to this rare character may be found in Heinz's motto: "To do a common thing uncommonly well, brings success." Nowhere has this been more amply demonstrated than with the 1876-recipe ketchup (then "catsup") that the Heinz company has bottled in essentially the same eight-facet American icon since 1906. From this, ketchup descends like Cleopatra from her royal launch, exuding the impassive dignity that comes with tradition-bound excellence. For here in the land where ketchup is Pharaoh, Heinz still reigns.

WEARING
APPAREL

131

##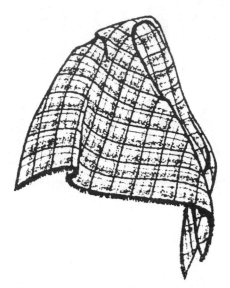

CLOTHING FROM LA PELLETERIE

In business for nearly four decades, La Pelleterie (the term for fur-trade establishments once given by French trappers) specializes in the accurate replication of historical garments, particularly those of the French and Indian War period (1754-1763), and the era of early westward expansion occurring between 1820 and 1850.

✦ "BOILED" COLLARLESS SHIRTS

The sombrero and the flannel shirt he scorned and sported a derby hat and "biled" goods instead.
— Outing, *February 1892*

Partly taking their name from the method used to launder them, boiled dress shirts were curiously favored by cowboys (as well as by clerks, bartenders and others) for working garments. Affixable to paper collars, River Junction Trading Company's replica of "this classic most common shirt of the 1880s to 1920s" has buttons and a collar stud made of genuine pearl. River Junction calls this garment its "Victorian" shirt, and most are fashioned in a striped or colored material, with white neckband and cuffs. The shirts are also available with bibs, which can be white, striped or colored and either pleated or ruffled.

Prices: $34, with a bib $3 additional unless it's pleated or ruffled, in which case an extra $8 will be required.

Catalog of replica western dry goods available, $3.50.

RIVER JUNCTION TRADING COMPANY
312 Main Street, P.O. Box 275
McGregor, IA 52157
Tel. 319/873-2387

▩ IRISH SCREEN

A great Hibernian babushka the use of which dates back to the eighteenth century, La Pelleterie's version of the Irish screen is 48 square inches of fine wool in traditional Irish plaids. State your preference for a predominantly red, dark blue, brown or green plaid.

Price: Woolen Irish Screen, $65.

✦ MERCHANT'S SHIRT

Full-bodied with a fold-over collar, this shirt was part of the standard apparel for men during the eighteenth and early nineteenth centuries.

Prices: Linen merchant's shirt, $90; Osnaburg, $55.

❈ BROADFALL TROUSERS

These broadfall trousers are similar to those found in the paintings of George Caleb Bingham depicting the lives of mid-century riverboatmen and fur traders. The trousers have pewter buttons, with waistband, gusset, drawstring and pockets all as on the full-length trousers. The broadfall trousers have been copied from a pair in the Randolph County, Illinois, collection.

Broadfall trousers, $310.

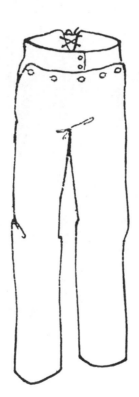

❈ WOMEN'S BODICE

A women's waistcoat available in either linen or wool, fully lined with linen with front lacing.

Price: $85.

▨ FULL-LENGTH TROUSERS

From the La Pelleterie Catalog:

Throughout the Eighteenth Century, knee breeches were the nether garments of most men. At times sailors and laborers wore full length trousers while the military used ankled coveralls during the Revolutionary War. By the turn of the Nineteenth Century, long trousers and pantaloons were replacing knee breeches, and by 1830 only 'old fogies' and servants wore short pants.

La Pelleterie's full-length trousers replicate those worn by laborers and others who wanted to protect their legs and hose. The trousers favor the looser straight leg style that was the common civilian style. The trousers have linen-lined waistbands and "dog-ear" pockets, drawstrings and gussets at the rear, pewter buttons and fall fronts.

Full-length trousers, $315.

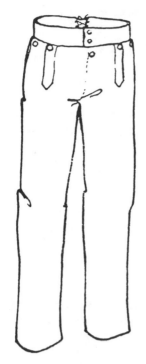

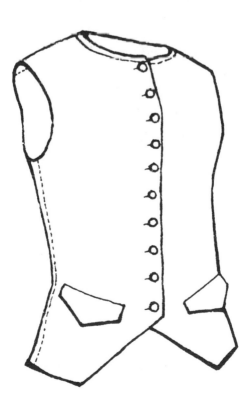

❀ SPORTSMAN'S WAISTCOAT

Eighteenth-century English sportsmen began to wear leather waistcoats such as these in pursuit of game. La Pelleterie's hip-length waistcoat has linen back panels and lining, leather-covered buttons, and functional pockets.

Price: Sportsman's weskit, $195.

The items listed each require $6 to cover the cost of UPS shipment when ordered within the continental U.S.

Catalog of historical clothing specializing in the fur trade of the eighteenth and nineteenth centuries, $5.

LA PELLETERIE
P.O. Box 127
Arrow Rock, MO 65320
Tel. 816/837-3261

▨ PIONEER SHIRT

A very democratic shirt, this pioneer garment was worn during the early nineteenth century "by most anyone of the period from blacksmiths to men of our government." It is comfortable and roomy, with dropped shoulder seams and wooden buttons. Made of unbleached muslin or lightweight unbleached cotton Osnaburg (a heavily woven cotton).

Sizes extra-small to extra-large.

Price: $24.95, ppd.

ALICE'S COUNTRY COTTAGE
Box 3, Rohrersville, MD 21779
Tel. 800/288-7977
Fax. 301/432-7265

❀ SHAKER CLOAKS

Hancock Shaker Village's coats are scrupulously fashioned in the traditional Shaker style but fit well with contemporary dress. The entire cloak, including shoulder cape and the pleated lined hood, is made from 100 percent wool melton cloth. The cloaks have been cut very full, so Hancock suggests that they be judged by shoulder width. The standard lengths are 52 and 55 inches, but special orders are accepted.

Specify size (small, medium or large) and color (black, red, gray, maroon, navy blue or forest green).

Price: $200 (plus $5 for shipping). Orders are taken year-round but are filled only from October through March.

HANCOCK SHAKER VILLAGE
Route 20, P.O. Box 898
Pittsfield, MA 01202
Tel. 413/443-0188

AMAZON DRYGOODS' LADIES AND GENTLEMEN'S FURNISHINGS

SUNBONNET

A woman dressed in bright-red calico... and shingle sunbonnet, sat there sewing on a muslin of gay colors.
—*Sara T. D. Robinson,* Kansas: Its Exterior and Interior Life, *1856*

Janet Burgess of Amazon Drygoods relates this bit of sunbonnet lore:

The original from which this pattern is made is 200 years old. The style was adapted from the bonnet that the French brought to America, although theirs were, without exception, starched pure white. We brought color and calico to the sunbonnet, thereby fashioning a distinctly American head covering. When you are inside its deep brim, you'll never wonder what people once did for lack of sunglasses. Fold the brim back on overcast days. The sunbonnet was worn in parts of the U.S. from the late eighteenth century to the Second World War.

Print pattern. Available in baby, child and women's sizes.
Price: $5.25 (plus $2 for shipping).

MAN'S FROCK COAT

The frock coat first appeared on the continent during the 1840s in marked contrast to the ostentatious pinched-waist and padded-shoulder coats of the previous decade. Amazon Drygoods' version, made of black gabardine with black collar and cuffs, is in the long "Abe Lincoln style" of the mid-to-late nineteenth century.

Sizes 36 to 48. (The coats are easily altered and run large, so Janet Burgess suggests that you order a size smaller than you normally would.)
Price: $92.95 (plus $3 for shipping).

VICTORIAN CORSET

Back lacings, front "busc" closing, and 37 bones. White. Washable, with lace and ribbon trim. To order, send waist measurement.
Price: $115.50 to $155.95, depending on style.

"GAY NINETIES" BATHING COSTUMES

In washable cottons for ladies and gents. The ladies' three-piece outfit consists of a tunic top with a middy collar and tie, ruffled pantalettes, and a matching mobcap. Color availability varies, so state preferences.
Sizes: small (8–10), medium (12–14), large (17–18).

The men's bathing suit is a striped, two-piece affair. It has a long top, with elbow-length sleeves, and pants that extend to below the knees. State color preference.
Sizes: small (16–18), medium (29–41), large (42–44).
Price: ladies' bathing costume, $79.50 (plus $3 for shipping); men's bathing costume, $59.95 (plus $3 for shipping).

❧ GIBSON GIRL SKIRT AND BLOUSE

"The Gibson Girl," as defined by Stuart Berg Flexner in his book *I Hear America Talking* (Van Nostrand Reinhold, 1978), was the

. . . typical, idealized 1890s girl as portrayed by (and in large measure created by) illustrator Charles Dana Gibson in his many drawings for such popular magazines as the old Life, Scribner's, *and* Collier's Weekly. *The Gibson girl's soft, wide pompadour, parasol, and clothing influenced styles until the late 1930s. Gibson drew her in what became known as a Gibson girl blouse, a starched, tailored shirtwaist (an 1879 word) with leg-of-mutton sleeves and a high collar with a ascot tie at the neck.*

Amazon Drygoods' Gibson Girl blouse is available in sizes 32 through 42. An accompanying skirt (appropriately black and floor-length) has a "flattering four-gore skirt back and self ruffle" in waist sizes 24 through 42.

Prices: Gibson girl blouse, $36.95; Gibson girl skirt, $49.95 (plus $3 for shipping either, or both when ordered together).

◉ TOP HATS AND DERBYS

Many [English tourists wear] various modifications of the Derby, with long, light veils draped thereon with studied carelessness.

—*Walter G. Marshall,* Through America, *1881*

The top hat was the essential piece of nineteenth-century head covering, first appearing in modified form as a kind of English equestrian crash helmet during the late eighteenth century, and still very proper for formal dress early in the twentieth.

Prices: Amazon Drygoods' top hats and derbies come in several styles, ranging from $25 to $65.

❧ HIGH LACED LADIES' SHOES

The expansive crinoline skirts worn during the 1840s were supposedly symbolic for the unapproachability of women. But in their constant state of agitation, there was also something seductive about the enormously expanded skirts, although they never revealed more than a glimpse of the wearer's ankle. This may be why it was during this period that the diminutive slipperlike shoes worn by women began to be replaced by high-topped boots, sensible shoes that would last until the Armistice.

Amazon Drygoods' high laced ladies' shoes are considered by the purveyor to be suitable for living history wear from the 1850s. The style was originally known as the "Balmoral Boot," having been designed by Prince Albert for Queen Victoria in 1852. The design became so popular that bright satin variations were produced for evening wear.

Kid leather and lined, these shoes have a 1⅜-inch stacked leather heel and extended leather sole. Available in 93 sizes.

Prices: Sizes 4 to 10, B to EEE, $98.50; 4 to 10, A and AA, $125.50.

Period shoe catalog of more than 150 styles, $5.

Catalog of "Items for the Nineteenth-Century Impression," $2.

AMAZON VINEGAR & PICKLING WORKS DRYGOODS
Dept. AH, 2218 East 11th Street Davenport, IA 52803 Tel. 800/798-7979 for orders Fax. 319/322-4003

✾ DETACHABLE COLLARS

Itself a compromise between the formal and unrestrained, the detachable collar was introduced in 1820—the same year Missouri was cutting a similar deal between slavery and abolitionism.

Gibson-Lee has been manufacturing detachable collars since the Civil War. While that conflict pretty well made the Mo Compromise moot, Gibson collars have continued to be turned out on their original machines to this day.

Gibson detachable collars are made of both paper (to which cloth has been laminated) and 100-percent cotton in 17 nineteenth- and twentieth-century styles. Neckband shirts, to which the collars attach, can be purchased in white, blue or various stripes.

Free catalog available.

GIBSON-LEE CORPORATION
78 Stone Place
Melrose, MA 02176
Tel. 617/662-6025

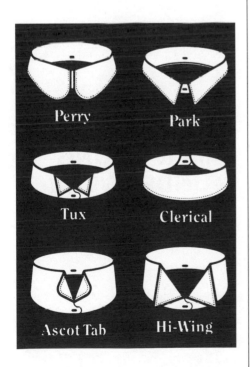

⸺ Sewing Patterns ⸺

❂ OLD WORLD ENTERPRISES

The Old World Enterprises features a line of full-size men's and women's patterns designed to faithfully represent the prevailing fashion trends of the nineteenth century, from its basic silhouettes to its most meticulous details and construction techniques. Printed on long-fiber paper (the very type used during the 1800s for this purpose), their current line comprises 22 female and 10 male patterns, including an 1805 Empire gown (reflecting the Napoleonic curtailment of extravagance in French fashion), 1860s men's evening suit, an 1860s crinoline walking gown, and an 1870s bustle ball gown.

Women's sizes 8, 10, 12 and 14. Men's sizes 38, 40 and 42.

Prices vary from $7.95 for shirts and accessories and from $9.95 to $13.95 for full gown or suit patterns.

Catalog available, $2.

OLD WORLD ENTERPRISES
29036 Kepler Court
Cold Spring, MN 56320

FOLKWEAR PATTERNS

Founded in 1975, Folkwear was the first company to provide sewers with patterns that, while not strictly authentic, were evocative of historical designs.

✤ MISSOURI RIVER BOATMAN'S SHIRT

Folkwear's pattern is for a shirt **"worn by men along the waterways of the American Midwest."** It is a roomy pullover, further described as popular as a workshirt in the 1880s. Men's sizes 34-38.

❀ VICTORIAN SHIRT

A pattern for a late-nineteenth-century men's dress shirt described by Folkwear as "also today's full 'tuxedo' shirt for women's 6-22, men's 32-46."

Catalog available, $2

TAUNTON PRESS
Folkwear Ordering Department
P.O. Box 5506
Newtown, CT 06470-5506

❧ EDWARDIAN UNDERWEAR

Everything was somewhat larger than life during the Edwardian period that followed the turn of the century. Edward VII's reported taste for "city men, millionaires...American heiresses and pretty women" was in part reflected by the appearance of frilly cotton underthings sometimes called flimsies, or trousseau sets. Folkwear's Edwardian undergarment patterns are available in women's sizes 6 to 16.

✿ TRADITIONAL NIGHTCAP

A homemade red flannel nightcap is periodically offered by Putnam Antiques of Middlefield, Massachusetts. Hand-finished with tassel.

PUTNAM ANTIQUES
3 Pond Road
Middlefield, MA 01243

▦ SUSPENDERS

Ordinary nineteenth-century suspenders were made of ticking, white linen or showed solid colors. Rich men wore floral braces or ones with somber stripes. Buffalo Enterprises carries each kind with the proper period buttons to attach them to the inside of your trousers. Measurements required.

Prices: Ordinary suspenders, $8. Dress, $18. An additional $5 required for shipping and handling.

"Period living" catalog, $4 ($6 for foreign destinations).

BUFFALO ENTERPRISES
308 West King Street, P.O. Box 183
East Berlin, PA 17316
Tel. 717/259-9081

❧ MEN'S LONG UNDERWEAR

The Crazy Crow Trading Post offers red and natural-color long-handled underwear (or long johns) for $23.50.

Catalog available, $3.

CRAZY CROW TRADING POST
P.O. Box 314-AMS
Denison, TX 75020
Tel. 903/463-1366

"Fur Trade Era" Clothing

Karalee Tearney, owner of La Pelleterie, has been offering authenticated replicas for more than 35 years. During this time, she has supplied numerous museums and movie companies with custom-manufactured historical garments.

⚜ TRAPPER'S SHIRT

Pat Tearney derived the design of his trapper's shirts from the portraits of George Caleb Bingham (1811-1879), whose citation in Eleanor S. Greenhill's *Dictionary of Art* **reads in part:**

To the following year [1845] belongs the celebrated canvas, Fur Traders Descending the Missouri...*in which the turquoise shirts of the two traders in the dugout and the subtle luminosity of the mists rising from the river—at once brilliant and soft—testify to his contact with sophisticated models.*

Prices: linen, $80; cotton, $60.

⚜ RIFLEMAN'S COAT

The buckskin rifleman's coat may have been worn as early as the French and Indian War; it was certainly still in use as late as the 1860s. The rifleman's coat was as popular with the mountain men of the 1830s as it was with the long hunters of the East. La Pelleterie's coat is a composite design derived from period drawings and from an original at the Valentine Museum in Richmond, Virginia.

The rifleman's coat hangs to the lower thigh, and is fringed at the collar, cuffs, bottom, and front and back sleeve seams. The attached cape is also fringed. These were often greased with bear oil for further weatherproofing. There are no buttons, as this style was meant to be closed with a sash.

Price: $350.

◼ TICONDEROGA SHIRT

In place of a coat, a slipover buckskin shirt such as one following an original at the Fort Ticonderoga Museum, was sometimes worn. This shirt is typical of those worn by eastern long hunters during the late eighteenth century.

Price: $285.

✿ MOCCASINS

Moccasins were the universal footwear of the fur-trade era. Customarily insulated with dried leaves or deer hair, they were quite comfortable in cold weather. But like any buckskin clothing, this was not the case when they were wet; after being soaked with water, moccasins were, according to one contemporary description, "just a decent way of going barefooted."

La Pelleterie's moccasins are made of soft tanned cowhide (the soles are of tough chrome-tan leather), and come in varieties styled after those worn by "plains and woodlands Indians from New York to the Rocky Mountain beaver country."

Price: Woodland: The eastern style—often called pucker toe—is made of heavy buckskin and has a hand-sewn center seam, $45. Rendezvous: An early plains moccasin popular ever since the early nineteenth century. Authentically soft soled, $35.

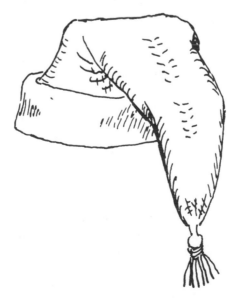

✿ WOOLEN TOQUE

Pronounced "tewk," this headgear was worn by the French voyageurs, the *coureurs des bois*, and early militiamen. Available in white, red and blue.

Price: $35.

Catalog of historical clothing specializing in the fur trade of the eighteenth and nineteenth centuries, $5.

LA PELLETERIE
P.O. Box 127
Arrow Rock, MO 65320
Tel. 816/837-3261

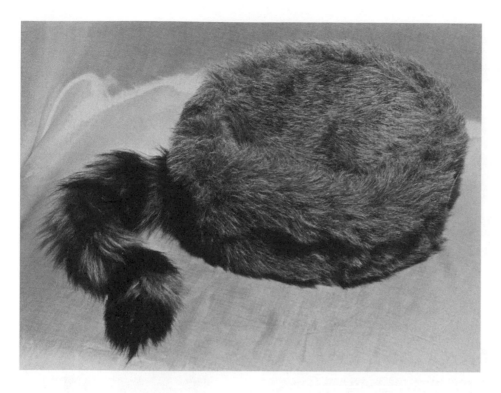

COONTAIL CAP

As for … plains-men and coonskin-capped hunters … of the 'West'… you see no more of them.
— Harper's Magazine, *April 1881*

And will not, it might have been added, until another century passes and the current revival of black-powder hunting begins.

Crazy Crow's cap is not referred to as "coonskin" because, while only genuine animal fur is used to make it, the tail is the raccoon's only contribution. Lined.

Catalog available, $3.

CRAZY CROW TRADING POST
P.O. Box 314-AMS
Denison, TX 75020
Tel. 903/463-1366
Fax. 903/463-7734

RIFLEMAN'S HUNTING FROCK

A tall backwoodsman, in a fringed hunting-frock, was stretched on several chairs.
—Charles Fenno Hoffman, *A Winter in the West, 1835*

A coat worn from the time of the French and Indian War through the nineteenth-century exploration of the frontier, the loose-fitting hunting frock sported two fringed capes to aid in keeping its wearer dry.

Catalog available, $3.

CRAZY CROW TRADING POST
P.O. Box 314-AMS
Denison, TX 75020
Tel. 903/463-1366
Fax. 903/463-7734

CAPOTES

Found a small red capot hung upon a tree; this my interpreter informed me was a sacrifice by some Indian to the bon Dieu.
—*Zebulon M. Pike,* An Account of Expeditions to the Sources of the Mississippi, *1810*

The capote is a long, loose-fitting blanket coat that was worn by the *coureur des bois* (the usually unlicensed traders of the eighteenth-century French-Canadian frontier), voyageurs (eighteenth- and nineteenth-century canoe-borne French trappers of the North American West) and long hunters (the eighteenth- and nineteenth-century frontiersmen who carried the "long rifle," or Kentucky rifle). Along with their kindred but more elaborately tailored "duffle coats," these fringed and hooded (or collared) coats are strikingly colorful garb, well suited to life in the woods.

Several types of capotes are made by Northwest Traders of Dayton, Ohio: Frontier, Coureur des Bois and Bourgeois ("booshway," or buffalo scout).

Prices are available on request.

Brochure of frontier clothing, accouterments, and supplies available.

NORTHWEST TRADERS
5055 W. Jackson Road
Enon, OH 45323
Tel. 513/767-9244
Fax. 513/767-9244

⚜ Camp Gear ⚜

◼ WOODEN CANTEENS

Crazy Crow's wooden canteen is a handmade replica of the type used during the American Revolution and up through the Civil War. It's made of paraffin-lined white pine, and furnished with a cloth strap and iron bands.

Also available is a single-quart wooden barrel canteen (paraffin-lined) replicating one used during the eighteenth century.

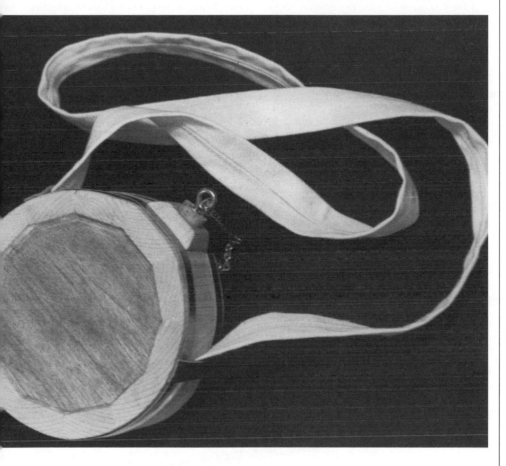

❈ WOODEN KEGS

Crazy Crow's wooden camp kegs range in size from one to ten gallons and are paraffin-lined.

Catalog available, $3.

CRAZY CROW TRADING POST
P.O. Box 314-AMS
Denison, TX 75020
Tel. 903/463-1366
Fax. 903/463-7734

◼ RATION BOX

Similar to an original in the collection of the Museum of the Fur Trade, this chest comes with brass hinges, handles and hasp. The bottom corners are each protected with brass pieces. The box is made from seasoned pine and all outer pieces are held together with wooden dowels. The chest is unfinished and requires staining or painting. Twenty inches long, 12½ inches wide and 13¼ inches tall. Shipping weight, 21 lbs. Price: $65.

Catalog of black-powder guns, shooting supplies and antique gun parts available, $4.

DIXIE GUN WORKS, INC.
Gunpowder Lane
Union City, TN 38261
Tel. 901/885-0700 or
*   800/238-6785 to order*
Fax. 901/885-0440

❋ HARD TACK BOX

Hard Tack was the stony bread ("tack" is an eighteenth-century word for food) used by hunters and trappers. Buffalo Enterprises hard tack box is made of sold pine boards and measures 24 inches by 16 inches by 10½ inches.

"Period living" catalog, $4 ($6 to foreign destinations).

BUFFALO ENTERPRISES
308 West King Street
P.O. Box 183
East Berlin, PA 17316
Tel. 717/259-9081

▨ VOYAGEUR'S LEAN-TO

My canoes were three times unladen…and carried on the shoulders of voyageurs.
—*Alexander Henry,* Travels and Adventures in Canada and the Indian Territories,
  1760–1776

In pursuit of the fur trade, French Canadian voyageurs would paddle all day, portage loads of more than 100 pounds, cordelle upriver, and if they hadn't finished off their supply of rum the very first night, carouse drunkenly before the campfire.

When the voyageur finally did retire, it was sometimes to a lean-to like the one replicated by the Log Cabin Shop. Made of 10-ounce canvas duck, this primitive tent has a floor measuring 8 feet by 8 feet at its widest points. It includes all ropes and ties necessary for erection (poles and stakes not included). Weight: 16 lbs. Log Cabin catalog #81010. Price: $95.

▨ HAND-FORGED COOKING UTENSILS

Forged to meet the demands of primitive camp use, these tools are all approximately 17 inches long, with handles formed from ¼-inch round-bar stock. The bowl of the spoon and the spatula blade are hammered from 16-gauge sheet steel. A 19-inch "ram's horn" wall bracket is optional.

Prices: fork, $9; spoon, $10; spatula, $9.50; bracket, $9. Postage and handling are additional.

COMBINATION TRIPOD AND CROSSBAR COOKING SET

Hand-forged in the traditional manner, this set consists of three interlocking bars of ⅜-inch-square steel. The upper ends of two bars are hammered to form hooks, and the third locks all three securely to form a tripod. To use as a crossbar, stick the two hooked-end bars vertically (and securely) into the ground, and place the third in between as a horizontal cross-member. Strong enough for coffee pots and heavy cooking kettles. Log Cabin catalog #81FTCS (32 inches long). Price: $23.50. Log Cabin catalog #81020 (44 inches long). Price: $25.50.

Catalog of black-powder supplies and accessories available, $4. Visitors welcome.

THE LOG CABIN SHOP
P.O. Box 275
Lodi, OH 44254
Tel. 216/948-1082

BIRCHBARK CANOES

The product of primeval northeastern woodlands, the bark canoe first emerged from its aboriginal home during the eighteenth century to carry French voyageurs westward in pursuit of the fur trade. So well suited was the bark canoe to wilderness travel that it seemed a part of it, as if the *forest's* expression of man's desire for passage within it. White men recognized the bark canoe's superiority from the moment of their arrival, and in time learned to use it to traverse the vast network of wilderness rivers and lakes that connected New York to the Northwest Territories.

From today's perspective the bark canoe seems almost as much a natural formation as a man-made object. Yet in a time when satellites can read the numbers off license plates—for strength, durability, beauty and versatility, nothing has come along to surpass it.

Possibly because its construction was the master craft of the eastern Indians, by the mid-nineteenth century the bark canoe seemed doomed: "It will ere long, perhaps, be ranked among the lost arts," wrote Henry David Thoreau in his *Journals*. But for the purpose of suddenly depositing the substance of the past on the banks of the present, rivers flow through time as well. Today in New Hampshire—a state where the old ground is broken most often to make way for software firms—Henri Vaillancourt wields his crooked knife to make a canoe of tree bark.

Mr. Vaillancourt has taught himself his craft by following the examples of early-twentieth-century Malecite Indian canoe builders and by assiduously studying the work of Edwin Tappan Adney (1868-1950), whose many sketches and models of various Indian bark canoes provided him with an apprenticeship. Of the very few men who can now build these canoes, Vaillancourt is the best; his craft are "Perfect in their symmetry," writes Vaillancourt's biographer, John McPhee. "Their ribs, thwarts, and planking suggest cabinetwork. Their authenticity is lashed in, undeniable."

Vaillancourt resists any romantic notions about his craft. In the modern world his work has simply provided him with a livelihood—while to the modern world it has returned the birchbark canoe.

Most of Henri Vaillancourt's canoes are patterned after the Malecite St. Lawrence River type and are made by hand in the ancient way, using axe, crooked knife, awl and froe. The woodwork—ribs, planking, stems, thwarts and gunwales—are made from white cedar and ash or birch. The canoe's skin is white birchbark, sewn with split spruce root in the traditional manner.

The flare-sided St. Lawrence River canoe has a beam of 34 inches and is 11 to 12 inches in depth. The tumblehome type (tumblehome is the area enclosed by this kind of canoe's large, parenthesis-shaped curves at the bow and stern), with either a high or low end, is available in 16- and 18-foot lengths only. Fur-trade canoes may be ordered in any length from 20 to 37 feet.

Prices for Henri Vaillaincourt's canoes range from $300 to $400 per linear foot, with fur-trade canoes quoted separately.

HENRI VAILLANCOURT
P.O. Box 142
Greenville, NH 03048

▧ THE CROOKED KNIFE

No book entitled _The Maine Woods_ can fail to refer to the crooked knife, the aboriginal carving tool from up in the forests of Down East. Henry Thoreau's book, derived from his journals and published in 1864, contains this passage:

When I awoke in the morning the weather was drizzling. One of the Indians was lying outside, rolled in the fire from want of room. Joe had neglected to wake my companion, and he had done no hunting that night. Tahmunt was making a crossbar for his canoe with a singularly shaped knife such as I have since seen other Indians using. The blade was thin, about three-quarters of an inch wide, but curved out of its plane into a hook, which he said made it more convenient to shave with.

Although this tool had been used by the Indians of the Maine woods (primarily to fashion the bark canoe) for thousands of years, a century after the publication of Thoreau's book it was about as extinct as transcendentalism. By the mid-twentieth century the only crooked knives to be found were likely in the weathered hands of New Brunswick's Malecite Indian tribesmen. Certainly the modern world has little use for the crooked knife, and there's small enough reason for Sears to carry it. Still, even for those who have diligently searched for it, the tool can be stubbornly evanescent—as if expressing a will to be part of history.

When Mainer John Gould was a boy, a Malecite whom he called Chief Pugwash made him a crooked knife. In 1947, when the knife was stolen from his toolbox in Freeport, Gould began the search for a replacement that has taken up almost all the intervening years.

Along the way Gould became an expert in the lore of the crooked knife, from its Stone Age origin to its probable inclusion among the articles carried west by Lewis and Clark in 1804. But as Gould was to learn, the knife is faithful to its home, and doesn't travel well too far from the misted Maine coast.

In 1975, a 21-year-old bark canoe builder named Henri Vaillancourt (whose canoes are described on page 146) was interviewed by John McPhee for _The New Yorker_ magazine. Despite his evidently French ancestry, New Hampshireman Vaillancourt is a singularly taciturn Yankee—yet when properly motivated he'll quote Thoreau with the verve that most of his peers reserve for hockey scores. While impressing McPhee with the crooked knife's Maine roots, Vaillancourt inadvertently mixed his tenses to reveal something of its recurrent nature as well: "Where the crooked knife was," he said, "the bark canoe was. People from Maine recognized the crooked knife. People from New Hampshire do not. All they knew was the draw knife."

As a builder of the traditional bark canoe, Vaillancourt is something of a historical recurrence himself. _His_ crooked knife, he told McPhee, was ordered from the Hudson's Bay Company.

John Gould finished reading the Vaillancourt interview exulting that his search was nearly over. "But of course," he would later write, "since 1760 the Hudson's Bay Company has outfitted the voyageurs, the _coureurs des bois_, the Indians and the Eskimos who made history not only in Canada but down the Mississippi....Think how many millions of knives that the Bay has sold from the Gaspé to the Aleutians!" Gould wrote off to Hudson's Bay straightaway, but got only a baffled letter in response. From its Toronto head-

Henry David Thoreau

quarters, the 300-year-old multinational was asking him what a crooked knife was and how it was used. "I'd just as soon expect a Full Gospel minister to ask me what the Bible was for," he lamented.

The knife had receded into the mists again, but today John Gould would be pleased to know that it has again chosen to reveal itself through the labors of another bark canoe builder—Ralph Frese. Packed in Styrofoam peanuts, Mr. Frese's knives arrive sheathed in the enduring history of the Indians of Maine.

Price: hand-forged and tempered blade, $25.

CHICAGO LAND CANOE BASE
4019 North Narragansett
Chicago, IL 60634
Tel. 312/777-1489

❧ SNOWSHOES

Henri Vaillancourt writes:

The natives of the northern U.S. and Canada have developed ways of coping with and using the environment that are unique among the world's peoples. They alone have mastered the skills necessary for independence and survival in an environment generally considered uninhabitable by modern man. Perhaps no more efficient harness for practical snowshoeing can be found than that used by the Indians of the north, despite the manufacturer's struggle to create a harnessing system that is more complicated and less efficient than that invented thousands of years before.

Snowshoes are Mr. Vaillancourt's wintertime occupation. Some, such as those he found still being made by the Indians of Quebec, are made of birchwood. Several, in Mr. Vaillancourt's own words, are "the fanciest of the traditional Indian kind."

In addition to a plain trail-style snowshoe are three with geometric woven patterns: the square-toe Penobscot, the long pointed-toe Cree and the Cree beavertail style.

Price: $600 per pair. Cree beavertail style by special order.

HENRI VAILLANCOURT
P.O. Box 142
Greenville, NH 03048

LOG CABIN SHOP'S EDGED WEAPONS

✿ HUDSON BAY CAMP KNIFE

This model is "copied directly from a knife so common among early North American fur trappers that it was dubbed the Hudson Bay knife after the famous fur company," writes Eric Kindig of the Log Cabin Shop. Their replica is fitted with horn slab handles that are secured by brass pins. Solid brass bolster. Overall length: 14 inches; blade length: 8 inches. Weight: 1¼ lbs. Price: $34.95.

▦ BLACK RIVER SKINNER

The Black River skinner is patterned after the Indian trade knives that were popular early in the 1800s. It is six inches long and has hardwood handles secured with rivets of brass. Weight, 6 ounces. Price: $24.50.

✿ FRENCH HAWK

A replica of a French tomahawk dating from the 1700s, this weapon's unusual shape is derived from its tapered eye. Made of investment cast steel and a hickory handle. Overall length, 17 inches; blade, 4 inches wide; weight, 1½ lbs. Price: $24.75.

✿ SHAWNEE TOMAHAWK

From the days of the earliest white settlers to the end of the fur-trade era, the steel tomahawk (in all its variations) was in constant use as a tool and weapon. The Log Cabin Shop's replica has been hand-forged and hammer-welded into a sturdy and functional axe. Overall length: 19 inches. Weight: 1½ lbs. Price: $29.95.

LOG CABIN SHOP
P.O. Box 275
Lodi, OH 44254
Tel. 216/948-1082

INDIAN WAR CLUBS

In his book of Native American poetry, *In the Trail of the Wind,* editor John Bierhorst notes the universal Indian belief in the magical power of words. This he claims is particularly true when words are used in sharp, coercive phrases like "Listen!" "Be still!" and "Drink my blood!" Bierhorst cites these as examples of a type of speaking known as "the formula" for its ability to influence and control events. More elaborate phrases, such as "around the roots the water foams" or "my god descended," are often spoken to *bring about* the action they describe.

Of the few authentically wrought Indian war clubs available, the name "Stone Headed Skull Cracker War Club" certainly has a formula ring. As advertised, the 18-inch weapon features a smoothly rounded stone mounted on a hidebound wooden handle. This is decorated with beading, beaver fur, buckskin fringes and simulated scalp lock and eagle feathers, the last painted by hand. Other war clubs available from the same supplier are the "Swinging Rock Stone Headed War Club," the "Horn Headed Medicine War Club" and the "Elk Antler Spiked War Club."

Prices range from $125 to $150, plus $10 for postage and insurance fees.

Illustrated catalog of fur-trade-era apparel and accouterments available, $3.

TECUMSEH'S FRONTIER TRADING POST
P.O. Box 369
Shartlesville, PA 19554
Tel. 215/488-6622

Firearms

KENTUCKY RIFLE
(.45 CALIBER)

But Jackson he was wide awake
and wasn't scared at trifles,
For well he knew what aim we
take with our Kentucky rifles;
So he led us down to Cypress
Swamp, the ground was low and
mucky,
There stood John Bull in
martial pomp, but here was
old Kentucky.
—From the original "Ballad of New Orleans," 1814

Rifling—the practice of cutting spiral grooves into the bore of a gun—has been used in the manufacture of firearms in Central Europe since the sixteenth century. Small wonder then that the Kentucky rifle (or Pennsylvania rifle, as it was originally known) was first developed by Swiss and German gunsmiths who had settled into Lancaster County, Pennsylvania.

No one can identify the exact year when the Kentucky rifle appeared, but it is recognized that after 1720 these artisans began adapting such old-world hunting rifles as the German jaeger to the requirements of the American frontier. They developed a longer, leaner weapon that carried a smaller charge, a rifle that would become as essential as the axe to life on the frontier.

"If your for a buck, or a little bear's meat, Judge," said James Fenimore Cooper's Natty Bumppo, "you'll have to take the long rifle, or you'll waste more powder than you'll fill stomachs." All frontiersmen, fictional or not, made use of the Kentucky rifle's deadly accuracy both to stock their larders and to protect themselves and their families from Indian raiders. And although the tactics of eighteenth-century warfare ensured the use of French and English smoothbores well past the Revolutionary War, General Washington once noted that even at 400 yards a rifleman using a long rifle could hit an 8-by-10-inch piece of paper three shots out of five. By comparison, a musket could send a ball only 150 yards, and wasn't accurate at all.

It wasn't until the ballad quoted above (celebrating Andrew Jackson and the 2,000 Kentuckians he led in the Battle of New Orleans in 1814) became popular that this rifle became known as a "Kaintuck." But by then the coming of percussion-fired weapons had numbered the days of the old Pennsylvania rifle, although many would be converted. In a short time, however, the era of the solitary gunsmith would be replaced by the early-nineteenth-century firearms factory.

But if such craftsmen gradually disappeared during the nineteenth century, they have gradually reappeared during the twentieth. One such is Michael Lea, a full-time gunsmith whose Kentucky rifles have twice won blue ribbons for carving, engraving and overall architecture at the Dixon Gunmaker's Fair in Kempton, Pennsylvania. Mr. Lea specializes in replicating the traditional Pennsylvania long rifle of 1780 to 1820, forging his own triggers, casting his own gun mounts—in fact, fashioning every piece of the rifle himself, except for its lock, barrel and rough, curly maple (or black walnut) blank.

Prices for Kentucky rifles range from $650 for a basic field piece to $3,400.

Free catalog available.

MICHAEL LEA, GUNSMITH
2109 Summit Street
Columbus, OH 43201
Tel. 614/291-4757

✻ HARPERS FERRY 1803 FLINTLOCK RIFLE (.58 CALIBER)

In May of 1804, Meriwether Lewis and William Clark departed from St. Louis on their advance to assert American claims to Louisiana, and—if possible—travel all the way to the Pacific Ocean. Hundreds of volunteers for the grueling expedition had been pared down to 14 soldiers, each carrying the most sophisticated firearm that the United States had yet produced: the Model 1803 .54-caliber flintlock musket. More than a year earlier, Lewis had chosen 15 of these weapons for the soldiers of the expedition while on a special visit to the federal arsenal at Harpers Ferry, Virginia. Navy Arms's replica of this historic flintlock features a blued, half round, half octagonal barrel, color-case-hardened lock, brass hardware and a push-button release patch box.

Overall length: 50 inches; barrel length, 35 inches. Weight: 8½ lbs. Price: $495 plus shipping.

Catalog of replica firearms and accouterments available, $2.

NAVY ARMS COMPANY
689 Bergen Boulevard
Ridgefield, NJ 07657
Tel. 201/945-2500

✻ HARPERS FERRY 1806 FLINTLOCK PISTOL (.58 CALIBER)

Made at Harpers Ferry between 1806 and 1809, this weapon was one of the first military handguns ever to be manufactured at a national armory. Navy Arms's replica features a round barrel with brown finish, polished brass hardware. The case-hardened lock is stamped "Harpers Ferry 1807" at the rear of the plate, exactly as on the original.

The walnut stock extends to half the 10-inch barrel length. Overall length: 16½ inches. Weight: 2½ lbs. Price: $265. Add postage and a $4 handling charge.

POSSIBLES BAG

Along with a powder horn, or gourd, carriers of the early muzzle-loading firearms would require a buckskin bag to load their "possibles"—flint, tobacco, striker knife, etc.

Navy Arms' replica possibles bags are available in rust-colored buckskin.

Price: $20, plus shipping costs.

Catalog of replica firearms and accouterments available, $2.

NAVY ARMS COMPANY
689 Bergen Boulevard
Ridgefield, NJ 07657
Tel. 201/945-2500

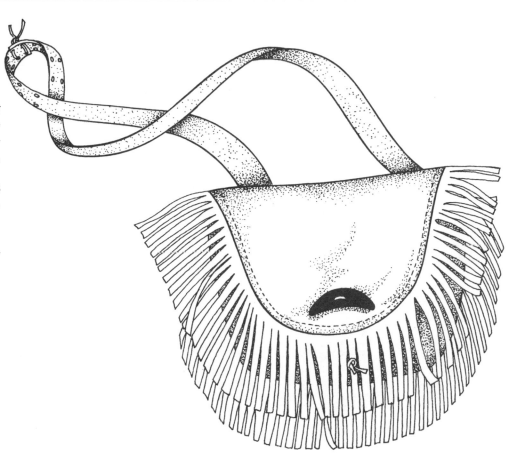

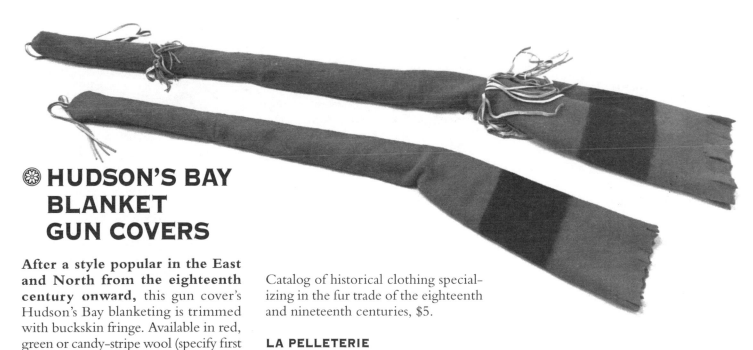

HUDSON'S BAY BLANKET GUN COVERS

After a style popular in the East and North from the eighteenth century onward, this gun cover's Hudson's Bay blanketing is trimmed with buckskin fringe. Available in red, green or candy-stripe wool (specify first and second color choice).

Price: Gun covers, $35 (kit, $25); add $3 each for postage.

Catalog of historical clothing specializing in the fur trade of the eighteenth and nineteenth centuries, $5.

LA PELLETERIE
P.O. Box 127
Arrow Rock, MO 65320
Tel. 816/837-3261

▨ RANGER'S COMPASS

A brass compass typical of those used during the early part of the nineteenth century, this accurate instrument includes a sundial with a folding gnomon.

Price: Ranger's compass, $19.50.

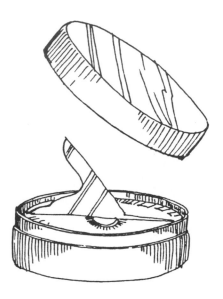

✲ VOYAGEUR BAG

This bag is particularly suited to early rifles and trade guns. It has pockets for small tools and flints, a partition and a gusseted bottom.

Dimensions: 7 inches by 8 inches. Price: Voyageur bag, $39.

The above items each require $6 to cover the cost of UPS shipment when ordered within the continental U.S.

Catalog of historical clothing specializing in the fur trade of the eighteenth and nineteenth centuries, $5.

LA PELLETERIE
P.O. Box 127
Arrow Rock, MO 65320
Tel. 816/837-3261

LOG CABIN BLACK-POWDER SUPPLIES

✾ LEATHER HUNTING BAG

At his side were his tobacco pouch, fire-tongs, pipe, and knife, his hunting-bag and powder-horn.
—David Zeisberger, Diary of David Zeisberger's Journey to the Ohio, 1885

Like the powder horn, its constant companion the hunting bag was a standard part of every backwoodsman's equipment. It was made of whatever leather was available and was treated hard and repaired often. Few of the original hunting bags of the nineteenth century have survived to the present day.

The Log Cabin Shop's replica leather hunting bag is 7½ inches wide and 9 inches deep. It's made of heavy top-grain cowhide and contains several inside pockets. A ¾-inch-wide carrying strap and patch knife sheath are included. Weight: 10 oz. Log Cabin catalog #3830. Price: $45.75. Add postage and a $1 handling charge.

▨ TINDERBOX

Before matches came into use, one of the fastest fire-starting methods required striking flint against steel. These items were carried in tinderboxes similar to this one available through the Log Cabin Shop. Copied from original fur-trade-era boxes, it measures 3½ by 2¼ by ⅞ inches. Flint, steel and charred cloth are not included. Available in solid brass or German silver. Weight: 3 oz.

Brass tinderbox, Log Cabin catalog #77TB2. Price: $14.95. Silver tinderbox, Log Cabin catalog #77TB3. Price $16.95.

THE LOG CABIN SHOP
P.O. Box 275
Lodi, OH 44254
Tel. 215/948-1082

LATE

FRONTIER ITEMS

(1846 - 1893)

153

RED RIVER FRONTIER OUTFITTERS

"We don't cater to the shoot-'em-up crowd," confided Phil Spangenberger of Red River Frontier Outfitters. "We are striving to satisfy the purist, and to maintain a high degree of both quality and authenticity."

These winning remarks are borne out by Red River's track record. Since going into business in 1970, the company has been supplying living-history buffs and the National Park Service with an impressive array of authentic frontier clothing and accessories. Red River's list of customers includes the U.S. Army's 1st Cavalry Regiment at Fort Hood, the Fort Laramie National Historic Site and the Golden Spike

National Historic Site, among others.

Also, Red River's stock in Hollywood has risen along the angle traced by the growing sensitivity of filmmakers to the value of straightforward depictions of the nineteenth-century West. In past years the firm has supplied historical props, clothing and leather goods to the Disney Studios, Stembridge Gun Rentals, Ellis Merchantile (Hollywood's major rental houses for firearms), and for the films *The Legend of the Lone Ranger,* Clint Eastwood's *Pale Rider*, and *Barbarosa* (here they made star Willie Nelson's personal holsters and belts). Their television credits include "How the West Was Won," "Hearts of the West," "Father Murphy" and "Little House on the Prairie." Naturally, all of Red River's customers can expect to benefit from their serious approach to historical replication: "Don't call our outfits 'costumes,'" Spangenberger unnecessarily insisted. "We make historical frontier clothing." Following are a few examples of these.

Style A

Style B

✳ 1880s WAISTCOATS

The remnant of a Victorian suit of clothing, the frontier waistcoat was a bit of Hart, Schaffner & Marx gone the way of Lewis & Clark. Although westerners donned waistcoats throughout the frontier period, woolen and corduroy vests were especially popular among cowboys for the way they provided warmth and extra pockets while retaining the freedom of movement needed for riding the range.

Red River offers Victorian-style waistcoats patterned from originals in its collection. These garments are made with pockets, polished cotton backs and linings, adjustable buckles in the rear, and the 1880-1910 style of "V" notch lapels (style A) or rounded "shawl" (style B). Red River's waistcoats are offered in regular suit sizes of: 36, 38, 40, 42, 44 and 46. Sizes 48 or larger must be specially ordered at extra cost

Price: $85, plus $5 for shipping and handling (Canada, $15).

BIB-FRONT SHIRTS

The 1800s "bib-front" or "shield-front" shirt was worn by every type of westerner—cowboy, miner, soldier and farmer—from the Canadian Rockies to the Rio Grande. Red River's 1870s bib-front shirts come in four styles and a range of authentic colors and fabrics. Available in small, medium, large and extra-large sizes.

Prices: Cotton bib shirt, $100; raw silk (a popular and durable nineteenth-century fabric), $115; wool flannel, $130. Ivory buttons and border braid trim are obtainable for $15 and $20 respectively. Allow several weeks for delivery and include $5 to cover shipping and handling.

SPLIT-EAR HEADSTALL

This was the cowboy's favorite type of bridle. With a single ear hole cut into the crown, this headstall simply slips over the horse's head behind the left ear and over the right. It's an exact replica of an original in the Red River collection, complete with solid-brass oval buckles. Available plain or with border stamp-tooling, and with or without concho. Natural (russet), oil finish only. Reins and bits not included. "Wyoming," "Outlaw" and "Texican" style headstalls also obtainable.

Prices: Plain headstall, $70. With conchos, add $7.50. Allow several weeks for delivery and include $5 to cover shipping and handling.

COWBOY BANDANAS

The frontier's face mask (although usually worn as a protection against dust, not detection), arm sling, bandage, water strainer, sweat mop and tobacco wrapper, cowboy neckerchiefs were available in every color and variety of floral and geometric design. Red River's 26-inch square bandanas are in the true 1870s-1880s style. State preference for first three colors when ordering. Price: $10 each. Include $5 to cover postage and handling (Canada, $15).

Catalog of frontier clothing, western and military Americana available, $3.

RED RIVER FRONTIER OUTFITTERS
P.O. Box 241
Tujunga, CA 91043

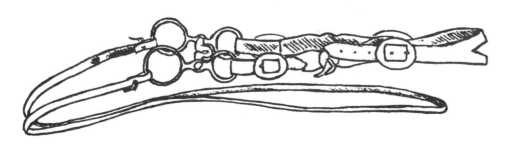

LEVI'S BUTTON-FLY DENIM TROUSERS

The television ad usually appears during the evening news, a jut-jawed cowboy silhouetted against a roseate sky. "In the last known photograph of the Dalton Gang," the voiceover intones as the cowboy wheels his horse and canters down a dry riverbed, "Bob and Brad Dalton were both wearing original Levi's Blue Jeans." The lone rider is joined by one, then another cowboy. Together they ride into the haze of the setting sun.

Well, shown here is what ought to be that last photograph. It was taken at Coffeyville, Kansas, on Wednesday, October 5, 1892, just after the Daltons' final bank raid—one aborted by a spontaneous uprising of townspeople against the robbers.

For the Coffeyville raid, Bob Dalton

can be seen wearing his glen plaid-pattern trousers. And as for brother "Brad"—well, despite the Levi's account, of the 10 Dalton boys, five were outlaws and five were not, but *not one* was Brad. Bob was joined in their last photo by brother Grot (really Grattan—brother Emmett survived Coffeyville but was later killed), a man expunged from the Levi's version of western history for not having a breezy enough name with which to sell blue jeans. Incidentally, Grot is wearing striped trousers. Now we know something of how those folks at Coffeyville must've felt.

Actually, the Levi Strauss Company has been making dungarees for far too long to have manufactured any history about them. In fact the Levi's 501 button-fly jeans sold today have been virtually unchanged (copper rivets were added in 1870 and belt loops replaced the cinch waist during the 1920s) since the first pair of denims were fashioned by Levi Strauss himself back in 1850. Strauss, a Bavarian immigrant, was

Levi Strauss

responding to the advice of an old forty-niner who told him that he "should've brought pants" along to sell on a visit to the California gold country. "Pants don't wear worth a hoot up in the diggins," the prospector is said to have told the merchant, giving him an idea with seemingly endless value.

To make tougher pants—or waist-high overalls, as they were then called—Strauss first used canvas and only later switched to denim (a strong cotton fabric loomed in Nimes, France, and called *serge de Nimes*). A special indigo dye, which could be depended on for its unvarying color quality, was then developed to color the overalls. From the time of their mid-nineteenth-century beginnings until their popularization east of the Rockies in the 1930s, Levi's jeans were the standard working clothing not just for cowboys, but also for the miners, loggers and railroad men of the West. Several pairs of these Levi's are today part of the Smithsonian Institution's Americana Collection.

Luckless and jeanless: The Dalton Gang in final repose. Coffeyville, Kansas, October 5,1892.
Courtesy Kansas Historical Society

⚜ Plains Indian Items ⚜

✳ WESTERN INDIAN WAR SHIRT

These were ceremonial shirts that were proudly worn among the warlike tribes of the West. La Pelleterie's war shirt replicates one now in the collection of the Museum of the Plains Indian at Cody, Wyoming; it follows the natural shape of the hides, retaining the animal's legs. It is decorated with long fringe at the shoulders and short fringe at the elbow, tabs, sides and bottom. The sleeves and sides are bound with buckskin thongs. Specify either leather triangular or woolen rectangular neck opening.

Price: $275 (plus $6 for postage).

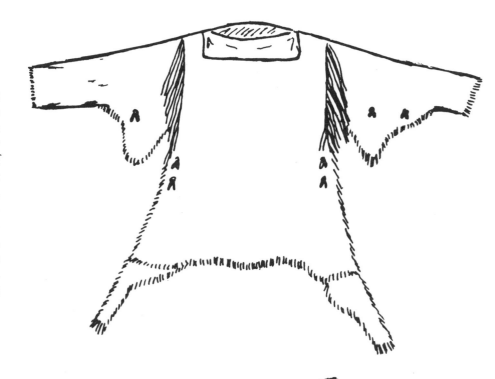

✳ PLAINS CREE COAT

This coat is a copy of one from the Cree tribe now in a private collection. Pat Tearney notes that it is nearly identical to those worn by other tribesmen, including two as geographically and chronologically distant as a 1700s Iroquois and an 1860s Crow.

The Plains Cree coat has fringed shoulder seams and fringed collar, cuffs and bottom. The front opening is buttonless, as if meant to be belted.

Price: $390 (plus $6 for postage).

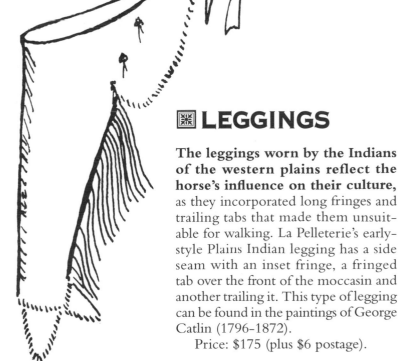

▦ LEGGINGS

The leggings worn by the Indians of the western plains reflect the horse's influence on their culture, as they incorporated long fringes and trailing tabs that made them unsuitable for walking. La Pelleterie's early-style Plains Indian legging has a side seam with an inset fringe, a fringed tab over the front of the moccasin and another trailing it. This type of legging can be found in the paintings of George Catlin (1796-1872).

Price: $175 (plus $6 postage).

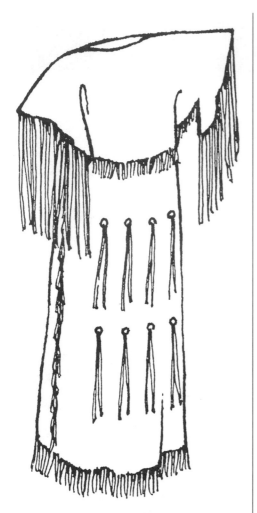

PRAIRIE EDGE STUDIOS

Just over a hundred years ago lived a proud people whose horsemanship, bravery, and colorful regalia captured the imagination of the world. They were the Cheyenne, Crow, Sioux, and Blackfoot of the northern plains. Their mystical lifestyle has inspired writers and artists for generations.

It was with deep respect for those proud people and their artistic traditions that Prairie Edge was created. We are located in the heart of the plains, at the very edge of the Paha Sapa, the sacred Black Hills.

In everything we offer, Prairie Edge strives to be faithful to the original spirit and design sensibilities of the finest artisans of these northern plains tribes. We use the same techniques and materials they did, except where impossible to do so.

Every single item in these entries is unique and made by hand. Because the detail work is so painstaking, and because of our vigorous insistence on authentic materials, quantities are limited.

—Ray Hillenbrand, Prairie Edge Studios

☒ CHEYENNE DRESS

After one in the Museum of the Plains Indian, this early-style northern plains dress was very popular among Cheyenne women. It's a full-length buckskin dress, fringed at the waist and hem and doubly fringed at the sleeves. The skirt is decorated with a thong-fringed back and front.

Price: Cheyenne dress, $350; with imitation elk teeth, $550 (plus $6 for postage).

Catalog of historical clothing specializing in the fur trade of the eighteenth and nineteenth centuries, $5.

LA PELLETERIE
P.O. Box 127
Arrow Rock, MO 65320
Tel. 816/837-3261

⚇ BUFFALO HONORING COLLECTION

To the Indian of the northern plains the buffalo was the center of life itself, providing food, medicine, clothing and shelter to the entire tribe. The western Sioux and other northern plains tribes believed that the buffalo was related directly to the Great Spirit and stood as a natural symbol for the universe. Many parts of the animal were used in religious and spiritual ceremonies.

The Buffalo-Honoring Collection is Prairie Edge's assemblage of those items with which the tribes of the northern plans would ceremoniously honor the buffalo. Included are the jaw knife and sheath, the buffalo ceremonial pipe tomahawk, and the buffalo-honoring skull, which honors the spiritual power of the beast.

❀ PAINTED BUFFALO ROBE

The Plains Indians recorded their history by painting their buffalo robes with depictions of true accounts. In this way a document was created that could be passed on to future generations.

Prairie Edge's painted buffalo robe portrays in an early geometric design the various parts of the sacred animal: heart, stomach, hump, legs and horns, emulating the work of a primitive Indian artist. The earthen paint colors (basically red and yellow with a blue-gray outline) have been applied with bone brushes in the traditional manner.

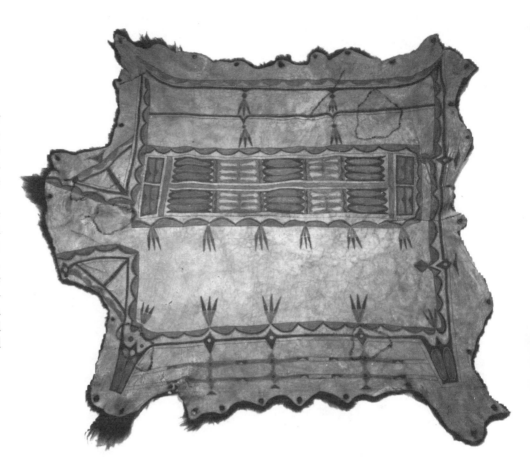

✺ HORSE DANCE STICK

A horse killed in battle was the Lakota Sioux warrior's fallen comrade, a brother to be honored by the creation of a piece of art in his memory. By making and then carrying the horse dance stick in warrior society dances, the Sioux brave would publicly demonstrate his grief for the loss of his horse.

The horse dance stick was uniquely Sioux. The honoring warrior would carve his horse's head and hoof onto it, embellishing the image with beads showing his family's colors. The brave would then use his horse's hair to fashion a mane on the stick, over which a bridle would be placed. The horse stick would be finished off with decorative brass tacks, brain-tanned hide, earth paints, wild turkey feathers and trade cloth.

✹ STAR QUILT

The first schools organized in the Sioux territory during the 1860s taught quilting as part of the curriculum. The Sioux star quilt marries the white man's craft with characteristic Indian use of color and design. The quilt's eight-pointed morning star is the traditional symbol of hope, accounting for its function as a wrapping for infants and a ceremonial covering for adopted relatives.

Prairie Edge's star quilts are made by Sioux women from the reservation communities of South Dakota and are stitched by hand.

⚙ THUNDERBIRD SHIELD

Among the tribes of the Paha Sapa, the mythical thunderbird came from the west—the direction of danger—as, wrote Francis Parkman in 1875, "all thunder storms are occasioned by his anger." The thunderbird flapped his wings to create thunder and blinked his eyes to produce lighting. His appearance signaled the end of drought.

Prairie Edge's artisans have replicated the shield used in the thunderbird portion of the Sun Dances, a Plains Indian ceremony conducted for the health of future generations. The shield's design depicts the thunderbird's wings and the mystical power believed to emanate from them.

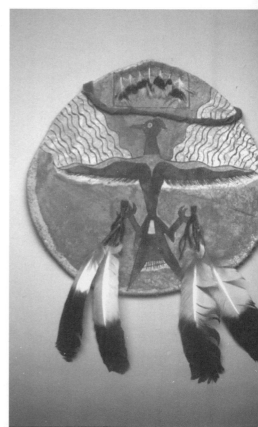

WAR ARROWS

Steel-pointed arrows with short, sturdy shafts and long feather fletchings were used by the Teton Lakota or western Sioux throughout the last century. The Indians abandoned the use of stone points as soon as metal became available from traders, often filing them from barrel hoops, as does Prairie Edge.

The arrow's shafts are short because the small and powerful bow that propelled the arrow was plucked rather than pulled. The arrow would be shot by the brave at hip level and at close range as he rode his horse at a gallop.

Earth paint and dye markings on an arrow identified its owner and established the credit for fallen enemies and game. Wild turkey feathers were used for fletching, and like the metal points, were attached to the shafts with sinew.

As it was considered the mark of a truly brave warrior to get close enough in battle to use a bow and arrow, they were carried long after firearms became prevalent on the plains.

WAR WEAPONS COLLECTION

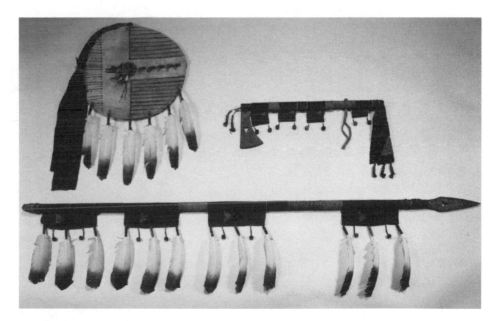

This collection, consisting of shield, tomahawk and lance, is Prairie Edge's tribute to both the bravery and success in battle of Plains Indian warriors.

The Bear Society shield, originally created by the Kiowa nation more than a century ago, imparted to its owner the spirit and fighting strength of the bear. It includes a medicine bundle for the owner's personal medicine—in this case scraps of buffalo wool, sweet grass and a buffalo tooth. The colors are earth pigments, authentically applied by bone brush.

Following tradition, the shield is arrayed with trailers of trade cloth onto which a warrior could attach charms and the coup feathers and scalp locks he earned in battle. The long length of the collection's tomahawk and lance reflect the requirements of mounted warfare.

The central design theme (in both beadwork and blade cutouts) is the forward-pointing triangle, symbolic of advancement in battle. The lance's dominant red coloration represents its power to shed the blood of an enemy; the yellow beadwork, symbolic of the sun, courts its power; dew claws of a deer are intended to impart that animal's speed and agility; and spent cartridges count the number of enemy warriors dispatched by the lance. Each eagle feather that hangs from the lance marks a coup, or the brazen and non-harmful touching of an enemy in battle, executed by its owner.

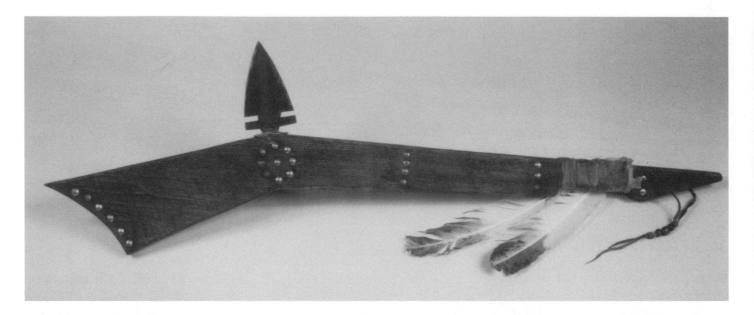

✹ GUN STOCK WAR CLUB

After the musket was introduced to the Sioux by eighteenth-century fur traders, the shape of the Indian's war clubs began to emulate those of guns in order to capture some of the latter's impressive power, or "medicine." That these efforts were unsuccessful may be seen in the musket's ability to eliminate much hand-to-hand combat, which made the war club obsolete.

Still, late-nineteenth-century Sioux warriors retained the gun stock war club as a part of their traditional regalia, and many are to be seen proudly displayed in period photographs.

Prairie Edge's replica war club has a heavy, hand-forged iron spear point and is decorated with brass tacks, red earth paint and feathers.

▦ BONE HAIR PIPE BREAST PLATE

Used early in the nineteenth-century as hair ornamentation, "hair pipes" were combined with brass trade beads to create the familiar Sioux Indian breast plate. By midcentury, this armor was the essential status symbol among all soldier society warriors of the plains.

🏵 GHOST DANCE SHIRT AND SHIELD

The Ghost Dance was a ceremonial religious dance connected with the Messiah doctrine originating among the Paviotso Indians in Nevada in 1888. An expression of the impending demise of the Indian way of life, it spread rapidly to include nearly all the tribes from the Missouri River to beyond the Rockies. The dance was predicated upon a revelation in which earthly floods washed all white people away. This deluge was accompanied by birds that lifted up those Indians who traveled the Red Road (the correct path) into the sky to be reunited with others who had already died. After the flood subsided, the Indians on the Red Road would be returned to the land where the grass, the buffalo and all the good things that had existed prior to the white man's arrival were restored. It was believed that the harder one danced, the sooner this deliverance would occur.

The blue and feathers on both shirt and shield represent the Ghost Dance's flood and birds respectively. The shirt's ability to repel bullets, according to a late nineteenth-century Sioux leader named Shortbull, was indicated by circles in its design. This belief is said to have led to more than 150 Sioux deaths during the Wounded Knee massacre of 1890.

Catalog available, $3.

PRAIRIE EDGE
P.O. Box 8303
Rapid City, SD 57709
Tel. 605/341-4525

🏵 PLAINS INDIAN BOTANICALS

In their beliefs and talismans, all Indian religions are rooted in the immediate natural environment. To almost every Indian, all men, plants and animals have souls permeated by a supernatural overforce. Indian priests and medicine men used grasses and herbs not only for the ritual communication with this spirit world, but also in conjunction with it as curatives. Although many whites considered Indian medicine men to be charlatans, their use of these botanicals was routinely effective, and their belief in the supernatural deeply held.

The Crazy Crow Trading Post offers several varieties of botanicals used by the Indians of the plains. Among these are sage, a fragrant plant used as incense and burned at religious ceremonies; sweet flag root, a Sioux medicine chewed for sore throats and toothaches; cedar, used by Native American Church members and dancers as a perfume; and sweet grass.

Catalog available, $3.

CRAZY CROW TRADING POST
P.O. Box 314-AMS
Denison, TX 75020
Tel. 903/463-1366
Fax. 903/463-7734

✽ PLAINS INDIAN TIPIS

The Sioux word *tipi* (meaning a place in which to dwell) succinctly captures a sense of the conical tent's serenity and comfort. Throughout all the seasons of their long use, in fact, tipis have provided room and agreeable shelter at every latitude of the Great Plains—a matter of some consequence to its nomadic buffalo hunters. Moreover, the tipi was easily broken down for transport into a travois, which could then be dragged by either dog or horse to a new site where the tipi could be resurrected by a single man, if need be. Even the most modern tents must strive unevenly against a tendency to be cramped, poorly lit and ventilated, or ugly looking—but the tipi simply has none of these failings; it is rather a stately dwelling that combines its naturalistic beauty with human cunning to reflect the dignity and grace so important to the everyday life of the Plains Indians.

The tipi can be distinguished from the smoky dens that were the skin tents of other native peoples by its use of smoke flaps—the external wings that flank the tipi's smoke hole and are infinitely adjustable by means of outside poles. These flaps ensure amenity by regulating the draft of the tipi, ventilating it and carrying its smoke out and away from its occupants. The unique smoke flaps were alluded to in the explorer Don Juan de Onate's 1599 account of an encounter with Apaches.

Here he described an assembly of "...50 tents made of tanned hides, very bright red and white in color and bell-shaped, with flaps and openings, and built as skillfully as those of Italy..."

The tipi's refined adaptation to both its purpose and environment has left it virtually unchanged (save for the regular substitution of canvas for hide during the late 1800s) for centuries. During their early winter campaigns on the frontier, U.S. cavalrymen so envied the Indians their warm tipis that elements of the design were later incorporated into the Silbey tent used during the Civil War. Tipis served as the setting for many historic councils, and the homes, at times, for such frontier scouts, soldiers and writers as Kit Carson, Buffalo Bill Cody, Jim Bridger, Joe Meed, William Bent and Gen. John Charles Fremont.

The Blue Star Company of Missoula, Montana, offers both three- and four-pole canvas tipis, the former based on the designs of the Blackfeet and Crow, the latter upon those of the Sioux and Cheyenne. These range in size from 12 to 24 feet. Interior liners, *ozans* (Sioux for "cover"—a flat interior ceiling to retain heat) and lodgepoles are also available.

Detailed price list and brochure available.

BLUE STAR TIPIS
300 West Main
Missoula, MT 59806
Tel. 406/728-1738 or
*   800/777-9964*
Fax. 406/728-1757

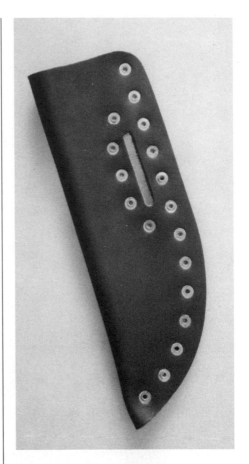

❀ MOUNTAIN SHEATH

The Dixie Gun Works replica of an 1840s knife sheath is held together with nickel-plated rivets and is made from top-grain natural cowhide. Its total length is 9½ inches, and it will hold blades of up to 1½ inches in width. The leather has been left unfinished. Shipping weight, 1 lb.

Prices: Mountain sheath, $6.25.

Catalog of black-powder guns, shooting supplies and antique gun parts available, $4.

DIXIE GUN WORKS
Union City, TN 38261
Tel. 901/885-0700 or
*   800/238-6785 to order*
Fax. 901/885-0440

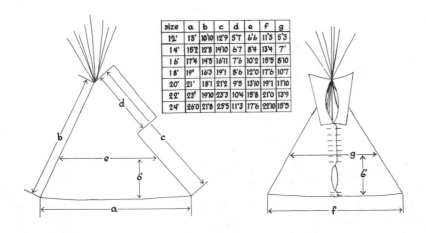

size	a	b	c	d	e	f	g
12'	13'	10'10	12'9	5'7	6'6	11'3	5'3
14'	15'2	12'8	14'10	6'7	8'4	13'4	7'
16'	17'4	14'5	16'11	7'6	10'2	15'5	8'10
18'	19'	16'3	19'1	8'6	12'0	17'6	10'7
20'	21'	18'1	21'2	9'5	13'10	19'1	11'10
22'	23'	19'10	23'3	10'4	15'8	21'0	13'9
24'	26'0	21'8	25'5	11'3	17'6	22'10	15'5

❧ BOWIE KNIFE

Scarcely were these words uttered when another of the party reached over and struck Joaquin a severe blow to the face. The latter sprang for his Bowie knife... when Rosita, instinct with the danger such rashness threatened, threw herself before him and... frantically held him. For the intruders to thrust aside the woman and strike the unarmed man senseless was the work of the moment. Joaquin awoke to consciousness, it was to find Rosita prostrate, her face buried in her clothes, sobbing hysterically. Then he knew the worst.
  —Hubert Howe Bancroft, "Joaquin Murieta: The Terror of the Stanislaus," California Pastoral: 1769-1848, 1888

His blade was tempered and so was he; indestructible steel was he. Jim Bowie, Jim Bowie, he was a fightin' and fearless, and mighty adventurin' man.
  —Theme from the 1950s television series "Jim Bowie"

The Bowie knife, long associated with Jim Bowie, the valorous Texican defender of the Alamo, was actually named for Jim's brother Rezin, its original maker. The early Bowie knife was a large 9- to 15-inch sheath knife, often fashioned by frontier blacksmiths from old files and horse rasps. The Bowie knives therefore varied widely in pattern and use.

Crazy Crow's "Alamo Bowie Knife" has a 12¾ inch overall length and features a sawback blade, large brass guard, finely finished handle and hand-laced leather sheath.

Dimensions: 7-inch blade, 12 inches overall. Weight: 1 lb. Available fully finished or as a kit.

Price: $39.95 plus $3.50 for shipping, insurance and handling.

Catalog available, $3.

CRAZY CROW TRADING POST
P.O. Box 314-AMS
Denison, TX 75020
Tel. 903/463-1366
Fax. 903/463-7734

❋ HAWKEN RIFLE (.50 & .54 CALIBER)

It was 1822 when brothers Jacob and Samuel Hawken began to make rifles in their St. Louis shop. As Sam's account of an event that took place the following year shows, acceptance of the gun was nearly immediate:

Paul Anderson's expedition was the first I fitted out. He and Chambers went to Santa Fe and gave such good reports about my guns that every man going west wanted one. [Gen.] William Ashley's men were the next to go out... The boys... ran out of provisions and had to kill a mule. Ashley told me that he was riding on a white horse looking for game one day and sighted a buffalo. He could hardly believe the shot was effective at so great a distance, and rode up to take another shot at short range, but found the buffalo dead, shot through... Ashley was offered $150.00 [for the gun] out west, but he would not take it.
  —"Testimony re Hawken's Rifles," Jefferson National Expansion Memorial, St. Louis

The fame of the Hawken half-stock rifle grew steadily throughout the era of westward expansion, and it became a favored weapon among such adventurers, explorers and scouts as Kit Carson, Jeremiah Johnson, Jim Bridger and Francis Parkman.

The Aldo Uberti company of Gardone, Italy, is recognized as one of the world's leading manufacturers of historically accurate replica firearms. The quality of workmanship becomes evident the moment one of their guns is taken to hand, and a guarantee of authenticity comes with the claim that their weapons are "accepted by various reenactment ... organizations as perfect duplicates of the originals in all aspects." Reenactors are known to have very exacting requirements.

Uberti USA's Hawken Santa Fe rifles are available as .50 and .54 caliber, one-shot, muzzle-loading firearms. They have brown-finished octagonal barrels and double trigger sets. Their lockplates are color-case-hardened, and they have German silver stock ferrules and wedge plates. Stocks are of genuine walnut with a beavertail cheekpiece.

Overall length, 50 inches; barrel length, 32 inches; weight, 9.480 lbs.

Prices: Santa Fe Hawken .50 caliber, $485; kit, $439. Santa Fe Hawken, .54 caliber, $485; kit, $439.

Color catalog available.

UBERTI USA INC.
P.O. Box 469
Lakeville, CT 06039
Tel. 203/435-8068
Fax. 203/435-8146

⊰ Western Handguns ⊱

The following account by John Reno, "inventor" of train robbery, describes the train ride to the Jefferson City, Missouri, prison after his capture by Pinkertons in 1868. Because it was planned that during this journey Reno's brother Frank and their comrades would raid the train and rescue him, John anxiously sizes up his guards:

I was a little uneasy on the morning we left Gallatin to see the guard so strong—

there were six or eight armed soldiers, well weaponed, but I knew they were not all going on the train and hoped they would leave us before my brother might make his attack. As I did not know where the attack was to be made however, I was very restless, watching for them at every station… I dreaded to see the time come, for I feared there would be some hard fighting. The guards were all provided with long 'navies' and had a reputation of being men with steel nerves.

Because gang members had "missed train connections at Quincy," Frank never mounted his attack. If John Reno was disappointed when he entered the Missouri pen, he hid it manfully:

When we arrived at the prison gate I looked up and read in large letters over the entrance: 'THE WAY OF THE TRANSGRESSOR IS HARD. Admission, twenty-five cents,' but I was on the dead-head list and went in free.

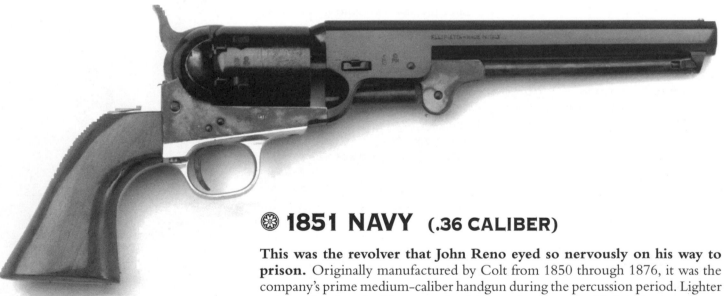

✹ 1851 NAVY (.36 CALIBER)

This was the revolver that John Reno eyed so nervously on his way to prison. Originally manufactured by Colt from 1850 through 1876, it was the company's prime medium-caliber handgun during the percussion period. Lighter and handier than the Dragoon pistol, it was also a popular Union Army weapon. Navy Arms notes that the original Colt was also a favorite dueling weapon during the California Gold Rush.

The Navy Arms replica features a steel frame, octagonal barrel, and a six-shot cylinder engraved with a period naval battle scene. The backstrap and trigger guard are both of polished brass.

Dimensions: Overall length, 14 inches; barrel length, 7½ inches. Weight: 2 lbs.

Price: Finished model, $135.

1873 SINGLE-ACTION 'PEACEMAKER' REVOLVER (.44, .40 OR .45 CALIBER)

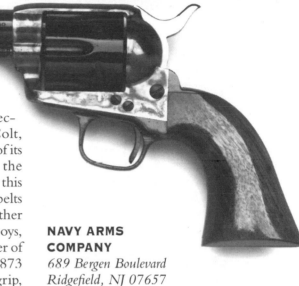

Our men with their deadly Colts told with terrible effect.
—William Thomas Hamilton, *My Sixty Years on the Plains,* 1905

Late in the 1860s, the Smith and Wesson Company developed a new revolver that would revolutionize the design of such weapons. Known as the single-action type, the gun had its barrel and part of its frame hinged at the lower front end. When a latch just in front of the hammer was released, the barrel and cylinder pivoted forward, causing a spring-held ejector to simultaneously discard empty shell casings.

Quick to appreciate the accelerated loading qualities of the single-action revolver, the Imperial Russian Government placed a large order with Smith and Wesson. This effectively left the U.S. market to Colt, which brought out a single-action of its own in 1873. Known as the 'Peacemaker' or 'Frontiers' model, this revolver found its way to the gun belts of Wyatt Earp, who, along with other western lawmen, outlaws and cowboys, made it the most famous six-shooter of its time. Navy Arms's replica 1873 'Colt-Style' S.A.A. has a walnut grip, a color-case-hardened frame and blued-steel parts.

Dimensions: Barrel length, 3, 4¾, 5½ or 7½ inches.

Prices: Finished model, $345.

Color catalog of replica arms and accessories available, $2.

NAVY ARMS COMPANY
689 Bergen Boulevard
Ridgefield, NJ 07657
Tel. 201/945-2500

PATERSON REVOLVER (.36 CALIBER)

In their quality, Uberti replicas are said to surpass the originals made by Samuel Colt during the 1850s and 1860s. Uberti's Paterson revolver continues the history of this, the first repeating handgun, with a variation known as the "Texas Paterson." Consistent with the original Texas Paterson used by the Navy of the Republic of Texas and the Texas Rangers, the Uberti replica features all-steel construction with color-case-hardened hammer, trigger, frame plate and backstrap, with all other metal parts available in the original charcoal blue, or in a more durable gunmetal blue. Other authentic features include a square-cut five-cylinder engraved with the famous stagecoach hold-up scene;

one-piece, tightly fitted flared grips; fine checking on hammer spur; and a folding trigger that drops into position when the hammer is cocked.

Overall length, 12½ inches; barrel length, 7½ inches; weight, 2½ lbs.

Color catalog available.

UBERTI USA INC.
P.O. Box 469
Lakeville, CT 06039
Tel. 203/435-8068
Fax. 203/435-8146

Western Accouterments

◈ FRONTIER CARTRIDGE BELTS

A re-creation of an early-style belt, handmade of the same weight leather as were the originals. "These authentic cartridge belts bring to mind the old towns of Tucson, Denver, Abilene, and El Paso, as well as the men who tamed them," says the Red River catalog.

Each belt is made with 30–36 cartridge loops to accommodate either .38, .44 or .45 caliber bullets. Heavy, old-style buckles are used, and each belt is available either plain or border-stamped. Natural oil-finish only.

Prices: Plain belt, $70; border-stamped, $75; frontier floral carved, $100. Include $5 per item to cover postage and handling.

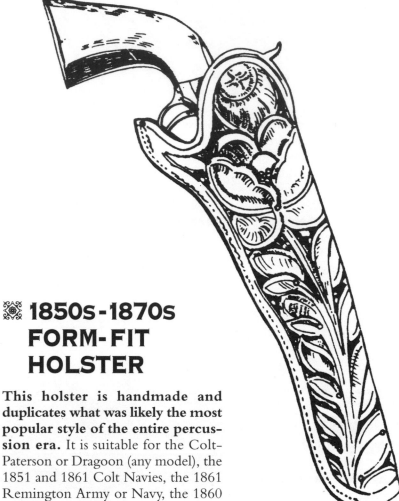

◈ 1850s-1870s FORM-FIT HOLSTER

This holster is handmade and duplicates what was likely the most popular style of the entire percussion era. It is suitable for the Colt-Paterson or Dragoon (any model), the 1851 and 1861 Colt Navies, the 1861 Remington Army or Navy, the 1860 Colt Army, and the 1873 Colt single-action Army revolvers. Available plain or with border-stamping, natural oil-finish only. Indicate preference for butt-forward or reverse style, right or left side.

Prices: Plain form-fit, $47.50; border-stamp tooled, $55; frontier floral carved, $75.

Catalog of frontier clothing, western and military Americana available, $3.

RED RIVER FRONTIER OUTFITTERS
P.O. Box 241
Tujunga, CA 91043

...ly Compartment Tents.

...with square ends. Weights without poles, ...pounds.

...de of 8 oz. double filling, brown and white ...white stripe, same as 10 ounce double fil-

...ts are especially designed for families ...o must have separate rooms. It is accou ...erfectly as at home. It is divided into fou ...on sides and dining room in center. Th ...shown in this tent is not extra to the ten ...the wall lifted up, thus forming an aw ...ng free circulation of air through the ten ...omplete shade. The prices include ever ...lete, ready for putting up.

...ze.	Wall.	Pole	White 10-ounce double filling or 8-ounce army duck.	White 1...ounce dou...ble filling o...10-o u n c...army duck
...x16½	6 ft	10 ft	$20.90	$23.70
...x19	6 ft	10 ft	22.75	26.00
...x19	6 ft	11 ft	26.90	30.60
...x21½	6 ft	11 ft	29.20	33.35
...x21½	6 ft	12 ft	32.20	36.60
...x23½	6 ft	12 ft	34.25	38.90
...x23½	6 ft	13 ft	38.85	44.40

...nsions of bed rooms and dining room.

...	...5½x9	Dining room	5 x9
...	6 x9	Dining room	6½x9
...	6 x6	Dining room	7¾x12
...	6 x7	Dining room	7¼x12
...	7 x7	Dining room	7¼x14
...	7 x7	Dining room	7½x14
...	8½x8½	Dining room	7½x16½

...e prices include everything complete ready ...up.
...hen 8 oz. stripe blue or brown is wanted the ...e the same as 10 oz., double filling.

The Protean Tent.

49200

...best all 'round tent for camping purposes ...d. It is compact, roomy, easy to put up, ...e for both hot and cold weather; only one ...ed. The tent has a sod cloth 9 inches wide ...to keep out wind and mosquitoes. The tent ..."fly" that can be used in many ways, as a fly ...the roof and part of sides or as an awning ...tent, or as a store house. It has other ad-...o numerous to mention here, and circulars ...e different shapes it can be made into with ...ns free.
...Protean tents, including fly, sod cloth, ash ...ns complete ready to set up.
... 49,200.

Height Rear Wall.	Height of Pole.	8-oz. Duck Single Filling	10-oz. Duck, Single Filling	Additional for 3 Joint Pole.	Additional for Com-stock's Carry Bag With Shoulder Straps

Comstock's Carry Bag.

49201 It is a very simple and inex-pensive bag for carrying tent, jointed pole, pegs and blankets or extra cloth-ing. It is light and convenient, and carries the load in comfortable posi-tion on the back. The bag can be in-stantly opened without removing the straps. The straps and cords can be instantly detached and stowed in top of bag for shipment. When ordering these bags for Protean tents, column in tent list above marked "additional for patent carry bags with shoulder straps" will give price of bag for any sized tent. Tent, jointed pole. etc., when packed in this bag can be checked as bag-gage. Each...........................$1.20

Comstock's Malleable Iron Tent Peg.

We can make to order all kinds of tents, canopies, etc.

...ordering give catalogue num-ber, length and breadth and price.

Wall Tents.

Wall Tent No. 49215

Weights without poles, 7x7, 30 lbs.; 9½x12, 40 to 50 lbs.; 14x16, 66 to 76 lbs.; 16x24, 120 to 130 lbs; 18x32, 147 to 160 lbs. Ridge poles weigh 22 ounces to the foot. Upright poles, 14 oz. to the foot Pins weigh ¼ to ¾ pounds each. All of our 12 ounce duck tents are double filling, best quality.

No.	Length and Breadth Feet	Height Wall Feet	Height Pole Feet	Price with Poles, Pins, Guys, etc. Complete ready to set up		
				8 oz. Duck.	10 oz. Duck.	12 oz. Duck.
Order 49215	7 x 7	3	7	$3.70	$4.30	$5.80
	7 x 9	3	7	4.35	5.10	6.70
	9 x 9	3	7½	5.05	5.90	7.50
	9½ x 12	3	7½	5.95	6.95	9.20
	9½ x 14	3	7½	6.75	7.85	10.40
	12 x 12	3½	8	7.05	8.25	10.90
	12 x 14	3½	8	7.95	9.30	12.35
	12 x 16	3½	8	8.85	10.30	13.75
	12 x 18	3½	8	9.80	11.45	15.05
	14 x 14	4	9	9.45	11.10	14.75
	14 x 16	4	9	10.45	12.25	16.30
	14 x 18	4	9	11.63	13.70	18.15
	14 x 20	4	9	12.95	15.05	19.70
	14 x 24	4	9	14.60	17.00	22.10
	16 x 16	5	11	12.95	15.25	20.25
	16 x 18	5	11	14.25	16.65	22.60
	16 x 20	5	11	15.70	18.30	23.95
	16 x 24	5	11	17.85	20.80	27.15
	16 x 30	5	11	21.62	26.00	32.90
	16 x 35	5	11	24.20	28.25	36.90

Photographers' Tents.

49220 Weight, without poles, 66 to 176 pounds. Ridge poles, 22 to 25 oz. per foot in length.

Size.	Pole.	Wall	Price, complete, without dark room.		
			8 oz. single fill'g duck.	10 oz. sin-gle filling duck.	10 oz. double fill'g duck.
12x16 ft....	11 ft.	6 ft.	$13.55	$15.20	$18.20
12x21 ft....	11 ft.	6 ft.	16.55	19.10	22.54
	11 ft.	6 ft.	18.40	21.15	24.85
	12 ft.	6 ft.	15.20	17.95	21.60
	12 ft.	6 ft	18.40	21.15	25.55
	12 ft.	6 ft.	20.00	23.25	27.60
	12 ft.	6 ft.	22.75	26.45	31.30
	13 ft.	6 ft.	17.95	20.95	25.05
	13 ft.	6 ft.	22.10	25.75	30.60
	13 ft.	6 ft.	25.10	29.20	34.75
	13 ft.	6 ft.	26.90	31.30	37.25

...ou tents include poles, pins, guys, etc. Tent ...ready to set up.
...ooms extra, 6x6 feet, $7.80; 4½x4½ feet $6.50.
...k rooms are made of same material, same ...nd color as the tent—all white. We make the ...y, the artist can darken it to suit his own taste. ...black silesia, some yellow, etc.
...ove prices include poles, pins, guys, etc., ready ... tent. Quotation on other sizes on application ...ottom prices.
...on stable tents, stable, tops, Sibley tents, cano-...without wall, photographers' tents, square hip-...s, or any other style, given on application and ...prices.

Palmetto, or Lawn Tents.

49225 Positively the best tent in use for lawn, croquet or archery parties They are made of 8 ounce awn-ing duck, color, blue and white or brown and white, internate shades. They have but one pole, and that in center. Top is supported by wood frame, umbrella shape. It can be set up in three to five minutes and taken down as speedily as the closing of an umbrella. The cut shows this tent with awning extension.

Size of Base.	Size of Top.	Height in Center.	Height at Side.	Price, without Awning.	Price, with Awning.
7x 7......	2 ft. 4 in.	7 ft. 6 in.	6 ft.	$4.30	$5.95
8x 8......	2 ft. 4 in.	8 ft.	6 ft.	4.95	6.50
9x 9......	3 ft. 6 in.	8 ft. 6 in.	7 ft.	6.25	7 95
10x10......	3 ft. 6 in.	9 ft.	7 ft. 6 in.	7.00	9.00

Black Oiled Wagon Cover.

These covers are made from 8 oz. duck and although black and called tar pualins, have no tar in their compo-sition. Our water proof dressing is an oil prepara-tion, and is entirely free from anything calculated to rot or burn the canvas, but adds to the durability of the cover being impervious to water, and very soft and pliable. It will neither rot nor mildew from damp, nor break from being too hard. They are invaluable to all persons who are shipping and receiving goods which are liable to damage from wet weather. In ordering, give catalogue number, size and price.
Weight 9 to 28 pounds. 6x12, 12 lbs; 6x9, 9 lbs; 7x12, 16 lbs; 7x14, 19 lbs.

No.	Size.	Price.	Size.	Price.	Size.	Price
49227	6x 8 ft	$2.50	7x 9 ft	$3.30	8x10 ft	$4.00
	6x 9 ft	2.85	7x10 ft	3.65	8x12 ft	5.8...
	6x10 ft	3.10	7x12 ft	4.40	8x14 ft	...
	6x12 ft	3.75	7x14 ft	5.10	8x16 ft	6.6...
	6x14 ft	4.35	7x16 ft	5.80	9x14 ft	...

Civil War Uniforms

The C&D Jarnagin Company of Corinth, Mississippi, manufactures replica nineteenth-century military (primarily Civil War) uniforms, equipment and accouterments. Regarding the authenticity of these, a single fact culled from a sidebar in their catalog can make the point standing alone: For its Confederate uniforms, Jarnagin identifies and replicates five shades of gray (including the brownish Tuscaloosa gray that was earmarked for the Eastern Theater; and the dark Richmond gray, so called because it was worn by soldiers who defended the Confederate capital) and four shades of butternut. This attention to detail extends to each cut, stitch and drape of every item produced. "We're not a merchandise mart," said John Jarnagin while leveling a gaze at me over the telephone, "we're a military reproduction service."

"Service" is very much the operative word here. Prospective customers are invited to fill out "Service Cards" as long as passport applications. These address special fitting problems, inquire after favored activities involving use of the item, and assign a "seniority number" to the customer. All this fidelity to both authenticity and customer care on the part of the Jarnagin Company evokes a strong bond with the customer, and a sense of family pervades the place. John Jarnagin will not suffer fools (or the "frivolous"—nonhistorical—use of uniforms) gladly, but he works long hours in aid of the serious educator, historian and military-history buff. "Here at least," he advised me, "nice guys come in first."

Although I spent a good deal of time both in correspondence and on the telephone with Mr. Jarnagin, when his company's catalog finally arrived the range of items it contained was still startling. Following (and elsewhere in this section) is a sampling of these:

UNITED STATES ARMY

✿ FATIGUE JACKET

This is the four-button "sack" coat that was the mainstay of all service branches during the war. The fatigue jacket is fashioned of 12-ounce dark-blue wool, unlined, with scalloped cuffs and an inside breast pocket (lined jackets were supposedly issued to recruits). The comfort and usefulness of the sack coat made it a popular garment during the war.

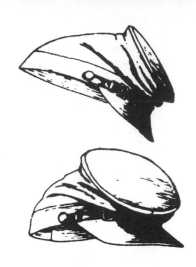

◉ FORAGE CAP

In 1858, a board of officers designed the forage cap—closely following the French "kepi"—for general use by the army. The design was adopted in part because it allowed for machine manufacture and thereby reduced expenses. During the war, literally all enlisted men were issued a regulation forage cap of dark-blue wool stiffened with buckram and having a paste-board crown reinforcement, a polished cotton lining, a crescent-shaped leather visor and two General Service brass buttons. The only acceptable substitute for the regulation forage caps were those brought into service through private means. Sometimes scorned as "shapeless feedbags," these forage caps stood high on the head and were relatively unattractive.

John Jarnagin's forage caps are styled from originals in his collection as well as from those in private and public collections. They have polished cotton linings, leather sweatbands and harness-leather bills with a chin strap with the correct slide. This is the standard cap of the Federal Army, Pattern of 1858.

MODEL 1851 JEFFERSON BROGAN

Although quality varied, the "bootees" or shoes that were issued to the troops were better made than their civilian counterparts. Also called "mudscows" or "gunboats," these brogans were rights and lefts, unlike the straight-last types that preceded them. Other changes included a shortening of the upper so that it came to just above the ankle, and a reduction of the lace holes from five or six down to four.

Available in sizes 7D through 14D, and 8 EEE through 12½ EEE, the Jarnagin Company's Jefferson Brogans are made of moderately heavy oak-tanned leather, rough-side out. The soles are fashioned with two layers of prime sole leather, fastened with pegs.

ARMY-PATTERN UNDERWEAR

The soldier of the 1850s and 1860s was issued underwear of a heavy cotton "canton" flannel. John Jarnagin noted that the undershirt was mainly used (except during cold weather) as a regular shirt worn around camp. The drawers, he continued, were worn long as issued during the winter, and cut off above the knee in spring. In addition to canton flannel, C&D Jarnagin offers lightweight underdrawers and shirts of lightweight 100 percent cotton Osnaburg.

MOUNTED SERVICES OVERCOAT

Made of heavy, sky-blue Kersey wool, this mounted troops' overcoat follows an original owned by the Jarnagin company. It is double-breasted, wool-lined, and has a wrist-length cape and stand-and-fall collar. Should they wish, mounted officers could substitute dark-blue wool.

ISSUE PATTERN SHIRT WHITE MUSLIN

Prior to the issuance of this shirt, the army acquired shirts on the open market, contracting for them to no specific pattern. The issue-pattern shirt is a four-button pullover with a yoke in the back, single-button cuffs and a square-bottom plaquet in front. Before the war a gray wool shirt was specified, but during it a white muslin shirt of the same pattern was very much in evidence. Civilian production provided colored and print shirts of a similar cut.

CONFEDERATE ARMY

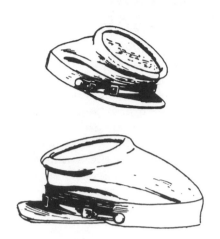

Confederate Army Regulations prescribed uniforms for all branches of the service, but particularly in the last years of the war, few Confederates were well supplied with them. Many 1861 volunteers wore militia uniforms and homespun clothing, and in some instances stripped the uniforms from the bodies of the enemy dead. Shorn of their insignia and (in some commands) dyed gray, these then served the Confederate cause. Especially prized were "Yankee overcoats," also known as the foot overcoat.

C&D Jarnagin's Confederate uniforms follow the regulations of the Confederate War Department and, worn together, would not represent a "mustering out." The typical uniform of the rebel guerrilla would be a hodgepodge of homespun and official garb.

COMMON SHELL JACKET

The common shell or roundabout jacket was the basic style used throughout the war in all theaters and by all service branches. It's a reasonably close-fitting, waist-length jacket, with a stand-up collar. Each jacket is lined with either muslin or polished cotton and has an inside breast pocket. Fronts have five to ten buttons, seven or nine being most common in the Eastern Theater (and in the early war everywhere), six or eight in the Western, or Trans-Mississippi, Theater. These jackets may have service-branch-trimmed collars or cuffs, and either solid-color or piped edges.

CONFEDERATE FROCK COAT

"The uniform shall be a double-breasted tunic of gray cloth, known as cadet gray, with the skirt extending halfway between the hip and the knee." So stated the Confederate War Department regulations promulgated in 1861, but as C&D Jarnagin notes, seemingly never enacted. While very few of these double-breasted coats were worn, these are what the Jarnagin Company replicates.

The single-breasted Confederate frock coats are fully lined in heavy muslin and have inside breast and tail pockets. They also have either seven- or nine-button fronts, and may be dressed plain or with trimmed collar and cuffs.

KEPI, CHASSEUR-STYLE FORAGE CAP

Somewhat more stylish than the Federal-based forage cap, the rakish *chasseur*-style hat was very popular among Confederate forces. C&D Jarnagin's replicas have been patterned after originals, featuring a heavy leather brim and a lining of polished cotton with drawstring adjustment. These caps are distinctly more substantial than the U.S. model 1872 forage caps with which they are often confused. As with the regulation C.S. forage caps, the Jarnagin Company's chasseur-style kepis may be ordered either in a solid color or with a dark-blue bottom band and tops distinguished by arms-of-service colors—red (artillery), light blue (infantry) or yellow (cavalry).

Catalog and price list of nineteenth-century military uniforms and equipment available, $3.

C&D JARNAGIN COMPANY
P.O. Box 13529
Jackson, MS 39236
Tel. 601/287-4977
Fax. 601/287-6033

CIVIL WAR FLAGS

The Hebrew poet whose idea of awe inspiring was expressed by the phrase 'terrible as an army with banners' [doubtless] had his view from the top of a mountain.
— Confederate Gen. Harvey Hill before the Battle of South Mountain, September 1862

The single star of the Bonnie Blue Flag represented South Carolina, first state of the Confederacy. Despite the rebellion it helped foment, the C.S.A. never adopted the pale-blue secessionist standard. The flag nevertheless stood unchallenged as a symbol of "The Cause" until after the first Battle of Bull Run (July 1861) when the Confederate battle flag was approved.

This flag, with its starry blue St. Andrew's Cross shielding a red field, is today the country's second most popular. Revived in the South during this century to protest the civil rights movement, it became a salient emblem of "Surrender, Hell!" obduracy and was greatly in evidence the day that Governor George Wallace stood in the schoolhouse door to block integration of the University of Alabama.

During the observation of the Civil War's centennial, use of the Confederate battle flag coincided with a new period of national upheaval, one that included a presidential assassination with its attendant roster of Lincoln-Kennedy coincidences. But the rebellion of the 1960s was a tepid affair compared to that of 100 years before. As a high-water mark, Woodstock was no Bloody Angle, even if it did close the New York Thruway all afternoon.

Since those hippie days, the "stars and bars" (actually the name of the first Confederate *national* flag) has variously represented country-and-western bands; an angry, biker-to-blue-collar type of rugged individualism; and, if you are European—Elvis. Many southern blacks still cannot look at the Confederate battle flag without seeing the colors of oppression; while a

great number of their white countrymen only recall what was for them a historic moment of valor and independence (their bumper sticker: "Heritage, not Hate"). As of this writing, a controversy flares over whether to fly the Confederate battle flag above Southern state capitols. It is the latest skirmish in that Civil War for which Appomattox was just a pause to water the horses.

Prices:

Bonnie Blue	$125.50
First Confederate National	$74.25
Confederate Battle	$174.95
Cavalry	$94.25
Artillery	$129.95
Second Confederate National	$147.75
Third Confederate National	$147.75

Add $2.50 for shipping and handling.

AUTHENTIC REPRODUCTIONS
1031 Old Nankin Road, R-3
Ashland, OH 44805
Tel. 419/289-6642 or
419/289-8688
Fax. 419/289-8688

BONNIE BLUE
In 1860, the BONNIE BLUE flag was unofficially used throughout the south. This flag was never adopted by the Confederate States of America. Solid light blue field with white star in center. White star represents SOUTH CAROLINA, first state to secede from the Union.
SIZE: 3' x 5'

FIRST CONFEDERATE NATIONAL
Adopted March 4, 1861, this was the first flag of the Confederacy. Also called the "STARS AND BARS." Red and white bars with blue field and white stars.
SIZE: 3' x 5'

BATTLE FLAG
The second flag of the Confederacy, this flag was red with a blue St. Andrews Cross containing 13 white stars.
SIZE: 3' x 5'
REGULATION SIZE:
Cavalry: 32" x 32"
Artillery: 38" x 38"
Infantry: 51" x 51"

SECOND CONFEDERATE NATIONAL
Also called the "JACKSON FLAG," this was the third flag of the Confederacy and was adopted May 1, 1863 to replace the "stars and bars."
SIZE: 3' x 5'

THIRD CONFEDERATE NATIONAL
This was the fourth flag of the Confederacy, adopted March 4, 1865. A broad vertical red bar was added to the right hand edge of the "Second Confederate National" flag so that it could not be mistaken for a flag of truce.
SIZE: 3' x 5'

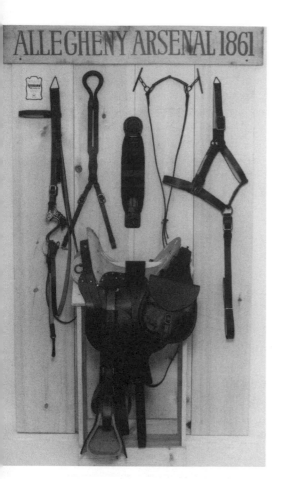

✾ U.S. CAVALRY EQUIPMENTS

Highly regarded for their workmanship and fealty to historic originals are the hand-stitched military saddlery and horse equipment offered by F. Burgess & Company. These are generally nineteenth-century items—saddles, girths, bridles, halters, spurs, scabbards, carbine boots and a great deal more—all replicated with devout attention to the accurate reproduction of period materials, techniques and industrial specifications.

Characteristic of the F. Burgess company's cavalry items is the "Allegheny Arsenal 1861," depicted. Consisting of the complete McClellan saddle, bridles (including a watering bridle), halter, hitching strap, saddlebags, surcingle, lariat and picket pin—the cavalry service horse equipments are precisely as manufactured by the U.S. Allegheny Arsenal at the outbreak of the Civil War. According to the Burgess company's literature, more than a dozen Allegheny saddles were compared and studied prior to undertaking the 1861 McClellan's replication and all sewing was done in the nineteenth-century manner—eight stitches to the inch, without aid of sewing machine. Even the blue woolen webbing used was woven to original specifications of a company in existence since before the Civil War. This assembly has been produced by the F. Burgess company for discriminating collectors in recognition of the special status accorded arsenal-produced equipments of this period.

Price: Allegheny Arsenal Horse Equipments, $2,900 per set.
Brochure of horse equipments and cavalry accouterments available, $3.

F. BURGESS & COMPANY
200 Pine Place
Red Bank, NJ 07701
Tel. 908/576-1624

✾ INDIAN WARS CAMPAIGN HATS, 1883—1900

Following the poorly received folding U.S. Army campaign hat of 1872, and the blue 1876 hat of the Little Big Horn, these drab-colored campaign hats were introduced the year that Buffalo Bill organized the first Wild West Show. They served through the closing of the frontier and well into the twentieth century.

Brochure of horse equipments and cavalry accouterments available, $3.

F. BURGESS & COMPANY
200 Pine Place
Red Bank, NJ 07701
Tel. 908/576-1624

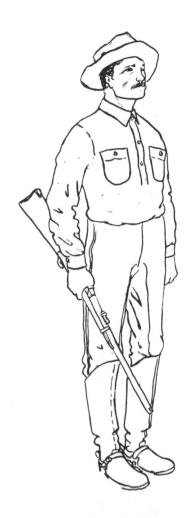

◫ 1883 ARMY CAMPAIGN SHIRT

Designated the "Model 1883 Army Overshirt," this blue wool garment was adopted as an alternative to the heavier five-button blouse that had seen earlier service on the frontier. A simple, practical and comfortable shirt, the Model 1883 found ready favor among the officers and enlisted men of all branches of the army.

The 1883 campaign shirt clad the backs of the cavalry and infantrymen who for many months guarded the waterholes and mountain passes in the Arizona and New Mexico Territories during the Geronimo Campaign of 1885-1886; it was standard issue to troops on the northern plains, and saw service during the last, cold campaign that devastated the already defeated Sioux near the Pine Ridge Agency at the end of 1890. Later, this shirt was used as the standard uniform blouse in Cuba during the Spanish-American War, and was worn by the Rough Riders. Before the Model 1883 was retired it also saw duty in the Philippines and at the Chinese Boxer Rebellion.

Red River's replica has been copied from existing original shirts and conforms to period army regulations. Its accuracy in style, detailing, buttons and material extends to its use of cotton ivory-glaze cloth and an inner yoke as per the originals. Made to your measurements.

Price: $130 (plus $5 for shipping and handling).

Catalog of frontier clothing, western and military Americana available, $3.

RED RIVER FRONTIER OUTFITTERS
P.O. Box 241
Tujunga, CA 91043

⇥ Civil War Accouterments ⇤

During the Civil War the term was the Gallic "accoutrements," meaning equipment other than weapons and clothing that was carried by a soldier. Here they are mentioned in Ambrose Bierce's late-nineteenth-century short story "An Affair of Outposts":

The Governor went forward alone and on foot. In a half-hour he had pushed through a tangled undergrowth covering a boggy soil and entered upon more firm and open ground. Here he found a half-company of infantry lounging behind a line of stacked rifles. The men wore their accoutrements—their belts, cartridge boxes, haversacks, and canteens. Some lying full length on the dry leaves were fast asleep; others in small groups gossiped idly of this and that; a few played at cards; none were far from the line of stacked arms. To the civilian's eye the scene was one of carelessness, confusion, indifference; a soldier would have observed expectancy and readiness.

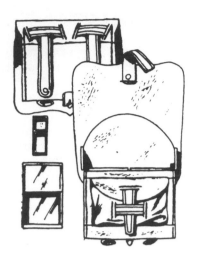

CARTRIDGE BOXES

These replica cartridge boxes, all made of oak-tanned leather and stitched with natural linen thread, extend back to the Revolutionary War. Each box uses interior tin liners and wooden cartridge blocks as per the original upon which they're based. Included are the militia-type cartridge box for flintlock musket (the "Lafayette"); the improved U.S. Model 1808; the U.S. Model 1841, designed for use with the Mississippi rifle; the British Enfield Infantry, circa 1853, which was imported for use during the Civil War; the U.S. Model 1855 .58-caliber box; and several purely Confederate cartridge boxes, including three types for muskets.

U.S. MODEL 1858 "SMOOTHSIDE" CANTEEN

The following appears as written in the C&D Jarnagin catalog:

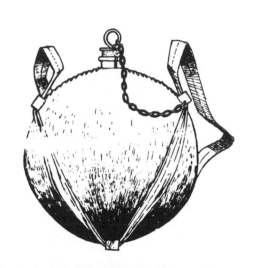

This is the first general-issue "modern-style" canteen of the U.S. Army. The first lot delivered—over 20,000—was covered with sky-blue wool. During the war years, covers were also issued in dark blue, various grays, and several shades of brown or tan.

The canteen consists of two dish-shaped sides, so formed that they seal together with a solder joint. On the top, a shaped shield mounts a pewter spout. Three strap carriers are soldered to the body. The whole is then covered by wool and a strap attached…of natural white military drill. This is three-quarters-of-an-inch wide, double-folded and sewn up on each side.

We offer the Model 1858 canteen in sky blue, dark blue, brown, and gray covers; each having an inspector's cartouche on the strap, as per the originals. This canteen was one of the most essential items of a Federal soldier's gear, and was also preferred by many Confederates when they could get them.

The Jarnagin company also offers the general-issue round-drum C.S. canteen, the oval-drum canteen, the U.S. "Bullseye" canteen, and many other nineteenth- (and eighteenth-) century types.

BELTS

Naturally, the Jarnagin company manufactures a full complement of replica nineteenth-century military belts. These include the U.S. Model 1839 Regulation waistbelt often used in the early part of the Civil War, the U.S. Model 1856 waistbelt, the most frequently encountered federal belt of the war, and the Confederate States Waistbelt, Selma Arsenal manufacture.

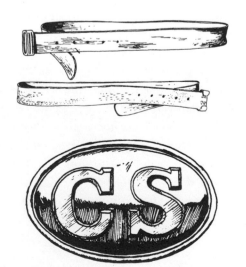

OVAL CONFEDERATE BELT PLATE

The Civil War waistbelt was fastened by a lead-filled belt plate of stamped brass, generally oval in shape and with its block lettering indicating either a "C.S." or "U.S." issue. This was the type most often found in all fields of conflict during the war.

The Jarnagin company also has available an oval U.S. belt plate and several box plates representing both sides.

FEDERAL REGULATION HAVERSACK, EARLY WAR

When in the field, each soldier would carry his rations in a haversack made of either canvas or leather. In theory these were waterproof affairs, but a downpour would usually render them as unprotective as any cloth bag. The effects that this would have both on the haversack's contents and on the bag itself (most were issued white) were often barely tolerable, even by a foot-soldier's standards. As one wrote: "By the time one of these haversacks had been in use for a few weeks as a receptacle for chunks of fat bacon and fresh meat, damp sugar tied up in a rag—perhaps a piece of an old shirt—potatoes and other vegetables that might be picked up along the route, it took on the color of a printing office towel."

The early-war haversack was first issued to U.S. soldiers during the 1850s and carried into the Civil War by the First Massachusetts Volunteer Infantry, among other regular troops. It is similar to, but smaller than the wartime version (also offered by the Jarnagin Company) and is made with special military drillcloth treated with black weatherproofing. The early-war haversack contains an inner bag fastened by three bone buttons; the outside strap closure is effected by means of a leather strap and buckle, which bear inspector's marks.

The Jarnagin Company also manufactures an early 1800s haversack known as the U.S. Regulation Mexican War and Later Militia type, and two eighteenth-century haversacks.

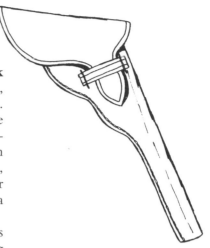

CONFEDERATE HOLSTER

"Be aware," cautions the Jarnagin catalog, "that very many Confederates wore their sidearms on the right side, butt to the rear." The firm's replica C.S. holster is finished in black or russet leather, has a strap-and-tab fastener, and no bottom plug. It is but one of a great variety of holsters that were employed by the Confederacy. Jarnagin's replica offers the most protection to the weapon. A black leather U.S. holster with a brass tab latch (after an original in the Jarnagin collection) is also available.

NONREGULATION SINGLE-BAG KNAPSACK

Civil War knapsacks were notoriously punishing to carry, but this was one of the more comfortable ones. Modeled after an original in the Jarnagin collection, it was one of three types most used by Confederate forces. The original is made of black weatherproofed drill, has leather strappage that has been sewn by hand with linen thread, and includes separate blanket straps. The large bag is divided by a wall of ticking. The Jarnagin replica is also available in untreated white drill "to illustrate the Southern lack of resources."

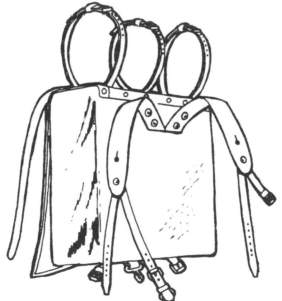

C&D Jarnagin also makes the U.S. regulation 1851 (hardpack, or Mexican War) knapsack; and the U.S. double-bag knapsacks, Types I, II and III. The Type III double-bag made up more than 90 percent of all the knapsacks used by Federal forces during the war.

OTHER MILITARY ACCOUTERMENTS

In addition to all the above, the C&D Jarnagin Company offers a similar range of replica nineteenth-century scabbards, frogs, cap pouches and slings.

Catalog and price list of nineteenth-century military uniforms and equipment available, $3.

C&D JARNAGIN COMPANY
P.O. Box 13529
Jackson, MS 39236
Tel. 601/287-4977
Fax. 601/287-6033

⊞ U.S. 1860 CAVALRY SABER

In 1860, a lighter military saber was introduced to replace the 1840 "Old Wristbreaker" model that had previously been used by the cavalry. The narrower bladed Light Model 1860 saw extensive service during the war.

Characterized as a "good representative modern copy," Dixie Gun Works's replica 1860 cavalry saber features a 35½-inch plated blade, with both hilt and guard made of polished brass. The wooden handle is covered with brown leather and wire-wrapped in the original fashion. The scabbard features an authentic trail drag and rings for attaching to a sword belt.

Catalog of black-powder guns, shooting supplies and antique gun parts available, $4.

DIXIE GUN WORKS, INC.
Gunpowder Lane
Union City, TN 38261
Tel. 901/885-0700 or
*   800/235-6875 to order*
Fax. 901/885-0440

⟿ Civil War Camp Items ⟻

❧ FEDERAL-ISSUE SHELTER TENT

Also known as the *tente d'abri,* pup, or dog tent, the shelter tent became available in early 1862 when 300,000 of them were issued to Federal forces. The shelter tent was the most common type of the war.

Troops gave them the "dog tent" name in derision, but in time their versatility—as sunshades, lean-tos, and ground cloths—made them favored gear.

The shelter tent was comprised of two pieces, usually of cotton drill, each carried by a single soldier. The first of these was 5 feet 2 inches by 4 feet 8 inches. The men would combine in threes and use the extra half to block up one end of the structure; or two men would use an overcoat or ground cloth for the same effect. In 1864 a larger tent was issued, complete with a triangular endpiece.

The Jarnagin company offers replicas of both the 1862 and 1864 model shelter tents. Each half is fully buttonholed on three sides and comes with stamped corner reinforcements on which brass grommets have been fixed.

C&D Jarnagin also replicates two wedge tents, old army standbys that saw service back before the Mexican War. These tents have end flaps covering a canvas cabin measuring either six or nine feet in length.

❋ 1851 ARMY CUP WITH BAIL HANDLE

No top, but possessing bail tabs this "original manufacture" cup follows one at the Museum of the Confederacy in Richmond. A field-modified version is available, along with a domed "billie cup," and a cup used throughout the period from the Indian Wars to the Great War.

❋ U.S. ARMY BLANKET, CIRCA 1861

Blankets were normally issued before soldiers left their home states, but early in the war an influx of volunteers and militia had exhausted supplies. In order to allow regular mills to run blankets, an emergency type was created.

These blankets were sent into the field in rolls and issued by cutting a length for each soldier. This left the blankets with frayed ends, as soldiers evidently wasted no time in separating their lengths into two halves. Raw ends, combined with the 1861 model's brown color (and darker end-stripes) distinguish what some assert were the most frequently used blankets of the Civil War.

LARGE COFFEEPOT

What John Jarnagin claims must by now be "the most famous coffeepot of the Civil War" was excavated at the site of the camp occupied by (U.S.) Gen. William S. Rosencrans's Army of the Cumberland prior to the Battle of Iuka. This boiler, which may have had something to do with the caffeinated quality of Rosencrans's September 1862 push to within two miles of the Mississippi town, became the model for Jarnagin's handmade replica. The top of the pot, the spout and handle are all wired; all parts are riveted and soldered with lead-free solder on the contact surfaces. 8½ inches wide by 9 inches high.

A smaller coffee pot, an eighteenth-century pot, a domed-lid camp pot, "mucket" (mug-bucket) and teapot are also available.

PLAYING CARDS

Bristol threw down a flyspecked ten,
"Theah," he said in the soft, sweet drawl
That could turn as hard as a Minie-ball,
"This heah day is my lucky day,
And Shepley nevah could play piquet,"
He stretched his arms in a giant yawn,
"Gentlemen, when are we movin' on?
I have no desire for a soldier's end,
While I still have winnin's that I can spend.
And they's certain appointments with certain ladies
Which I'd miss right smart if I went to Hades,
Especially one little black-eyed charmer
Whose virtue, one hopes, is her only armor,
So if Sargent Wingate's mended his saddle
I suggest that we all of us now skedaddle
To employ a term that the Yankees favor—"
—Stephen Vincent Benet, John Brown's Body, *1927*

Poker was the game in most regiments. Francis Lord's *Civil War Collector's Encyclopedia* notes that in the 150th Pennsylvania it was described after the war as the "absorbing occupation" of private soldiers and officers alike—the former "risking his scanty allowance as heedlessly as the latter their liberal stipend." Both sides also enjoyed playing cribbage and euchre.

The Jarnagin Company's Civil War playing cards have been "painstakingly reproduced" from an original deck. Their patriotic military motif is reminiscent of those made by the American Card Company, "the first and only genuine American cards ever produced," according to one contemporary advertisement. The replica cards employ the highest quality color-separation techniques, and have been shellacked by hand in the old way. Each deck has been boxed.

Catalog and price list of nineteenth-century military uniforms and equipment available, $3.

C&D JARNAGIN COMPANY
P.O. Box 13529
Jackson, MS 39236
Tel. 601/287-4977
Fax. 601/287-6033

CIVIL WAR WALLET

Although styles varied greatly, most wallets used during the Civil War were made of pliable brown leather and simply designed. Francis A. Lord's *Civil War Collector's Encyclopedia* notes that most were 4 to 4½ inches long and 2½ to 3 inches wide. Dixie Gun Works offers what it believes to be a highly representational replica of the Civil War Wallet, measuring 3 by 5¼ inches and including four inside pockets. Shipping weight: 1 lb.
Price: $11.95.

DEERSKIN GAUNTLETS

Part of the Civil War officer's dress uniform included gauntlets, many of which were elaborately embroidered. Due in part to their utilitarian value, the popularity of these gauntlets continued on after the war, well into the late 1800s.

Dixie Gun Works of Union City, Tennessee, offers deerskin gauntlets very similar to those worn during the Civil War. These are large-cuffed and tight-fitting, but are extremely soft and flexible. Machine stitched.
Price per pair: $59.95.

Price: Five packages of 16 bills each, $1. Catalog of black-powder guns, shooting supplies and antique gun parts available, $4.

DIXIE GUN WORKS
Gunpowder Lane
Union City, TN 38261
Tel. 901/885-0700 or
*   800/238-6785 to order*
Fax. 901/885-0440

❄ CONFEDERATE MONEY

"In the North a carpenter got three dollars," said Mark Twain's Connecticut Yankee, "in the South he got fifty—payable in Confederate shinplasters worth a dollar a bushel." Actually, in 1863 you could exchange a U.S. gold dollar for four Confederate bills (with the exception of four half-dollars struck in New Orleans just before that city's fall, the Confederacy never minted any coins), and even a loathsome Yankee greenback brought $2.50 in rebel "shinplasters," so named because a soldier once used a fistful to cover a tibia wound.

Dixie Gun Works describes its Confederate bills as "reasonable facsimiles." They are sold in $1, $5, $10, $50 and $100 denominations at a Reconstruction price.

Price: Five packages of 16 bills each, $1. Catalog of black-powder guns, shooting supplies and antique gun parts available, $4.

DIXIE GUN WORKS
Gunpowder Lane
Union City, TN 38261
Tel. 901/885-0700 or
*   800/238-6785 to order*
Fax. 901/885-0440

⊰ Pistols and Revolvers ⊱

Val Forgett founded the Navy Arms Company back in 1958 after his experience with the North-South Skirmish Association (an early Civil War reenactment group) triggered in him an awareness of the need for authentically replicated historic firearms. All of Navy Arms' guns are shooting pieces, far safer than their "guess and by God" antecedents.

The word "navy" had been used to identify U.S. military firearms for nearly two centuries before the Navy Company got started. The earliest citation appears in a 1777 description of battle by an officer in the Continental Navy, and later the word most often referred to the .36-caliber 1851 Colt revolver described in the section on "Late Frontier Items" (page 166).

⊞ "REB" MODEL 1860 REVOLVER
(.36 OR .44 CALIBER)

At the beginning of the Civil War, the largely agricultural South faced difficulties in procuring arms for the fight. Other than the old flintlock and percussion rifle muskets that volunteers could bring into battle from home, before the Confederacy developed sufficient importation of arms (mainly from England) it had to rely on captured weapons and the product of its smattering of arms manufacturers. The most consequential of these was the firm of Griswold and Gunnison, of Griswold, Georgia. Under contract to the C.S.A. from 1862 to 1864, the company produced the Model 1860 percussion revolver.

Navy Arms' replica features a brass frame and backstrap with a steel barrel and cylinder.

Dimensions: overall length, 13 inches; barrel length, 7½ inches. Weight: 2 lbs. 12 oz.

Prices: Finished .36-caliber piece, $100; finished .44-caliber piece, $100.

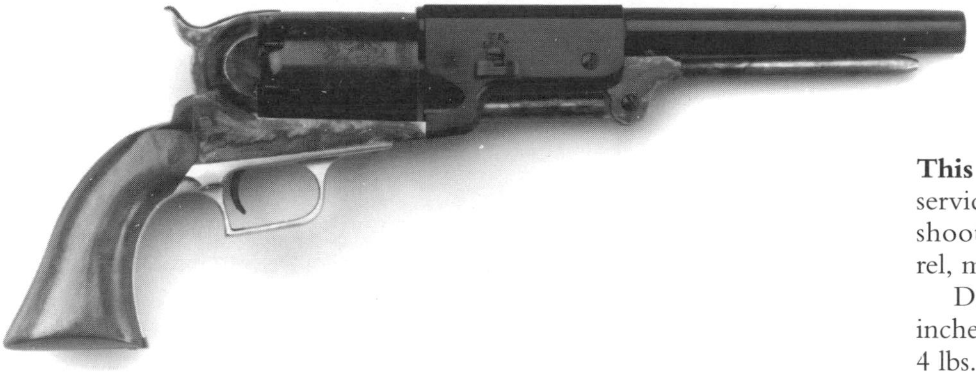

1847 COLT-WALKER REVOLVER (.44 CALIBER)

This famous magnum saw extensive service in the Mexican War. It's a six-shooter, with a precision-rifled barrel, marked "U.S. 1847."

Dimensions: Overall length, 16 inches; barrel length, 9 inches. Weight: 4 lbs. 11 oz.

Price: Finished piece, $250.

LE MAT REVOLVERS (.44 CALIBER)

This Parisian-made firearm, invented by a French seafarer and perfected with the help of General Beauregard, ran the Union blockade to become the favorite gun of J.E.B. Stuart and many other rebel navy and infantry officers. Its lower (approximately .65 caliber) barrel was designed to fire shot.

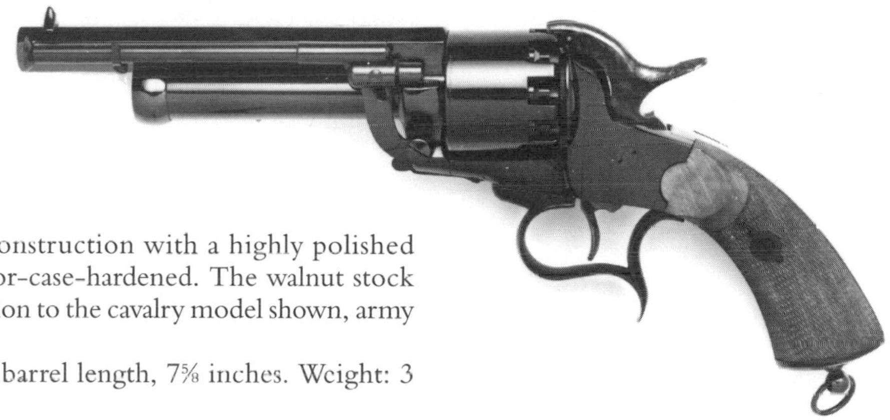

The Navy Arms Le Mat has all-steel construction with a highly polished blue finish. Its hammer and trigger are color-case-hardened. The walnut stock is hand-checkered with an oil finish. In addition to the cavalry model shown, army and navy models are also available.

Dimensions: Overall length, 14 inches; barrel length, 7⅝ inches. Weight: 3 lbs. 7 oz.

Price: Finished piece, $595.

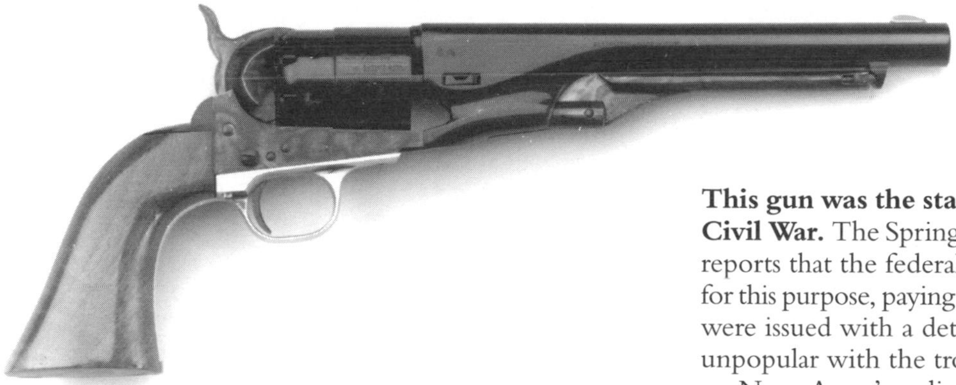

1860 ARMY REVOLVER (.44 CALIBER)

This gun was the standard U.S. firearm used during the Civil War. The Springfield Armory Museum in Massachusetts reports that the federal government bought 129,730 of them for this purpose, paying $17.69 each. Some 1860 Army revolvers were issued with a detachable shoulder stock, but these were unpopular with the troops and promptly "lost."

Navy Arms' replica has a blued barrel and roll-engraved cylinder, a brass trigger guard, steel backstrap and case-hardened frame.

Dimensions: Overall length, 13½ inches; barrel length, 8 inches. Weight: 2 lbs. 9 oz.

Price: Finished piece, $150.

SPILLER & BURR REVOLVER (.36 CALIBER)

This percussion revolver was originally produced for the Confederacy by Spiller & Burr of Atlanta between 1862 and 1864. After the company proved unable to comply with an order for 15,000 pieces, the Confederate government purchased it and moved it to the Macon Armory.

Navy Arms' replica comes with a brass frame, trigger guard, backstrap and top strap. It has an octagonal blued barrel and cylinder.

Dimensions: Overall length, 12½ inches; barrel length, 7 inches. Weight: 2 lbs. 8 oz.

Price: Finished piece, $125. When ordering from Navy Arms, include $4 to cover shipping, handling and insurance.

Catalog of replica firearms and accessories available, $2.

NAVY ARMS COMPANY
689 Bergen Boulevard
Ridgefield, NJ 07657
Tel. 201/945-2500

1858 REMINGTON ARMY

This is the gun that Colt's closest competitor, the firm of E. Remington & Sons, placed on the market following the expiration of Sam Colt's patent on muzzle-loading revolvers. Despite the difficulty of cleaning it, the 1858 Army's sturdy construction and precision aim made it a favorite among Civil War troops. In fact, after Appomattox, when the U.S. government offered to sell each of its soldiers the weapon they had been issued, the Remingtons were most often selected.

Cimarron Firearms' replica 1858 Remington is a six-shot muzzle-loader with a blued-steel frame and brass trigger guard. It has a two-piece walnut grip and a tapered octagonal barrel.

Dimensions: overall length, 13¾ inches; barrel length, 7½ inches. Weight: 2.65 lbs.

Price: $199.95, plus shipping.

TEXAS CONFEDERATE DRAGOON (.44 CALIBER)

In 1862, the Confederate State of Texas commissioned Tucker, Sherrard & Company of Lancaster, Texas, to make 3,000 revolvers in lots of a .44 caliber (navy). Cimarron Firearms's Texas Dragoon model replicates the characteristics of the original faithfully, right down to their cylinder engravings.

Dimensions: overall length, 13½ inches; barrel length, 7½ inches. Weight: 3.97 lbs.

Catalog of firearms and accessories available.

CIMARRON FIREARMS COMPANY
1106 Wisterwood
Houston, TX 77043
Tel. 713/468-2007

Rifles

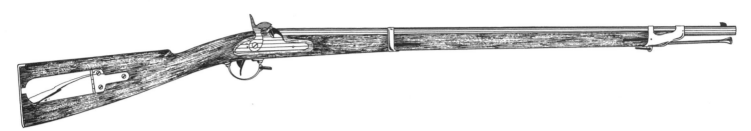

❊ 1841 MISSISSIPPI RIFLE

The old Mississippi Rifle, carrying a half-ounce ball, is a favorite with them.
—Rodney Glisan, *Journal of Army Life*, 1874

This .58-caliber percussion-lock weapon gained its name during the 1846 Mexican War after Jefferson Davis's Mississippi Regiment used it to turn back Santa Anna at the decisive battle of Buena Vista. Although the rifle was obsolete by 1855, its reputation caused the Colt Company to rebuild it to accommodate the Union Army's .58-caliber mini-ball in 1861.

Dixie Gun Works' replica Mississippi rifle is trimmed with solid brass furniture and has a case-hardened percussion lock with an eagle emblazoned above its "U.S." stamping. The stock is made of walnut-stained beech wood.

Dimensions: overall length, 49½ inches; barrel length 33½ inches.
Price: Dixie catalog #PR0401, $430.

⚙ 1853 ENFIELD RIFLED MUSKET

The .58 caliber Enfield Model 1853 **was made chiefly at the London Armoury Company in Enfield, England,** and was considered to be one of the best of the foreign arms to see service during the Civil War.

Similar to the Springfield Rifle (the machine tools at the Enfield armory were direct copies of those at the U.S. armory at Springfield, Massachusetts),

the Enfield was admired in one contemporary account as "a beautiful arm [that] presented a natty appearance." Enfields were purchased in large amounts by both the U.S. and C.S. governments.

The Dixie Gun Works replica is produced by Parker-Hale, a company recognized for its exacting standards. The Enfield has a walnut stock with a brass buttplate, triggerguard, nosecap and sidelock escutcheons. There is an authentically graduated leaf rear sight and case-hardened lockplate and hammer, forward of which are the mark-

ings "1853 Enfield."

Barrel length, 39 inches; shipping weight, 15 lbs.

Price: $615, plus postage and handling.

Catalog of black-powder guns, shooting supplies and antique gun parts available, $4.

DIXIE GUN WORKS
Union City, TN 38261
Tel. 901/885-0700 or
*   800/238-6785 to order*
Fax. 901/885-0440

1863 SPRINGFIELD RIFLE

America's "most historical firearm" was the .58-caliber muzzle-loading Springfield percussion rifle, brought into the Civil War for its ability to stabilize the dreaded mini-ball. As described in the *Civil War Collector's Encyclopedia*, the 1863 Springfield was a variation of the 1861 model (a.k.a. the U.S. Rifle-Musket) that was so advanced for its time as to cause one of the 52nd Massachusetts Volunteers to write home in a torrent of admiration:

Our guns were issued to us the other day, beautiful pieces; of the most improved pattern—the Springfield rifled musket.... Mine is behind me now, dark black—walnut stock, well oiled, so that the beauty of the wood is brought out, hollowed at the base, and smoothly fitted with steel, to correspond exactly to the curve of the shoulder, against which I shall have to press it many a time. The spring of the lock, just stiff and just limber enough; the eagle and stamp of the government pressed into the steel plate; barrel, long and glistening— bound into its bed by gleaming rings— long and straight and so bright that when I present arms, and bring it before my face, I can see the nose and spectacles and the heavy beard on lip and chin...

Navy Arms claims to have carefully replicated the 1863 Springfield rifle down to its most minute detail. Their piece is a full-size three-band musket with a precision-rifled barrel that is identical to the original.

Dimensions: Overall length, 56 inches; barrel length, 40 inches. Weight: 9½ lbs.

Price: Finished piece, $550 (plus $6 for shipping, handling and insurance).

Color catalog of replica arms and accessories available, $2.

NAVY ARMS COMPANY
689 Bergen Boulevard
Ridgefield, NJ 07657
Tel. 201/945-2500

MINI-BALLS AND MOLD

The mini-ball was the 1848 invention of Capt. Claude Minie of the army of France. It was a bullet that revolutionized nineteenth-century warfare.

Cast as a projectile, the true mini-ball was hollowed at the base for about one-third of its length. When the gun was fired, this configuration allowed the explosive gases to force the lead into the barrel's riflings with increased velocity, giving the bullet greater smashing power. The U.S. Army adopted the mini-ball in 1855, and it was used extensively in the .58-caliber rifle muskets.

Prices: .58-caliber mini-balls, twenty for $5.50; mini-ball mold, $50 (plus $2 each for shipping and handling).

Catalog of replica firearms and accessories available.

NAVY ARMS COMPANY
689 Bergen Boulevard
Ridgefield, NJ 07657
Tel. 201/945-2500

ARTILLERY

Functioning full-scale gun barrels, solid-cast and drilled in accordance with eighteenth- and nineteenth-century principles of gunmaking, are available from Indiana's South Bend Replicas. After drilling, the ordnance are fitted with breeched steel sleeves and—except in instances where lathe-turning best conforms to the demands of historical accuracy—meticulously ground by hand. Stock artillery ranges in price from $297 for a 1792 King howitzer to $8,861 for the 24-pound siege howitzer shown here. This gun is a replica of one of 40 that unsuccessfully defended Fort Pulaski, Georgia, in "the first combat of rifled guns and masonry forts" on April 11, 1862.

Catalog of replica miniature to full-scale artillery available, $7.

SOUTH BEND REPLICAS, INC.
61650 Oak Road
South Bend, IN 46614
Tel. 219/289-4500

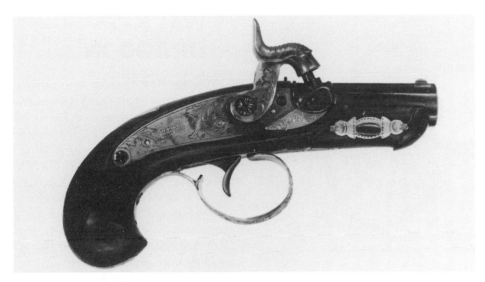

BOOTH'S DERRINGER

During the April 14, 1865, performance of *Our American Cousin* at Ford's Theatre, young Julia Shephard sat in the audience excitedly writing a note to her father back home:

The President is in yonder upper right hand private box so handsomely decked with silken flags festooned over a picture of George Washington. The young and lovely daughter of Senator Harris is the only one of the party we can see, as flags hide the rest. But we know 'Father Abraham' is there, like a father watching what interests his children....How sociable it seems, like one family sitting around their parlor fire....The American Cousin has just been making love to a young lady who says she will never marry but for love, yet when her mother and herself find he has lost his property they retreat in disgust at the left of the stage, while the American Cousin goes out at the right. We are waiting for the next scene.

The next scene would be the final one in a chapter of American history: the crack of the assassin's pistol and his leap onto the stage. Many recognized the actor John Wilkes Booth, and until they learned of the President's mortal wound, believed his dramatics to be a new part of the play. Lincoln was carried across the street to the Petersen House, where he died the next morning.

Dixie Gun Works offers a replica of the .41-caliber pistol wielded by Booth at Ford's Theatre that they call the "Lincoln Derringer." As described in their catalog, the gun has a "two-inch browned barrel...and will shoot a .400 patched ball. Top barrel flat and lock is marked 'Deringer Philadela.'...German silver furniture includes triggerguard with pineapple finial, wedge plates, nose inlay, wrist inlay, side inlay and tear-drop inlay on the birdhead grip. Walnut-stained wood with a checkered grip. Brass front sight with rear sight positioned on the tang of the breechplug. Case-hardened lock, hammer and trigger....An excellent high-quality reproduction....Made in Italy."

Prices: Lincoln Derringer, finished $285; kit, $89.95.

Catalog of black-powder guns, shooting supplies and antique gun parts available, $4.

DIXIE GUN WORKS
Gunpowder Lane
Union City, TN 38261
Tel. 901/885-0700, or 800/238-6785 to order
Fax. 901/885-0440

ORDNANCE RIFLE BARREL

Here is a three-quarter-scale replica of the Federal gun that opposed the 24-pound howitzer at Fort Pulaski. It is said to have revolutionized siege warfare when 10 such rifled guns (and 26 smoothbores) enabled Gen. Quincy Adams Gillmore to breach the 7½-foot-thick brick walls at the fort defending Savannah. The siege lasted only 24 hours, and Gillmore's batteries fired from a point one mile from their target. The 3-inch rifled guns were manufactured in large quantities and were considered among the most important weapons of the war.

Dixie Gun Works's ordnance rifle barrel has an overall length of 55⅛ inches and a smooth bore of 2⁵⁄₁₆ inches. Weight: 340 lbs.

A 2⁵⁄₁₆-inch smoothbore carriage-mounted replica Civil War field cannon and a replica 1836 mountain howitzer barrel are also available.

Catalog of gun supplies available, $4.

DIXIE GUN WORKS
Gunpowder Lane
Union City, TN 38261

1861 PATTERN PISTOL HOLSTER

This is a hand-stitched replica of the holster used by the Federal cavalry troopers throughout the War Between the States. It is made of vegetable-tanned leather and waxed linen thread, per the original. An 1881 pattern pistol holster is also available.

Price: $48 each.

Photo illustrated catalog of period horse equipments and cavalry accouterments, $3.

F. BURGESS & CO.
200 Pine Place
Red Bank, NJ 07701
Tel. 908/576-1624

GATLING GUN

From the windows of the *New York Tribune*, two machine guns faced the mobs storming through the streets below. Publisher Horace Greeley had received the Gatlings as a promotion, and while the New York Draft Riots raged, he used them to discourage any rabble advancing in his direction.

Improving on the technology provided by the 1852 Ager Union gun and the 1856 Barnes Machine Cannon, Dr. Richard Jordan Gatling patented his "revolving gun battery" in November 1862. Like the discredited Ager, the Gatling used .58 caliber charges fired by a crank-operated action. But unlike the Union gun (which was also known as the "Ager Coffee Mill"), the Gatling's six rotating barrels had time to cool during firing, enabling the gun to discharge faster and for a greater time.

As stated in a letter to President Lincoln, Gatling believed that use of his rapid-fire gun was "just the thing needed to aid in crushing the present rebellion"; but all efforts to sell the U.S. Army on his repeater met with bureaucratic stonewalling. This may have been because the doctor originally hailed from North Carolina, a circumstance that created some suspicion about his loyalties. Gatling persisted, however, and by the spring of 1863 induced Gen. Benjamin F. Butler to observe a demonstration in Baltimore. Highly impressed, "Spoons" Butler (characterized as stealing the silver during his occupation of New Orleans, Butler was also known as "Beast Butler" there) plunked down a grand of his own money for each of 12 Gatlings, and is said by historian Frederick Myatt to have directed their use during the siege of Petersburg, Virginia.

The U.S. Army's untimely adoption of the Gatling gun took place in 1866, a year following Lee's surrender. But for generations thereafter, the weapon was used in every major conflict (including the Franco-Prussian and Spanish-American Wars) throughout the world.

George Shimek, a "forge and anvil" blacksmith out of Waterloo, Iowa, became interested in the Gatling gun after he saw a replica of one at a 1982 Civil War battle reenactment in East Davenport. Using copies of the original drawings submitted by Gatling for his patent, Shimek began building his replica in January 1983. It took about 250 hours for him to complete the piece. Mr. Shimek's .50-caliber Gatling is a scaled-down replica of the 1862 model. It will fire 200 rounds per minute, and according to Shimek, is highly accurate.

Dimensions: Overall length, 38 inches; barrel length, 22 inches. Weight (without carriage): 135 lbs.

Price: $10,000; complete mechanical blueprints, $25.

CUSTOM BLACKSMITHING AND MANUFACTURING
827 Commercial
Waterloo, IA 50702
Tel. 319/291-2095

WALKER-DRAGOON FLASK

During the 1830s and 1840s the powder flask gradually replaced the horn, although there are accounts of some rural Confederates' using the latter in the early days of the Civil War. The Log Cabin Shop's powder flask is a replica of one originally used to charge such large muzzle-loading revolvers as the famous Colt-Walker or the Dragoon. This flask features an adjustable charger head that automatically throws a correctly measured charge.

Dimensions: 8½ inches high. Weight: 9 oz. Price: $32.95.

Catalog of black-powder supplies and accessories available, $4.

THE LOG CABIN SHOP
P.O. Box 275
Lodi, OH 44254
Tel. 216/948-1082

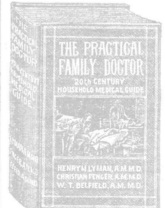

WASHINGTON IRVING FACSIMILE LIBRARY

Hailed by William Makepeace Thackeray as "the first ambassador whom the New World of Letters sent to the Old," Washington Irving (1783-1859) was indeed the first American writer to attain recognition abroad for his literary works. Historic Hudson Valley (which owns and maintains several historic sites in the lower Hudson Valley, including Sunnyside, Irving's Tarrytown, New York, home) has reprinted a series of Irving's nineteenth-century editions, first published by G.P. Putnam. "Faithful to the original editions as contemporary book manufacturing and materials will allow," Sleepy Hollow Press has made a great effort to match the original volumes in both quality and authenticity.

DIEDRICH KNICKERBOCKER'S A HISTORY OF NEW YORK

Diedrich Knickerbocker *I have worn to death in my pocket.*
—*Charles Dickens*

Although Washington Irving had a close friend named Herman Knickerbocker, he stoutly maintained that he fashioned the name of his book's hero from the Dutch words *knicker,* to nod, and *boeken,* a book. The doughty Knickerbocker, then, was one who dozes over books.

This satirical depiction of the period when the Dutch ruled New York was America's first humorous book and signaled a coming of age for American letters. That the English loved the book is hardly surprising, and Sir Walter Scott's report that "our sides were absolutely sore with laughing [at the story]" was not echoed by anyone in Holland's aristocracy. This book is a facsimile of G.P. Putnam's 1854 illustrated edition, 496 pages, with 16 illustrations by F.O.C. Darley. Introduction by the noted Irving scholar Andrew B. Myers.

Price: Clothbound, $23.95.

THE ALHAMBRA

Irving served as a U.S. diplomat in Spain between 1826 and 1829, and remains a popular and often-read figure there. This is in some measure due to the warmth and brilliance of his portrayal of Moorish Spain in *The Alhambra* (1832), which according to a contemporary review in the Richmond (Virginia) *News Leader* "retells the legends of the area with all the grace of the tales of Scheherazade." Sleepy Hollow's facsimile edition replicates G.P. Putnam's 1851 book, with text from the Author's Revised Edition of 1848. 464 pages with 15 illustrations by F.O.C. Darley. Introduction by Andrew B. Myers.

Price: Clothbound, $23.95.

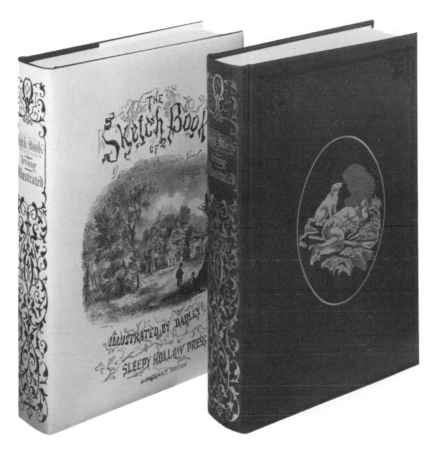

✻THE SKETCH BOOK

Every reader has his first book: I mean to say, one book among all the others which in early youth first fascinates his imagination, and at once excites and satisfies the desires of his mind. To me, this first book was The Sketch Book *of Washington Irving.*
—Henry Wadsworth Longfellow

The Sketch Book was originally published in seven parts during 1819 and 1820. Containing such universally beloved stories as "Rip Van Winkle" and "The Legend of Sleepy Hollow," the book is pervaded by Irving's clear, colorful and humorous American style. Sleepy Hollow's facsimile of the 1852 G.P. Putnam edition takes its text from the 520-page Author's Revised Edition of 1848 and includes 22 original illustrations by F.O.C. Darley.

Price: Clothbound, $23.95; leatherbound, $47.50.

✽BRACEBRIDGE HALL

Like *The Sketch Book,* which it followed, *Bracebridge Hall* also emphasized English settings, but was Irving's least successful book. This is a facsimile of a first edition published by the MacMillan Company in 1876. It numbers 320 pages containing 118 illustrations by Randolph Caldecott. Introduction by Andrew B. Myers.

Price: Clothbound, $12.

Books in the Washington Irving Facsimile Library may be ordered directly from the publisher if accompanied by a check or money order. Postage and handling require $1.25 for the first book in each order, plus 25 cents for each additional copy. Retail discount schedule available.

HISTORIC HUDSON VALLEY
150 White Plains Road
Tarrytown, NY 10591
Tel. 914/631-8200

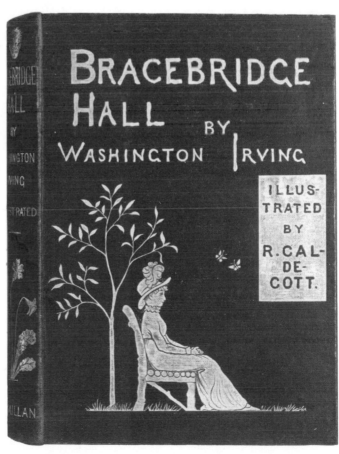

⌁ Books on Lighting and Architecture ⌁

❧ VICTORIAN LIGHTING: THE DIETZ CATALOGUE OF 1860

The complete 1840-1860 catalog of the R.E. Dietz Company of Syracuse, New York, America's leading manufacturer of Victorian kerosene lamps. Ulysses G. Dietz, a descendant of the company's founder and now curator of decorative arts at the Newark Museum, discovered the sole remaining original from which this facsimile has been taken. 128 pages, 41 plates (six of which are in color), with a new history of "Dietz and Victorian Lighting" by Ulysses G. Dietz. Published in 1982.

    Price: $40 (plus $2 for shipping).

❦ PHOTOGRAPHIC VIEWS OF SHERMAN'S CAMPAIGN

A reprinting of a landmark 1866 volume containing 61 plates of his campaign, many by Matthew Brady. 80 pages.

    Price: $6.95 (plus $2 for shipping).

❂ THE AMERICAN BUILDER'S COMPANION
BY ASHER BENJAMIN

First published in 1827, this book was widely used as an architectural style book covering the Colonial through the Greek Revival periods. Seventy plates show construction details, floor plans and elevations. 114 pages.

    Price: $8.95 (plus $2 for shipping).

❂ THE OCTAGON HOUSE
BY O.S. FOWLER

This reprint of an 1853 edition focuses on the curious octagon house, many examples of which can still be found in Connecticut and other areas. Construction plans include such innovations for the time as central heating and an indoor water closet. 192 pages.

    Price: $5.95 (plus $2 for shipping).

Catalog of "Items for the 19th-Century Impression," $2.

AMAZON VINEGAR & PICKLING WORKS DRYGOODS, LTD.
Dept. AH, 2218 East 11th Street
Davenport, IA 52803
Tel. 319/322-6800 or
*   800/798-7979 to order*
Fax. 309/312-4003

McGUFFEY'S READERS

The Author has long been of the opinion that a mischievous error pervades the public mind, on the subject of juvenile understanding. Nothing is so difficult as "nonsense." Nothing so clear and easy to comprehend as the simplicity of wisdom.

So wrote William Holmes McGuffey in the preface to one of his early *Eclectic Readers,* the schoolbooks first published in 1836 that would dominate classroom education for the following three-quarters of a century. Widely regarded as a monument in American education, more than 122 million copies of the *Readers* were to be published prior to their decline in the 1920s. South of the Mason-Dixon line, their popularity was exceeded only by that of the Bible.

In terms of marketing the books, all of the simple wisdom involved was comprehended by McGuffey's nineteenth-century publishers, who paid the author no more than $1,000 for his work and craftily billed him on the title pages as a "late professor at the University of Oxford." If the reader surmised that the Oxford referred to was England's great gothic academy and not *Ohio's,* so much the better.

Except for his leather bullwhip, McGuffey himself was every inch the didact. The whip—a red one—was used by McGuffey to keep at bay the mud-slinging schoolboys (in winter, they used snowballs) that he somehow attracted wherever he lived. It was as if the boys could calculate the number of hours of study that 122 million textbooks would in time bring upon their class. But the *Readers* were extremely well suited to the requirements of nineteenth-century study. Beginning with a primer and going on through six volumes of increasing difficulty, schoolhouse students not segregated by grade could advance each at his own pace.

The *McGuffey's Readers* never shrank from lessons in morality, except where certain contemporary nineteenth-century controversies were involved. The books stoutly advocated temperance, but carefully sidestepped such other political issues of their time as slavery, secession and trade unionism. Similarly, although the *Readers* included selections from the works of the highest order of poets and writers (Shakespeare, Dickens, Hawthorne and Wordsworth are all represented), they also much preferred the hale verse of Longfellow and Holmes to Poe's fevered images or Emerson's abolitionism.

Yet these criticisms are made negligible by the *McGuffey's Readers'* effective value. They may not be *Catcher in the Rye,* as a Van Nostrand Reinhold spokesman said, but a leisurely perusal of the books soon has one marveling at their richness and gently graduated complexity. What's more, their moral and religious philosophy seems more quaint than overbearing, and the values taught—honesty, industry, courage, charity and politeness—are all old American ones sorely in need of restoration.

And this brings me to a modern matter known in some circles as the "McGuffey's Phenomenon." Although the *Readers* have not been out of print since they were first introduced, recent sales of the books have climbed from 10,000 in 1975 to a 1982 figure ten times that! Several school districts have

returned to using the books as a part of their recommended curriculum, winning the approval of parents, teachers and students in each case.

The Van Nostrand Reinhold Company of New York began publishing their current series of *McGuffey's Readers* after one of their authors discovered the original copper plates of the 1879 editions while doing some research in the (now-defunct) American Book Company's printing plant in Cincinnati. These were then used to prepare the facsimile editions that Van Nostrand Reinhold has been selling since 1969, seven to the set. The publisher claims these facsimile editions to be authentic down to the point of forsaking a new introduction. Furthermore, the binding used is "as closely matched to the original as modern bookbinding permits."

Price: Complete set, $47.95, ppd.

VAN NOSTRAND REINHOLD CO., INC.
VNR Order Processing
P.O. Box 668
Florence, KY 41022-0668
Tel. 800/926-2665
Fax. 606/525-7778

WESTERN LITERATURE FROM BENNETT-WALLS

Bennett-Walls is a mail-order concern offering books about Texas and the American West. The following are a couple of their facsimile editions:

The Best-Selling Handbook for America's Pioneers

THE PRAIRIE TRAVELER

RANDOLPH B. MARCY
Captain, U.S. Army

INCLUDES
Routes · First Aid
Recommended Clothing, Shelter, Provisions
Wagon Maintenance and the Selection and Care of Horses
Information Concerning the Habits of Indians

◪ THE PRAIRIE TRAVELER
BY CAPT. RANDOLPH B. MARCY

Published in 1859 at the behest of the War Department as a guide for western emigrants, this book became their principal manual. Its detailed information on recommended routes, clothing, shelter, provisions, wagon maintenance and "the sagacity of the Indians" is illustrated by more than 25 woodcuts.

Price: $10.95, plus 6¼ percent sales tax within the state of Texas.

THE GRIZZLY.

THE SIBLEY TENT.

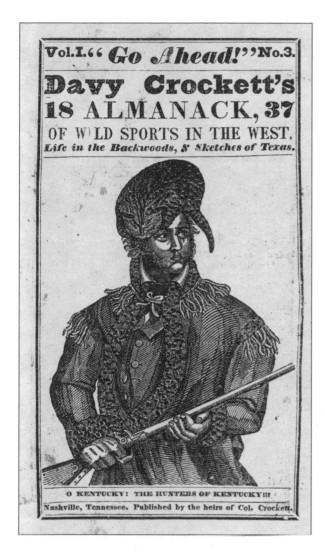

Method of Catching Wild Horses on the Prairies of Texas.

An Unexpected and Lucky Elk Hunt.

DAVY CROCKETT'S 1837 ALMANACK OF WILD SPORTS IN THE WEST

The Crockett "Almanacks" were nineteenth-century pamphlets of broad appeal. Published in the name of Davy Crockett—the backwoodsman, soldier and Congressman who died a martyr in the 1836 fight for Texas independence—the pamphlets interspersed the information typically found in almanacs of this era with accounts of Crockett's "man-alligator" feats wrestling bear, men and alligators. Between 1835 (Crockett had become a legend within his own lifetime) and 1856, some 50 Crockett almanacs poured out of Nashville, New York, Boston, Philadelphia and elsewhere by the tens of thousands. Although the nineteenth-century appetite for them seemed inexhaustible, by the twentieth their pulpy medium had made them rare and costly collector's items.

Reproduced from an original in the Henry E. Huntington Library in San Marino, California, this facsimile edition almanac typically depicts the life of Crockett complete with tall tales, told mostly in dialect. It also recounts much straightforward Crockett lore, such as in the "Method of Catching Wild Horses on the Prairie in Texas" and "Useful Hints to Persons Lost." The book's 48 pages include more than a dozen primitive woodcuts and a glowing account of the hero's fall at the Alamo.

Price: $3, plus 6¼ percent sales tax within the state of Texas. A $2 shipping charge accompanies all orders.

Book catalog available.

BENNETT-WALLS
P.O. Drawer 1
Rotan, TX 79546
Tel. 800/624-1739

🔲 ALICE'S ADVENTURES IN WONDERLAND

What is the use of a book without pictures?
—Alice, in Wonderland

It's likely that those were also Lewis Carroll's sentiments when he chose artist John Tenniel to illustrate his 1865 novel about the Victorian waif with the pluck to stand up to blood-thirsty queens and talking caterpillars. Tenniel was one of the most accomplished illustrators of his day, and Carroll worked in close collaboration with him for more than a year and a half to ensure that each of the 42 drawings that were to be published was faithful to his idea of Alice. Carroll then hired the Brothers Daziel, the era's best wood engravers, to carve the blocks that the printer would copy with metal electroplates.

For more than 125 years, those plates of *Alice's Adventures in Wonderland* were used to produce unending editions, their images losing detail as the plates wore down with use. Like so many frog footmen slowly set to the boil, generations of Alice's readers were unaware of how far away she had actually gone, receding bit by bit into a wonderland of crosshatching.

But in 1985 the original wooden blocks were found in a London bank vault. That discovery led to the publication of this beautiful new edition by William Morrow—the first with prints taken directly from the blocks.

Price: $15.

At bookstores, or through:

WILLIAM MORROW & COMPANY, PUBLISHERS
1350 Avenue of the Americas
New York, NY 10019
Tel. 212/261-6500

❋ MERRIMACK PUBLISHING COMPANY

Merrimack Publishing is the imprint of the B. Shackman Company, a firm that has been in business on Manhattan's lower Fifth Avenue since 1898. Merrimack specializes in the replication of nineteenth-century printed paper products including postcards, valentines and children's books. They are exclusively wholesalers but will be pleased to provide the name of a nearby retailer to those readers interested in purchasing their Victorian children's book facsimile editions. Included among these are: *Kate Greenaway's Tiny A-B-C Book, Kate Greenaway's Book of Games, Old Fashioned Red Riding Hood, Little Snow White, Animal Frolics, Hansel & Gretel, The Three Bears, Railroad A-B-C, Frog Frolics, Jumbo Dolly at the Seaside, The World's Great Circus, Story of the Firemen, What Next?, Peter Rabbit's Birthday* and *Peter Rabbit's Easter.*

Wholesale catalog available.

MERRIMACK PUBLISHING COMPANY
85 Fifth Avenue at 16th Street
New York, NY 10003
Tel. 212/989-5162

✳ "POP-UP" AND "DISSOLVING VIEW" BOOKS

Toward the end of the nineteenth century, "pop-up" and "dissolving-view" books achieved enormous popularity on both sides of the Atlantic. The dissolving-view, or revolving-picture, books incorporated scenes that a child could "magically" change by rotating a ribboned tab. The movable books manufactured between 1891 and 1900 by Ernest Nister are considered the finest of the genre.

Philomel Books has replicated a series of three of these books: *Magic Windows* (originally published as *In Wonderland*, 1895), *Land of Sweet Surprises* and *Merry Magic Go-Round* (both 1897). In addition Philomel has republished the pop-up book *The Little Actor's Theater*, originally published in Germany in 1883.

Prices: *Magic Windows, Land of Sweet Surprises* and *Merry Magic Go-Round*, $8.95 each; *The Little Actor's Theater*, $10.95.

PHILOMEL BOOKS
The Putnam Publishing Company
200 Madison Avenue
New York, NY 10016
Tel. 212/951-8400 or
800/631-8571 to order

▥ N.C. WYETH ILLUSTRATED EDITIONS

Facsimile editions of children's classics illustrated by N.C. Wyeth are available from Charles Scribner's Sons Books. These reprints of books originally published during the eighteenth, nineteenth and early-twentieth centuries include *The Black Arrow* and *Kidnapped* (1888 and 1913 respectively) authored by Robert Louis Stevenson; *The Deerslayer* (1841) by James Fenimore Cooper; *Robinson Crusoe* (1719) by Daniel Defoe; and *The Scottish Chiefs* (1809) by Jane Porter. Illustrated by the most renowned book artist in U.S. history, each volume is rich in color plates made from paintings that now hang in the Brandywine Museum in Chadds Ford, Pennsylvania.

"This reprint is a model of restoration," enthused *Time* magazine's reviewer about the 1982 reprinting of *Kidnapped*. "The very typeface bespeaks adventure, and the artworks are reproduced with even greater fidelity than the plates in the rare first edition."

Prices: *Black Arrow,* $22.95, deluxe limited edition, $75; *Kidnapped,* $24.95; *The Deerslayer,* $24.95; *Robinson Crusoe,* $24.95; *The Scottish Chiefs,* $26.95, deluxe limited edition, $75.

CHARLES SCRIBNER'S SONS BOOKS FOR YOUNG READERS
MacMillan Publishing Company
866 Third Avenue
New York, NY 10022
Tel. 800/323-7445

OFFER THE

ARS SPECIAL

LM CAMERAS

e equal of other Film
eras sold at from
0 to $12.00.

WE HAVE THIS SEASON closed a contract with the leading manufacturer of Film Cameras, which enables us to furnish the highest grade film cameras at prices heretofore unknown in the camera business.

OUR FILM CAMERAS are manufactured exclusively for us; they are made under contract that calls for the very best materials, the very best of

ACHROMATIC LENSES.........

...OUR...

FILM CAMERAS use the

CARTRIDGE SYSTEM OF DAYLIGHT LOADING FILMS

and they may be loaded and unloaded in broad daylight.

FILM CARTRIDGES are unbreakable; their weight and bulk as compared with glass plates is practically noth-

---

PHOTOGRAPHIC
❋❋
GOODS

. 1 SEARS SPECIAL FIL
ments, 4¼x4½x5½ inches.
20R2116 Price.........
THESE PRICES DO

EARS SPECIAL FILM CA
removable parts. They are f
chromatic lenses, and are pro
UTTER is suitable for bot
and the speed may
ss of the light.

OF THESE FILM CAMERAS is provided with an automatic registering device, which shows at exactly how many pictures have been taken and how many unex-
ms remain in the camera.

EARS SPECIAL FILM CAMERAS are provided with brilliant view finders and tripod. The covering is the best quality of black morocco leather, and all arts are finely nickel plated.

CAMERA, for 4x5 picture
Weight, 28 oune
ty, twelve exposures. $5.

INCLUDE FILMS.

FILM CAMERAS. This Film put up to go into the camera, and may ht.

n Cartridge, for six exposures,

sures, 3⅓x3⅓. Price.........
extra, 3 cents.
n Cartridge, for twelve expo-
If by mail, postage extra, 4 cents.
No. 20R2127 Daylight Loading Film Cartridge, for six exposures, 4x5. Price.........
If by mail, postage extra, 4 cents.
No. 20R2128 Daylight Loading Film Cartridge, for twelve exposures, 4x5. Price.........
If by mail, postage extra, 5 cents.

1.98 BUYS THE COMPLETE PERFECTION VIEWING OUTFIT
FOR 5 x 7 PICTURES.

R2135

THE PERFECTION VIEW CAMERA is a thoroughly up to date, well made, substantial camera. It is made from the best seasoned mahogany, finely finished and highly polished, and all metal parts are nickel plated.

THE PERFECTION VIEW CAMERA
FOLDS UP COMPACTLY, has rising and falling front for adjusting relative amount of sky or foreground, and is provided with a first class swing back, a very valuable feature, especially when photographing buildings.

THE LENS is our Monarch Single Achromatic, a strictly high grade lens, manufactured especially for us by the Bausch & Lomb Optical Co., and guaranteed to be

The Best Single Achromatic Lens that can be made.

The Monarch Single Achromatic Lens is suitable for general all around photography including landscapes, groups, portraits, etc.

THE PERFECTION VIEW CAMERA
is made with **REVERSIBLE BACK**, thus permitting the camera to be used for either vertical or horizontal pictures without changing its position on the tripod.

THE BELLOWS is made from the very best quality of black gossamer cloth of double thickness and is cone shaped. Both the cone shaped bellows and the reversible back are features which have never before been offered except in high priced cameras.

THE COMPLETE OUTFIT CONTAINS:

rfection Viewing Camera, with
rch Achromatic Lens, Sliding
od, Canvas Carrying Case, and
Double Plate Holder.
Ruby Lamp.
ressed Fiber Trays for develop-
xing and toning.
e Measuring Glass.
inting Frame.
Ruler.
Paste Brush.

2 Dozen Sensitized Paper.
1 Dozen Dry Plates.
25 Card Mounts.
1 Package Concentrated Developer.
1 Package Concentrated Toning and Fixing Solution.
1 Package Hypo.
1 Tube of Paste.
1 Fine Gossamer Focus Cloth.
1 Copy of "Complete Instructions in Photography."
20R2135 The Complete Perfection Viewing Outfit. Price, **$11.98**

THE PERFECTION VIEWING
CAMERA makes pictures 5x7 inches; the most popular e both for professional and amateur rposes.

THE TRIPOD is our best quality sliding tripod, thoroughly substantial and rigid.

REMEMBER $11.98 includes the entire outfit just as listed and describ There are no extras to buy before you can co mence work. The outfit contains absolutely everything necessary

DEVELOPING, FINISHING AND MATERIAL OUTFIT.

197

◉ DAGUERREO-TYPE CAMERA

Invented in 1839 by the Frenchman Louis J. Daguerre, the daguerreotype process recorded an image on a silver plate made light-sensitive with iodine. The first American daguerreotypes were made with the aid of Samuel F. B. Morse, inventor (in 1837) of the "American electromagnetic telegraph."

The working daguerreotype camera replicated by Douglas Jordan of St. Petersburg, Florida, is fashioned after the William & Henry Lewis camera popular in the 1850s and '60s. "Special care is taken to ensure that each are [sic] as close to the original as can be," claims Mr. Jordan, who offers his Lewis-style cameras with either mahogany or rosewood bodies, fully assembled or in kit form. The cameras measure 9 inches high by 6 inches wide by 14 inches deep, including their bases. They use standard 4-by-5-inch sheet film and holders. Approximately 30 days are required for delivery. Lenses and tripod are also available.

Prices available upon request.

DOUGLAS JORDAN
P.O. Box 20194
St. Petersburg, FL 33702

PHOTOGRAPHIC PRINTING PAPER

Taking its name partly from the prevailing nineteenth-century photographic printing process, Chicago Albumen specializes in the printing, duplication and conservation of nineteenth- and early-twentieth-century photographic negatives.

In this work, the company uses gelatin chloride printing-out paper, which was the standard photographic paper for the decades following its 1885 introduction. The paper's uses now range from the production of exhibition-quality prints (the beautiful hues characteristic of turn-of-the-century prints can be achieved through the use of a simple gold-chloride toning solution) to "sun printing" projects for children. Chicago Albumen is the sole U.S. distributor of this paper, which is made in France by the firm of R. Guilleminot Boespflug & Cie.

Available in 8-by-10-, 11-by-14- and 20-by-24-inch sheets.

Ordering information and data sheets available.

CHICAGO ALBUMEN WORKS
Front Street
Housatonic, MA 01236
Tel. 413/274-6901

THREE-DIMENSIONAL STEREOVIEWS

The Victorian belief in eternal truths never interfered with a delight taken in the period's technological advances. Of these, photographs were perhaps most emblematic of the progressive life, particularly when observed on the three-dimensional cards of the stereoscopic viewer.

Replicas of this ubiquitous Victorian parlor accessory have only recently gone out of production, but some of their companion photo cards are still available new. Produced from originals from the then-famous Keystone and Underwood Studios, sets of 18 stereoviews depicting the Civil War, "Unique & New York City," "Industry," the San Francisco earthquake, the Great War, "Suffragettes and the Alaskan Gold

16259 British Battle Cruiser *Indomitable*, Which Sunk the German Battle Cruiser *Bluecher*.

Rush" and "Victorian Risqué" can be obtained at a cost of $3.45 each postpaid. Implying that these too are now just out of production, the supplier warns that the availability of these sets is limited.

Literature available.

T.M. VISUAL INDUSTRIES, INC.
212 West 35th Street
New York, NY 10036
Tel. 212/757-7700

THIS IS ONE OF THE FINE LINES of band instruments which we have been handling for years and which have given such immense satisfaction.

MUSIC RACKS and INSTRUCTION BOOKS are sent with all of these Instruments.

WE GUARANTEE EVERY INSTRUMENT in this line and sell the same terms that all of our other band instruments. Each horn is fitted with celebrated piston light action valves and is splendid in model and finish. of the cheap lines of instruments handled by dealers throughout the They only sell a very limited quantity of goods, and no manufactu reputation whatsoever can entrust his agency to them.

Marceau E Flat Cornet.

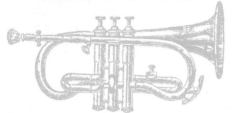

A clear toned, splendid instrument for the use of enders. Guaranteed in every w model, perfect in tune and tone. ever used except for playing in a cornet for general playing, yo B flat cornet.
No. 12K7980 Brass, highly pol
No. 12K7981 Nickel plated, high

Marceau B Flat C
SINGLE WATER

This is a fine B Flat Cornet in uitable for use in either band or c with it an A shank for use in orchestra, and it is a splendid instrument in every way.
No. 12K7984 Brass, highly polished..... $6.85
No. 12K7985 Nickel plated, highly polished 7.75

Marceau C Cornet.
We can also furnish this cornet in the key of C at the following prices:
No. 12K7988 Brass. Price.................. $6.95
No. 12K7989 Nickel plated. Price.......... 7.85

Marceau B Flat Cornet.
DOUBLE WATER KEY.

This Double Water Key Cornet has been a favorite with bandmen for a long time on account of its beautiful model and splendid tone. It is furnished with an A shank for use in orchestra and is a fine instrument in every way.
No. 12K7992 Brass, polished. Price..... $7.95
No. 12K7994 Nickel plated, highly polished. Price...... 8.95

Marceau Solo Altos.

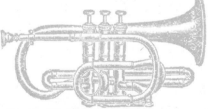

7-inch Bell.

These instruments are manufactured for solo alto purposes and have been great favorites ever since their appearance. They are easy blowing, have a splendid tone and a handsome appearance.
No. 12K8011 Brass, highly polished........... $10.45
No. 12K8012 Nickel plated, highly polished.... 11.95

Marceau Valve Trombones.
SPECIAL HILLYARD LONG MODEL.

No. 12K8023 6½-inch Bell.   No. 12K8029 7-inch Bell.

These Trombones are all fine in every respect and have that deep, rich tone so peculiar to trombones. Each band should be fitted with at least two of these, as they give a coloring harmony, which could be obtained in no other way.
No. 12K8023 E Flat Alto Trombone, brass. Price $11.65

Marceau E Flat Altos and B Flat Tenors.

Altos 8-inch Bell.

Tenors

These instruments are splendid for harmony work in a band, and we recommend them highly for those who desire fine altos and tenors at extremely low prices. They have a splendid tone, a beautiful model and a handsome appearance. They are perfect in tune and tone and so well constructed that they will last a lifetime. The action of the valves is extremely

---

MUSICAL INSTRUMENTS

Instrument Catalogue

Marceau B Flat Baritone.

9½-inch Bell.

These instruments have been used with great success in all sorts of solo playing and general band work. A large number of bandmen have pronounced them the finest baritones on the market for less than double the price given below. Their tone is full and sonorous without being dull, and is light and clear without being too snappy. The model is handsome and the general workmanship on the instruments is all that can be desired. We recommend these baritones highly to baritone players throughout the country and we are always willing to have them compared with instruments offered by other dealers for twice the price.
No. 12K8017 Brass, highly polished. Price................... $14.15
No. 12K8018 Nickel plated, highly polished. Price................... $16.65

Marceau F Circular Alto. 10-inch Bell.
This style of alto horn has become very popular with all kinds of military and concert bands in the last few years on account of its beautiful mellow tone. It is used almost exclusively by all of the larger bands and we recommend its use to all bandmen. Its circular model makes it a very easy blowing and sensitive instrument and not only does it add to the appearance of the band, but it gives the music a coloring which can be obtained in no other way. It is made by the same celebrated makers who manufacture the balance of this line, and is a valuable addition to the well known Marceau & Co. band instruments which we have handled so successfully for years. If your band does not possess altos of this model you should by all means procure them without delay, and you will find that the beautiful effect which you will obtain will much more than compensate for the small expense incurred. It is furnished with three additional crooks, Eb, D and C; thus enabling the performer to play in four different keys. All crooks are fitted with water key, enabling the performer to quickly remove the accumulation of saliva, a feature to be found only on our instruments.
No. 12K8033 Brass, highly polished. Price............... $19.95
No. 12K8034 Nickel plated. Price. 22.45

Marceau Slide Trombones.

7-inch Be

We know that these instruments will appeal to all trombone who desire good, serviceable trombones at an extremely low pr

---

Marceau B Flat Bass.

10¼-inch Bell.

These instruments can be used with excellent effect to fill in between the E Flat Bass and the B Flat Baritone. They are very effective when used in the bass solos which frequently occur in band selections and
19
.40
20
7.95

Marceau E Flat Bass.

excellent bass for any b It has enough answer for a k mentation an is full and sw for use, if de chestras. The fine and the thoroughly reinforced th break down u use. The va quick and resp we guarantee ment to be s in every part
No. 12K80 highly polished. Price.
No. 12K80 plated, highly Price.....

Marceau E Flat bass. 15-inch

This instrument is of exactly the same splendid mod struction as our No. 12K8021, only it is of extra lar tions, and is very deep and rich in tone. We recomm highly to all band organizations. The bell of this is of a flaring model.
No. 12K8021½ Brass, highly polished.....
No. 12K8022½ Nickel plated, highly polishe

200

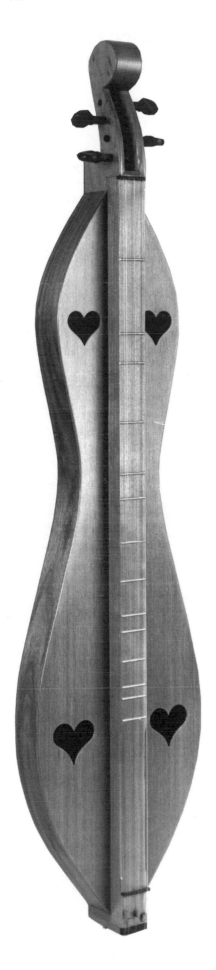

❄ APPALACHIAN DULCIMER

Among the many ancient things carried into this century by our mountain culture is a biblical instrument—the dulcimer. The sound of the dulcimer, a haunting fusion of the wild and lyrical, somehow reflects the character of Appalachia itself—both in culture and terrain.

Jeremy Seeger has been handcrafting traditional Appalachian-style (or mountain) dulcimers for more than 20 years. Each instrument is individually built of selected woods and is crafted to produce consistently excellent sound. A variety of wood combinations and designs are available.

Prices range from $250 to $600.

Free brochure available.

JEREMY SEEGER DULCIMERS
P.O. Box 117, Fassett Hill
Hancock, VT 05748
Tel. 802/767-3790

▦ CLASSIC KEYBOARDS

Geoffrion Keyboards replicates Italian, Flemish, French, German and English keyboard instruments that date back to the tenth century in design. Available to a clientele of musicians, reenactors and museums are custom-built clavichords, spinets, virginals and harpsichords. The luthiers will also reproduce original antique fretted instruments in exact detail.

The beginning price for clavichords is $1,000; for spinets, $4,500; for virginals, $4,200; for single manual harpsichords, $5,000; for double manual harpsichords, $7,500.

Further information available.

GEOFFRION KEYBOARDS
Route 1, Box 273
Pomona, IL 62975
Tel. 618/687-2159

▦ JAW HARP

Once commonly called "Jew's" or "mouth" harps, the jaw harp is a traditional folk instrument.
Price: $1.95.

DIXIE GUN WORKS
Gunpowder Lane
Union City, TN 38261

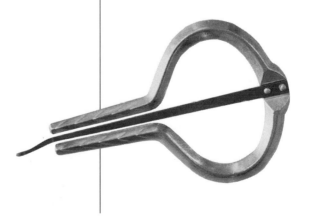

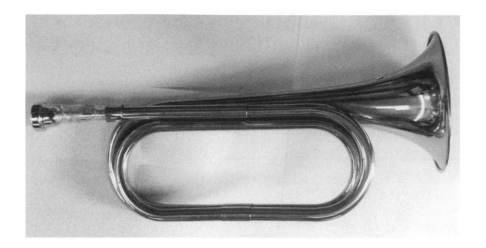

⧚ CONFEDERATE BUGLE

Dixie Gun Works's Confederate infantry bugle is a copy of one dug up at the site of the Battle of Stone's River, near Murfreesboro, Tennessee. It is a genuine musical instrument that replicates the original down to its use of a double-thickness brass bell, made entirely of polished brass. Overall length: 10½ inches.

Price: $54.95.

Catalog of gun supplies available, $3.

DIXIE GUN WORKS
Gunpowder Lane
Union City, TN 38261
Tel. 901/885-0700 or
*   800/238-6785 to order*
Fax. 901/885-0440

❋ HOHNER HARMONICAS

A Danbury boy of ten winters…stole a harmonica Friday evening to serenade his girl with.
—James M. Bailey, Life in Danbury, 1893

It's a dubious distinction, but the harmonica still produces more music for its size than any other instrument known to the world, and at the least cost.

Since Matthias Hohner turned out his first 650 harmonicas in 1857, his name has been virtually interchangeable with the word "harmonica."

As the accompanying old catalog entries show, many Hohner harmonicas produced today are the same as they were at the turn of the century and before.

Catalog of harmonicas, melodicas and accordions available.

HOHNER, INCORPORATED
Lakeridge Park
P.O. Box 15035
Richmond, VA 23227-5035

No. 1896. "MARINE BAND." Hohner Harmonica. Length 4 inches. The instrument with an international reputation. Its accuracy of tone and simplicity have made it the choice of music teachers and professional players everywhere. 10 single holes, 20 reeds, brass plates, heavy convex covers, finely nickel-plated. In hinged box bearing photograph of The United States Marine Band. Available in all keys.

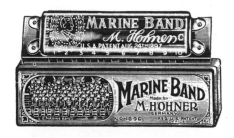

No. 34B. "OLD STANDBY." Hohner Harmonica. Length 4 inches. An ideal instrument, and popular everywhere. 10 single holes, 20 reeds, brass plates, finely nickel-plated covers. Furnished in a neat hinged box. Available in all keys.

No. 607. "ECHO." Hohner Harmonica. Length 6⅛ inches. Large double sided tremolo instrument in two different keys, having 40 double holes and 80 perfectly tuned reeds, brass plates, finely nickel-plated covers with turned in ends. Packed in a very attractive hinged box with pictorial design in many colors. Available in key combinations "A-D," "Bb-F," "C-G."

CHILD'S FURNITURE.

Order No. 25238.

...ription and the illustration of crib does not ...ce to this line of goods. The pieces are imita- ...amel, corrugated, finished in white and gold, ...large enough to be of practical value.

Beds.
. Price, each.................$1
. Price, each.................
. Price, each.................

Cribs.
. Price, each.................
. Price, each.................
. Price, each.................
Rocker. Price, each ....
Chair. Price, each ....
Settee. Price, each ....
..hair. Price, each.............
Chair. Price, each............
Table. Price, each............
Table. Price, each............

Black Boards.

25240 One of the finest most complete blackboards made. A well arranged c..bination of easel and de..having a movable sawed ex-tension, with designs for drawing on either side. The board is made of new material of best quality, smooth and warranted not to check. The desk is provided with an ex-tra large drawer with orna-mented front. The board drops forward to form the desk, showing additional designs for drawing. It is made in a substantial man-ner and folds very closely for shipping. Height, 48 in. Size of board, 16x19 in. Price....................$1.00

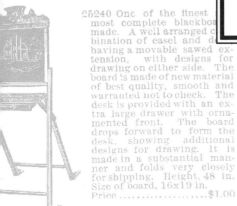

A perfect Blackboard and Easel; no cut. ..tuted standards. Complete alphabet on the ..e of the board. A movable extension hav-..esigns for drawing on both sides. The back sup-..n be easily removed so as to make a very thin ..e: height, 41 inches. Size of board, 18½x12½
.................................$0.45

DOLLS.

..ted Dolls, Bisque ..ds, with Chemise.

..Jointed Dolls, bisque ..s, flowing hair, teeth, ..ong plaited chemise. ..th, 15½ inches.
..................$0.50
..Jointed Dolls, with ..e heads, flowing hair, ..and long chemise. ..th, 19 inches.
.90
..Jointed Dolls, extra ..and fine, with flow-..hair, teeth and long ..ise, bisque heads, ..th, 25 inches.
1.90

Kid Body Dolls, Not Dressed, Jointed.

25252 Kid Body Dolls with bisque heads, flowing hair, teeth and solid eyes. Length, 12 inches. Price......................$0.25
25253 Kid Body Dolls with bisque heads, woven wig, flowing hair, teeth and solid eyes. Length 15 in. Price.......................50
25254 Kid Body Dolls, bisque heads, woven wig, flowing hair, and teeth. Length, 17 inches. Price.......................75
25255 Kid Body Dolls, with bisque heads, flowing hair woven wig, teeth and solid eyes. Length, 21 inches. Price...................1.25

Dressed Dolls, Patent Indestruct ible Heads.

25267 Indestructible Head Dressed Doll, cloth body hair stuffed, painted hair, cloth shoes. Length, 17 inches. Price...................$0.40
25268 Indestructible Head Dressed Doll. Same as above, 20 inches long. Price.... $0.60
25269 Indestructible Head Dressed Doll, largest size, 24 in. long. Price............$0.80

Dressed Dolls, Cloth Bodies, with Kid Joints.

25275 Dressed Dolls, with kid joints, bisque heads and arms, teeth and flowing hair. Dress-ed in handsome costume; length, 13 inches. Price......................$0.50
25276 Dressed Dolls, cloth body, kid joints, bisque heads and arms, flowing hair, teeth, shoes, stockings. Dressed in costume of handsome design and good material; length, 14½ inches. Price...................$0.85
25277 Dressed Dolls, cloth body, kid joints, bisque head and arms, flowing hair, teeth, solid eyes, shoes and stockings; dress is of the best *materials*, in fashionable colors and well made; length, 17 inches. Price.............$1.00
25278 Dressed Dolls, cloth..d kid joints, bisque heads, flowing hair, teeth ..d eyes, shoes and stockings, dressed in an elaborate costume of satin, with large turned-up hat, length 20 inches. Price.................................2.00

Dressed Baby Dolls, Jointe..

25280 Full Jointed Do.. finest bisque head, flow.. hair, solid eyes; long b.. dress of woolen stuff silk, neatly trimmed, cut. Price.............1
25281 Same description larger size, and more e.. orate dress. Price..1

25282 Superior quality, superfine dolls; ..jointed, with bisque heads, flowing ..ity dolls. Dress made of cotton stuff, trim.. ..ssed in "Baby" costume of nun's ..ing, with cap to match. Length. ..inches.
................$0.65
.. Same description as above, ..larger. Each $0.90
.. Large size "Baby" doll. ..gth, 16 inches. Price..... $1.50

Jointed Dolls, Dressed.

25285 Finest bisque heads, solid eyes, flowing hair, teeth, shoes and stockings. Superior qual-ity dolls. Dress made of cotton stuff, trim-med, silk bonnet. Price......................$
25287 Same description; dress of muslin and lace, bonnet trimmed with ribbon. Price......
25288 Same description, dress and bonnet of changeable silk trimmed with ribbons. Price....
25289 Same description; dress, finest muslin woven through with ribbons. Full silk bonnet with silk strings and balls. Price.............
25290 Same description; dress of fine woolen goods, trimmed with silk ribbons or embroider-ed. Some hair lace hats, some bonnets. Price....................
25291 Same description; dress, fine cashmere trimmed with silk and lace. Full silk bonnet, lace trimmed. Price...................
25292 Same description; dress, full winter cos-tume of fine woolen goods, trimmed with plush and ribbons. Bonnet to match. Price.........

Columbus Dress.. Dolls.

The costumes are works of .. made of the finest silk velvet .. satin, in contrasting colors. E.. Cavalier wears at his side a .. sword. The broad cap is .. mounted with an ostrich plu.. while the inscription, "149.. Columbus, 1893" is emblazo.. upon its front.
25293 Columbus Doll, join.. bisque head, flowing hair, te.. solid eyes. Length, 15 inc.. Price.................
25294 Columbus Doll, same.. scription as above. Length.. inches. Price............
25295 Columbus Doll, large size. Length, 21 inches. Price.................$

203

▣ DOLL HOUSE KIT

This is not the replica of an antique doll house so much as it's a modern kit depicting a period building. In the Enchanted Doll House's characteristically diabetes-inducing prose, it is characterized as "An extraordinary structure of Victorian grandeur, its fourteen rooms provide tremendous space in which you can recreate the settings of the late 19th-century." Dimensions: 44 inches high by 61 inches long by 26 inches deep.
   Price: Doll House Kit, $738.

Catalog available.

THE ENCHANTED DOLL HOUSE
Manchester Center, VT 05255-0697
Tel. 802/362-1327

▣ SLED

The Snow King was introduced in 1861, as rebel guns on the Charleston Battery were seeing to it that the Union was in for its roughest sledding ever. Made today in much the same way it was then, the Snow King's solid oak runners are joined with tenoned cross-members and the original hand-painted deck and runner embellishments have been faithfully reproduced. The Snow King measures 42 inches in length by 11 inches in width by 3¾ inches high.
   Price: $62.

General Merchandise Catalog available, $3.

CUMBERLAND GENERAL STORE
Route 3, Box 81
Crossville, TN 38555
Tel. 615/484-8481 or
     800/334-4640 to order

✻TOY BLOCKS

This set of toy blocks replicates one produced in 1888 by the renowned McLoughlin Brothers Publication House of New York to promote their line of chromo-lithographed story-books for children. Gates, Inc., the new manufacturer, claims to have taken "pains-taking measures" in order to ensure that the same methods and materials were used to fashion the replica as were once employed to make the original.

The nine nesting blocks are derived from the work of illustrator William Roger Snow (1834–1907), and include "Three Bears," "Babes in the Wood," "Tom Thumb" and "Jack in the Beanstalk."

Prices: $75 per set, including domestic U.S. delivery charges.

GATES, INCORPORATED
P.O. Box 90
West Peterborough, NH 03468
Tel. 800/669-4903 or
603/924-3394 in New Hampshire
Fax. 603/924-0011

⊛ NOAH'S ARK TOY

In the nineteenth century, the Noah's Ark was a Sabbath Day toy allowable on Sunday because it imparted biblical knowledge. Blue Ridge Arks' solid wood replica spares 10 pairs of hand-carved animals from the righteous deluge. It is fully painted, dated and signed, and includes a ramp.

Brochure available, $1.

BLUE RIDGE ARKS, CRAFTS & CRADLES
Route 1, P.O. Box 39
Blue Ridge, VA 24064

▓ 1890 FIELD DRUM

In the winter of 1854, Silas Noble and James P. Cooley began the manufacture of drums in the kitchen of Noble's farmhouse. So great was their initial success that by 1856 they were able to build their first factory. In 1860, Noble and Cooley made a drum from a rail split by Abe Lincoln—this was used by the Great Emancipator in political rallies in Connecticut and Massachusetts, and may even have had something to do with the company's landing of several contracts for regimental drums.

By 1873, Noble and Cooley were manufacturing 100,000 drums a year, including toys. These required special machinery to aid in the difficult process of steam bending, decorating and fabricating the drum parts. The 1890 Field Drum is still made by this nineteenth-century equipment.

The 1890 "cord and ear" Field Drum is an authentic vintage toy. It features a brightly lithographed and embossed shell 9 inches in diameter, strung with white cord through leather ears. Drumsticks and carrying sling included.

Price: $10.95.

NOBLE & COOLEY COMPANY
P.O. Box 131
Granville, MA 01034
Tel. 413/562-9694

CAST-IRON BANKS

Shortly after the Civil War, brightly painted cast-iron mechanical banks made their appearance. Although parents bought them as devices to encourage thrift among children, the youngsters became so enthralled by their ingenious mechanisms that many buttons were stolen out of sewing boxes to be saved when pennies were scarce. The complex movements of the banks often depicted actions and characters reflecting the cultural and political atmosphere of the time: from a circus dog jumping through a hoop to deposit a coin in a barrel, to a smiling Uncle Sam salting his coins away in a valise.

By the 1880s, mechanical banks had become so popular that the *Book of Knowledge*, a highly respected source of information, published a compilation of the most popular ones. Handpainted, cast and assembled according to nineteenth-century methods, Cumberland General Store's replicas include Trick Dog, Trick Pony and Colorful Clown banks.

The Organ Grinder bank depicted was first crafted in 1892. As you turn the handle, the boy and girl begin to dance, bells chime, and the monkey deposits the coin from his tray while politely tipping his hat. Other penny banks available are Jonah and the Whale (1890), American Eagle (1883), Hometown Battery (1890) and William Tell (1896).

General Merchandise Catalog available, $3.

CUMBERLAND GENERAL STORE
Route 3, Box 81
Crossville, TN 38555
Tel. 615/484-8481 or
*   800/334-4640 to order*

FARKEL

Farkel is an old gambling game said to have been played by French sailors and marines to pass the time on lengthy ocean voyages. Along with the game's history and instructions, this set includes five dice in a linen or buckskin carrying bag.

Prices: game set in buckskin bag, $7.95; game set in embroidered linen bag, $9.95. An additional $3 is due to cover the cost of U.P.S. shipment when ordered within the continental U.S.

Catalog of historical clothing specializing in the fur trade of the eighteenth and nineteenth centuries, $5.

LA PELLETERIE
P.O. Box 127
Arrow Rock, MO 65320
Tel. 816/837-3261

BILLIARD AND POOL TABLES

Pre-1900 Brunswick and English Thurston pool tables are replicated by the Adler company of Los Angeles. The Adlers offer a range of types, each handcrafted from $1\frac{1}{16}$-inch Pennsylvania slate and kiln-dried hardwoods. Weighing more than 1,600 pounds apiece, the pool tables may be ordered with any one of several finishes, cloths, frieze and pocket treatments. Each is built to meet the commercial specifications of the Billiard Congress of America.

Prices range from $2,800 to $15,750.

Catalog available, $5 (refundable with purchase).

POOL TABLES BY ADLER
10100 Aviation Boulevard
Los Angeles, CA 90005
Tel. 213/382-6334

▦ BALL BEARING COASTER WAGON

Beginning in the year 1900 and for three decades thereafter, the Janesville Ball Bearing Coaster Wagon was the standard, as the copy line goes, by which all other such toys were judged. The solid-oak Janesville wagon was the model of versatility—it was a racer, a covered wagon (when properly fitted out), a farm wagon and a bus. When necessary, the durable plaything could also be pressed into service aiding adults with shopping and laundry—serious tasks that it performed with happy aplomb. The Janesvilles got passed on from one generation to the next, and today they are valuable collector's items.

The Wisconsin Wagon Company began producing the "Series II" Janesville Ball Bearing Wagon in 1979, intent on sacrificing none of the quality of the originals to contemporary standards of workmanship and design. As a result, the Series II is said to precisely replicate their design details, retaining the solid-oak body, the ball-bearing wheels, the unique bracing, the front-axle pivot system and stainless-steel bodywork.

Dimensions: 16-by-33-inch box with 4-inch sides.

Price: $185 (plus $10.50 UPS charge).

Brochure available.

WISCONSIN WAGON COMPANY
507 Laurel Avenue
Janesville, WI 53545
Tel. 608/754-0026

knowledged as one of the **GREATEST REMEDIES** of the age.

A GREAT BLOOD purifier and nerve tonic. Cures all diseases arising from a poor and wasted condition of the blood, such as pale and sallow complexion, general weakness of the muscles, loss of appetite, depression of spirits, lack of ambition, anæmia, chlorosis or green sickness, palpitation of the heart, shortness of breath on slight exertion, coldness of hands and feet, swelling of the feet and limbs, pain in the back, nervous headache, dizziness,

DR. WORDEN'S FEMALE PILLS
FOR WEAK WOMEN.
COMPLEXION, BEAUTY, NERVE AND BLOOD MAKER

mory, feebleness of will, ringing in the ears, early decay. ALL OF FEMALE WEAKNESS—leucorrhœa, tardy or irregular periods, on of the menses, hysteria, locomotor ataxia, partial paralysis, heumatism, neuralgia. Cures all diseases depending on vitiated n the blood, causing scrofula, swelled glands, fever sores, rickets, liseases, hunchback, acquired deformities, decayed bones, chronic consumption of the bowels and lungs. In invigorating the blood hen broken down by overwork, worry, excesses and indiscretions of living, most wonderful medicine.

MALE PILLS are not a purg... icine; they are... contain nothing that could... ate system but act upon t... upon poor and watery... state of that fluid.

AN BE BEAUTIFUL, their... perfect... rmal, circulation perfect. disease removed by taking... n have been cured by us... and physicians had failed...

ANTEE A CURE. One singl... are usuall... tanding, while ten to twel... hich these pills are prep... of female weakness if the... anner, and for a reasonab... R39 Our special price, per... If by mail, postage...

Cathartic Pills, On...
price........... ice, per box........... ice, per dozen boxes........... $0.10
.90

THE OLD FASHIONED
ATED CATHARTIC PILL
S. Pharmacopœia, the... Ayer's, Brandreth's,... nd other much adver-... They act principally... r, and move the bowels... thout griping. These... arefully prepared from... etable extracts, and can be thoroughly relied upon. For this reason... much superior to many others sold at double their price. R42 Price, per dozen boxes, 90c; per box containing 25 pills.....10c
If by mail, postage extra, per box, 2 cents.

Wonderful Little Liver Pills.
price........... 25c
ice, each........... $0.13
ice, per dozen........... 1.00
vegetable in their composition. These wonderful little pills oper-... ate without disturbance to the system, diet or occupation.

WONDERFUL LITTLE LIVER PILLS
ONLY BY SEARS, ROEBUCK & CO. INC. CHI.

CONSTIPATION, that most hide-... ous and deathly demon of sickness, is an easy enough thing to cure if you will only persist in taking proper treatment. It is one of the com-... monest troubles and often thought to be a very little thing. Yet we say that nine-tenths of

n sickness is due to this one thing. When the bowels do not move the natural drainage tract in the human system is dammed up, sition ensues and poisonous gases and liquids are carried all the system. The result is jaundice, torpid liver, biliousness, in, indigestion, foul breath, coated tongue, loss of appetite, belching foul gases, blotches, boils, dizziness, headache, cramps,
You can easily avoid all these troubles and keep your system healthy by taking from time to time one or two of our **WONDER-TLE LIVER PILLS**. Some of our customers call them "**LITTLE** " they are so small in size and so easy to swallow, yet so effective in their operation. Whenever your stomach, liver and bowels get er take one or two of our **LITTLE WONDERS** and notice the ct and great relief you will experience. Keep a box always beside them occasionally and you will always feel well and look the health.
R45 Price, per dozen boxes, $1.00; each........... 13c
If by mail, postage extra, per box, 2 cents.

Do You Sneeze? Camphor Pills.
price........... 25c and $1.00
ice, 25c size, each........... $0.18
ice, 25c size, per dozen........... 1.50
ice, $1.00 size, each........... .50
ice, $1.00 size, per dozen........... 4.80

EN LONG USED BY THE OLD SCHOOL PHYSICIANS,
edy for cold in the head, cramps, colic, diarrhœa and orbus and other annoying troubles resulting from catch-... Also for menstrual colic. A bottle of these pills ought ied in the pocket continually by those who are travel-... tside most of the day exposed to all weathers. Though tive in performing cures, they are small and can be con-... kept in the vest pocket.
48 Price, regular size, per dozen $1.50; each........... 18c
If by mail, postage, extra, small, 2 cents.

Retail price........... $1.00
Our price, each........... $0.60
Our price, per dozen........... 6.00

SIX BOXES POS
TIVELY GUARAN
TEED TO CURE AN

Dr Hammond's NERVE AND BRAIN PILLS
FOR THE CURE OF

DISEASE for whic... theyarei... tended. This wil... cure you if you fe... generally miserab... or suffer with a thou... sand and one inde... scribable bad fee... ings, both mental an... physical, amon... them low spirit... nervousness, wea... ness, lifelessnes... weakness, dizzines... feeling of fullne... like bloating aft... eating, or sense... goneness or empt... ness of stomach...

...eadache, blurring of eyesigh... bility, poor memory, chillines... bing, gurgling or rumbling se... ins occasionally; palpitation... on of blood, cold feet, pain ar... loins, aching and weariness... nervous wakefulness at nigh... f dread, as if something awf...

...our **NERVE AND BRAI... PILLS** will cure you. No matt... trouble is, **DR. HAMMOND... you. These pills have a r... They cannot be equaled t... r, spermatorrhœa, night swea... kness of both brain and bod... They will tone up the who... a out, overworked or depress... made strong and bold agai... f life to the old.

...to scare men into paying mone...
BEWARE OF QUACK DOCTORS for remedies which have no merit. Our Ner... and Brain Pills are compounded from a prescription of one of the not... German scientists, and are the same as have been used in German hospitals fo... years with marvelous success. **HOW TO CURE YOURSELF** and full and e... plicit directions are enclosed with every box. All orders and inquiries co... cerning these pills will be treated confidentially, and all shipments made... plain sealed package.
ONLY $3.00 FOR SIX BOXES. Enough to cure almost any case, no matt... how severe, no matter how long standin... whether old or young, no matter from what cause. Send us $3.00 and v... will send you six boxes by return mail, postpaid, in plain sealed package, wi... full instructions.
If you need these pills don't delay. This is the first time the Americ... people have had an opportunity of getting the genuine Dr. Hammond's Pil... and the first time they have been sold anywhere at anything like our price
No. 8R51 Price, per dozen boxes, $6.00; each........... 6...
If by mail, postage extra, per box, 2 cents.

Our Famous Blood Pills.
A WONDERFUL PURIFIER.
Retail price........... 50c
Our price, each........... $0.22
Our price, per dozen........... 1.80
For men and women that require a nerve tonic, blood purifier or builder.
Over one hundred thousand sold last year, which shows what is thought of these pills when known. Others sell them at 50 cents per box.
FOR FEMALE TROUBLE they are an unfailing remedy, and guaran-... teed far superior to any other pills on the market at any price.

DR. M. BAINS' FAMOUS BLOOD PILLS
TAKEN THE WORLD OVER BY THE
WEAK AND SALLOW COMPLEXIONED

They give tone to the whole system, making the eyes bright, the cheek ros... and, through strength and buoyancy, the step is firm and elastic.
OUR BLOOD PILLS can be taken according to directions without any da... ger, by either sex, and if carefully followed will gi... quick results and permanent relief. Weakness, poor, thin blood, giving... sallow or pale complexion, loss of appetite, chlorosis or green sickne... pain in the back, palpitation of the heart, nervous headaches, suppre... sion of menses, leucorrhœa, tardy or irregular periods, hysteria, pa... alysis, and all diseases resulting from humors in the blood, which cause er... sipelas, sores, swellings, and even consumption, also in cases where t... system is broken down by overwork of mind or body, or from excesses a... indiscretions of living.
THE EFFECT IS WONDERFUL. These pills are not of a cathartic natur... they do not, nor are they intended to pur... They are intended to act on the blood, and supply what is needed in resto... ing the tone and lacking constituents, stimulating to activity the slugg... system.
FOR WOMEN in case of suppression of menses, leucorrhœa or whit... chlorosis, anæmia, locomotor ataxia, a quick and perm... nent cure can be effected; in fact, it is the greatest remedy known.
MEN these pills stand without a rival, and should be used in all ca... where the patient is suffering from a tainted condition of th... blood. They have proved especially valuable in the treatment of blo... and skin diseases, and as a rule are prescribed by the most successful... sicians in cases of eczema and blood poison. A similar class of pills reta... everywhere from 50 cents to $1.00, but they cannot be compared with t... famous Blood Pills, which are the grandest prescription in existence... restoring the blood to a natural, healthy and normal condition.

✢ Cologne ✢

▨ NUMBER SIX COLOGNE

The Caswell-Massey Company's claim to being "the oldest chemists and perfumers in America" is certainly no idle boast. In fact, if by America we mean the United States, then the New York chemists are older than America.

The apothecary was founded in 1752 by Dr. William Hunter, a patron of the arts who helped support Gilbert Stuart when he was a young portraitist. Dr. Hunter was also the first person in America to lecture on anatomy, and displayed an interest in affairs both cultural and scientific reminiscent of those of the Founding Fathers who were his peers. The difference was that Dr. Hunter was a Tory, and one who died with his cause during the Revolutionary War.

Hunter's apothecary was then located in Newport, Rhode Island. Following the Revolution, his widow sold this store to a clerk, thereby beginning a tradition that has held on ever since, with one assistant after another succeeding the previous owner.

Until a few years ago, Caswell-Massey still sold leeches; other products of theirs—since discontinued—were used by historic Americans. The Tory Dr. Hunter's Number Six Cologne was slapped on, ironically enough, by the Father of our Country.

Still made from the formula that Dr. Hunter brought over from England, Number Six Cologne contains 27 natural ingredients—including bergamot, musk, orange blossom and lemon—and was so favored by George Washington that as President he sent two bottles over to France for his friend and ally, the Marquis de Lafayette, to enjoy. Although this formulation is somewhat stronger than the original (in those days

"cologne-water" was used for sponge bathing), Dr. Hunter's stipulation that the aging casks be rolled from one end of the laboratory to the other once monthly is still followed faithfully. Available in the traditional "Caswell Round" bottles in 3-, 8- and 16-ounce sizes.

Prices: 3 oz., $20; 8 oz., $40 (plus shipping and handling for orders up to $60).

Free seasonal catalog available.

CASWELL-MASSEY CO., LTD.
Catalogue Division
100 Enterprise Place
Dover, DE 19901
Tel. 800/362-0500

❋ LILAC VEGETAL

According to the Nestle-LeMur Company, makers of Lilac Vegetal, the lilac-scented after-shave tonic was developed during the 1850s by Edouard Pinaud, *parfumeur* to the court of Napoleon III. Pinaud was charged with the task of creating a distinctive scent for the contingent of Hungarian cavalry then attached to the monarch's court; the lime-green lotion still to be found in most drugstores was then produced by Pinaud after several months' work.

❋ SLOAN'S

As the early records regarding Dr. Earl Sloan and the liniment he developed in 1885 have been lost, little is known about the beginnings of the product that bears his name. Warner-Lambert, the company that now manufactures Sloan's Liniment according to its original formula, does tell us that at the time he first produced his capsicum-based compound, Dr. Sloan was a veterinarian for the St. Louis Street Car Company. Thus it may be assumed that Sloan's Liniment was preceded by a stronger potion used to relieve the muscular distress of horses.

The packaging of Dr. Sloan's liniment appears unchanged, and features the benign veterinarian, contemplative behind his massive (and from the looks of it, spinning) handlebar mustache.

WARNER-LAMBERT
201 Tabor Road
Morris Plains, NJ 07950

❋ FLORIDA WATER

Merchandise includes lavender and Florida waters; perfumed toilet and pearl powders.
—New Orleans Picayune, *July 28, 1840*

With a label by Du Maurier depicting the Fountain of Youth, Florida Water was first brought to the U.S. from France in 1808. Modern Ponce de Leons may search for it in apothecary and specialty stores, or contact the manufacturer.

Free color brochure and wholesale price list available.

LANMAN & KEMP BARCLAY & COMPANY, INC.
25 Woodland Avenue, P.O. Box 241
Westwood, NJ 07675
Tel. 201/666-4990
Fax. 201/666-5836

❋ PRAIRIE CHIEF

For internal and external use. Contains methyl salicylate, thymol, oil of eucalyptus, oil of camphor, refined oil petrolatum, D&C color. 8 fluid oz. Shipping weight: 2 lbs.
Price: $2.73.

❋ HARDY'S GENUINE SALVE

As it's been around since 1836, Hardy's Genuine Salve is old enough to remember the Alamo. Unfortunately, as a treatment for "lame backs, cracked hands and many more minor wounds—even warts," it wouldn't have been much use to the mission's defenders, who were unspared by Santa Anna's troops. Average weight 1¼ oz. Shipping weight ½ lb.
Price: $6.50.

❋ SMITH'S MENTHOLATED SALVE

Formerly Tholene, Smith's is a cooling menthol-camphor salve that is used toward the relief of minor irritations of the nose, minor burns and insect stings. Shipped weight, 1 lb.
Price: $2.95.

CUMBERLAND GENERAL STORE
Route 3, Box 81
Crossville, TN 38555
Tel. 615/484-8481 or
800/334-4640 to order

DR. PIERCE'S GOLDEN MEDICAL DISCOVERY

This **"aid to indigestion and heartburn"** contains blood root, also used in the nineteenth century as a treatment for "costiveness"—or constipation. Other ingredients contained in the good doctor's 8-oz. bottle are gentian root and Oregon grape root. Shipped weight, 1 lb.
   Price: $8.80.

DR. KILMER'S SWAMP ROOT

A natural diuretic extracted from organic roots in a 10.5 percent alcohol base. Aids the kidneys in eliminating waste. Contains extractives of buchu leaves, cape aloes and peppermint herb, oil of juniper, venice turpentine and subrose. Eight oz. Shipped weight, 1 lb.
   Price: $7.60.

CUMBERLAND GENERAL STORE
Route 3, Box 81
Crossville, TN 38555
Tel. 615/484-8481 or
800/334-4640 to order

THE FARMER'S MUSEUM PHARMACEUTICAL PREPARATIONS

The Farmer's Museum of Cooperstown, New York, offers a range of medicinal items. Historically researched and packaged, they each bear the likeness of an upstate New York personage from sometime between 1820 and 1850.

ACHING NERVES CAUSE
AGONY!
Doctor Davis's Pain Killer
BRINGS
RELIEF!

Neuralgia - Sciatica - Earache
And the whole noxious family of
NERVE DISEASES are CURED by
Perry Davis's Pain Killer
Contains Essence of
ANISE

Doctor O Dells'
EUPHONIAL LUBICATORS

DOCTOR O DELL

A Sure Relief For
HORSENESS COUGHS COLDS
CROUP CATARRH ASTHMA
LOSS of VOICE SORE THROAT
CONSUMPTION   IN ITS FIRST STAGES

MOTHER MINER'S
Marvellous Medicine

This GREAT REMEDY
Positively CURES All Diseases of the
Stomach - Liver and Kidneys
BILIOUSNESS
FEVER & AGUE
and All DISORDERS of the BLOOD
It Contains Natures Herbal Remedy
SPEARMINT

Also available from the Farmer's Museum are Dr. LaDuke's Infallible Health Pills (sassafras drops) and Dr. Fong's Secret of the Orient Aphrodisiac Remedy. All are priced at $1 per single package, with shipping charged at cost. A 7 percent sales tax is applicable if ordered within the state of New York.

THE FARMER'S MUSEUM, INC.
Lake Road, P.O. Box 800
Cooperstown, NY 13326
Tel. 607/547-2593

ALLCOCK'S POROUS PLASTER

An old-time poultice that "draws out" temporary muscle pain by "counter-irritant action." Contains: burgundy pitch, frankincense, orris root, capsicum, beeswax, camphor, gum of elemi and gum of myrrh on a natural-rubber base.

Price: $6 (plus $5.50 shipping and handling).

Seasonal catalog available.

CASWELL-MASSEY CO., LTD.
Catalogue Division
100 Enterprise Place
Dover, DE 19901
Tel. 800/362-0500

Genuine ALLCOCK'S POROUS PLASTER

 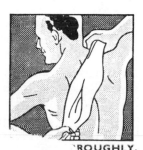 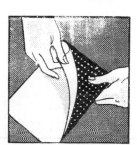

❶ Wash the skin well us. plenty of soap.

...ROUGHLY. If necessary shave the skin to facilitate removal of the Plaster.

❸ Gently remove the covering from the face of the Plaster.

  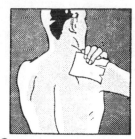

❹ If necessary, cut the Plaster to make it fit.

❺ Warm the Plaster until it is sticky.

❻ Place the Plaster over the pain, and smooth it down.

 The Plaster may be worn from one day to three weeks, as required. If pain persists after three days, remove the Plaster and apply a new one.

Give the Plaster a quick, firm pull from one corner. Do not pull it a little at a time, because if it is removed with one pull you will feel no discomfort. If your skin is tender moisten the Plaster with cotton wool dipped in Eau de Cologne, Lavender Water or Surgical Spirit. This will soften the rubber and make removal easy.

GRANDPA'S SOAP

Grandpa's is a pine-tar soap unchanged from the product introduced by the Beaver-Remmer Graham Company in 1878, and sold without advertising ever since. Entirely devoid of coloring and perfuming agents, the soap is reputed to have germicidal qualities and circulatory benefits.

For retailer information, contact:

GRANDPA SOAP COMPANY
317-321 East Eighth Street
Cincinnati, OH 45202
Tel. 513/241-1677
Fax. 513/241-1676

SASSAFRAS TEA

The matron of the house boiled him some hot 'sass-tea' which, the old man said, relieved him mightily.
—*John S. Robb,* Streaks of Squatter Life, *1847*

A root used by the Algonquin Indians since ancient times, sassafras was an early export to England where it was used as a cure for such ills as the agues, stomach ulcers, skin troubles, lung fevers, dropsy, catarrh, gout, dysentery, sore eyes, ingrowing toenails, bad breath and baldness. Dixie Gun Works' sassafras, for which it claims no medicinal properties, comes packed with six to twelve sticks to a bundle, each stick cut from the sassafras tree root by the light of the moon and only when the sap is down. Simmer the bundle one-half hour to make three quarts of tea, then re-use the roots by simmering one hour to make another three quarts.

Price $3, plus shipping and handling.

Catalog of black-powder guns, shooting supplies and antique gun parts available, $4.

DIXIE GUN WORKS
Union City, TN 38261
Tel. 901/885-0700 or
    800/238-6785 to order
Fax. 901/885-0440

No. 37.   7½ inch

No. 192.   9 inch

No. 203.   9 inch

ACE HARD-RUBBER COMBS

Made from the material accidentally discovered by Nelson Goodyear in 1851, Ace hard-rubber combs were reputedly found among the remains of Civil War soldiers during archaeological excavations of battlefield sites. Found today at drug counters everywhere.

...8R5534 This splendid ...r is a French brier, bull-...ape bowl, with amberold ...piece; the stem between ...d mouthpiece is genuine ...el wood, and will not ...our tongue; worth 75 ...e regular pipe stores. ...each.................27c ...mail, postage extra, 5 cents.

...rench Brier Pipe for 39 Cents.

No. 18R5538 Handsome French Brier Pipe, straight bulldog shape, with clear Chinese amber stem and decorated band and bowl, latest design. ...hly recommend this pipe. ...each...............39c

The Distiller Pipe, 44 Cents.

...8R5542 The Distil-...e. Greatest success ...entury. Brier bowl ...ard rubber stem. ...n bowl and stem is ...tube which takes up the nicotine and sa... ...ut the mouthpiece and let out the nico... ...easily replaced. ...each....

German Porcelain Pipes.

No. 18R5546 German Porcelain ...handsomely decorated; just the t... for a good old-fashioned smoke. Th... an exceptionally fine and handsome ...man Porcelain Pipe. Made with very long stem, fitted with flexible top...extra fine hard rubber mouthp... Long, genuine porcelain bowl artistic... and handsomely decorated. The ...can readily be taken apart for clea... thus insuring a clean, cool smoke. Price, each.... If by mail, postage extra, 28 cents.

69 Cents for this Chip M... schaum Pipe.

No. 18R5550 Large Sized Fine Vienna chip Meerschaum Pipe, large egg shaped bowl and handsome cherry stem with silk cord and tassel

and Chinese amber mouthpiece. An exceptionally handsome article.

No. 18R5550 Price, each...........69c

If by mail, postage extra, 6 cents.

...sh Water Pipe.

...8R5554 A genuine ...a Water pipe; the ...made of fine color-..., prettily decorated, ...a long flexible stem, ...mall amber mouth-...nnected to pipe. In ...er of head is a thin ...abe through which ...ke passes. The cup ...olds the tobacco is ...f Vienna Meer-..., which can be re-...if desired, by the ...Meerschaum cigar ...which comes with ...Entire height of ...about 10 inches ...each...........$1.94 ...g weight, 1 pound.

...R5558 Turkish Water Pipe, same as above, ...ng two flexible stems from which two per-...smoke at the same time. The bowl is more ...tely decorated than the above, and a little ...Entire height about 10½ inches. ...each. (Shipping weight, 1 pound)... $2.75

...es in Leather Covered Cases.

No. 18R5562 Genuine French Brier Pipe, English bulldog shape. Length, 5 inches. Handsome Vienna amber mouthpiece. Each one of these pipes is put up in a handsome leather covered case, with silk and velvet lining. Price, each...........73c If by mail, postage extra, each, 5 cents.

---

79 Cents for a Rosewood Pipe.

No. 18R5566 This is certainly one of the very handsomest pipes made. It is made from highly polished rosewood with removable set in bowl of genuine meerschaum, which can be unscrewed and easily cleaned. Genuine Chinese amber mouthpiece; length, 5¼ inches. Put up in handsome leather covered, satin lined case. Price, each...........79c

If by mail, postage extra, 4 cents.

Most Stores get $1.50 for this Grade.

No. 18R5567 Flat Stem French Brier Pipe, with 1½-inch genuine amber mouthpiece. Has a medium small size bowl and is a very desirable shape

Bull Dog Style, $1.47.

No. 18R5571 French Brier Pipe, bulldog shape, with 2¼-inch genuine amber mouthpiece and trimmed with a sterling silver band between stem and pipe. Entire length of pipe, 5¼ inches. Large size, highly polished bowl.

Inlaid in fine leather plush lined case. Price, each....................$1.47

If by mail, postage extra, 5 cents.

A Beauty for a Present.

No. 18R5573 Fine French Brier Pipe, bulldog shape, with genuine amber mouthpiece, 3 inches long, highly polished bowl, with band of chased gold, also on stem, in elegant plush lined leather case. $3.75 value. Our price....................$2.29

If by mail, postage extra, 6 cents.

This $5.00 Pipe for $3.25.

No. 18R5575 Finest Quality French Brier Pipe, with heavy, wide, 3½-inch genuine amber mouthpiece. The bowl is ornamented with a heavy 14-karat gold band, and a heavy 14-karat gold band also connects the amber mouthpiece with the brier bowl.

Total length of pipe, 6½ inches. Inlaid in an elegant plush lined chamois covered case. There are no finer goods made; real $5.00 value. Price, each....................$3.25

If by mail, postage extra, 6 cents.

Fancy Egg Shape.

No. 18R5579 This is a fancy egg shape, French Brier Pipe, ...and stem and ½-inch gold band and 4-inch amber mouthpiece. Entire length of pipe is 11 inches, mak-...ing a delight-

---

Finest Quality French Brier Pipe.

No. 18R5581 Finest Quality French Brier Pipe, Bull bitch shape. This handsome pipe has a thick curved genuine amber stem, heavily mounted in real gold, such a pipe as you never expect to pay less than $7.50 for elsewhere. Price, each....................$3.7...

If by mail, postage extra, each, 6 cents.

A Novelty Ball Shape Pipe, $1.85.

No. 18R5583 Fine French Brier Pipe, ball shape. Highly polished bowl, with curved square, genuine amber stem and trimmed with small, gold band. Inlaid in leather lined case. A very desirable small pipe. Price, each..............$1.8...

If by mail, postage extra, 5 cents.

Special Value at $2.75.

...8R5585 Highly ...ed, Fine French ...Pipe, bulldog shape, ...urved 2½-inch genuine amber square stem; ...d with gold band at ...the stem between the ...and bowl. A very ...me pipe. Inlaid in ...plush lined case. Price, each.........$2.7...

If by mail, postage extra, 5 cents.

Handy Set Pipe, 87 Cents.

No. 18R5586 Well Shape French Brier Pipe, with clear ben Chinese amber stem, inlaid i plush lined pocket case. A rea bargain. Price, each..........87... If by mail, postage extra, 4 cent...

No. 18R5587 Fine French Brier Pipe, with a well shaped, large size, egg bowl; trimmed with curved sterling silver band and 2¾-inch genuine amber curved shove bit. Pipe inlaid in chamois, plush lined pocket case. Price, each................$1.89 If by mail, postage extra, 4 cents.

No. 18R5589 A well shaped genuine French Brier Pipe. Highly polished, with handsom chased gold bands on stem an top of bowl; genuine amber curve shove bit, 2¾ inches in length Pipe is inlaid in handsome chan ois, plush lined pocket case. Price, each................$2.9... If by mail, postage extra, 5 cent...

No. 18R5591 Square Stem, French Brier Bowl, very highly polished, heavy sterling silver band between stem and pipe; 2¾-inch genuine amber shove bit; medium large bowl for a good long smoke. Inlaid in fine chamois plush lined pocket case. Price, each....... $1.97

If by mail, postage extra, 4 cents.

Smoker's Companion.

No. 18R5594 Smoker Companion, consisting of two pipes, on straight French brier bulldog shape, with 2 inch genuine amber mouthpiece, solid gold band, and one bent egg shape, highly polished French brier pipe with curved 2-inch genuine amber mouthpiece, solid gold band around stem both pipes inlaid in beautiful chamois covered and silk plush lined case. Price, per set....................$2.0...

If by mail, postage extra, 6 cents.

FINE MEERSCHAUM PIPES.

No. 18R5597 Chip Meerschaum Pipe, bulldog shape bowl, best English amber mouthpiece. We warrant this pipe to color; with satin lined leather covered case. Do not unscrew stem to...

⪦ Pipes ⪧

▨ MARK TWAIN'S 1896 PETERSON

Samuel Clemens's well-known love of tobacco was not without its limits: "I have made it a rule," the Bard of Hannibal, Missouri, was once quoted as saying, "never to smoke more than one cigar at a time." As the accompanying photograph shows, this rule applied to pipes as well. But while it may be assumed that Twain smoked a single stogie at a time out of his sense of proper restraint, he kept to one pipe because, from 1896 until his death in 1910, he favored one above the others.

For years it rested almost unnoticed in the Mark Twain Museum, mercilessly misshapen as a result of the author's frequent cleanings. Then one day in 1980, Henry Sweets, curator of the Hannibal museum, received a telephone call from Bill Sweeney, president of Peterson Pipes of Dublin, Ireland. Sweeney had come across the picture of Twain we see here and believed that the pipe cradled in his hand was once made by the Peterson Company and discontinued early in this century. One look by the curator at the original pipe in the museum's collection instantly confirmed Mr. Sweeney's suspicion.

Sweeney immediately dispatched a company expert from Dublin to Hannibal to record the precise dimensions of Mark Twain's 1896 Peterson pipe. Then, after carefully selecting proper blocks of aged briar with which to reproduce it, in 1981 the Peterson company manufactured a limited run of 400 "Mark Twain Deluxe Quality System Pipes," dedicated to the great American writer's memory and works.

For retailer information contact:

PETERSON OF DUBLIN
20717 Marilla Street
Chatsworth, CA 91311

CLAY PIPES

Replicated to faithfully follow eighteenth- and early-nineteenth-century originals, clay pipes like those offered by the Crazy Crow Trading Post were likely to have been found in every Hudson's Bay and Northwest Company trader's pack. With cherrywood stems.

TRAPPER'S PIPES

For making the bowls of their calumets, the Indians of the upper Missouri River region used a red pipestone found only in one Minnesota quarry. This quarry and the territory around it were considered neutral land, accessible to those of any tribe who came for the sacred pipestone. In time this Minnesota catlinite was used to fashion the compact, stowable pipes that were smoked (and often worn as pendants) by eighteenth- and early-nineteenth-century trappers. Today this material is still used by Crazy Crow to make its unique replica trapper's pipes.

Catalog available, $3.

CRAZY CROW TRADING POST
P.O. Box 314-AMS
Denison, TX 75020
Tel. 903/463-1366
Fax. 903/463-7734

RIBBED CLAY PIPE

As the Ohio Valley was settled in the early part of the nineteenth century, pottery factories were soon established to fulfill the pioneers' requirements for crocks, jugs and tableware. These places also made clay pipe bowls in great quantities, each usually to be fitted onto a reed stem. The Log Cabin Shop's ribbed clay pipe comes from the descendant of one such pottery and measures six inches from bit to bowl.

Price: $4.50 plus postage and handling.

Catalog of black-powder supplies and accessories available, $4.

THE LOG CABIN SHOP
P.O. Box 275
Lodi, OH 44254
Tel. 216/948-1082

KINNIKINNICK

In its various forms, the word "kinnikinnick" comes from the Cree or Chippewa dialects of the Algonquin language and means "what is mixed." What was mixed by the Indians was originally dried sumac leaves together with other ingredients. As a name for the smoking mixtures used by both red men and white, "kinnikinnick" was widely employed throughout the nineteenth century—Kinnikinnick-brand tobacco was sold to Federal troops by Civil War sutlers for a dollar a pound.

The Crazy Crow Trading Post offers several blends of Indian kinnikinnick, loosely replicating what may have been smoked early in the nineteenth century: Northern Plains, "a mild blend of...tobacco, leaves, and herbs common to the Indians of the upper Missouri River country"; Eastern Woodlands, "a...blend of tobacco, roots, and bark preferred by the Indian forest dwellers of the Eastern United States"; Comanche Straight, "a non-tobacco blend of herbs, bark, and leaves from the Southern Plains"; and Great Lakes Straight, "an all-herbal blend based upon an old 'good medicine' recipe. The herbs that are used were common to the Indian people of the midwestern woodlands, the Appalachians, and the Ozarks."

CRAZY CROW TRADING POST
P.O. Box 314-AMS
Denison, TX 75020
Tel. 903/463-1366
Fax. 903/463-7734

✿ TWIST

At eight o'clock, the Posscossohe, Black Cat, grand chief of the Mandans, came to see us. After showing these chiefs many things which were curiosities to them, and giving a few presents of curious handkerchiefs, arm bands, and paint, with a twist of tobacco, they departed at 1 o'clock much pleased.
—*The Journal of William Clark, Captain, The Corps of Discovery, November 28, 1804*

From the eighteenth century, when it was used in trade with the Indians, through the Civil War, when it was bought from sutlers, the convenient tobacco twist was a familiar sight. These would be chewed or smoked, and the Indians would make use of them in medicine bundles.

The Crazy Crow Trading Post offers the following varieties of tobacco twist: American Fur Company Brand, a sweet chew or smoke; Rocky Mountain Pride, described as "natural" by the store; and Astorian Twist, a burley tobacco.

Catalog available, $3.

CRAZY CROW TRADING POST
P.O. Box 314-AMS
Denison, TX 75020
Tel. 903/463-1366
Fax. 903/463-7734

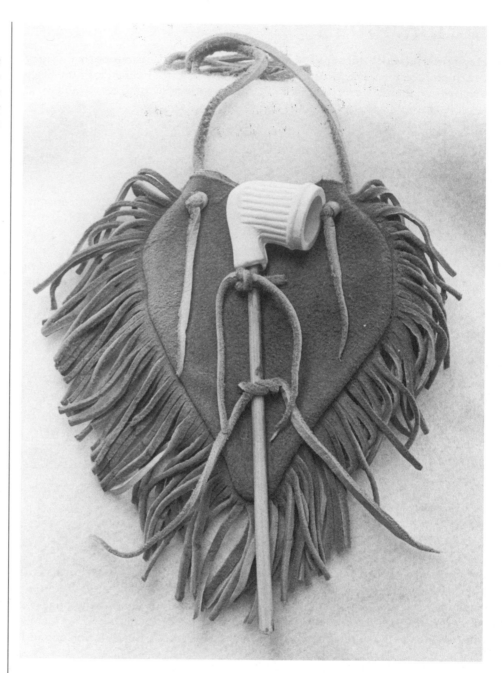

▨ GAGE D'AMOUR

La Pelleterie's heart-shaped tobacco bag (its name means "token of love") has been copied from early drawings of the Plains Indians. Made of finely fringed buckskin, it holds tobacco and carries a clay pipe.
Price: $19.95, plus postage and handling.

Catalog of historical clothing specializing in the fur trade of the eighteenth and nineteenth centuries, $5.

LA PELLETERIE
P.O. Box 127
Arrow Rock, MO 65320
Tel. 816/837-3261

◼ TOBACCO BOX

A faithful replica of an early-nine-teenth-century tobacco box that might have been found on a trade blanket in an Indian camp or in a Boston gentleman's coat. Available in solid brass or German silver, it measures 4 inches by 2 inches by ⅝ inch. Weight: 4 oz.

Prices: Brass tobacco box, $19.25. German silver tobacco box, $18.25. Postage and handling additional.

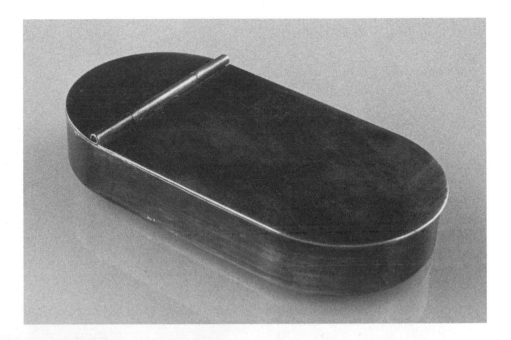

❋ SNUFF BOX

Made of brass, 2½ inches in diameter and 1 inch high. Press-on lid. Weight: 3 oz.

Price: $6.95, plus postage and a $1 handling charge.

Catalog of black-powder accessories and supplies available, $4.

THE LOG CABIN SHOP, INC.
P.O. Box 275
Lodi, OH 44254
Tel. 216/948-1082

❀ TOBACCO CANTEEN

Crazy Crow's hand-crafted replica tobacco canteens are rawhide flasks, each with a willow end-plug and braided leather thong.

Catalog available, $3.

CRAZY CROW TRADING POST
P.O. Box 314-AMS
Denison, TX 75020
Tel. 903/463-1366

CIGAR STORE INDIANS

Unseen in the forest surrounding Claremont, New Hampshire, numberless Indians yet lurk. These are not wild men, but wooden; and once freed from the tree trunks that conceal them, are more likely to brandish a fistful of cheroots than a tomahawk. They exist today because of the craftsmanship of Edward Boggis, a former logger, wrestler and woodcarving instructor who is presently the country's only full-time maker of cigar-store Indians.

Since he began to carve them full size back in 1972, the 70-year-old Mr. Boggis has turned out well over a thousand wooden chiefs, squaws and scouts, each crowned with either feathers or (as was often the case historically) tobacco leaves. Mr. Boggis's wooden Indians cleave closely to the traditional and are made by means of a painstakingly authentic process that takes up to nine months to complete. Until the store closed in the mid-1970s, the wooden Indians were sold by New York's Abercrombie & Fitch on Fifth Avenue.

When and where the first cigar-store figures appeared is not known for certain, but several sources point to an early-eighteenth-century London tobacconist as their originator. This cigar store "Indian" was more likely a Negro, or "black boy" as they came to be called, wooden facsimiles of the West Indian slaves that (along with imported African ones) did the work of the American tobacco industry. Perhaps because Europeans had become aware of both simultaneously, the wild Indian was also associated with tobacco, and in time fanciful red men and women came to replace the wooden slaves at their cigar-store stations. Toward the end of the nineteenth century the use of wooden figures had spread to other establishments, as Chinese mandarins bowed before tea shops, German kings greeted tavern-goers with foaming steins, and legions of carved Punches, Columbines, Turks and others populated city sidewalks. Early in the 1900s all these fell victim to the traffic ordinances of meddlesome local governments whose ferocious action against them was such that today few survive. Few, that is, except those in the museums, those in our memories, and those still unseen in the forests a short haul from Ed Boggis's shop.

Price: $3,000.

Brochure available.

ARTIST IN WOOD
Ed Boggis
Old Church Road, R.R. 2, Box 387
Claremont, NH 03743
Tel. 603/542-2082

No. 20K3515 We recommend this glass particularly to those who are willing to pay a little more money for the sake of quality. This instrument comes from a Paris maker, who is noted for the quality of his telescopes, particularly the...

...which are of higher grade and better quality than the lenses used by other makers. The object glass in this telescope is a very fine achromatic lens, insuring magnifying power and fine definition. This instrument is strongly and substantially made throughout, finely finished, fitted with the special patented hinge cap cover in the eyepiece, draw tubes of highly burnished brass, and trimmings of bronzed brass, lacquered. Length, closed, 6¾ inches; extended, 16¾ inches. Price......(If by mail, postage extra, 15 cents)......**$3.95**

This Big Marine Telescope, $5.55.

20K3520 This telescope, although designed especially for use on ship... is a fine instrument for general purposes. It is a one draw telescope, the ... the made of highly burnished brass, and all exterior metal work of lacquered brass. ... the object lens and the eyepiece are protected by sliding covers, and the body is ... with a special corded material made from pure linen, ornamental in appearance, ... stronger and more durable than leather. The diameter of this telescope is 2½ ... The length, closed, is 14½ inches; extended, 24 inches; the magnifying power, ...two times. Price......**$5.55**

If by mail, postage extra, 37 cents.

No. 20K3520 partly extended.

Metal Hinge Cap Telescope, $8.40.

This special hinge cap telescope is an e... telescope in every way, material and wor... best, extra quality achromatic lenses, car... adjusted, giving high power and fine defi... parts, including the outside trimmings and t... erfect working of the draw tubes so long as t... is perfectly protected by a sliding cover. T... rays of the sun when viewing objects where ...inches long when closed, and 23¾ inches lo...

......**$8.40**

...ubes, are made with the finest gunmetal ... ...ent may be used. The patented hinged ... ...pe is made with extension sun shade, by ... ...sary to look toward the west in the eve... ...lly extended. The diameter of the obje...

20K3530 This high grade, first qu... ...d shoulder strap, is an ideal instrument ... ...tc., the leather caps and the strong leat... ...the instrument, no matter how roughly i... ...pe is covered with fine quality, pebbled n... ...urable material, made extra heavy and st... ...ead black oxidized finish and the workmanship throughout is the best. This ... ...pe is provided with specially ground achromatic lenses of the highest degree of ... ...ice, carefully and accurately adjusted, and we particularly recommend this ... ...pe to anyone desiring a serviceable, strongly made instrument, of the highest ... ...of optical perfection. The diameter of the object glass is twenty-two ligues; ... ...gth, closed and with the caps on, is 10¾ inches; the length when fully extended is 35¾ inches, and the magnifying power is thirty diameters. ...ice......(If by mail, postage extra, 47 cents.)......**$11.95**

...elescope partly extended.

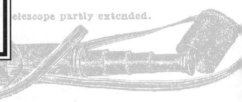

Large Field Extra Luminous Telescope, $17.25.

No. 20K3540 This telescope is the highest grade telescope that c... be manufactured, representing the very highest degree of excellence in instr... ments of this kind.

IT IS FITTED WITH GENUINE ANASTIGMAT LENSES, lens... that a... perfectly corrected, not only for spherical and chromatic aberration, but a... for astigmatism, thereby securing the finest possible definition, combined wi... the highest possible magnifying power.

No. 20K3540 partly extended.

TELESCOPE embraces a wider angle of view than any other telescope made of corresponding size and power, and the peculiar construction of t... lenses, both the objective lens and the lenses in the eyepiece, is such as to admit an unusually large amount of light, from which fact t... ...ents are known as "Extra Luminous." This desirable quality is particularly advantageous on dark, cloudy days or when using the instrument alo... evening.

RSTAND, that so far as magnifying power and definition are concerned this is the best telescope that can be manufactured, fully equal in ... optical and mechanical perfection to the very finest astronomical telescopes.

WORKMANSHIP, FINISH AND MATERIALS used in this telescope are made to correspond with its unsurpassed optical qualities, all me... parts, both the draw tubes and the external fittings, being made with the finest gunmetal finish and t... ...g is a very fine quality of blue levant leather. Made with patented hinge cap for protection of the object glass, sliding cover for the eyepiece, two draw ...closed, 10¾ inches; extended, 24 inches; diameter of object glass, 19 lignes; magnifying power, thirty diameters. Price......**$17.25**

If by mail, postage extra, 33 cents.

25-Ligne Hinge Cap Telescope, $19.70.

0. 20K3545 This is the most powerful telescope that we handle, a much higher grade telescope ... to be found in the best optical stores in the United States. **It is the lenses** which make this ...ent so much superior to ordinary telescopes, these lenses being especially ground from the finest ... glass, very carefully centered and accurately adjusted. They are made to combine to the greatest ... extent the finest definition and highest magnifying power. For astronomical work this telescope ... an ideal instrument, showing clearly and distinctly the interesting changes and mysterious spots on ...rface of the sun, the wonderful mountain ranges and apparently extinct craters of the moon, the ...es and the surface markings of the planet Jupiter, the wonderful rings of Saturn, the canals on the ...Mars, nebulae, double stars, etc. For the observation of the sun a dark glass is mounted in the ...ver of the eyepiece. The magnifying power is 50 diameters.

Genuine Stanhope Lens Floro-scope, 30 Cents.

No. 20K3600 This Microscope is fitted wi... an exceedingly powerful Stanhope lens, by mea... of which the animalculae in stagnant water, entire... invisible to the naked eye, can be distinctly seen. ... drop of vinegar seen by this instrument is found ... be swarming with living creatures, and yeast wate... alive with wriggling germs. Besides the high pow... Stanhope lens, this Floroscope is also fitted with an or... nary long focus magnifying glass for the examinat... of insects, flowers, etc. An intensely interest... instrument. Finished in lacquered brass. Price......(If by mail, postage extra, 3 cents)......**30¢**

Astronomical Eyepiece, $5.20.

No. 20K3546 This Eyepiece is made for use with our No. 20K3545 telescope, for astronomical observations only and increases the power...

The draw tubes, trimmings, and all exposed metal parts are made with fine gunmetal finish, the very best and most expensive finish known for optical instruments. **This fine steel blue gunmetal finish will never tarnish** nor rust and the draw tubes always work smoothly and easily. The body of the instrument is covered with a fine grade of pebbled morocco leather. **This telescope is made with sunshade,** and instead of the ordinary cap, it is provided...

221

Tripod Microscope

No. 20K3605 Tripod Mic... scope, adapted to a variety of ... where a short focus and high m... nifying power is desirable. Adj... able focus, extra high grade ... strong, heavy brass mountings...

⬛ HANDMADE SHIP MODELS

Handcrafted miniatures of eighteenth- and nineteenth-century sailing ships are the work Piel Craftsmen. From their shop in Newburyport, Massachusetts (where many of the original vessels were built), Piel Craftsmen have been carving their ship models from selected, well-seasoned wood for more than 35 years.

The completed models measure from 13½ to 18½ inches in length, and from 11 to 17¼ inches in height. Included are the cargo carrier *Benjamin Hale* (Newburyport, 1882); the small merchant brig *Topaz* (Newburyport, 1807), with her characteristic "cod's head, mackerel tail" lines; the clipper *Sea Witch* (New York, 1846), the first ship to sail from New York to San Francisco; the clipper *Red Jacket* (Rockland, Maine, 1853), "one of the seven fastest sailing ships in all history"; the lordly *Sovereign of the Seas* (East Boston, 1852); the *Charles W. Morgan* (Newburyport, 1841); the famous clipper *Flying Cloud* (East Boston, 1851); and the *U.S.S. Constitution*, illustrated.

Prices: $75 to $510 (plus $5 for postage).

Brochure available.

PIEL CRAFTSMEN
307 High Street
Newburyport, MA 01950
Tel. 508/462-7012

※ SCRIMSHAW CARVINGS

Although Europeans hunted whales at least as long ago as the ninth century, among white settlers of North America whaling began during the seventeenth century, after the Indians of Nantucket Island taught it to them. Within a hundred years of this modest beginning, Nantucket whalers were voyaging to the Pacific Ocean, plying the sperm whale's sea lanes in pursuit of its valuable oil. So dependent was nineteenth-century America on the products of whaling that from its industrial centers of New Bedford, Massachusetts, and San Francisco, California, several species of leviathan were hunted to extinction, or nearly so.

In those days a whale hunt might last from three to five years, and it was during the seaman's long periods of idleness that scrimshaw—the art of carving and decoratively engraving whalebone—emerged. Some of the finest artifacts of nineteenth-century scrimshanders are in the collection of the Nantucket Whaling Museum, which has granted Artek, Inc. the exclusive rights to their replication and sale. Using a polymer "ivory" to replicate the weight, the color, and even the flawed texture of the whalebone originals, Artek's copies can barely be distinguished from them. Shown here is "A Susan Tooth," depicting the whaler *Susan* as it was carved by the renowned nineteenth-century scrimshander Frederick Myrick. The original of this polymer replica is in the Nantucket Museum.

Catalog available, $2.

ARTEK, INC.
P.O. Box 145
Elm Avenue
Antrim, NH 03440
Tel. 603/588-6825
Fax. 603/588-6894

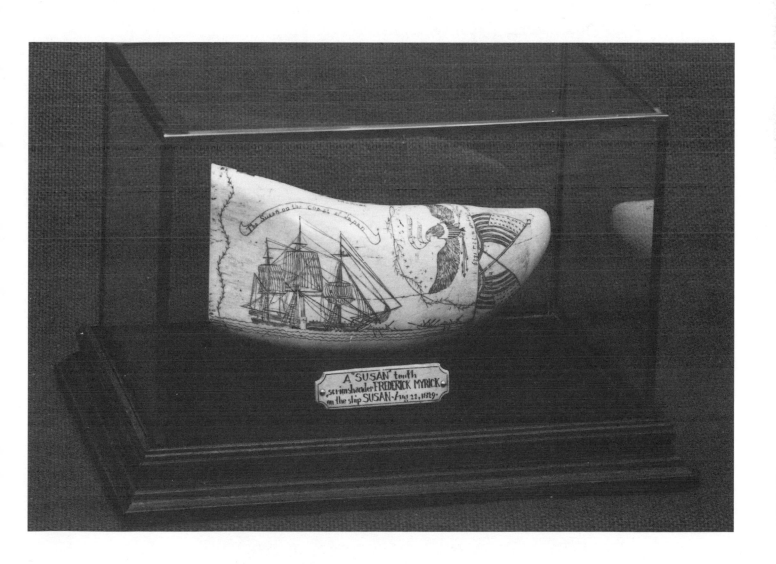

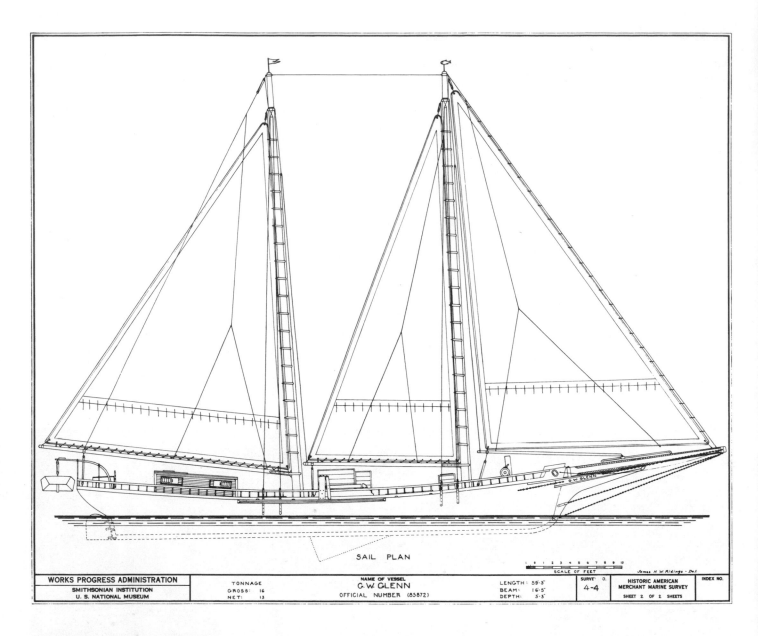

SAIL PLAN

SCALE OF FEET

James H W Ridings - Del.

WORKS PROGRESS ADMINISTRATION	TONNAGE	NAME OF VESSEL	LENGTH: 59-3"	SURVEY D.	HISTORIC AMERICAN	INDEX NO.
SMITHSONIAN INSTITUTION U. S. NATIONAL MUSEUM	GROSS: 16 NET: 13	G. W. GLENN OFFICIAL NUMBER (85872)	BEAM: 16-5" DEPTH: 5-3"	4-4	MERCHANT MARINE SURVEY SHEET 2 OF 2 SHEETS	

◈ WATERCRAFT PLANS

The Smithsonian Institution's National Museum of American History has ship plans available from its National Watercraft Collection. Derived primarily from the works of the naval historian H.I. Chapelle, these are obtainable in two sets: *The Smithsonian Collection of Warship Plans,* and the 250-page *Ship Plan List of the Maritime Collection.* Naval designs range from the mid-eighteenth to the early twentieth-centuries, comprising vessels from the Continental Navy, Confederate States Navy and U.S.

Navy; and the *Ship Plan List* contains design drawings of such varied and/or historic vessels as Columbus's flagship, the *Santa Maria*; the 1775 tobacco ship *Brilliant*; and 15 Seattle fishing boats from the period 1910 to 1930. In both collections some vessels are represented by a single line drawing or inboard profiles, while others—such as the original frigate *Constitution* or Revolutionary War gunboat *Philadelphia*—are rendered in as many as 16 sheets of drawings. Income from sale of the plans goes toward making masters of older, more fragile drawings in addition to further-ing other aspects of the publication process.

Contact:

SHIP PLANS
*NMAH 5010 / MRC 628
Smithsonian Institution
Washington, D.C. 20560*

❀SAILING DINGHY

The *Columbia* sailing dinghy was originally designed in the 1880s by the famous boatwright Nathan Herreshoff as a lifeboat or tender to his large sloops and ketches. The replica, which accommodates three or four adults, is planked in western red cedar over white-oak backbone and ribs. Her trim is made of Honduras mahogany, brightly finished, with the outboard painted in colors of the owner's choosing. According to the Columbia dinghy's maker, Anthony R. Bries, this boat rows easily and is extremely seaworthy.

Price, complete with sail and spruce oars: $9,254.

Freedom Boatworks is a custom builder of historic and contemporary wooden boats. It offers no catalog per se, but invites prospective buyers to call or write with a description of the type of craft in which they are interested.

FREEDOM BOATWORKS
P.O. Box 511
Baraboo, WI 53913
Tel. 608/356-5861

❁ ROSE 20 STEAM LAUNCH

With their exposed boilers and tall funnels, turn-of-the-century steam launches were generally used on rivers and as yacht tenders. The Rose 20 steam launch features the Townsend hull—a fiberglass design combining the finer points of several antique hulls—which measures 20 feet in length, 4 feet 3 inches in width and 1 foot 10 inches in depth.

The boat's power plant, assembled from currently available off-the-shelf components, includes either a Semple or a Tiny Power "M"—both single-cylinder engines with reverse valving—and a steam boiler fired by either propane, diesel or solid fuel. Both engines are capable of generating 5 h.p., an amount deemed more than necessary due to the hull's low drag configuration.

The Rose 20 is available in two kits

and a completed "Steamaway" version. The Standard kit includes everything an amateur builder requires to complete the launch except the wood; and the Deluxe kit includes "the necessary woods for hull and boiler," plus a bilge system, all deck hardware and an insulated brass boiler stack.

Price: $16,950.

Catalog available, $12.

WALTER C. BECKMANN, LTD.
P. O. Box 97, Point Judith
Wakefield, RI 02880
Tel. 401/783-1859

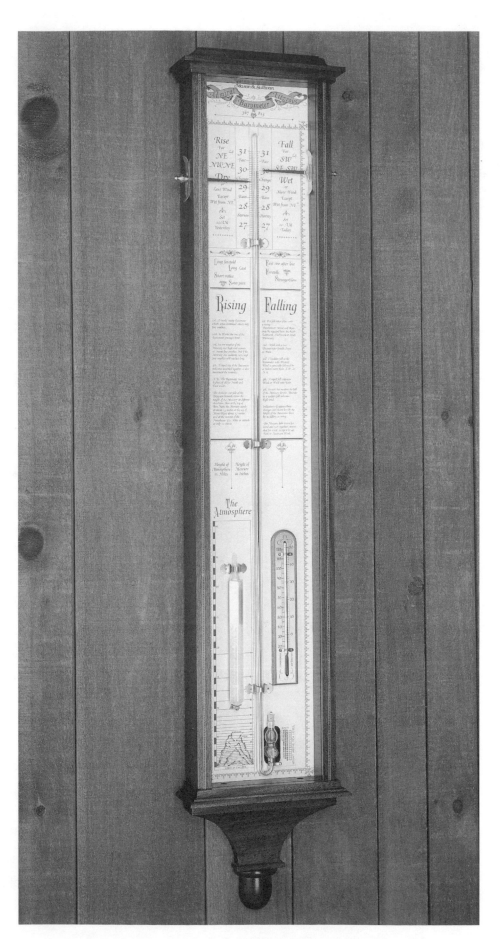

❧ **FITZROY BAROMETER**

This barometer was designed by Admiral Fitzroy, captain of the H.M.S. Beagle, which sailed the world from 1831 to 1836 with Charles Darwin as its naturalist. This voyage embarked Darwin on a career that resulted in his formulation of the concept of natural evolution. Fitzroy is less well remembered as the first man to set up a formalized system for forecasting weather.

The replica of Admiral Fitzroy's barometer is made of Honduras mahogany with a solid wood inlay. The blown-glass mercury-filled tube, the glass atmospheric storm tube, and the alcohol thermometer with mahogany plaque and scale are all mounted on a gold and black chart. Hardware and fittings are of solid brass and are imported from England.

Dimensions: 45 inches high, 9 inches wide and 3¼ inches deep.

Seasonal catalog of replica clocks available.

MASON & SULLIVAN COMPANY
586 Higgins Crowell Road
West Yarmouth, MA 02673
Tel. 800/933-3010
Fax. 508/775-5581

Sole Leather Trunks.

56690 Canvas covered, sole leather bottom, heavy leather bound corners riveted, linen lined, steel springs; high set up tray with hat box, with sateen finish, large packing partition, linen lined throughout, leatherbound duck cover.
30 inches..$19.00
32 " .. 20.00
34 " .. 21.00

56692 Genuine sole leather, heavy duck leather cover, frame, springs, stitch, French Excelsior with sol er pro sole bottom set up natio with silk ha covered divided
artments underneath for collars, cuffs, shi d morocco faced. The trunk is Holland throughout. The finest men's sole leathe e market. 30 inches
ches......$35.00   34 inches....

Portmanteau.
SOLE LEATHER.

56694 Iron frame, steel springs hand stitched French edge, Excelsior lock, with sole leather lock protector, hand stitched sliding handles. The trunk opens in the center and is lined throughout with linen. The interior is especially arranged for tourists.
26 inches..$27.00
28 " .. 29.00
30 " .. 31.00
32 " .. 33.00

Straight Back Trunks.
SOMETHING NEW.

56696 The straight back or wall trunk, canvas covered, iron bound, steel clamps, generally known as the wall trunk, as the lid opens straight up without pulling from the wall; has a heavy brass lock, all steel clamps and heavy side bolt locks, linen faced, heavy iron centre band around body and hoop iron band on each end; a serviceable, convenient and in every respect a practical trunk for either home or traveling purposes. See cut of 56697 for closed appearance.
32 inches long, price.......$7.50
34 " " 8.00

56697 Wall Trunk, see cut of 56696 for open appearance; canvas covered, iron bound, steel clamps; this is an elegant and strongly made trunk, best Excelsior lock and heavy side bolts, steel corner clamps, and linen lined throughout; it is also provided a linen web dress tray.
ches long, price.... ....$9.00
.... 9.50

well built. See cut of 56696 for open appearance.
32 inch. long, price.$13.00 34 inch. long, price.$14.00

Grain Leather and Canvas Satchels, Telescopes, Coat Cases, Etc.
Note reduced prices.

The Gladstone style of traveling bag is the most desirable of any, as under the straps on the outside as much can be secured as the inside will hold; convenient for carrying shawls, blankets, etc. Satchels weight

56699 Canvas Covered Wall Trunk, leather bound, brass trimmings; has solid brass clamps, heavy brass Excelsior lock, is full linen lined and an extra dress tray beneath a large body tray. This is a neat, compact and very desirable trunk; has a stylish appearance and is

double hasp lock, flat key, English nickel side catches, nickel plated, heavy leather handle.

Each.			Each
14 inch............$2.55		20 inch..........$3.56
16 inch............ 2.85		22 inch.......... 3.90
18 inch............ 3.23		24 inch.......... 4.75

56710 Grained Leather Gladstone, leather covered frame, nickel lock, spring catch, patent corner protections. This bag is lined with pigskin, the outside straps are stitched, and has an English handle; is handsomely finished and very strong and durable.

Each.			Each
14 inches.... ....$4.75		20 inches.. ....$6.25
16 inches.... 5.25		22 inches.. 6.75
18 inches.......... 5.75		24 inches.......... 7.25

56712 Fitted Gladstone Bag, made of best selected leather, Spanish olive or light brown, leather covered steel frame with English corner snap catches, bottom shoes, handsome lock and trimmings, full leather lined with fine set of toilet trimmings.

Length.	Price.
16 inches..... .$8.67
18 inches..... 9.35
20 inches....... 10.00
22 inches....... 10.67

56715 Large Size Bag made from bright rubber cloth, alligator grained, heavy double flange frame, long lock, nickel trimmings, strong handle, leather straps

---

56719 Canvas stone" Traveling made of drab duck, with straps, nickel corners bound grained leather lined; will out leather satchel.

Each.		
14 inches..........$1.40	20 inches..........
16 inches.......... 1.50	22 inches..........
18 inches.......... 1.67	24 inches..........

56720 Canvas Bag, strong and substantial, makes a handy desirable very low c opens on and is f by means spring c one on t one on ea

| 4 inches price....$0.75 | 20 inches, price... |
| 0 inches, price.... .85 | 22 inches, price... |
| 8 inches, price.... 1.00 |

56722 The "Cabin," and very popular opens on top, very pack, as the top of sides open up t width of the sate very stylish and made of the best grained leather, lin leather, strong handle, strong nick and catches. This dered the best bag on the market for the mo
inches Each......$4.35 | 16 inches Each.......
14 inches Each...... 5.00 | 18 inches Each.......

56724 Grain Cabin Bag, ja frame, strong English band brown imit leather lining; a very popula bag and is fas the place of th stone shape.
14 inches, eac
16 inches, eac
18 inches, cac
20 inches, eac

56725 Engli ford Alligat natural bro or, entirely style, very h wide. The best selecte are used in t heavy steel covered, stitched a n entire fram lock and trim English cate inside stay bag open

leather lining. Price.
14 inches long......$8.00 | 17 inches long..
15 inches long...... 8.35 | 18 inches long..
16 inches long...... 8.70 |

56727 Genuine tor Skin Gladstone made from s stock, leather steel frame han to bag, heavy f brass set in l snap catches, double jointed shoe, heavy st around, Englis tor handle, full lined, Englis pocket on one flap, and shirt on the other.

16 inches.....Each$12.50 | 20 inches....Each
18 inches.....Each 13.50 | 22 inches....Each

56729 English Sewed Gladstone Traveling steel frame, padloc chain; made from stock with heavy leut ered steel frame. to bag is hand stitched nickel plated with chain, leather

✸ THE DEARBORN INN

As improbable as it seems on the face of it, Detroit's Dearborn Inn ("Colonial Homes and Motor House") offers its guests lodging in any one of five homes replicating the original dwellings of historic American figures. This means that midway between downtown Motown and the airport you can pass the night in a house an awful lot like the Frederick, Maryland, one from which Barbara Fritchie (1766-1862) waved the flag as the Confederate troop rode through town; or like the Long Island farmhouse where Walt Whitman was born in 1819.

Located near Greenfield Village and the Henry Ford Museums, the Dearborn Inn's replica homes were built in 1937 as a way of accommodating more guests. For a private area behind the hotel, Charles M. Hart ("the father of the historic village idea") designed the homes, and landscape architect Marshall Johnson surrounded each with flora appropriate to its original site.

The exteriors of the replica homes are the same size and made from the same materials as the originals. Although the interiors have been modified both in terms of structural space and to allow for modern conveniences, the entrance halls, stairs and sitting rooms are "exact copies or close adaptations" of those in the original structures, their sconces and candelabra copied and electrified. Many of the furnishings are reproductions of pieces used in the original homes.

The original of the Dearborn Inn's Poe Cottage still stands near where it was first built in the Bronx (euphemistically, if authentically, called "Fordham, New York" in the hotel brochure) in a tiny park where it now marinates in the rap music from ghetto-blasters. Even in the far more civilized Bronx of the 1950s the simple frame house invited protective worry, walled in as it was by the Grand Concourse's imposing art deco apartment buildings. The

The Walt Whitman House

The Edgar Allan Poe Cottage

poverty of Poe's life is reflected by the primitive workmanship of the white cottage, with its cut nails, crude laths and mud plaster. A colonial influence can be seen in the paneled doors, broad mantels and small-paned windows. Here is where Poe wrote "The Bells," "Annabel Lee," "Ulalume" and "Eureka."

In addition to the Poe Cottage, the Barbara Fritchie House and the Whitman farm, there are replicas of the

Red Hill, Virginia, home that Patrick Henry bought in 1794; and of the Litchfield, Connecticut, home that was built by Gov. Oliver Wolcott (1726-1797) in 1754, and where Alexander Hamilton, the Marquis de Lafayette and Gen. George Washington all stayed.

THE DEARBORN INN
20301 Oakwood Boulevard
Dearborn, MI 48124-4099
Tel. 313/271-2700

❧ HANCOCK SHAKER VILLAGE

Following a visit to the Hancock Shaker community in 1827, James Fenimore Cooper declared, "I have never seen, in any country, villages so neat, and so perfectly beautiful...without, however, being picturesque or ornamented, as those of the Shakers." This atmosphere, born of Shaker design and reflecting the sect's spirit of "consecration, peace, order, simplicity, and quiet industry," can still be found at Hancock Shaker Village. Shaker functionalism is said to anticipate that of the twentieth century, while in the other ways mentioned, it provides a refreshing contrast to it.

At the time of Cooper's visit the Hancock Shaker community was just about reaching its peak in members and productivity. During the middle of the nineteenth century its population began to dwindle (as Shakers' celibacy makes almost inevitable), and the last eldress, Sister Frances Hall, died and was buried there in 1959.

Today Hancock Shaker Village is operated by a nonprofit group as a public museum presenting the sect's unique culture as it unfolded during parts of three centuries. Of the museum's 21 structures, most are restored originals, although in 1962 the Meetinghouse was moved to Hancock from a closed Shaker community in Shirley, Massachusetts, and the schoolhouse is a reproduction. The 1830 Brick Dwelling, the Trustee's Office and the 1826 Round Stone Bar are each of special interest.

During the summer, demonstrations of Shaker crafts and domestic industries can be observed, including a working farm with nineteenth-century breeds of livestock. Extensive gardens represent the Shaker's profitable seed and medicinal herb businesses. Special events include Shearing Days (May), candlelight dinners in the Believer's Dining Room (Saturday evenings July through October), the Americana Artisan's Show (July), the annual antiques show (August), and the Festival of Shaker Crafts and Industries (October).

Open May 1 through October 31 daily, 9:30 a.m. to 5 p.m., and April and November, 10 a.m. to 3 p.m.

Color brochure and events calendar available.

HANCOCK SHAKER VILLAGE
Route 20, P.O. Box 898
Pittsfield, MA 01202
Tel. 413/443-0188

◪ LIVING HISTORY FARMS

The lamentable fading of the traditional family farm over recent decades has created outdoor farm museums to record and preserve their way of life. One of these museums, Living History Farms, is situated on 600 acres some eight miles northwest of Des Moines, Iowa.

Using diligently researched historical lore, the museum's 85 staff members and 200 volunteers demonstrate Midwestern life as it existed from the 1840s to the turn of the century. Included at Living History Farms are reconstructions of an 1850 farmstead, an Iowa town of 1875 and a 1900 farm. The museum's newest addition reflects its oldest period: an Ioway Indian village of about 1700.

The Living History Farms are true working farms, where all the spinning, canning, soapmaking, cheesemaking,

cabinetmaking, threshing and harvesting are done to produce actual goods, as well as to instruct.

Open May 1 through October 30, Monday through Saturday, from 9 a.m. to 5 p.m. (on Sunday from 11 a.m. to 6 p.m.). Admission: $7 for adults, $6 for seniors and $4 for children.

LIVING HISTORY FARMS
2600 N.W. 111th Street
Des Moines, IA 50322
Tel. 515/278-5286

◪ BLACK CREEK PIONEER VILLAGE

At Black Creek Pioneer Village in North York, Ontario, more than 30 buildings have been restored and furnished in the manner of a typical crossroads Ontario community of the 1860s. In addition to the livestock and gardens representative of Canada's early years there is a working pioneer farm, a harness shop, general store, blacksmith shop, printing office, weaver's shop, tinsmith, flour mill, school and church. Demonstrators in period costume appear throughout the village. Special events are scheduled seasonally.

Open seven days a week, 10 a.m. to 4:30 p.m.

BLACK CREEK PIONEER VILLAGE
1000 Murray Ross Parkway
North York, ON
Canada M3J 2P3
Tel. 416/736-1733

John Schippers
79

⊠ CONNER PRAIRIE

"A microcosm of Indiana as it was in the 1830s, an exciting period of expansion for the state and region," Conner Prairie is located only a few miles from downtown Indianapolis.

The museum began in 1934 when Eli Lilly, grandson of the well-known pharmaceutical pioneer, purchased the estate of William Conner, an Indian trader who was one of the area's first settlers. Conner was the husband of a Delaware Indian woman named Mekinges, and fathered six children by her. In 1820, when the Delawares were forced to withdraw to the western side of the Mississippi River by the Treaties of St. Mary's, Ohio,

Mekinges and her children accompanied her tribe on their overland journey. Conner stayed behind, took a new wife, and became a merchant. In 1823, his brick Federal-style house was built (now included in the National Historic Register), and is today a part of the Conner Prairie Pioneer Settlement.

After buying the 200-acre estate, Lilly and his wife immediately set about restoring it into a village that would reflect southern Indiana as it existed in the year 1836. At Conner Prairie costumed blacksmiths, weavers and farmers conduct themselves as if past were present; and much of the fruit of their labor—including salt glaze and spatterware pottery, ironware and wooden objects—is available in the Museum Shop.

Open April through November, with special programs scheduled regularly.

CONNER PRAIRIE
13400 Allisonville Road
Fishers, IN 46038
Tel. 317/776-6000

⬧ SCHOONER HARVEY GAMAGE

Then it was that Mr. Haveby sent Bunster to Lord Howe, the falling-off place. He had celebrated his landing by mopping up half a case of the schooner's gin and by thrashing the elderly and wheezy mate who had offered it. When the schooner departed, he called the kanakas down to the beach and challenged them to throw him in a wrestling bout, promising a case of tobacco to the one who succeeded. Three kanakas he threw, but was promptly thrown by a fourth, who, instead of receiving the tobacco, got a bullet through his lungs.

> —*Jack London, "Mauki," South Sea Tales,* 1909

Designed in the style of the swift packet boats of the 1860s, the schooner *Harvey Gamage* **was launched from the Harvey Gamage shipyard in South Bristol, Maine, in 1973.** She's of traditional wood construction, displaces 129 tons, is 95 feet in length and carries 4,200 square feet of sail on her 91-foot masts. The schooner also has 14 private cabins, shared toilet facilities and a library. Defying old schooner traditions, however, she's strictly BYOB.

A score of times each winter, the *Harvey Gamage* departs St. Thomas in the U.S. Virgin Islands to follow the tradewinds to St. John, Jost Van Dyke, Tortola, Virgin Gorda and Norman Island. Her 30 passengers (there is also a professional crew of seven) are free to either loll about while aboard or learn how to work the lines with the crew. Summertimes, passengers may sign on for a variety of week-long voyages departing from Bar Harbor, Maine; Mystic, Connecticut; and Annapolis, Maryland. Some of these trips have some sort of special content—such as a Summer Studies program carrying graduate credit—and there are races, nature tours and whale watches as well. On voyages departing from Bermuda and Annapolis in the spring and fall, courses on piloting and celestial navigation are available.

Winter-program passenger fares per person: Adults, $645; young adults and children (18 and under), $545; senior citizens (50 and older) $545; companions to senior citizens, $445. Prices include meals beginning the first full day, port charges and British Virgin Island cruising permits.

Literature and video available.

SCHOONER HARVEY GAMAGE
Dirigo Cruises
39 Waterside Lane
Clinton, CT 06413
Tel. 800/845-5520

✳ FORD'S THEATRE

With the play "Octaroon," John T. Ford had expected to reopen his E Street theater, two-and-a-half months after President Lincoln's April 1865 assassination. Undeterred by an outpouring of letters threatening both to burn the theater and to murder him, Ford sold 200 tickets for the play's July 7 opening; but that night the War Department ordered Ford's Theatre closed, stationed guards in front of it, and demanded that the proprietor refund the ticket holders' money. It would be more than a century before the boards of Ford's Theatre would again groan underneath the performance of a stage play.

In August 1865, the War Department purchased Ford's Theatre for $100,000 and began to dismantle the interior. Over the following century the building would variously be used as a War Department office building, as the home of the Army Medical Museum, and for the storage of government documents. In 1931, it passed into the hands of the Department of the Interior.

On July 7, 1964—99 years to the day after the army stopped the curtain from rising on "Octaroon"—the 88th Congress appropriated more than $2 million for the full restoration of Ford's Theatre, a painstaking process that involved tracking down elements of the original interior; it took almost three years to complete. On February 13, 1968, Ford's Theatre was again open to the public under the direction of the National Park Service.

In cooperation with the Ford's Theatre Society, performances are scheduled throughout the year. Also available are free 15-minute programs recounting the story of President Lincoln's assassination, an exhibition of the Oldroyd collection of Lincolniana, and visits to the 1849 William Petersen house, directly across the street, where the president expired.

Open all year, 9 a.m. to 5 p.m.

Closed for matinees on Thursday, Saturday and Sunday, October through June. Closed December 25.

FORD'S THEATRE NATIONAL HISTORIC SITE
10th Street N.W.
Washington, DC 20001
Tel. 202/426-6924

MOHONK MOUNTAIN HOUSE

Perched dramatically on a jagged rock cliff that frames a glacial lake in New York State's Catskill Mountains, the Mohonk Mountain House began in 1869 after two Quaker schoolteachers, Albert and Alfred Smiley, purchased the 10-room tavern that was standing at the site. The sale of the tavern must have come as a disappointment to the revelers of the nearby old Dutch village of New Paltz, for not only were the Smileys strictly religious, but they intended to convert the tavern into their home.

Still, the size of both the Smileys' debt and their newly acquired building was such that in quick order it made sense for them to take in boarders. They somewhat moderated their religious reservations against drinking and smok-

ing (although at Mohonk there is still no bar, and smoking is not permitted in the hotel's dining room) and soon Victorian New Yorkers were finding the inn to be an ideal retreat from city life. Greatly in aid of this was the Smileys' interest in conversation and their Victorian notions of landscape design, which today has lent the stately air of an English garden setting to the grounds. Furthermore, the hotel's magnificent 5,000 acres of woodlands (through which several trails and bridle paths wind) have been spared development by the device of a preservation trust.

The hotel's massive lakefront main building was added to incrementally until it reached its present form at about the turn of the century. Its piecemeal architecture was described thus by Elizabeth Cromley in an essay entitled "A Room with a View":

Buildings, additions, and replacements for outmoded parts join together in a long,

irregular line along the edge of the rock-bordered lake to form the hotel. Wood meets stone, shingle shifts to tile, browns and grays give way to greens and reds—creating a disturbing eclecticism or an enchantingly varied romantic fantasy, depending upon the eye of the beholder.

The list of the Mohonk Mountain House's beholders includes naturalist William Burroughs, industrialist Andrew Carnegie, and four presidents: Theodore Roosevelt, William Howard Taft, Rutherford B. Hayes and Chester A. Arthur.

Open all year. A Victorian Holiday theme program is available in early July.

MOHONK MOUNTAIN HOUSE
Lake Mohonk
New Paltz, NY 12561
For reservations: from area codes 212 and 718, call 914/255-4500; otherwise 800/772-6646 or call your travel agent. Fax. 914/256-2161

NORLANDS

I hear the talk goin' round about you but I want you ta know I don't believe t'word of it.

—Mystifying announcement made by "Emeline Hilton" to "Brooksey Waters" at the time of the latter's arrival at Norlands

For those contemplating a trip to Maine there are plenty of nice places to visit, but anyone traveling back into 1870 must book a bedchamber at Norlands.

Norlands, named for the loud whirlwinds that blow through Alfred Lord Tennyson's "Ballad of Oriana," is a working nineteenth-century farm located on 430 acres in Livermore, Maine. Originally conceived as a downeast Old Sturbridge Village, Norlands (under the direction of Mrs. Billie Gammon) has created so keen an experience of the last century as to make visits to other "living history" museums seem like watching daytime television. The Norlands program even awes the professionals: "A Norlands live-in is the most in-depth experience in America of life as it was lived 100 years ago," says Terry Sharer, secretary-treasurer of the Smithsonian-based Association of Living Historical Farms and Agriculture Museums. "I can't think of anything quite like it."

The Norlands' live-in program is a four-day, three-night visit for adults (shorter sessions are available for families with children at least eight years old) conducted from February through November—and it generally begins by making participants a bit uneasy. Clothed "appropriately" in late-nineteenth-century agricultural garb, newly arrived visitors will find themselves addressed as a member of one of two local farm families (the Waters and the Prays) of the period. Moreover, conversation is conducted in the infectious Maine dialect of the time and concerns matters that have long since receded into the pages of the *Farmer's Almanac.* Initially this ritual just seems like play, but it serves the real purpose of an initiation, a baptism into the past.

A stay at Norlands is as little like a visit to a New England inn as it is to the Superbowl. There is no plumbing or electrical wiring at the farm; and wristwatches, cigarettes and flashlights must be left at home. Mornings begin at dawn, with the crowing of the cock and the clanging of pots (a warning that breakfast—which might include either fried liver or ham, scrambled eggs, oatmeal, toast and plenty of strong, dark coffee—follows early chores at 8:30). Then a day of more work around the farm commences—perhaps including the mucking of the oxen stalls or, in winter, cutting ice—and in evening there's a quiet gathering around the kitchen cookstove where "Shouting Proverbs" may be played over cocoa, and soapstones warmed to be wrapped in flannel and carried off into the cornhusk beds. Any notion of "quaintness" here is sure to die with the rooster that is slaughtered for dinner, or the necessity of using a frigid chamberpot on a midwinter night, but every visitor seems to take home the experience of a unique moment that these deprivations may have helped to bring about.

It usually comes at a quiet time that has been spent perhaps watching Nathan Bartlett, the farm blacksmith, tending the oxen; or noting with pleasure how vast the stardome is, and how luminous its planets. It is inevitably triggered by a small thing, like the flutter of a flame as a draft passes over a lantern's chimney, but as with Emerson's "crossing of a bare common, in snow puddles, at twilight, under a clouded sky," it is the most mundane circumstance that is also the most transcendent. Suddenly it's the world of car-jackings and 124-channel cable that seems fantastic, and dreadful. If anything beyond the farm seems real at all, it's the course of Reconstruction, and the possibility of continued drought until harvest.

In addition to the live-in program, Norlands holds a variety of 1½- to 4-hour programs for school groups, and four public festivals a year: Autumn Harvest (in October), Christmas at Norlands, Maple Days (in March) and Heritage Days (in late June). The adult live-in program carries three teacher recertification credits through the Maine Department of Education and Cultural Service, and/or three college credits.

Prices for live-in program: $195 for adults, half price for children aged 8 to 12, and $150 for teenagers.

Free brochure available.

NORLANDS
Mrs. Alfred Q. Gammon
R.D. 2
Livermore Falls, ME 04254

❀ WHITE HOUSE RANCH

The White House Ranch Historic Site is located in the Garden of the Gods Park in Colorado Springs, Colorado. This living-history farm depicts three periods in the history of the state, beginning with a working reconstruction of an 1868 homestead and including an 1895 farm and the restored Orchard House, a country estate built in 1907. Interpreters in period garb depict life as it was lived on this property, which is listed in the National Register of Historic Places.

Open from early June through Labor Day, Wednesday through Sunday from 10 a.m. to 4 p.m. During the period from Labor Day to Christmas, the site is open on weekends only, Saturdays from 10 a.m. to 4 p.m., and Sundays from noon to 4 p.m.

Admission: adults, $3; senior citizens, $2; children 6 to 12, $1.

WHITE HOUSE RANCH
Living History Program
1401 Recreation Way
Colorado Springs, CO 80906
Tel. 719/578-6777

❧ HUBBELL TRADING POST NATIONAL HISTORIC SITE

Inside its long, low stone walls is a rectangular iron stove, the center of the "bull pen." During winter it was always stocked with piñon and juniper wood, and the Navajos, talking and laughing, lingered in the warmth. Behind the massive counters are shelves filled with coffee, flour, sugar, candy, Pendleton blankets, tobacco, calico, pocketknives and canned goods. Hardware and harness hang from the ceiling.
—A nineteenth-century description of the Hubbell Trading Post

GANADO ARIZ.

The Hubbell Trading Post is part of a historic Arizona site operated today by the National Park Service. The trading post itself has been in continuous operation since it was started by John Lorenzo Hubbell in 1878. Hubbell, a Spanish-American, was a trusted friend of the Navajo, often acting as a lawyer, doctor, undertaker and translator for them. Throughout his career, Hubbell was also sheriff, chairman of the Arizona Territorial Council and one of the state's first senators. The trading post is still active. Locals and visitors can buy groceries, general merchandise and Navajo and Hopi crafts. The National Park Service offers daily tours of Hubbell's home.

Free admission. Summer hours are 8 a.m. to 6 p.m.; winter hours are 8 a.m. to 5 p.m.

**HUBBELL TRADING POST
NATIONAL HISTORIC SITE**
P.O. Box 150
Ganado, AZ 86505
Tel. 602/755-3475

RIDING THE CARS

The story of a town's being created or becoming successful because of the arrival of the railroad is a familiar one. Particularly during the late nineteenth century, when the railroad companies had power comparable to today's multinationals, many towns were also founded by them. Such was the case with Durango, Colorado, which came into existence in 1879 by dint of the Denver & Rio Grande Railway's need for it. In July 1882, a link to Silverton was completed for the purpose of hauling gold and silver down from the San Juan Mountains, and over the years to follow more than $300 million in precious metals were carried on its narrow-gauge rails.

Ninety-nine years later, with the ore long gone, the (renamed) Denver & Rio Grande Western Railroad sold the Silverton Branch to the Durango & Silverton Narrow Gauge Railroad Company (D&SNG), which put into operation what is now the country's only regulated, 100 percent coal-fired, narrow-gauge railroad.

Faithful to the pledge of the company's president, Charles E. Bradshaw, Jr., that "there will never be a diesel run on the D&SNG tracks," the Silverton train employs two early-1920s-vintage steam locomotives to pull their 1880 coaches and open-air gondolas. Many of these cars, such as the parlor car Alamosa, were rolling back when the James-Younger gang was riding; and

now they make the run between Durango and Silverton in every season but winter, when there's an abbreviated schedule.

The Silverton train travels through a wilderness area, part of the 2-million-acre San Juan National Forest, following the Animas River into Silverton. Any other access into this area may only be made on horseback or on foot, making the train a favorite among backpackers and fishermen, for whom it calls at Needleton and Elk Park en route. The Silverton train also serves the Tall Timber Resort, as well as continuing to haul freight.

Round-trip fares from Durango to Silverton are $37.15 per adult and $18.65 per child.

Free brochure available.

DURANGO & SILVERTON NARROW GAUGE RAILROAD
479 Main Avenue
Durango, CO 81301
Tel. 303/247-2733

GOLDEN NORTH HOTEL

Built in the "Days of '98" during the era of the Klondike Gold Rush, the Golden North is the oldest operating hotel in Alaska, and was once considered the territory's finest accommodation. The hotel's furnishings include many original pieces brought around Cape Horn at the turn of the century—tintypes, four-poster beds, porcelain water pitchers, oil lamps and a days-of-'98-vintage piano.

Open all year.

GOLDEN NORTH HOTEL
P.O. Box 343
Skagway, AK 99840
Tel. 907/983-2451
Fax. 907/983-2755

▨ HOTEL DEL CORONADO

The Hotel Del Coronado, a seaside Victorian castle dominating San Diego's Coronado peninsula, is generally considered to be the last of that era's extravagantly conceived ocean resorts. The hotel was the brainchild of Elisha Babcock, a wealthy Hoosier who acquired the 4,100-acre peninsula in 1885 as the future site of a resort hotel that would be the "talk of the Western world."

As a pipeline under the bay from San Diego had to be constructed to supply fresh water to the peninsula, and since both lumber and carpenters needed to be imported from San Francisco, the Hotel Del Coronado took three years to complete. On opening day in February 1888, thousands of people from all over the country passed beneath its great lighthouse turrets and gingerbread arches.

Although minor structural changes have taken place over the past century, many of the original facilities are intact. Notable among these are the Crown Room where the Prince of Wales was introduced to Wallis Simpson in 1920, and the Grand Ballroom.

Brochure and historical literature available.

HOTEL DEL CORONADO
1500 Orange Avenue
Coronado, CA 92118
Tel. 619/435-6611; for reservations 800/HOTEL DEL

K 13367 Our finest quality Foliage Effect in combination with buds. Good buyers will appreciate offer. Comes in natural foliage with pink, tea or American beauty red. State color wanted.......... 48c
by mail, postage extra, 7 cents.

A Novelty Wreath.

K 13369 Foliage Wreath. Full for one hat. Made up of handsome foliage, liberally mixed with tiny natural shaded foliage with pink, tea, an beauty red buds as wanted. 42c
y mail, postage extra, 7 cents.

37 had qual nium with con wen aves, only ity—

18c
y mail, postage extra, 6 cents.

Styles in Fruite with Foliage.

No. 18K13373 Very showy spray of fine quality imported Cherries, branched with natural foliage. Finest quality unbreakable cherries. Very showy trimming. Price, per bunch. 21c
If by mail, postage extra, 6 cents.

38C

No. 18K13376 Beautiful bunch of imported Cherries branched in three sprays with natural foliage and rubber stems. Very attractive number. Comes in natural shades only. 38c
er bunch.. (Postage extra 8c)

A SPLENDID STYLE. GREAT VALUE.

o. 18K13378 Handsome Cherry ath, branched very long. Made up kable cherries and natural shaded Exceptional value at our 38c
ice, per wreath.............
y mail, postage extra, 8 cents.

No. 18K13380 Our very finest Cherry Wreath Effect, beautifully sprayed with imported foliage and quantities of soft effect. A very attractive trimming. Price, per 48c
by mail, postage extra, 8c)..

Grapes Are Very Popular.

No. 18K13382 A very pretty cluster of natural shaded Grapes, sprayed with natural grape foliage

---

67C

No. 18K13384 This beautiful wreath is made up of finest quality Grapes, sprayed with natural foliage and stems. Enough to trim the entire brim of a hat. Nothing better at any price. Price, per wreath. 67c
If by mail, postage extra, 9 cents.

Handsome June Rose Clusters

No. 18K13387 Showy cluster of twelve good quality June Roses, branched with foliage and long stems. Colors, pink, white, light blue or American beauty red. 25-cent value. State color wanted.
Price, per bunch. 15c
If by mail, postage extra, 5 cents.

38c

lin Ju leaves bargai blue o wante

No. 18K13392 Our finest June Rose Effect of best quality silk and muslin flowers in combination with buds and beautiful sea moss. Very handsome front trimming with the present style hats, soft and fluffy. Colors, pink, tea or American beauty red. State color wanted. Price, per bunch, 59c
If by mail, postage extra, 8 cents.

No. 18K13394 All silk and muslin June Rose Wreath, branched very long with natural moss and imported foliage. Colors, white, pink, tea or American beauty red. State color wanted.
Price, per wreath...... 45c
If by mail, postage extra, 8c.

Best Muslin Roses.

No. 18K13396 Good quality three in a bunch muslin Crush Roses, with full centers. Colors, pink, white, tea, light blue or American beauty red. State color wanted. Price, per bunch.. 14c
If by mail, postage extra, 5 cents.

No. 18K13398 Our best quality all muslin, six in a bunch Cup Roses, with rubber stems. Colors, white, pink, light blue or American beauty red. State color wanted.
Price, per bunch.. 23c
If by mail, postage extra, 5 cents.

Silk and Velvet Crush Roses.

No. 18K13403 All silk and velvet, three in a bunch Crush Roses. First class materials. Colors, white, pink, light blue, tea or American beauty red. State color wanted.
Price, per bunch.. 13c
Postage extra, 5c.

No. 18K13413 These beautiful three in a bunch Crush Roses are made of a combination of finest quality silk, velvet and muslin. Our illustration does not show its real beauty. Colors, pink, white, or American beauty red, brown

---

No. 18K13417 Our very finest quality all silk and velvet Crush Roses, three in a bunch. No better flower at any price than this. Colors, pink, old rose, brown, gray or American beauty red. State color wanted.
Price per bunch 49c
If by mail, postage extra, 6 cents.

No. 18K13424 Great value in silk and velvet Crush Roses with rubber stems, six in a bunch. Made of good quality materials. Colors, pink, white, light blue, tea, or American beauty red, 50-cent value.
Price, per bunch... 29c
If by mail, postage extra, 7 cents.

No. 18K13430 Our finest quality six in a bunch all

No. 18K13434 Natural American Beauty Roses are always popular. This number contains two beautiful, full blown roses with a bud and natural imported rose foliage. A rich trimming. Colors, white, pink, tea or American beauty red.
Price, per bunch 27c
If by mail, postage extra, 6 cents.

No. 18K13436 Our very finest two in a bunch, Half Blown Rose Effect. Made of silk, velvet and muslin in handsome combination with natural rose foliage and moss. Our illustration does not begin to show the real beauty of these flowers. Comes in white, pink, tea or American beauty red.
Price, per bunch.. (Postage extra, 7c). 46c

No. 18K13438 Handsome spray of six medium size Cup Roses of fine quality lawn, sprayed with soft sea moss, giving it a very dainty effect. Colors, white, pink, tea or American beauty red. State color wanted. Price, per bunch. (Postage extra, 7c). 33c

Rose Wreaths Trim Easily.

No. 18K13440 Our leading value in velvet and muslin Rose Wreath, six velvet and muslin roses, wreath effect, sprayed with foliage on chenille stems. One of the biggest bargains ever offered. Colors, white, pink, light blue, tea or American beauty red.
Price, per wreath...(Postage 8c).... 27c

No. 18K13442 A very showy wreath effect

No. 18K13444 This handsome cluster contains four half blown muslin Roses of good quality, branched with quantities of finest imported foliage and tiny buds. Colors, pink, white, tea or American beauty red.
State Color Wanted

Price, 48c
per bunch .... If by mail, postage extra, 6 cents.

No. 18K13446 Beautiful wreath of half blown muslin Roses, branched with June rose foliage, natural soft moss and tiny buds. Others ask $1.25 for no better value. Colors, pink, white, tea or American beauty red. State color wanted. Our price, per wreath............ 67c
If by mail, postage extra, 8 cents.

88c

No. 18K13448 Our most beautiful Crush Rose Wreath. The daintiest effect is our complete line. Something entirely new and very attractive. Our illustration does not show the exquisite beauty of these roses. Come in white, pink, tea or American beauty red. State color wanted. Price, per wreath. 88c
If by mail, postage extra, 8 cents.

Black Foliage.

No. 18K13450 Good quality black Mercerized Satin Foliage for use with black crush roses. Regular 35-cent value. Price, per bunch 19c
If by mail, postage extra, 7 cents.

No. 18K13452 Our very finest All Satin Foliage in black only. No better black foliage than this can be bought at any price. Contains twenty-four beautiful leaves handsomely sprayed. Price, per bunch 33c
If by mail, postage extra, 8c.

Best Black Flowers.

No. 18K13454 Good quality black Crush Roses with all silk centers, three in a bunch. Great value at our price. Price, per bunch .. 14c
If by mail, postage extra, 5 cents.

No. 18K13456 Fine quality, six in a bunch, black Crush Roses, made of combination of silk, satin and muslin. Regular 50-cent value. Price, per bunch............ 33c
If by mail, postage extra, 5 cents.

No. 18K13487 Extra fine quality all silk and satin black Crush Roses with very full centers. Three in a bunch. Price, bunch... 46c
If by mail, postage extra, 5 cents.

No. 18K13489 Very handsome black Crush Rose and Foliage Spray, branched in double sunburst effect. Best silk flowers and all satin foliage. This is a very bunch 33c

---

239

⬚ SCRAP RELIEF PICTURES

During the Victorian era, the filling of scrapbooks with such novelties as these chromolithographic pictures was a popular pastime. Embossed and die-cut, inexpensive scrap pictures were also used to decorate Christmas ornaments, gingerbread cookies and valentines. The pictures shown here are part of a collection reprinted from antique originals in England and sold here by the D. Blümchen company.

Price: $1.50 per double sheet, plus $5 per order for shipping.

A catalog, "The Best of Christmas Past," available, $3.

D. BLÜMCHEN & COMPANY, INC.
P.O. Box 1210-AHS
Ridgewood, NJ 07451-1210

⬚ DECORATIONS AND STOCKING STUFFERS

B. Shackman & Company has been doing business at the same Fifth Avenue location since 1897, and sells many novelty items reminiscent of that time. Their Christmas catalog contains a wonderful array of paper and tinsel Victorian Santas, angels, tree decorations and cards. A minimum $10 order is required.

Catalog available.

B. SHACKMAN & COMPANY
85 Fifth Avenue at 16th Street
New York, NY 10003
Tel. 212/989-5162

OLD CHRISTMAS BY WASHINGTON IRVING

As a part of their Washington Irving Facsimile Library, the Sleepy Hollow Press has also republished *Old Christmas,* a series of Irving's Christmas tales that predate Dickens' *A Christmas Carol* by a quarter century.

Price: clothbound, $10. 208 pages with 106 illustrations. *Old Christmas* may be ordered directly from Sleepy Hollow Press when accompanied by a money order. Postage and handling require $1.25 for the first book, plus 25 cents for each additional copy. A retail discount schedule is available.

HISTORIC HUDSON VALLEY
150 White Plains Road
Tarrytown, NY 10591
Tel. 914/631-8200

❀ CHRISTMAS POSTCARDS

The first printed Christmas post-card was brought out by Louis Prang, a Boston lithographer, in 1874. Along with the Thomas Nast Santa of 1881, the Christmas bonus of 1899 and the electric Christmas tree of 1902, yuletide cards are examples of Victorian America's commercialization of what had been a quiet folk holiday in antebellum times.

Replicas of Victorian Christmas Postcards (and reprints of other cards on a variety of period subjects) are available from the Evergreen Press.

❊ THE NIGHT BEFORE CHRISTMAS
BY CLEMENT CLARK MOORE

Originally calling it "A Visit from St. Nicholas," this poem was written by the Hebrew scholar Clement Clark Moore as a Christmas gift for his six children in 1822. A family friend gave the poem to the Troy (New York) *Sentinel* where it was published anonymously on December 23, 1823.

For years, newspapers everywhere copied the poem without attribution until finally Mrs. Sarah Joseph Hale, editor of Godey's *Lady's Book*, discovered the identity of the author. An edition of Moore's verse published in 1844 included the poem as his own for the first time.

Evergreen Press of Walnut Creek, California, has published a facsimile of the 1870 "Charles Graham" edition of *The Night Before Christmas*. The book's artwork recalls the first time that holly was associated with Christmas and the first representation of Santa Claus dressed in a red cloth coat trimmed with white fur.

Other Victorian Christmas books published by Evergreen are: *Christmas Delights* (turn of the century), *Christmas ABC*, and *Santa Claus and His Works* (first published around 1870) with illustrations by Thomas Nast.

Price: $5.00.

Free catalog sheets of antique reproduction books, postcards, scrap and certificates available.

THE EVERGREEN PRESS
3380 Vincent Road
Pleasant Hill, CA 94523
Tel. 510/933-9700
Fax. 510/256-7782

Index of Suppliers & Manufacturers

R.E. DIETZ COMPANY 67
225 Wilkinson Street
Syracuse, NY 13204
Tel. 315/424-7400

DIXIE GUN WORKS 143, 164, 178, 179, 180, 183, 185, 201, 202, 214
Gunpowder Lane
Union City, TN 38261
Tel. 901/885-0700 or
    800/238-6785 to order
Fax. 901/885-0440

DURANGO & SILVERTON NARROW GAUGE RAILROAD 237
479 Main Avenue
Durango, CO 81301
Tel. 303-247-2733

EDWARDS HORSE-DRAWN BUGGY WORKS AND HARNESSES 114
U.S. Highway 19 South
Putney, GA 31782
Tel. 912/787-5307

ELECTRIC TIME COMPANY, INC. 90
45 West Street
Medfield, MA 02052
Tel. 508/359-4396
Fax. 508/359-4482

ENCHANTED DOLL HOUSE 204
Manchester Center, VT 05255-0697
Tel. 802/362-1327

EPOCH DESIGNS 88
P.O. Box 4033, Dept. 050
Elwyn, PA 19063

EVERGREEN PRESS 242
3380 Vincent Road
Pleasant Hill, CA 94523
Tel. 510/933-9700
Fax. 510/256-7782

EXAMPLARERY 83
P.O. Box 2554
Dearborn, MI 48123
Tel. 313/278-3282

FAMOUS & HISTORIC TREES 103
P.O. Box 7040
Jacksonville, FL 32238
Tel. 800/677-0727
Fax. 904/768-2298

FARMER'S MUSEUM, INC. 212-213
Lake Road, P.O. Box 800
Cooperstown, NY 13326
Tel. 607/547-2593

FORD'S THEATRE NATIONAL HISTORIC SITE 233
10th Street NW
Washington, DC 20001
Tel. 202/426-6924

FORGE & ANVIL 108, 112
P.O. Box 51
Newman, IL 61942
Tel. 217/352-0803

FREEDOM BOATWORKS 225
P.O. Box 511
Baraboo, WI 53913
Tel. 608/356 5861

FRYE'S MEASURE MILL 53
Wilton, NH 03086
Tel. 603/654-6581

GATES, INCORPORATED 205
P.O. Box 90
West Peterborough, NH 03468
Tel. 800/669-4903 or
    603/924-3394 in NH
Fax. 603/924-0011

GENERAL HOUSEWARES CORPORATION 48
Consumer Services
P.O. Box 466
Terre Haute, IN 47804
Tel. 812/232-1000

GEOFFRION KEYBOARDS 201
Route 1, Box 273
Pomona, IL 62975
Tel. 618/687-2159

GIBSON-LEE CORPORATION 137
78 Stone Place
Melrose, MA 02176
Tel. 617/662-6025

GOHN BROTHERS 122
Box 111
Middlebury, IN 46540
Tel. 219/825-2400

GOLDEN NORTH HOTEL 237
P.O. Box 343
Skagway, AK 99840
Tel. 907/983-2451
Fax. 907/983-2755

GOOD DIRECTIONS, INC. 25
24 Ardmore Road
Stamford, CT 06902
Tel. 203/348-1836
Fax. 203/357-0092

GOOD TIME STOVE COMPANY 95
Route 112
Goshen, MA 01032
Tel. 413/268-3677

GRANDPA SOAP COMPANY 214
317-321 East Eighth Street
Cincinnati, OH 45202
Tel. 513/241-1677
Fax. 513/241-1676

GREEN ENTERPRISES 30
43 South Rogers Street
Hamilton, VA 22068
Tel. 703/338-3606

GROUND FLOOR 88
95 1/2 Broad Street
Charleston, SC 29401
Tel. 803/722-3576

HAMMERMARK ASSOCIATES 51
P.O. Box 201
Floral Park, NY 11002

HANCOCK SHAKER VILLAGE 134, 229
Route 20, P.O. Box 898
Pittsfield, MA 01202
Tel. 413/443-0188

HAROLD'S CABIN 128
In the Fabled Meeting Street Piggly
    Wiggly
445 Meeting Street
Charleston, SC 29403
Tel. 803/722-2766

HARRINGTON'S 125
618 Main Street
Richmond, VT 05477
Tel. 802/434-3411

HEARTHSTONE HOMES 15
Route 2, P.O. Box 434
Dandridge, TN 37725
Tel. 615/397-9425

HEARTLAND APPLIANCES, INC. 101
5 Hoffman Street
Kitchener, ON, Canada N2M 3M5
Tel. 519/743-8111
Fax. 519/743-1665

HELLER-ALLER COMPANY, INC. 104
Corner Perry & Oakwood
P.O. Box 29
Napoleon, OH 43545
Tel. 419/592-1856

HERITAGE RUGS 78
Sherry and Martin Shulewitz
Lahaska, PA 18931
Tel. 215/794-7229

HERITAGE SHOP 43
Dept. SC, P.O. Box 172
Boiling Springs, PA 17007

HISTORIC HUDSON VALLEY 188-189, 241
150 White Plains Road
Tarrytown, NY 10591
Tel. 914/631-8200

HISTORICAL REPLICATIONS 16
P.O. Box 13529
Jackson, MS 39236

HITCHCOCK CHAIR COMPANY 28
Riverton, CT 06065
Tel. 203/379-8531

HOHNER, INCORPORATED 202
Lakeridge Park
P.O. Box 15035
Richmond, VA 23227-5035

HOMESTEAD PAINTS & FINISHES 20
111 Mulpus Road, P.O. Box 1668
Lunenburg, MA 01462
Tel. 508/582-6426

HONEY ACRES 127
Ashippun, WI 53003
Tel. 414/474-4411

HOTEL DEL CORONADO 238
1500 Orange Avenue
Coronado, CA 92118
Tel. 619/435-6611; for reservations
    800/HOTEL DEL

HUBBELL TRADING POST NATIONAL HISTORIC SITE 236
P.O. Box 150
Ganado, AZ 86505
Tel. 602/755-3475

HUDSON RIVER MUSEUM OF WESTCHESTER 85
511 Warburton Avenue
Yonkers, NY 10701
Tel. 914/963-4550

HUNTER FAN COMPANY 20
2500 Frisco Avenue
Memphis, TN 38114
Tel. 901/743-1360

C&D JARNAGIN COMPANY 170-172, 176-177, 178-179
P.O. Box 13529
Jackson, MS 39236
Tel. 601/287-4977
Fax. 601/287-6033

JORDAN, DOUGLAS 198
P.O. Box 20194
St. Petersburg, FL 33702

DUDLEY KEBOW, INC. 47
2603 Industry Street
Oceanside, CA 92054
Tel. 619/439-3000, or 800/447-2600
Fax. 619/967-8032

LANMAN & KEMP BARCLAY & COMPANY, INC. 210-211
25 Woodland Avenue, P.O. Box 241
Westwood, NJ 07675
Tel. 201/666-4990
Fax. 201/666-5836

LEA, MICHAEL, GUNSMITH 149
2109 Summit Street
Columbus, OH 43201
Tel. 614/291-4757

LEHMAN HARDWARE & APPLIANCES 48, 51, 55, 105, 107
4779 Kidron Road
Kidron, OH 44636
Tel. 216/857-5441
Fax. 216/857-5785

LEONARD'S REPRODUC-TIONS AND ANTIQUES 27
600 Taunton Avenue
Seekonk, MA 02771
Tel. 508/336-8585
Fax. 508/336-4884

LIVING HISTORY FARMS 230
2600 N.W. 111th Street
Des Moines, IA 50322
Tel. 515/278-5286

LODGE MANUFACTURING COMPANY 48, 76
P.O. Box 380, Railroad Avenue
South Pittsburgh, TN 37380
Tel. 615/837-7181

LOG CABIN SHOP 144-145, 148, 152, 186, 217, 219
P.O. Box 275
Lodi, OH 44254
Tel. 216/948-1082

MARLE COMPANY 66
35 Larkin Street, Box 4499
Stamford, CT 06907
Tel. 203/348-2625

MASON & SULLIVAN COMPANY 92-93, 226
586 Higgins Crowell Road
West Yarmouth, MA 02673
Tel. 800/933-3010
Fax. 508/775-5581

McGUIRE, JOHN C. 45
398 South Main Street
Geneva, NY 14456
Tel. 315/781-1251

McILHENNY TABASCO COMPANY 129
Avery Island, LA 70513

MERRIMACK PUBLISHING COMPANY 195
85 Fifth Avenue at 16th Street
New York, NY 10003
Tel. 212/989-5162

MOHONK MOUNTAIN HOUSE 234
Lake Mohonk
New Paltz, NY 12561
For reservations: from area codes 212 and 718, call 914/255-4500; otherwise 800/772-6646 or call your travel agent
Fax. 914/256-2161

WILLIAM MORROW & COMPANY, PUBLISHERS 194
1350 Avenue of the Americas
New York, NY 10019
Tel. 212/261-6500

MOULTRIE MANUFACTURING COMPANY 30
P.O. Box 1179
Moultrie, GA 31776-1179
Tel. 800/841-8674

MOUNTAIN LUMBER COMPANY 19
P.O. Box 289
Ruckersville, VA 22968
Tel. 804/985-3646
Fax. 804/985-4105

NAVY ARMS COMPANY 150-151, 166-167, 180-182, 184
689 Bergen Boulevard
Ridgefield, NJ 07657
Tel. 201/945-2500

THE NESTLE-LeMUR COMPANY 210
902 Broadway
New York, NY 10010

NOBLE & COOLEY COMPANY 206
P.O. Box 131
Granville, MA 01034
Tel. 413/562-9694

NORLANDS 235
Mrs. Alfred Q. Gammon
R.D. 2
Livermore Falls, ME 04254

NORTHWEST TRADERS 142
5055 W. Jackson Road
Enon, OH 45323
Tel. 513/767-9244
Fax. 513/767-9244

NOSTALGIA DECORATING COMPANY 86
P.O. Box 1312
Kingston, PA 18704
Tel. 717/472-3764
Fax. 717/472-3331

NOWELL'S, INC. 69-73
P.O. Box 295
Sausalito, CA 94966
Tel. 415/332-4933
Fax. 415/332-4936

OLD GRANGE GRAPHICS 82
P.O. Box 297, 12-14 Mercer Street
Hopewell, NJ 08525
Tel. 800/282-7776

OLD SOUTH COMPANY 14
3301 Highway 101 North
Woodruff, SC 29388
Tel. 803/877-0538
Fax. 803/848-0025

OLD STURBRIDGE VILLAGE 42, 63
One Old Sturbridge Village Road
Sturbridge, MA 01566
Tel. 508/347-3362

OLD WEST OUTFITTERS 126
7213 East First Avenue
Scottsdale, AZ 85251
Tel. 800/447-5277
Fax. 602/951-8633

OLD WORLD ENTERPRISES 137
29036 Kepler Court
Cold Spring, MN 56320

PANEK, BRUCE, TINSMITH 49
Ohio Historical Society
1985 Velma Avenue
Columbus, OH 43211
Tel. 614/297-2680

PEARCE WOOLEN MILLS 76
Woolrich, PA 17779

LA PELLETERIE 132-133, 140-141, 151, 152, 157-158, 207, 218
P.O. Box 127
Arrow Rock, MO 65320
Tel. 816/837-3261

PENNSYLVANIA FIREBACKS, INC. 41
2237 Bethel Road
Lansdale, PA 19446
Tel. 215/699-0805

PETERSON OF DUBLIN 216
20717 Marilla Street
Chatsworth, CA 91311

PHILOMEL BOOKS 196
The Putnam Publishing Company
200 Madison Avenue
New York, NY 10016
Tel. 212/951-8400 or
     800/631-8571 to order

PHOENIX FOUNDRY 110-111
P.O. Box 68 H
Marcus, WA 99151
Tel. 509/684-5434

PIEL CRAFTSMEN 222
307 High Street
Newburyport, MA 01950
Tel. 508/462-7012

PLYMOUTH CHEESE COMPANY 124
P.O. Box 1
Plymouth, VT 05056

POOL TABLES BY ADLER 207
10100 Aviation Boulevard
Los Angeles, CA 90005
Tel. 213/382-6334

PORTLAND STOVE COMPANY 98-99
P.O. Box 37, Fickett Road
N. Pownal, ME 04069
Tel. 207/688-2254

PORTSMOUTH CLOCK COMPANY 92
P.O. Box 4247
Portsmouth, NH 03802-4247
Tel. 603/433-6120

POTTING SHED 59
P.O. Box 1287
Concord, MA 01742
Tel. 508/369-1382
Fax. 508/369-1416

PRAIRIE EDGE 158-163
P.O. Box 8303
Rapid City, SD 57709
Tel. 605/341-4525

PROGRESS LIGHTING 68
Erie Avenue and G Street
Philadelphia, PA 19134
Tel. 215/289-1200
Fax. 215/537-0887

PUTNAM ANTIQUES 138
3 Pond Road
Middlefield, MA 01243

QUILT ROOM 80
Old Country Store
Main Street
P.O. Box 419
Intercourse, PA 17534

**RED RIVER FRONTIER
OUTFITTERS 154-155, 168, 175**
P.O. Box 241
Tujunga, CA 91043

**REGGIO REGISTER
COMPANY 24**
P.O. Box 511
Ayer, MA 01432
Tel. 508/772-3495
Fax. 508/772-5513

**RIDEABLE ANTIQUE
BICYCLE REPLICAS 122**
2329 Eagle Avenue
Alameda, CA 94501
Tel. 510/769-0980
Fax. 510/521-7145

**RIVER JUNCTION TRADING
COMPANY 132**
312 Main Street
P.O. Box 275
McGregor, IA 52157
Tel. 319/873-2387

**ROCKY MOUNTAIN
BROOMWORKS 45**
The Victor Trading Company and
Manufacturing Works
114 South Third Street
P.O. Box 53-M
Victor, CO 80860
Tel. 719/689-2346

**CHARLES P. ROGERS BRASS
BEDS 32**
899 First Avenue
New York, NY 10022
Tel. 212/935-6900 or 800/272-7726
(outside New York State)

ROMANCING THE WOODS 15
33 Raycliffe Drive
Woodstock, NY 12498
Tel. 914/246-6976

ROSS FARM MUSEUM 109
New Ross Route 12
Lunenburg County
Nova Scotia, Canada B0J 2M0
Tel. 902/689-2210

**ROTH, McKIE WING, JR.,
DESIGNER 16**
Box 31
Castine, Maine 04421
Tel. 800/232-7684

ROWANTREE'S POTTERY 59
Blue Hill, ME 04614
Tel. 207/374-5535

**ROXBURY FLYTRAP
COMPANY 41**
P.O. Box 33
Roxbury, KS 67476

**SCHOONER HARVEY
GAMAGE 232**
Dirigo Cruises
39 Waterside Lane
Clinton, CT 06413
Tel. 800/845-5520

**CHARLES SCRIBNER'S SONS
BOOKS FOR YOUNG
READERS 196**
MacMillan Publishing Company
866 Third Avenue
New York, NY 10022
Tel. 800/323-7445

SEED SAVERS EXCHANGE 103
Route 3, Box 239
Decorah, IA 52101

**JEREMY SEEGER
DULCIMERS 201**
P.O. Box 117, Fassett Hill
Hancock, VT 05748
Tel. 802/767-3790

**B. SHACKMAN & COMPANY
240**
85 Fifth Avenue at 16th Street
New York, NY 10003
Tel. 212/989-5162

**SHAKER WORKSHOPS 35-38,
46, 87**
P.O. Box 1028
Concord, MA 01742
Tel. 508/646-8985

**SMITH & HAWKEN TOOL
COMPANY 112**
25 Corte Madera
Mill Valley, CA 94941
Tel. 415/383-2000

**SMITHSONIAN
INSTITUTION 224**
NMAH 5010 / MRC 628
Washington, D.C. 20560

**SOUTH BEND REPLICAS, INC.
184**
61650 Oak Road
South Bend, IN 46614
Tel. 219/289-4500

STANLEY IRON WORKS 96
64 Taylor Street
Nashua, NH 03060
Tel. 603/881-8335

STEPTOE & WIFE 22
322 Geary Avenue
Toronto, ON, Canada M6H 2C7
Tel. 416/530-4204 or 800/461-0060
Fax. 416/530-4666

SUNRISE SPECIALTY 23
5540 Doyle Street
Emeryville, CA
Tel. 510/654-1794
Fax. 510/654-5775

T.M. VISUAL INDUSTRIES, INC. 199
212 West 35th Street
New York, NY 10036
Tel. 212/757-7700

TAUNTON PRESS 138
Folkwear Ordering Department
P.O. Box 5506
Newtown, CT 06470-5506

TECUMSEH'S FRONTIER TRADING POST 149
P.O. Box 369
Shartlesville, PA 19554
Tel. 215/488-6622

THREE FEATHERS PEWTER 63
P.O. Box 232, 221 Jones Street
Shreve, OH 44676
Tel. 216/567-2047

TRADITIONAL LEATHER-WORK COMPANY 43
4030 East 225th Street
Cicero, IN 46034
Tel. 317/877-0314

TRAVIS, MARTY 109
Rural Route 1, P.O. Box 96
Fairbury, IL 61739
Tel. 309/377-2271

UBERTI USA INC. 165, 167
P.O. Box 469
Lakeville, CT 06039
Tel. 203/435-8068
Fax. 203/435-8146

VAILLANCOURT, HENRI 146, 148
P.O. Box 142
Greenville, NH 03048

VAN NOSTRAND REINHOLD CO., INC. 191
VNR Order Processing
P.O. Box 668
Florence, KY 41022-0668
Tel. 800/926-2665
Fax. 606/525-7778

VINTAGE WOODWORKS 18
Highway 34 South, P.O. Drawer R
Quinlan, TX 75474
Tel. 903/356-2158

WAKEFIELD-SCEARCE GALLERIES 61
Historic Science Hill
Shelbyville, KY 40065
Tel. 502/633-4382

WAREHAM NAIL COMPANY 108
8 Elm Street, P.O. Box 111
Wareham, MA 02571
Tel. 508/295-0038

WARNER-LAMBERT 211
201 Tabor Road
Morris Plains, NJ 07950

WATERFORD IRISH STOVES 100
16 Airpark Road, Suite 3
West Lebanon, NH 03784

WESTMOORE POTTERY 58
Route 2, Box 494
Seagrove, NC 27431
Tel. 919/464-3700

WHITE HOUSE RANCH 236
Living History Program
1401 Recreation Way
Colorado Springs, CO 80906
Tel. 719/578-6777

WHITE MOUNTAIN FREEZER COMPANY 56
Winchendon, MA 01475
Tel. 508/297-0015

WILBUR CHOCOLATE COMPANY, INC. 130
48 North Broad Street
Lititz, PA 17543
Tel. 717/626-1131

WINDMILL PUBLISHING COMPANY 16
2147 Windmill View Road
El Cajon, CA 92020

WISCONSIN WAGON COMPANY 208
507 Laurel Avenue
Janesville, WI 53545
Tel. 608/754-0026

WOODCRAFT SUPPLY CORPORATION 105
P.O. Box 4000
Woburn, MA 01888
Tel. 800/225-1153
Fax. 304/428-8271 to order

WOODSTOCK POTTERY 58
Woodstock Valley, CT 06282
Tel. 203/974-1673

WOODSTOCK SOAPSTONE STOVE COMPANY, INC. 97
Airpark Road, Box 37H
West Lebanon, NH 03784
Tel. 800/866-4344
Fax. 603/298-5958

ZAHN, CHARLES, IMPORT MERCHANT, LTD. 62
Post Office Box 75
Milford, NH 03055
Tel. 603/673-1908

Index

About the Author

Alan Wellikoff is a journalist and writer who holds a degree in American Civilization from George Washington University. His work has appeared in *Esquire, Smithsonian, Playboy,* and *Gentlemen's Quarterly*. He is the author of three books, including *The Modern Man's Guide to Life*. He lives in Baltimore, Maryland.